When Mexicans Could Play Ball

When Mexicans Could Play Ball

BASKETBALL, RACE, AND IDENTITY IN SAN ANTONIO, 1928–1945

By Ignacio M. García

University of Texas Press *Austin*

Printed in the United States of America
First edition, 2013

Requests for permission to reproduce material from this work should be sent to:

Permissions
University of Texas Press
P.O. Box 7819
Austin, TX 78713-7819
http://utpress.utexas.edu/index.php/rp-form

∞ The paper used in this book meets the minimum requirements of ANSI/NISO Z39.48-1992 (R1997) (Permanence of Paper).

LIBRARY OF CONGRESS CATALOGING-IN-PUBLICATION DATA
García, Ignacio M.
When Mexicans could play ball : basketball, race, and identity in San Antonio, 1928–1945 / by Ignacio M. García. — First edition.
pages cm.
Includes bibliographical references and index.
ISBN 978-0-292-75377-8 (cloth : alk. paper)
1. Basketball—Texas—San Antonio. 2. Basketball—Social aspects—Texas—San Antonio. 3. Sports—Texas—San Antonio—History. 4. Mexican Americans—Texas—San Antonio. 5. Mexican Americans—Social life and customs. 6. San Antonio (Tex.)—Social conditions. 7. Hispanic American basketball players—Texas—San Antonio. I. Title.
GV885.73.S34G37 2013
796.32309764′351—dc23

2013008527

doi: 10.7560/753778

This book was made possible by some incredible young basketball players, and so it is to them that I dedicate this book: Tony, Joe, David, Henry, Raul, Ruben, Ramiro, Kino, Frank, David, Indio, Mosca, Santos, Carlos, Jesse, Walter. . . . And to their coach, William Carson "Nemo" Herrera, who saw their worth and helped them become the best they could be.

Contents

Acknowledgments ix

INTRODUCTION. The Punch Heard 'round the Barrio 1

CHAPTER 1. A Coach Comes to Sidney Lanier 18

CHAPTER 2. Mexicans Can Play, but Not Everyone Is Pleased 41

CHAPTER 3. Lanier Makes Its Run at State and Finds Its First Stars 62

CHAPTER 4. Sidney Lanier: An American-Mexican Landscape 89

CHAPTER 5. War Comes to the West Side, and Lanierites Respond 111

CHAPTER 6. Adjusting to War and Getting Back to State 132

CHAPTER 7. The Voks Finally Make It to the Top 153

CHAPTER 8. On the Summit Looking Up 175

CHAPTER 9. The Rodríguez Boys Must Be Stopped 195

CHAPTER 10. An Era Comes to an End, but a School Remains 218

Notes 229

Bibliography 259

Index 267

Photo section follows p. 110.

Acknowledgments

Books are usually made possible by lots of passion and good sources, and for this book I had an ample supply of both. My passion for this story comes from my having grown up in the barrios of the West Side of San Antonio and attending Sidney Lanier High School. Like the basketball players I write about, I spent much of my life across the street from the high school or within a short walking distance. My family bought their food at the H-E-B a block away from our home and half a block from the school, got our hot and tasty Mexican bread across the street on the corner, our tortillas—handmade—a block the other way, and our medicine—and shakes—at the corner pharmacy only about thirty yards from our front door. On the way there, we'd pass the local theater, separated from my family's duplex by an alley. Across the street from the movie house was the restaurant where my father worked. From the big storefront window he could see both our house across the street to the west, and my elementary school—also across the street—to the east. Mine was what President Jimmy Carter once described as an "ethnically pure" neighborhood.

The extended version of that Lanier community was also the fertile ground in which grew those young men who donned the basketball uniform of the Voks on their way to numerous championships. Like me, they became lifelong "Lanierites" and thus natural allies in the writing of this book. I was lucky enough to interview seven former Lanier players, two sons, two spouses, and several die-hard fans. Their recollections of their playing time and of their friends and former teammates provided the foundation for this story.

The first two players I interviewed, and probably the biggest fans of Lanier, were brothers Jesse and Carlos Camacho, who played in the late 1930s and early 1940s. I spent two days in two different years talking about the team, the players, the school, and 1940s San Antonio with them. Later I followed up the interviews with Jesse in his home and had the pleasure of meeting and interviewing his wife, Jessie, a former member of the pep squad and later a secretary at Lanier. The next player I interviewed was Tony Rivera, two-time all-state player and the hero of the first state championship team. More than any other player, he spoke openly about the hostilities he and his teammates faced from white players and the discrimination in out-of-town gymnasiums.

Those three led me to the one player that proved to be the most helpful and the one I most pestered with questions and engaged in long conversations with: David Rodríguez, all-state player, who played in the two state championship teams and would later go on to coach alongside William Carson "Nemo" Herrera, the legendary coach who guided these young West Side boys to five regional titles, two third-place finishes, one second-place, and two state titles. I interviewed this junior college All-American in his home in El Paso. He was the only player to have a scrapbook handy. We spoke for hours the first time and then spent numerous hours on the phone every time a new question arose and when I simply needed to have someone provide me feedback on a thought I had about the Lanier Voks or the West Side of San Antonio. His scrapbook turned out to be crucial in reconstructing the basketball seasons from 1942 to 1945. I had tried the school to find old school newspapers and yearbooks, but of the former they had none, and it took the school district almost two years to provide me copies of the yearbooks from 1940 to 1945.

I then interviewed Walter Kelley, the "half-gringo" on the 1943 team whom players lovingly called "Rough-House Kelley" because he was all of one hundred pounds but could still play a mean defensive game. He exuded love for Lanier during the interview, and because of him—and his brother, whom I did not interview—Chapter 9 became a discussion of the partly Mexican students at Lanier.

And just when I thought I would not be able to, I got to interview Tony Cardona, the all-state guard/forward, who helped win Lanier's first regional title and helped me open the book with the story of the riot his last-second shot caused. Other than Jesse and Carlos Camacho, no other player had married a Lanier girl. Rebecca, a tall, sophisticated, and charming woman, gave me insights that none of the other players had even thought about. To my dismay, Tony Cardona and Walter Kelley passed away before I finished the book. They joined team captain and all-around athlete Henry Escobedo, the only player alive at the time that I did not interview (because he was ill), in the basketball courts up in heaven.

The final player to be interviewed was the one who had started it all with an anecdote he gave a research assistant of mine almost twenty years earlier, when I was working on another book. It was then that I found out that Mexicans could play basketball and that at one time they had dominated Class 1A basketball in Texas. Joe Bernal provided not only memories of his time in high school, but as a veteran civil rights legislator he provided a perspective on race relations, segregation, and growing up Mexican American that few others could. David Rodríguez and he were the ones with the sharpest minds, and they were only in their eighties when interviewed.

Through the players, I contacted Charles Herrera, one of Nemo Herrera's sons, who has a scrapbook kept by his father. It is a large scrapbook that covers Nemo Herrera's sports career, from middle school to the years after he retired from coaching. It has poems, slogans, and picture upon picture of his youth, his players—both football and basketball—and a number of articles and news clippings that covered his life. Charles became a good source and a strong supporter of this project. One other person, Raul Zuniga—himself a basketball player, but after the Nemo era—was helpful in providing perspective on Lanier sports and the community around the school.

Also extremely helpful were some friends who graduated with me twenty-four years after the last state basketball championship. They gave me tidbits about their growing years, the places where the students hung out—I was always too poor to attend most dances and student activities—their lives in the Alazan federal housing projects, the nicknames we used, the teachers and the administrators who watched over us, and so forth. Why was this important? Because many of the players lived in the same housing projects, hung out in some of the same places years before, gave each other nicknames—some similar to the ones we used—and knew teachers who were still there when my cohorts and I arrived at Lanier. This allowed me to tie the 1940s to the 1960s and in some way to connect all Mexicans and Mexican Americans that have ever attended a segregated school and lived in the barrios of the United States.

One former classmate to whom I owe much is Benjamin Dominguez, who became my volunteer research assistant at the start of the project. Ben did the first initial interview with the Camacho brothers and Tony Rivera, along with interviews of other people who lived during that era. His enthusiasm for the project and the occasional document he found kept me enthused about the book.

My research was made possible by funding from the Charles Redd Center for Western Studies at Brigham Young University through the Lemuel Hardison Redd Jr. Professorship in Western and Latino History that I currently hold. Friend and colleague—and department chair—Donald J. Harreld provided me a key semester off that allowed me to finish most of my research. Allison Faust, Sponsoring Editor, of the University of Texas Press believed in the idea of the book and was very encouraging when the project took longer than expected. Two reviewers, Jorge Iber and José M. Alamillo, provided the kind of criticism that makes scholars cringe but that makes any work better. Much better sports historians than I would ever hope to be, they helped me improve this work tremendously.

Angela Ashurst-McGee, editor extraordinaire, helped greatly with her editing and her incisive comments on the manuscript. She made it easier to move paragraphs and even ideas around. And, of course, she helped get the manuscript ready for submission, as no matter the books I've written and the years in this business, I'm still all thumbs when it comes to giving the press what it wants.

Finally, my Alejandra made this project happen with her support and her company. While my sweet wife has not been in full health for a number of years, she still accompanied me on several trips and kept me excited by asking good questions about the players, the team, and the school. And she listened attentively—though probably rolled her eyes occasionally—while I discussed the research and reminisced about my old Lanier days.

When Mexicans Could Play Ball

INTRODUCTION

The Punch Heard 'round the Barrio

IN THE CONFUSION OF THE CELEBRATION, NO ONE SAW the fist coming. It landed on the back of the head of its intended target, sending Tony Cardona, the future all-state guard, reeling toward the wooden floor as his teammates watched in shock. It was not what he expected just moments after dribbling across mid-court and evading several opposing players to score the winning bucket thirty seconds into sudden-death play in the 1939 San Antonio city basketball championship game. The shot clinched a title that the Sidney Lanier High School Voks had come close to winning for the last three years. The "Speedy Mexicans," "who dart[ed] in and out like a bunch of *mosquitoes*,"[1] had finally gone over the top, and hundreds of Mexican American fans leapt to their feet to release their pent-up emotions.

Lanier fans hugged, flung their arms up high, and cried out, their accented voices rising to the top of the gymnasium to proclaim the Voks city champs. Some simply looked around at those celebrating, basking in a sense of pride that Mexicans could play a "white man's game" and win. Possibly they stole a glance at the other side, where their opponents' fans stood around stunned, wondering how their expected triumph had slipped away in mere seconds. After all, the Brackenridge High School Eagles had been the dominant basketball school in town the last few years, and they had always known how to beat the Mexicans from across the tracks. The Eagles and the Voks had played excruciatingly close games in the past, and even this season the teams had split their two contests, with each team winning on the road.

For the celebrants, it was not just a sports victory for their school but a collective triumph for Mexican Americans throughout the city and the surrounding area. Years of discrimination, racial conflict, disdain by word or deed, and inferiority complexes disappeared for just that one moment. The Voks, most of the city had learned by now, were tenacious and extremely competitive but were usually the smallest and always the ones with the least equipment and flatbed trucks for transportation. Nearly always the disadvantages took their toll when the Voks competed against the bigger players from the more affluent schools. Victories did not seem to come easy for Mexicans and Mexican Americans in this city where the biggest civic celebrations commemorated the battles of the Alamo and San Jacinto. In one, Mexicans were the massacrers of brave Texans defending freedom, and in the other they were in turn massacred by "liberty-loving" Texans.

Theirs was a city that held a grand celebration in the spring called Fiesta Week, where horses, vaqueros, and other Mexican motifs were common but where white Texans made sure Mexican participation in the major events was as invisible as possible.[2] But in this case, Mexican Americans were central to the event even if it were just a game. Too often in the Alamo city Mexican Americans were props to be manipulated for the benefit of tourism or to fill the labor needs of the manufacturing and agricultural industries in the area. Their revelry following the championship win, however, was all about them, their players' skill, and their own loyalty to a group of tenacious young men who had proved to be the best basketball players in the city.

The euphoria, however, lasted only as long as it took an opposing fan—maybe even a player's relative—to sprint from the bleachers and express his outrage with a right cross to the guard/forward's head. For some observers, things were moving too quickly. Seeing Mexicans grasp victory from the jaws of defeat and celebrate as if they had actually accomplished something significant was a bit too much to swallow, even in a sporting event. It is possible, though, that the punch didn't come from someone who harbored racial insensitivities or thought that Mexicans shouldn't win championship games against strong Christian white boys; maybe it was just some father who had taken his son's defeat to heart. But either way, the blow awakened all the pent-up hostilities between the two groups and led to a full-scale riot that brought both sides into a mid-court battle that soon spilled out into the sidewalks and streets, where rocks replaced fists as the weapon of choice. Numerous busted chins, black eyes, bruised backs, sore shins, and even a couple of stabbings resulted from the mêlée over a close overtime game between two very different people.

The fight unveiled two aspects of sports and race relations in this segregated Southwestern city. First was that Mexicans and Mexican Americans were out of the mainstream of both sports and society, and second, that they, nonetheless, could play basketball well enough to dominate the city's basketball arenas for most of the World War II years. Their Mexican American coach, William Carson "Nemo" Herrera, had trained them well, sacrificing their bodies with exhausting practices and filling their minds with confidence to compete at a level above what people who saw their small and skinny frames believed they were capable of. More important, he prepared them emotionally to withstand opposing player and fan hostility that sought to do on the court what it did out in the streets, factories, and public spaces: intimidate. By 1939, Mexican Americans were fighting back in all arenas of the public domain, and in the case of Sidney Lanier, they were proving that their athletes were just as talented and mentally tough as those in the city's top sports teams.

When Mexicans Could Play Ball then is the story of a group of young men who went beyond the purview allotted to them, winning two state basketball titles and coming in second once and third twice when few people expected them to play the sport. Even today, or maybe more so today, most people are astonished that Mexican Americans can dominate in a sport where height and speed are considered fundamental. Mexicans and Mexican Americans, says the common wisdom, are soccer and baseball players or even boxers, and while they often can be found in the park playing on open basketball courts, they are not considered natural to the game. Yet they were, and in many ways basketball was a more natural game for them given that it required only a ball and a rim—and little money.

Basketball is a game that requires individual effort and talent, as well as team play. Before the advent of the better coaching, equipment, and diet that today's more affluent teams enjoy, Mexican Americans in the 1940s confronted a more level playing field, and there they competed on equal terms in spite of their small frames and shorter height. For a community awakening to its American reality, sports triumphs provided an important impetus to their integration into the larger society. Victory meant they belonged, but more important, it meant they could belong while maintaining their identity as people of Mexican descent. Besting whites in a white man's game eliminated one area in which they could be demeaned or thought of as less than equal. For some players and fans it affirmed their feelings of muscular parity, but for most, it strengthened their pride in community.

The young men on the Lanier team did not speak of their victories in terms of race, but they were not blind to the fact that brown victories shifted the racial fault lines in the Texas sports world and even in the social arena. Their wins forced sportswriters to cover their games, extoll their skills, and predict their final standing in the state playoffs. Over time, the Voks became San Antonio's "team" because they were the most likely of the city squads to win a regional title, do well in state, or even win it all. They did not capture the hearts of all white fans but often did earn grudging respect, especially from those who prized good basketball. Their Spanish surnames became a regular feature in the local and area newspapers, and it was positive coverage.

Mexican Americans in the West Side of town saw these triumphs in a more visceral way, just as they did discrimination and prejudices. Unlike Herrera or Lanier school officials who sought to maintain social and cultural neutrality, many in the community saw the battle as one between a white community that discriminated and the Mexican American barrios that were fighting for the right to live in peace. It wasn't about which group was better, only about how one was not unequal.

This story is not only about sports; it stretches into a search for identity and community building as well. The athletes' world was not limited to the basketball court, the practice gym, or the hostile arenas where they were verbally and sometimes physically threatened. Much of what they became on and off the field was shaped in the classrooms, clubs, and activities that took place at Sidney Lanier High School and the surrounding barrios. Named after the nineteenth-century poet, Sidney Lanier was originally an elementary school, and then a junior high that was later expanded to serve grades 6–11 and eventually grade 12 as the only high school serving San Antonio's West Side. The largely white school board, administration, and staff implemented an educational vision of delivering basic education and vocational training to prepare their Mexican students to furnish the labor to meet the region's industrial appetite.

It was also a place in which Mexican students were to learn how to become American. Few educators expected the students to become proud of their Mexican ancestry or to reject the limitations that society and even the school placed on them. Yet groups of students—and particularly the players—did. Lanier might have had all the limitations of a segregated school in the middle of a poor barrio, but it also had bright students, dedicated teachers—though they did not always understand their students—and a principal who loved and defended them—though he did not always understand their yearnings. Sidney Lanier both limited and lifted its students, preparing them to participate in Americanism while holding them separate from full inclusion.

Lanier became a laboratory in which students, teachers, administrators, and even community members navigated the troubled racial waters of American society. The lack of college preparatory courses or academic counseling services to educate students on college options limited the opportunities for many of the students. The barrios around the school suffered from the fact that many Lanierites did not graduate. Yet those who did graduate, who went on to college, or who learned a skill and opened their own businesses helped create a vibrancy that constantly pushed back against the ills that often existed in places such as the West Side of San Antonio. The fan loyalty and the sense of school pride for students, former students, and West Side residents served as glue for a community that faced very difficult challenges, and it provided a hope that things could get better. In this case—as in the case of many similar communities, both Mexican American and white—sports served as a foundation for developing a communal identity, complete with heroes, memorable moments, painful disappointments, and tangible results such as titles, winning streaks, and individual accomplishments. Seventy-plus years later, many Lanierites still feel proud of their Voks and their community, even as the sports victories have been less frequent.

Writing this story had been on my mind for over twenty-five years. Ironically, the initial idea came while I was conducting an interview with a former basketball player turned legislator for my first book on Mexican American civil rights. I thought of it as such a great topic that I stored it in the back of my mind until I could fully dedicate myself to it. I had labored as a sportswriter before becoming a historian and always longed to do a project on sports and community. This story seemed a perfect topic for me because I graduated from Sidney Lanier High School twenty-four years after the last basketball state title and I lived in a neighborhood adjacent to the school for most of my growing-up years. The two principals I had during my high school years were also the top two administrators during the years I cover in the book. I even had one of the basketball players as a science teacher. It was a particularly enticing story because I had witnessed only defeats and mediocre seasons as an avid Voks fan and was fascinated with an era in which the Lanier basketball teams reigned supreme.

In preparing to write this book, I read works on Chicano sports and then reflected on how new and limited the field was. The paucity of monograph-length sports histories available was striking. I could count the number in both hands, and most were anthologies that tried to provide a framework for understanding sport in the life of the barrios of this country.[3] Only a few of the articles and book chapters actually dealt with the sport itself; instead, they talked about poverty, discrimination, segregation, or the common theme that sports built communal cohesion, prepared Mexican Americans for the outside world, developed ethnic identity, and so on. While important, most of those concepts are so common in Mexican American studies that they can be applied to any kind of history that you want to write on Chicanos and Mexican Americas.

Scholars Jorge Iber, Samuel O. Regalado, José M. Alamillo, and well-known Tejano historian Arnoldo De León followed in part this approach when they co-wrote *Latinos in U.S. Sport: A History of Isolation, Cultural Identity, and Acceptance*, the most extensive and comprehensive view of Latinos in all sports written to date. The book covers Latinos and sport since the Pre-Columbian era to 2010. But despite their coverage of basketball in San Antonio and throughout the country, they make no mention of Sidney

Lanier's state titles. They, in fact, only mention a team from Miami, Arizona, that played eight Mexican Americans along with several white players when it won the state title in 1951, six years after the Voks won their second state title with an all–Mexican American team.[4] In their holistic conclusion, they write:

> At all levels of sport, Latinos are breaking barriers, forging friendships, and demonstrating in a very effective way that they are as spirited and dedicated as the rest of the American populace. In addition, recent immigrants are using sport in order to hold on to important parts of their cultural heritage as they fight to establish themselves in new territory.[5]

In one regard, *When Mexicans Could Play Ball* is different because it does not attempt to provide an overarching theme that is applicable to all Latinos or Mexican Americans in all sports and in all communities, though I do posit that many of the experiences of the Lanier basketball players and their fellow students are similar to those of other Mexican Americans who might find themselves in a similar space and time.[6] This book also differs in that it tells multiple stories but does not downplay the actual sport, whether we are talking about box scores, individual heroics, game strategies, or the role of the coach. *When Mexicans Could Play Ball* has all of these and yet weaves them into a history of community and the creation of identity. Without that history—that is, details, time, space, and individuals—it is presumptuous to create hard-and-fast theoretical or analytical frameworks.[7]

Once I focused on the story, I tracked down the available press clippings, interviewed seven of the eight players still alive (one was too ill to be interviewed and died before the manuscript was finished), and collected copies of the six high school yearbooks that covered the World War II period (only one was produced before 1940). The school newspapers were never collected in one place and are mostly unavailable. I cringe over how much was lost to carelessness. I found that most of the city newspapers had huge gaps in their coverage of the basketball scene of the period, and what was available, with the exception of a few features and columns, was straightforward reporting with a little racial commentary. The documents I collected told a very small part of the story, and the interviewees were sixty-five-plus years removed from their playing years and had long ago forgotten game details or routine school activities that would have added color and depth to the story. What I most needed, I realized, was perspective.

I decided, then, to fill in the holes of the story with experiences, thoughts, and tales from those who went to school with me in the late 1960s. A risky proposition for a historian, I know, but I engaged in it because my research revealed to me that as Lanierites and as residents of that vast area known as the San Antonio West Side, my classmates and I had experienced many of the same things these players and their fellow students did twenty-odd years earlier. We both attended a segregated and predominantly vocational school deep in the Mexican side of town. When I talk about discrimination at the sporting events, life in the federal housing projects, nicknames, the campus environment, favorite teachers and administrators, and the search for identity, the discussion touches on quite similar experiences. I remembered that as a Vok fan I encountered a riot similar to the one that starts this book. In my case, it was a football game, but the anger expressed toward us was just as intense.

My generation of Lanier graduates grew up in the same, only slightly less dilapidated barrios as most of the basketball players did. Like many of them, I lived in a home with its privy and showers outside, with little room for our family of four, in conditions that would have been designated as unlivable on the better side of town. Many of our parents worked in menial or low-skill jobs, most could not speak English, and most had little formal education—though a few more than in the 1930s. Few of them—as was the case with those of the earlier periods—ever stepped on campus except to attend the occasional school carnival. Historian Richard A. García called the area that surrounded the high school a "town within a city" because in custom, economic interaction, and cultural expression it was an entity quite different from the rest of the city. This area was often referred to as the "Latin Quarter" or "Mexican Town" in the 1940s.[8] In the 1960s, we simply called it *el barrio*.

I am mindful of the differences and the dangers of collapsing the experiences of Lanier students in the 1940s and 1960s into one, so I include from my own experience only those events and places that provide a frame of reference to what occurred or existed in the war years. These insertions play only a small part in the story, but they provide a bridge to the experiences of other Mexican Americans from different generations. Most often our experiences from generation to generation differed only by the fact that some of us lived in more segregated areas than others, had greater social or economic fluidity, or lived within slightly less rigid boundaries. But the isolation, powerlessness, hostility, and misunderstanding we faced from those outside the barrio varied only in intensity. Most Mexican Americans who attended fully segregated high schools and lived in poor neighborhoods can relate well to this story because it speaks to being Mexican in American society.

My family came to the West Side of San Antonio only eleven years after the last championship team. By then the barrio had a few more street lights, better roads, and more small businesses, but much of the housing was left over from the pre-war years. Most homes were old, decaying places where others had once lived but had long since left. Many still lacked indoor plumbing or sewer connections, and when night came, we found ourselves in the dark or with anemic light since electrical services were limited. Many of the streets had no sidewalks and no drainage ditches for the rainwater. When the usual San Antonio downpours came, the streets would flood and create rivers and small lakes throughout the barrio, making the whole area almost impassable to both pedestrians and the few automobiles available.[9] With the water came debris, mud, animal carcasses, and often disease. I remember navigating flooded streets on the way to school, as did many of an earlier period, though we were lucky enough to have more street pavement.

Those lucky enough back then to live in the federal housing projects known as the Alazan–Apache Courts were better off, but only because their houses were made of cement and brick. Their poverty, however, was only less extreme than those who had no luck in securing one of these prized apartments. The units, simple one- or two-story buildings of hollow tile and concrete with three to six rooms and built to last at least sixty years, were adjacent to the school and later extended several blocks south. They had little gardens, walkways, and with time, small recreational areas for the children. There were about 1,180 units built during the New Deal era at a cost of $5 million. They covered an area of sixty acres, or ten city blocks, making them the largest "subdivision" in the West Side and surely the sturdiest. The rents were based on income, and so residents would pay anywhere from nine to fifty dollars. By the mid to late 1940s, nearly 4,500 residents lived there, more than half of them children.[10]

I, too, lived in the Apache–Alazan Courts, as did many of my friends. By then the federal housing had expanded dramatically and spilled over to just across the street from Sidney Lanier's ROTC building. Like many of the people who lived there, my family was poor, though most of my peers had working parents and by then few of them were following the migratory stream. Back in the 1940s, however, the residents were required to be American citizens and to have lived previously in slum housing, been displaced by public slum clearances, or been migrant workers. Of youth living in federal housing during World War II, 77 percent were born and raised in the United States. Forty percent of their parents and 90 percent of their grandparents had been born in Mexico. Eighty-five percent of federal housing residents spoke English but preferred to speak mostly Spanish at home. Only 10 percent of those who knew both languages spoke English at home. Thirty percent of the residents had less than three years of schooling, and only about 6 percent had "finished school," which often meant completing the sixth grade or possibly the eighth, which was the last year of junior high then.[11]

In the mid-twentieth century, federal housing residents occupied the second tier of the class structure of Mexican San Antonio, as did most of the Lanier basketball players who brought fame to the barrio. Two-time all-state forward Tony Rivera remembered that "most (of the players) lived in the courts—the majority of us." Rudy Bernal, son of popular point guard Ramiro Bernal, knew from his father that few of the players came out of "regular homes," given that most were poor and their families worked in the local West Side economy. "I guess the courts, you would say, [were] the barrio."[12]

In the Lanier area, there were at least four elementary schools and two Catholic parochial schools within walking distance. The Mexican Christian Institute provided a kindergarten for about forty-five students, while numerous other community centers offered adult education classes.[13] But in the 1940s, at least 25 percent of Latin Quarter residents left school because of migrant work or to help support the family, because they felt uncomfortable not speaking the language, or because they had only hand-me-down rags to wear. Still others dropped out because the education they received had little impact on the kinds of jobs they got upon graduation. Often those who finished school were still found working as mechanic assistants, janitors, night watchmen, or pecan shellers alongside those who had dropped out or rarely attended school. My father was a waiter, and he often worked with young men who had either finished high school or at least reached high school—still an accomplishment given that in the 1960s Mexican Americans had an average of less than six years of schooling. For many young men in the barrio of my time, like those of the 1940s, there simply was little incentive to keep going to school.[14]

Yet in spite of the problems they confronted in getting an education or with the schooling itself, most Mexican families considered education important. A survey of the housing project in the late 1940s found that 75 percent of parents with teenage kids enrolled them in high school. The same survey also found that most children were interested in educating themselves, although interestingly, many of their parents were more impressed with the Mexican school system they left behind because they thought it was more rigorous. While the Mexican children struggled with the language and the school culture, some teachers found them superior to other students in writing, drawing, and music.[15] Most of the students who stayed in school back then must have enjoyed it, otherwise most would have found a reason to drop out.

For the most part, basketball players interviewed years later felt comfortable in their barrios, liked school, and appreciated their teachers. Stella Molina, a student in the early 1940s, remembered Lanier as a "good, sharp school," though admittedly a bit too strict for her taste.[16] Rudy Bernal remembered his father as having fond memories of the school and the faculty: "He talked real good about the teachers that were [there]. Mr. Brewer was the principal . . . and he had a lot of good things to say about him. . . . I never heard a whole lot of negative things from him about the school."[17] The school offered its students an opportunity to be with their friends, to engage in activities that were often unavailable to them in the outside world, and to be part of clubs and sports teams. Most important, the students could go to school in an environment where they were all Mexican or Mexican Americans, and so they did not confront racism in the schoolyard, clubs, activities, or with a few exceptions, the classroom.

It is important to note—and the reader is likely to notice—that I do not deal with the problems of education for the Lanier students in any profound way. I do not ignore the fact that schools like Lanier had high drop-out rates or were known for producing students who lacked the skills for either college or white-collar jobs. In 1968, I would be part of school protests to expand the school's curriculum to better train students for college. Our efforts were not meant to eliminate vocational training but to enhance educational opportunities for those interested in going to college. In an interesting irony, one of those who mentored us during those days of protest was none other than one of the former players, Joe Bernal, the state legislator whose interview first gave me the idea of writing this book.

My interest in writing this book revolved around the desire to see how Lanier played a part in assimilating and acculturating Mexican American students into American society, even if at times it was only to the lowest rung of that society. I had no desire to victimize Mexican Americans all over again by seeing their lives only as flawed products of a flawed educational system. As these players proved both by their athletic achievements and their post–high school careers, Lanierites could go on to have productive and enjoyable lives. Even for those students who would go on to live just above poverty, Lanier still provided them enough skills to survive, something their parents and many of their neighbors never had. It also provided them knowledge of American ideals, habits, and culture. It allowed them to become Mexican American at a time when their identity was evolving from predominantly Mexican to partly American. I attempt here to validate the efforts of the students themselves to create their own personae to help them navigate the larger society. For the first time in their lives, these young people were given opportunities to participate in clubs and activities that they had a hand in planning. They were leaders and, for the most part, were responsible for the success or failure of their clubs and activities. This was particularly true in the case of athletics. While Lanier students suffered from outside-imposed limitations, the gap between their facilities, teachers, and mode of education in the war years was smaller than it would come to be after the war, when segregation and discrimination would in some places take on an even more insidious nature.

The Lanier teachers of the post-war era were often young, single, and imbued with a progressive spirit of helping immigrant children. In the interviews I conducted, I heard no one accuse the Anglo teachers of racial prejudice. Some interviewees believed they could have gotten a better education or have had more sensitive teachers, but none of them believed the teachers were particularly hostile. Since almost all of the interviewees saw themselves as successful in life, they expressed few regrets in attending the school. They could recite all the things wrong in the school, but most of them believed the whole was better than the sum of its parts. This generation saw an opening in American society that was not there for their parents, and they found educational, political, and professional crevices previously unavailable. This allowed them to navigate a landscape that while still hostile was more fluid. In taking advantage of these openings and in seeing the growth of their numbers and their successes in limited areas in the broader community, they became more confident about their place in American society.[18]

The existence of Lanier, as noted earlier, was made essential by the need for skilled labor—especially during and immediately following the war years. Competing with the idea of developing a labor force was the insistence by educators, intellectuals, politicians, and social advocates that Lanier students also be assimilated into the larger society. While there was a belief that each could be done effectively without disrupting the other, such a balance proved not to be easy or popular with some sectors of the American public. Segregation's importance thus grew as a strategy by which Mexican Americans could be both prepared for jobs that the area industries produced and assimilated into their proper place in the larger society's pecking order. Lanier became a place where students could be both trained for American industry and yet be Americanized away from the Anglo side of town. While their parents were constructing a Mexican community to retain their dignity and find space for their culture and sociability, the students, sometimes with the unknowing help of their teachers, were creating a space that was much closer to the America they knew would be their permanent home.

Still, even while trying to assimilate Mexican youth, some educators and politicians believed that Mexicans did not value education or have a serious outlook toward life. One researcher in the 1940s called them "romantic" and as "seasonal and migratory" as any bird.[19] Another wrote that they tended to live beyond their means: "There is no spirit of thrift, no foresight; 'today we spend all we have and as for tomorrow, God will provide.'"[20] This perception was held by many social scientists who studied Mexicans and Mexican

Americans. Sister Mary John Murray, in her master's thesis on the federal housing projects in the 1940s, wrote about a Mexican woman who complained that her husband spent his money on alcohol and "[ran] around with other women and neglect[ed] his family." Sister Mary also pointed out that Anglo-American "leaders" believed that any kind of economic betterment of the Mexican always brought out the worst. The more Mexicans received, according to these unidentified individuals, the more they wanted, and that usually led them to crime, to spending time away from their families, to the delinquency of their children, and to the breakdown of the family.[21]

These perceptions were typical of white residents when they saw hundreds of Mexicans and Mexican Americans living in substandard conditions. Whites often saw Mexicans as fully responsible for their squalor. The reality, however, was that too many Mexican men and a large number of Mexican women found themselves in a cycle or, even worse, a downward spiral of low pay, inconsistent work, unsafe working conditions, and verbal abuse from foremen and supervisors, and this made it difficult to be cheerful employees or to see the possibility of upward mobility. That many men fell into vices or spent much of their money on alcohol or illicit affairs underscores the hard life that many faced. Unable to provide well for their families, keep their children in school, construct a better future, or see any light at the end of their tunnel, many men were tempted to shirk the responsibilities of life outside of work, though they were far from the majority of the men in the barrio. Most did the best they could with the life they were given.

Said one man, "I have worked in a variety of hard labor jobs, mines, smelting, stone quarries, railroad tracks, street cleaning, etc. I have also been a traveling salesman and at one time I even dressed statues. Now, I'm old and sick and I'm learning to be a tailor." Income studies for those who lived in federal housing projects reveal a woeful situation that explains many of the problems in the West Side community. In 1939, the housing authority estimated that 45 percent of Latin Americans earned less than $550 a year and that 75 percent earned less than $950 a year.[22] Annual household income nationally by the end of the 1940s ranged from less than $500 to $3,400, but the average income was around $1,400 per individual worker.[23] Pauline R. Kibbe in her book, *Latin Americans in Texas*, quotes a public health report: "The most obvious reason why one Latin American out of twenty was found to have tuberculosis is poverty. These people have been exploited as a cheap source of labor; they harvest the crops, shell the pecans, wash the clothes, and dig the ditches. For this they receive barely enough to keep body and soul together."

The Reverend Carmelo Tranchese, a Jesuit priest of the Lady of Guadalupe Parish, which served the predominantly Catholic community around the high school, remembered the deplorable conditions in which the people lived in 1936. In a trip through San Antonio before he came to serve his ministry there, he found a cluster of homes serviced by two toilets, one of which had been broken for a long while, and one water faucet with no handle that could be opened only with a set of pliers. Those who did not live in tenement-type housing or in multiple-family structures lived in what historian Richard A. García describes as "corrals," rows of wooden shacks "built very close together and facing each other without running water, without window screens, with no indoor baths or toilets, and with millions of mosquitos and flies."[24]

Many of the residents in this area found the steadiest work as pecan shellers. García estimates that during the November–March season, the Southern Pecan Shelling Company hired at least 12,000 to as many as 20,000 workers, almost all Mexican, to do the tedious, dirty, and often dangerous job of separating pecans from their shells.[25] The work was tedious because of the small size of the nut and dirty and dangerous because of the powder that pecan shelling let off when the cracking and peeling occurred. The powder caused respiratory problems that were often taken home since many Mexican residents—thousands of them, in fact—took the nuts home and did the work around family and children. There were major distribution centers for this product in San Antonio, but many, maybe even hundreds, of small shops throughout the West Side did the work and then delivered the product to the larger outlets.

Local historian David Mercado Gonzalez remembers his mother telling him about *las nuecerías*, the pecan-shelling plants. "Everybody here in the West Side at one time or another worked or took *nueces* (pecans) home to crack and then . . . back to the *nuecerías*." His mother also told him about *el polvito*, the residue that flew freely around the air as the pecans were cracked and that led to "all kinds of respiratory diseases."[26] Mom-and-pop shops, no more than a family with a small shack for a home, would do much of the work of pecan shelling. For the employers, at-home workers were cheaper than wage employees. For the workers, working at home was better than working in large, unsafe, unventilated buildings with rude supervisors for body-depleting long hours. Having control of one's hours and the right to move around at leisure made work at home more bearable, though not any more profitable or easy.

Horrible working conditions at the large pecan-shelling factories would lead to the formation of numerous unions in Texas, such as the El Nogal Union, Cooperativa de Nueceros de San Antonio, and the Mandadores de Nuez, which demanded better wages and working conditions. In 1938, the refusal by the industry to negotiate would lead to one of the most famous strikes in Texas labor history. Led by a diminutive and young labor and communist agitator, Emma Tenayuca Brooks, thousands of pecan shellers went out on the picket line to protest the wages and the conditions. Gonzalez remembers his father and uncles being part of that protest in which the workers were gassed, beaten, and arrested. The strikers persevered until they won a better contract only to see it come to naught when a year later the pecan companies switched to machines and laid off thousands of workers.[27]

Pamela Grundy, in her book *Learning to Win*, describes how in North Carolina "athletics . . . sat at the center of cross-cutting currents, becoming an arena in which individuals and communities negotiated aspects of their own identities as well as their position in the state's new social order."[28] This new order was the rise of industrial capitalism and its effects on Southern states. Sport served as a way to mitigate the disruptive nature of this new economic order in the lives of small communities and eventually integrate North Carolina into a sports and market culture that remains prevalent in the South today. Similarly, residents of the barrios surrounding Lanier were also affected by the rise of industrialization and the need for a labor force skilled enough to work in the factories of San Antonio. But because they were not white, their ability to negotiate was limited to that which they could influence in the West Side of San Antonio.[29]

Still, this limited negotiation—seen mostly through their cultural retention, social clubs, and political activity at the municipal level—was important for the residents of San Antonio's largest ethnic enclave because it allowed them some control over their lives and gave them a sense of ownership and pride in the things that they accomplished, things that were often ignored outside the boundaries of their barrio. This collective, though often unstructured, negotiating with the forces outside of the West Side provided the residents a sense of commonality in their lives and gave them a feeling that they were a "people" rather than just an "ethnic group."[30]

Given the hostilities—reflected in employment, housing, education, and law-enforcement discrimination—presented by the world outside the barrio for the players of the 1940s and us in the 1960s, partial segregation was welcomed, no matter how often education reformers decried the situation. Being with our own never made us feel inferior or destroyed our dreams, though it would limit the possibilities of many after they left school. Segregated schooling did much to hamper the possibilities of integrating into American society, particularly to that part which facilitated good jobs and upward mobility. But given that schooling in the few integrated schools in the city was rarely any better for Mexican Americans, Lanier represented a less hostile option for the West Side residents. Venturing outside the confines of our school was what usually made us feel different or diminished. The quality of schooling could have been much better, but in American society, good schooling is only for those who live in more affluent school districts. In many ways, Lanier was as good as it was going to get back then mainly because there were few educators or politicians before World War II who truly understood or cared about the problems Mexican Americans faced in becoming literate in American society. Even most Mexican American reformers concentrated on advocating for better facilities and did little to improve curriculum and college preparation. Not until the rise of the Chicano Movement in the 1960s did reformers begin to concentrate on curricular changes and college preparation and accessibility to higher education.

By being winners, however, Lanier's basketball players reinforced the notion preached by Mexican American reformers, politicians, and writers that Mexican Americans were a people capable of much if given the chance and provided the training, guidance, and resources. The boys of Lanier were not so much the exception as they were the example of what Mexican Americans could do.[31] This became clear when some of them went on to have successful professional, political, and community careers. There were many others from Lanier who became good citizens in their communities and in the larger society. By the time I attended Lanier, many Mexican Americans were involved in education, politics, and employment. Too few, I admit, but I came to understand that as our community kept growing, more Mexicans kept coming across the border; many dropped out of school or were pushed out, and that kept the pool of *gente pobre* (poor people) in my barrio replenished. There were also those whose ambition was simply to get a job, raise a family, and be part of their community. In the West Side of San Antonio, that usually meant being low-income and generally underemployed.

But if I stop to remember people as individuals, I recall printers, commercial artists, mechanics, body and fender repairmen, small business owners, teachers, secretaries, clerks, and civil service workers at the air field or with the city. Many of them got their skills at Lanier. We as students in the late 1960s and many in the Latin Quarter of San Antonio in the pre-war years wanted more, and we legitimately fought for what we wanted, but we did so because Lanier itself provided the environment in which we could expect more. Part of that environment was about placing boundaries on our passions, providing structure to learning, and creating a place where we could interact with each other and with figures of authority, which tended to be mostly white teachers and administrators. All of this served the purpose of putting us in our place. And yet that environment also provided us opportunities in school that were closed off to our peers in the predominantly white schools in the rest of the city. In our little segregated world, we could be all that we could be, though that usually translated into something better in the outside world only for the most capable.

The ball players in the 1930s and 1940s were those who conformed to the rules most rigidly—in order to stay on Nemo Herrera's good side—and yet transcended their effects because their experiences went beyond that of their fellow students. Getting out of the barrio allowed them to see that there was a bigger world. Being allowed to compete on whites' turf gave them a status not often afforded their fellow barrio residents. And winning instilled in them a confidence in their abilities. It also showed them that whites were beatable, or at least that they were simply human beings with a different shade of skin and different sets of talents and skills. More important, the players found that their victories, bolstered by their exemplary behavior on the court, won them support and praise from some in the Anglo community, allowing them to see diversity in behavior among those seen as the "others" by the people in the barrio.

World War II, which was under way by the time the 1939 San Antonio city basketball championship game ended in a riot, provides a unique and significant backdrop to this story. That conflict did what a hundred years of living in this country had not done for Mexicans and Mexican Americans: it made them feel like they belonged. The improvement in race relations—to the extent that it did improve among some—and the reenergizing of Mexican American civil rights and reform activities were a direct result of hundreds of thousands of Mexican American men serving in the armed forces and thousands of Mexican American women serving in defense industries and victory committees and going out to work outside the barrio. Being victorious in sports during the war added significance to the players' status as athletes, Americans, and Mexicans. Playing and winning in the American-created game when the nation hungered for victory made their accomplishments that much more significant. Winning without giving up their ethnic and racial identity made it even sweeter.

For the community of fans that followed the Voks' victories and bemoaned their losses, the skill, tenacity, and self-control the team exhibited, despite the trash talk and verbal abuse that came from opposing players and fans, was a sign that their boys were growing up to be men. I, too, remember as a student the excitement felt by the student body when the basketball team played well, when one of the track runners made regionals, or when the football team won a game they shouldn't have. When my companion and I went to the state quarterfinals in debate, our friends and teachers were not only surprised but also quite jubilant. Each little victory in the barrio or by barrio residents was a moment for celebration, not only because those victories came so rarely but because they reaffirmed our humanity and our abilities and countered all the negativity against us that came from other parts of the city.

In the end, of course, basketball was still just a game, and what these students did in school and at war was much more important. Yet the experience of the basketball players proved significant for them, for their families, and for those who remember their exploits on the basketball courts. In the darkest hours of the Depression and war, the players' success in proving that Mexicans could play ball went a long way toward making those years bearable and oftentimes quite enjoyable.

CHAPTER ONE

A Coach Comes to Sidney Lanier

William Carson "Nemo" Herrera wondered what he'd gotten himself into when he entered the Sidney Lanier Junior High campus in the fall of 1928. He knew he wanted to coach, but he also knew that those jobs were often maintained within an old coaches' network or given to former hometown heroes. He took what was available, even if it meant coming to a part of town he had often heard about when he played sports at G. W. Brackenridge High School. It was not a good part of town, was the word, and the school was about to enter its first year as a junior/senior high school. He didn't know what that meant or what to expect from Mexican kids. While Mexican American himself and a native of Brownsville, Texas, a predominantly Mexican American world, he had grown up playing sports with mostly white kids once his family moved to San Antonio. He attended Southwestern University in Georgetown, Texas, and had coached for the first time and for only one year at Beaumont High School in East Texas.[1] He had never coached Mexican kids—though he had coached adults in Mexico—and never been associated with a place as poor or as segregated as this school. No doubt he had confidence in his athletic knowledge but still wondered what he could do with these boys.

Herrera may have also cringed upon hearing the team's name, the Voks, a term whose definition quickly became mired in confusion. What was a Vok? became a question asked by every generation of Lanier students removed from the early years, when the name was hatched. My generation's best guess was that it was a gear because an image of one seemed to appear periodically in our yearbooks and in the large banners for the football games. Only in researching for this book did I learn that the name was meant to depict the vocational aspect of the school and the importance of the vocational worker as a small part in the large machine of industrialism.

Herrera, however, was a winner, a tenacious player in his time, and a successful baseball and basketball coach, if only for a short time, and so he stepped onto the campus with confidence mingled with a bit of trepidation. Whatever his misgivings about coming to a small vocational school—with little grass on the ground, poverty on all sides, eventually a large security fence, and a gear for a mascot—Herrera was determined to field winning teams in basketball, football, and baseball—though the last he would do only on his off time. And he did. More important, he helped build boys with character whose exploits on the competitive stage and whose demeanor both on and off the court brought credit to their school and community. He was a man whose legacy continued to be heralded twenty-five years after his death, and in his prime he became the darling of West Side parents, students, and community leaders. Though a Vok player commented years later that he never heard him utter a word in Spanish, Herrera came to represent what Mexican Americans were capable of doing when given the chance.

Herrera arrived at Sidney Lanier School just before the rise of what historian Mario T. García calls "the Mexican American Generation." This was a generation that fought for its civil rights, looked north instead of south for its future, and became the first group of Mexicans to see themselves as Americans first. Members of this generation were neither ashamed of nor indifferent to their Mexican heritage, but as the first predominantly American-born generation, they saw themselves with few real ties to the nation to the south. They believed in the concept of "Americans All," a slogan that would become popular during the massive struggle that came to engulf the nation during the 1940s.[2] They were the first generation to come of age after the massive deportations of the late 1920s and early 1930s that forced many Mexican families to focus on becoming American to avoid another such traumatic experience, where thousands of American-born Mexicans were repatriated to Mexico along with hundreds of thousands of Mexicans in the country both legally and illegally.[3]

But the formative events of this generation were not all tragic. For some, it was built on more schooling. Like Herrera, some in this generation went on to finish high school and attend college. They grew up going to school with white students, competing with them, and even earning their respect. Herrera, like a number of them, was engaged in being a "first." In his case, he was the first Mexican American coach at Lanier and in the whole city of San Antonio. Within a short time, Herrera and his peers saw numerous other firsts in Texas and other parts of the country where Mexican Americans lived and dreamed. Mario "Mike" de la Fuente pitched for the University of Texas in the late 1920s, went undefeated for two years, and eventually became a successful businessman. Coach E. C. Lerma was the first Mexican American quarterback at Texas A&I University (later renamed Texas A&M University–Kingsville) and went on to a successful football-coaching career in the Rio Grande Valley. Victor Rodríguez ran circles among most distance runners of his time, became a track coach at Lanier, and then became superintendent of schools in the San Antonio Independent School District.[4] There would also be social activists and politicians such as Hector P. García, a medical doctor and founder of the American GI Forum; Gustavo "Gus" García, successful litigator before the Supreme Court; Alonso Perales, co-founder of the League of United Latin American Citizens (LULAC) and the premier intellectual of his time; Edward Roybal, city councilman from Los Angeles and the first Mexican American congressman from California in the twentieth century; and George S. Sánchez and Carlos Castañeda, the top scholars of their generation.[5]

All these pioneers had one thing in common: the ability to navigate hostile territory and still find ways to succeed. Some, like Herrera, did it by staying close to their community, while others did it by diving into the white world to find friends and success. Still others had a mixed lineage after years of their families living in the United States. Herrera's own mother, Carolina, was part Anglo—the name Carson was from her side of the family—and her family claimed that she was a descendent of José Francisco Ruiz, one of the signers of the Texas Declaration of Independence from Mexico and a loyal citizen of the United States when Texas became a state.[6] Herrera's father, Rodolfo, came from Tampico, but while the family lived in the Rio Grande Valley and the extended family seems to have retained many of its Mexican roots, Herrera was quite comfortable in the English-speaking world.

What defined Herrera and his peers away from their immigrant world was their belief that the term "American" was as much for them as it was for others. On the inside cover of a scrapbook he put together, Herrera pasted William Tyler Page's "American Creed," which was adopted by an act of Congress on April 6, 1918, the same year he graduated from high school. Below it, he wrote:

> I believe in the United States of America, as a Government of the people, by the people, of the people, for the people, who [*sic*] just powers are [de]rived from the consent of the Government, a democracy [and] republic; a sovereign nation of many sovereign states; a perfect union. . . . I therefore believe it is my duty to my country to love it, to support its constitution, to obey its laws, to respect its flag, and to defend it against all enemies.[7]

Like a number of his Mexican American elite cohorts, Herrera lacked any insecurity in competing with whites for the fruits of the larger society. Having grown up with whites and navigating a white world gave them a perspective often missing in other Mexicans and Mexican Americans. Interestingly, many of them, though surely not all, would come back to work with their own, whether by choice or circumstance. They came back hoping to teach other Mexican Americans how to survive and succeed in an Anglo world. No doubt they often had a white mindset as believers in the American way of doing things. Yet in some way all of them reflected the reality that even they, as successful as they were, were mostly so in a Mexican environment. This was the contradictory reality of most of these men and the few women that formed this generation.[8]

From an early age, Herrera played ball with Anglo athletes and found himself quite successful among them. One of the first pictures in his scrapbook is of the Comanche Jrs., the city basketball champions. By the looks of the participants, this was likely a pre–high school league of some kind. Herrera is pictured seated in front, legs crossed, and looking rather confident. In his early years, he had eyes and a skin tone that made him look almost Southeast Asian. He had a small but lean body and a rather confident but not cocky air about him. Another picture has him seated on the floor, arms crossed and legs in a V shape. A handwritten caption on top of the picture indicates that this was in 1917, when he was a junior in high school. Below the picture is typed, "At Brackenridge High School I was fortunate to make both the basketball and baseball teams." Below that, he handwrote: "South Texas Champions." Under another picture, this one of the 1918 high school team, he pasted a little poem whose first line read, "I do not fear the road ahead, we know all men must tread."[9]

At Brackenridge High School, Herrera played baseball, football, and basketball and often had his name in the headlines reporting the school's exploits in basketball. He also stood "shoulder to shoulder" with football standouts of the late teens in San Antonio. He played left forward for the Brackenridge team that went to the state playoffs in 1918, his senior year. And he played second base for the baseball team.[10] In one article he is described as "shooting goals as fast as the guards could relay the ball."[11] The team was undefeated during the season, but no record survives of how far the team went in the playoffs that were then available. At the time, no official state playoffs existed, and basketball was still a sport in search of an identity in Texas. But as good as he was in basketball and football, he was just as good or even better as a baseball player, playing not only high school ball but also in the city leagues so common back then and eventually even in the minors. In a newspaper clipping in the scrapbook he is again seated in front of some adult baseball players. "Our Boy Nemo," says the caption. This was in 1913, when Herrera was named the batboy for the San Antonio Bronchos of the

Texas League, a position he held for three years and left only when he entered high school.

Herrera graduated in 1918, and in the scrapbook he explains how he got to Southwestern University:

> A fellow came to San Antonio during the summer of 1918 to recruit some 18 athletes for Southwestern University at Georgetown, Texas. This fellow's name was Pete Cawthom, who later became a legend as a high school and college coach in the state of Texas. When my name was called I was more than surprised to have been included as one of the 18. But I was confident that I could play not only college basketball or [in the] baseball team and this I did. I lettered 4 years in both . . . and during the summers . . . I played semi-pro ball to help me along with the expenses.

He was good enough to be inducted into the university's hall of fame. It was there where he also met Dick Brewer, the man who would be his boss at Sidney Lanier High School for most of his career.[12]

At the time, Texas universities were not welcoming to Mexican American athletes. The lives of two Mexican American athletes may help explain the typical experience of boys with Spanish surnames. As mentioned earlier, Mike de la Fuente was an excellent baseball player who got a pitching scholarship to the University of Texas, the premier university in the state then and now. The young man from South Texas remembers once when the University of Texas visited Texas A&M University for an important game. The Aggie school baseball team refused to play the Longhorns in a public arena with a Mexican pitching. So the athletic officials emptied the stands and played the game with no fans, and De la Fuente proceeded to pitch a no-hitter, prompting one opposing player to come to the locker room and apologize.[13]

E. C. Lerma confronted a similar situation in his beloved Texas A&I University in Kingsville, Texas. He grew up in the shadows of Javelina Stadium and yearned to play for the team. His high school football exploits got him into the university, and he got a chance to quarterback the team to one of its most successful seasons. But during his playing time, he stayed away from the homecoming games and any activity that might place him in proximity to a white girl, even as some of his burly white football friends provided him cover in those activities that he chose to attend. Years later he remembered the last football party he attended. There he learned just how destructive racial biases could be for a Mexican athlete like him. As he mingled with the players, he came upon a gathering of the coach and some of his teammates. He overheard the coach say, "We had a successful season with Lerma at quarterback, but can you imagine what it would have been if he had played halfback?" Simply put, white girls and the running-back slot were not for Mexicans no matter how good they were. This was a memory that Lerma never forgot.[14]

Having a name like "William Carson" may have initially helped Herrera navigate an Anglo world better than Lerma or De la Fuente. His pleasant and often humorous demeanor and even the fact that he did not broadcast his Spanish also may have eased his way because in his first year at the university he was initiated into the Phi Theta Delta Fraternity, creating a readymade group of friends.[15] Being in a fraternity was simply not common for Mexican American college students at the time.

But it was his athletic exploits, however, that facilitated his stay at the university. In his first year, 1918–1919, Herrera played end for the Southwestern football team, which won the Texas Intercollegiate Athletic Association title. In his second year, the baseball team also won the conference title with Herrera on the team. By his third year, Herrera was the top basketball player, scoring 230 of the team's season point total of 371. A newspaper said of him, "His playing was at all times above par and he was the shining light when everything else looked gloomy for the Pirates."[16]

Herrera's scrapbook is full of clippings that detail his athletic life as a Southwestern Pirate. His teams played teams from all over Texas, including the bigger state schools and sometimes even teams from outside the state. Southwestern more than held its own against these larger schools, and it seems that Herrera was always an important part of the victory. His name appears in most of the clippings—which is probably natural since he kept the scrapbook—but particularly those that talked about the Pirate basketball games. For someone who measured less than five-foot-five, Herrera's athletic exploits were stellar. No doubt that these performances, as well as his ability to get along with teammates, made his time at Southwestern pleasant. Interestingly, though, he did not graduate from Southwestern University but instead graduated several years later from the University of San Antonio (now Trinity University in San Antonio). It is possible that he ran out of money before he ran out of courses to meet graduation requirements.[17]

Herrera's first coaching job after college was at Beaumont High School in 1923, where his team had an outstanding season, winning nineteen out of twenty games. But Herrera lasted only one year there. Why? No explanation exists. While there, and even before, he played minor league baseball. If, as noted by one journalist, he had played in the Cotton State League or the Panhandle–Pecos Valley League, he would have traveled throughout the western part of the state, playing teams with such colorful names as the Amarillo Gassers, Clovis Buzzers, Ranger Nitros, and Sweetwater Swatters. Those small town baseball fields were connected by lonely dusty roads where the traveler found his nostrils full of oil fumes and the smell of manure. Anything but glamorous, this lifestyle hardly made anyone rich. It was not uncommon for players to hook up with a small-town team and be there for most of their athletic life. Hundreds of these teams existed throughout the nation, but particularly so in the South and Southwest.[18] Herrera, in an interview given at age eighty, remembers being a member of the Galveston Sandcrabs of the Texas League for a few weeks. "No wonder we didn't win," he recalled, "with a name like that we were more crawlers than hitters."[19]

We have no record of Herrera's play in the Cotton League as his name does not appear on its incomplete rosters. By his own account, he played mostly semi-pro ball, starting in 1919 with the Sulphur Refining Company, where he played with Eddie Dyer, who later coached the world champion St. Louis Cardinals. From there he went to Bay City, then in the summer of 1921 he played with the Lake Charles Athletics in Louisiana and roomed with Ted Lyons, who would be inducted into the Baseball Hall of Fame. In 1922 and 1923, he played at Monroe, Louisiana, but left in the middle of the last season to join the Galveston Sandcrabs in the Texas League.[20] One newspaper account announcing his induction into the Texas Hall of Fame describes Herrera as having spent "a couple of seasons [playing] minor league baseball."[21] It is quite possible that what he termed "semi-pro ball" was what later came to be known as the minors.

Baseball was Herrera's favorite sport and the one he best played. More interesting was how he fit into a game popular among Mexican Americans but one from which they were often excluded in small Texas towns, where segregation and discrimination were palpable. Mexican Americans in those towns did not participate in many public events that were not either sponsored by them or explicitly opened to them. Things might have been different in larger cities like San Antonio, Laredo, and El Paso—places where there was a larger Mexican American population—but in small towns such as Sweetwater, San Angelo, and Abilene, Mexicans and Mexican Americans understood well where they were wanted and where they were not. Historians in recent times have written that Mexicans and Mexican Americans were still being lynched in Texas in the mid- to late 1920s. Lynching was less common by then, but the possibility was hard to ignore, particularly during those passionate close games.

Surely Herrera was never in any danger of violence, but it is not difficult to imagine that he was conscious of it.[22] Given his approach to things, it was something that he probably did not entertain for long. Baseball was the game in both the Anglo and Mexican worlds, and one that Herrera loved. He played it while his legs could keep him running around the bases and his eyes kept the ball in front of him. He retired grudgingly, but even before he fully retired from baseball he began umpiring in the local leagues and eventually in Mexico.[23]

This is what we know of his coaching experience in Beaumont: He was an assistant to the football coach and the head basketball coach. He left the school two years before it went to the state playoffs and defeated San Antonio High School for the fifth official state title given in Texas. We know little of what occurred there, though he seemed excited about the boys he had when he first arrived. "I'll have the material for a championship club," Herrera told a reporter, "and if the breaks come my way, Beaumont should be at Austin when the interscholastic finals are being played." The little coach also revealed in that story the confidence and grit that motivated him: "I intend to teach the fellows everything I know about the game, and to instill a fighting spirit into them."[24] At Beaumont he met and worked with Lil Dimmitt, the head football coach and athletic director, whom he credited with helping him learn to mentor young men. We don't know how the people of that East Texas community reacted to this coach with the Mexican name and the light brown skin, but since Texans liked winners, it is likely that most soon warmed to him. What we do know is that he played basketball after work for the Good Gulf Oil Company of neighboring Port Arthur.

In the 1920s, most mid-size and large businesses sponsored athletic teams to create a sense of community and, in the words of the *Port Arthur Daily News*, "bring clean, wholesome fun to the city."[25] In her book *Learning to Win*, Pamela Grundy argues that sports became another part of the developing "American landscape" built by industrial capitalism, and its competitive nature allowed communities to see themselves as creating individuals who understood rules, had self-discipline, were self-assertive, and knew how to engage in teamwork. Basketball, in her words, fit with the "glamorous modernity" that was being promoted by capitalists throughout the nation.[26] This modernity required creating a new labor force of men and women willing to work long, hard hours for the company and show respect for authority. But the work was so tedious and conditions so miserable that employee turnover was often high. To counter this, companies sponsored teams and provided their workers a moment of glory by either playing or supporting their fellow workers. Over time, winning became important for the companies and businesses because their own reputations within the community rose with the success of their teams. Soon they hired athletes to come to play for them even if they did not work for the company.[27]

Herrera joined the Good Gulf Basketeers the same year he came to coach at Beaumont High School. Good Gulf, which became Gulf Oil Company and later part of Chevron Oil, was at the time a pioneer oil company that led gas exploration in the Gulf Coast and eventually into Mexico. The company dominated the economic and social life of Port Arthur, an ocean-side community with no other economic endeavor.[28] It is not clear how Herrera became part of the company team, but in the year he joined he became one of its stars, sometimes being called the "diminutive forward" and at other times the "midget forward." Herrera shone as a sharpshooter for a team that loved to "cut and slash their way" to victories. In one tournament game he hit six field goals and eight free throws to lead his team to victory. In another he "rang up one of the prettiest baskets of the contest." The Basketeers, in city and regional tournaments, played against other oil companies, against Herrera's alma mater Southwestern University, and even a team from Mexico City. Theirs was a busy schedule that often had the players practicing every day of the week for several hours.[29]

Given that schedule of games and practices, one might question how much coaching at the high school mattered to a young man who was still in his prime playing years. What we do know is that he left a year later and joined the Gulf Oil Company in Port Arthur, which then sent him to Mexico.[30] One newspaper account has him going to Mexico for a "four-season stint as a professional baseball player at Tampico, Mexico."[31] We don't know whether Herrera was hired simply to play ball or whether he went to work as a pipeliner and accountant. It is probable that he was recruited to do both, though he left the company after a short time and moved on to the East Oil Company in Tampico.[32]

His athletic skills became quite useful in Mexico to the oil company. As in the States, companies with international branches formed teams to keep them connected to their American roots. These teams were often quite skilled and talented, and it was not beyond company managers and supervisors to hire individuals and move them overseas for their athletic skills as much as for their labor talents. Whether the company knew about Herrera's baseball skills before they hired him, they soon found out and had him not only playing for their team but also coaching semi-pro teams, some of which they might have sponsored from 1923 to 1927. Baseball became an organized sport in Mexico in 1925, though there were teams, many replete with Cuban players, even earlier. Numerous leagues and teams were sponsored either by Mexican businesses, unions, or government ministries.[33] Herrera became so well known for both his athletic and coaching abilities that he was soon managing the Luz y Fuerza baseball team sponsored by the federal government's electrical company. This public monopoly fielded teams in various sports and was the one entity able to recruit and hire strong baseball players. Herrera found himself with several players that went on to compete with professional baseball teams in the States, and with them he won the Mexican national championship.[34]

His coaching exploits in Mexico, especially those with Luz y Fuerza, indicate that Herrera could coach both Anglo and Mexican players and win over Mexican officials, who at the time would have shared their countrymen's distrust of Americans and the disdain shown to Mexicans who lived in the United States. While Herrera never revealed an interest in Mexican American politics and seemed to lack familiarity with Mexican culture, he spent many summers umpiring in the Mexican leagues and probably counseled his players to participate in international basketball tournaments after they left school. Going back and forth across the border seemed a natural thing for him to continue as a part of baseball and to provide extra income to what would always be a meager salary for coaching basketball.[35] In fact, going to Mexico constantly got him some very good connections, and in his later years he umpired in the Mexican Professional Baseball League and was even invited to attend the opening of the Mexican Baseball Hall of Fame.[36]

It was during his three-plus-year stint in Mexico that he met his wife, Mary Leona Hatch, a young nurse from Louisiana who was working at an American hospital in Tampico. Mary was a tough-minded, no-nonsense orphaned woman who went to Mexico to practice her trade and possibly find a bit of adventure. Herrera, spiked on the foot in a baseball game, fell for the woman who tended his wound and who became his companion and his most loyal fan to the day he died. But her relationship with the in-laws would be conflicted, and the couple soon moved away from Herrera's family, either by her insistence or in his attempt to avoid family turmoil. Whatever the reasons, the familial conflict resulted in the loss of most contact with Herrera's immediate family, and his children would not know their cousins, aunts, and uncles until late in their own lives, when both their parents had passed away.[37] Perhaps this familial separation combined with his early schooling at Brackenridge High School, his university years at Southwestern, and his experience playing with predominantly white teams to create Herrera's white persona. Though he spent almost all of his years in the company of Mexicans and Mexican Americans, he never quite looked or acted like one of them. Yet it was with them that he found his greatest achievements and his greatest joys. And they in turn found a most important mentor.

By the late 1920s, numerous American oil companies began reconsidering their operations in Mexican for fear that Mexico's revolutionary government might renege on their contractual agreements and even expropriate their oil fields. These fears arose from the fact that both American businessmen and Mexican government officials recognized that the oil contracts negotiated shortly after the Mexican Revolution actually violated Article 17 of the post-revolutionary Mexican Constitution that gave Mexico greater soil rights than were agreed to by the oil companies and the government. By this time, Venezuela had become more attractive both politically and economically as an oil-producing nation, while Mexican domestic consumption had risen to a point that less gas was available for export.[38] Expropriation would not come for another decade and a half, but for Herrera and other Americans working in the oil fields, Mexico had lost its luster by the late 1920s. Of course, that work had often been for single men. Once married, most men wanted to raise their families in the States.

Herrera came back to his adopted hometown of San Antonio to work for the Public Service Company and soon found himself playing basketball in the afternoons for the company team. While back in the States, Herrera reacquainted himself with an old college classmate, R. H. Brewer, who directed athletics for the San Antonio school district and who had been on Herrera's Southwestern Pirate baseball team. It may have been a tip from this old buddy that led Herrera to apply to Sidney Lanier Junior High. He was hired in 1928 to coach all the junior high sports. The initial job lasted three months, but he then received permanent status the following year when Sidney Lanier went from a junior high school to a junior-senior vocational high school. This meant that students in the West Side of town would attend Sidney Lanier from the sixth to the eleventh grade, which at the time was the highest grade in American high schools.

That stint as head coach lasted until the fall of 1929, when the school hired Wright "Toady" Riley to coach varsity sports and relegated Herrera to the junior teams. Riley turned out to be a successful coach, and his teams won cage titles in 1930, 1931, and 1933. In 1933, Riley left to take over the coaching job at the newly constructed Fox Tech High School, and Herrera again assumed the head coaching job of all sports until 1935, when the high school hired a football coach and Herrera went to coaching basketball almost exclusively.[39] In the 1940s, Herrera would again coach football for Lanier.

When Herrera assumed the head coaching job, he entered a basketball world that was changing, with basketball becoming a faster game that depended more heavily on the role of the guards. For the first part of the twentieth century, basketball had been a methodical game more suited for the big man in the middle or the sharpshooter from the outside—although judging from the early low scores, there were not many of those. Up until the 1930s, not all players were allowed to cross mid-court, allowing the defense to have a player advantage over the offense. The teams also jumped for the ball after every score. Since there was no shot clock for either high school or college games at the time, coaches instructed their players to take their time to set up a shot either by the big man inside or the shooter from the perimeter. Dribbling as a game-breaking or game-changing skill was not taught. And it was not until the late 1930s that players began to dribble behind the back or with either hand. The slow pace gave an advantage to the methodically moving, basket-securing team with at least one good shooter and one good big man. It was particularly partial to the big man with a sure shot from the five- to ten-foot range. Physical play was not encouraged—at least not the slashing, driving, and posting-your-man type—but tall players still had an advantage because of their big elbows and larger bodies.

By the late thirties, there were still many teams that played a slow game because their coaches had either played or been trained in that style. Some teams, however, had transitioned to a much faster, wide-open game. The fact that all players could cross the mid-court line, that man-to-man and even full-court press defenses were developing, and that guards were becoming the real leaders on the court with their dribbling skills, all allowed a fast-moving team to become more dominant. Big men were always a necessity, but teams could win without them, and teams that had them required them to move up and down the court. With the faster game, passing became more important, and so did the idea of creating your own shot. Jump shooting came into existence—though not widespread until the late 1940s—and that also favored the faster and more athletic teams.

Herrera was still a young coach in 1933 when he took over varsity for the second and last time and so seemed more willing to try the new innovations in basketball. He saw the benefits of the new style because he understood that he was never going to have many tall and athletic players who could dominate inside. Every year when tryouts began, it dawned on him how short his fellow Mexicans were. Tony Rivera remembered that most of the guys on the team were around five-foot-two or five-foot-three, "so we always used a fast break."[40] It was not uncommon for the point guard to be just a notch above five feet and for the starting center to be shorter than most other teams' starting forwards or even guards. Compounding Herrera's disadvantage were the slim frames of most of his players. There are few pictures of large muscular kids in shorts and T-shirts playing for Lanier. But what his players offered was a love of the game.

Basketball was a game that many Mexican American youth knew well because they played it frequently in the schoolyard courts and at the community centers that dotted the barrios around Lanier. There was the Boys Club, the Mexican Christian Center, Wesley House Center, the House of Neighborly Service, the Good Samaritan Center, the Guadalupe Community Center, and a host of other centers, most sponsored or set up by the local churches in the barrio. Even the Alazan–Apache Courts had their own recreational activities for the residents and their children. While these centers offered a number of sewing, craft, and English classes, about the only sporting activities provided were basketball and occasionally volleyball. These sports were a less expensive alternative to baseball and football. At the time, soccer did not appear to be popular among Mexicans and Mexican Americans. It would not come into American high school until nearly the 1980s. Even in Mexico, soccer trailed basketball, baseball, and in some cases, American football in popularity.

In a community with few resources, it was always much easier to get a basketball than it was to get a glove, bat, and ball. Basketball, at least back then, was considered a real team sport, much more than others, and thus lent itself to a greater effort at Americanization, one of the main missions of most of these centers. "The original Boys Club was . . . where I used to hang out as soon as I got out of school," remembers Tony Rivera, future all-state player for the Lanier Voks. "They had all kinds of things going on . . . that's where I started playing basketball." It was also the place that many of the players from Lanier met each other and bonded on the court. They came to know each other's moves, strengths, and weak spots. It was also a place where younger players got a chance to play with older ones and learned what it took to start for Lanier.

Those who stopped to watch the pickup games were treated to a high level of basketball. Tony Rivera, two-time all-state forward and member of the 1943 team versus David Rodríguez, all-state center for the 1945 team, would have been a sight to see. The game must have been memorable because many years later a rather confident Rivera would continue to admire the underclassman because "he was good . . . and the only tall guy we had."[41] Rudy Bernal, who coached at Lanier decades later, remembers his father telling him about the Guadalupe Community Center, the Good Samaritan Center, and numerous "little areas" where "the guys grew up playing basketball." There was, according to Bernal's dad, simply nothing else to do. This kind of street-ball playing not only allowed players to refine their skills but, more important, to develop the chemistry that would make the championship runs possible.[42]

Jesse and Carlos Camacho, both who played in the early 1940s, learned basketball at the Wesley House community center located a block from where they lived. There Frank Bernal, who would have several family members play at Lanier, coached the kids from the barrio and taught them the fundamentals of the game. He also got them involved in weekend tournaments in the city and took them to the border town of Laredo to play teams down there. Carlos remembers starting to play at the age of eight. Aside from Wesley House, the Camacho brothers remember playing at the Boys Club and then with the city leagues. Most of the kids they played with, remembers Carlos, went on to play at Lanier: "When we got to Lanier we came trained [to play basketball], then Nemo got us and polished [our game]."[43] This constant playing together allowed the players to develop chemistry, to know each other's moves, and bond as friends.

It is probably there and on the outside courts where some of the players got their nicknames, a working-class ritual prevalent even today among Mexicans and Mexican Americans in the barrio where young men are named according to their skin complexion, the shape of their head, how tall or short they are, where they live, and how they talk. It can also come from the shortening or adulteration of a first name. Nicknaming is a ritual that seems to say that whatever you were named in the *pila bautisma*, or the baptismal font, here you have been christened in a way that people will know you and instantly recognize you. These nicknames had a way of making everyone equal or bringing someone down from their "high horse." It allowed for a descriptive renaming that made people famous or infamous—or at least memorable. It would not have been uncommon in the barrios of San Antonio to know someone by their nickname without ever knowing their full proper name. There are formal explanations of why nicknaming occurs, though most Mexicans would simply say that this is the way it has been since they can remember.[44]

While often a term of endearment, nicknames could also be unflattering. Rudy Bernal remembers his father telling him about the nicknames and hearing them when he met some of the players when he accompanied the older Bernal to play recreational or even city league ball. "Tony [Rivera] was "Molo" [given to those with big teeth] . . . my uncle Joe [who also played], they called "Chema" [usually reserved for those named José María] . . . my dad was "Ram" [for Ramiro]. There was another fellow who went by "Curro" [a name given to a flashy dresser]. They all had nicknames."[45]

A Lanier '69 graduate remembers an uncle telling him about a player who played at Lanier in the 1940s known as "Azteca," probably because he looked, in the minds of his teammates, like a Mexican Indian warrior. Carlos Camacho, team captain in 1941, was called "Mochito"—which could mean "Shorty"—or sometimes "Charlie." And he and his brother Jesse remember others who were named "Cebolla" (onion), "Dracula," and "King Kong." Another was known as "la Verdura" (the vegetable) for being green when he started playing. Jesse also remembered the best player he played with in 1940 was called "el Huevo" (the egg).[46] Before long, everyone knew the nicknames of those to whom they passed the ball. And of course they would also know their coach's nickname, "Nemo," though it is unlikely that anyone called him that while in practice or during the game, though many would after they left the school and continued their relationship—now a friendship among equals with him.

I asked some of my Lanier fellow graduates about their own nicknames and those they often heard in the barrio and the school grounds. One friend, Domingo Vasquez, I quote at length, as he explained better than most some of the reasons and ways people got their nicknames:

> Three of our friends were really dark, so one was nicknamed "Negro"; the second was Ramon, who was called "Handsome"; and the third was Robert Sánchez, who was called "Bobby Black" or "Boston Blackie." Everyone knew José Espinoza as "Devil" because he was always getting into trouble. Augustin Sánchez was nicknamed "Speedy" because he was a very fat kid, however he was pretty fast. . . . Leroy Garza was called "Lucky Leroy" because very few Mexican mothers would name their son Leroy. "Chale" was just short for Charles or Charlie. "Quequito" [pronounced *cake-ito*] was always eating cupcakes so the name stuck. Encarnación Flores was called "Carne" [meat] because who would want to call him by his long name every time? Fernando García was called "Horse" because he ran strong and tough. Ernest [Ernesto] Rodríguez was called "Neto" for short. This guy . . . in the El Paso Meat Market softball team was called "Venado" [deer] because he ran really fast. Finally, this boy in elementary school was called "Columpio" [swing] because he had broken his leg . . . [and] it did not heal correctly because he kept cutting the cast himself until his leg stayed messed up and he had to swing his leg in order to walk.[47]

Rosie Peña, head cheerleader in 1960, remembers her brother's friends "Nariz" (nose), "Troca" (Spanglish for "truck"), and "Mouse." One had a long nose, the other was built like a small truck, and the third had an obsession with cheese.[48] Other names popular in the barrios of San Antonio both in the 1940s and 1960s were "Tachuela" (thumbtack) for someone short, "Mayate" (beetle) for someone very dark, "Tartajas" for someone who stuttered, "la Polla" (the chick) for someone with pigeon toes, "Cacheton(a)" for someone with fluffy cheeks, "Tapon" (plug) for a snotty person, and "Rana" (frog) for someone who jumped far. Then there were those that were common for proper names: "Chayo" for Rosario, "Chuy" for Jesús, "Rules" for Raul, "Nacho" (my nickname) for Ignacio, "Tacho" for Anastasio—and the list could go on. This practice goes back even before the twentieth century, and it would not be surprising to have found an Aztec warrior with the name of "Chino" (Chinese), a common nickname among Mexicans and, as we learn in the movie *West Side Story*, among Puerto Ricans.[49]

These names were mostly had within the Mexican working class, as they might have seemed offensive to the *exiliados* and some of the more established middle class. Mexican movies of the 1930s and 1940s would add fuel to the nicknaming phenomenon with a parade of famous working-class, slapstick comedians such as "Resortes" (spring or rubber band), "Clavillaso" (nailing), "Capiruta," "Tin Tan," and the most famous, "Cantinflas." These actors became the definers of Mexican working-class culture and encouraged their audiences to *relajarse*, let their hair down and take life less seriously. The absence of formal names allowed the antics of these funny characters to become universal among the Mexican working class and free those who had little with which to express themselves. By empowering their difference, the working class could ignore or at least push back against high-brow culture. They showed they were capable of besting those who considered themselves better in the game of life.[50]

This Mexican working-class culture would see itself reaffirmed in the barrios of the Southwestern United States. In El Paso during the late 1930s and early 1940s would emerge what came to be known as *pachuco* culture.[51] Taking their cue from both the working-class movie characters and the underworld crime scene, these Texas-born or second-generation immigrant youth created a style of dress and a language that was at first only accessible to them but that later became common among barrio youth and older men who occasioned the bars and cantinas of the Mexican side of town. Eventually the bilingualism of many of the youth attending public schools affected the nicknaming tradition, yielding names such as Speedy, Spaceman, Horse, el Blue, Lefty, and Curly.

Many years after Herrera had left Lanier, his former players hosted a testimonial dinner where former players could gather to honor him. "But Herrera is worried," wrote sports columnist Dan Cook, "You see, when he was building champions and putting Lanier into the record books every Latin athlete with a pound of desire or an ounce of talent had a nickname. . . . The old man well remembers his boys but he remembers most by nicknames that have long since been dropped. Oscar Flores, for instance, isn't too willing to admit that for many years he was known simply as 'Dracula.' But Drac will be there Monday night. Along with Chivo (goat), La Chispa (the spark), Goofus, King Kong, El Pelón (the bald one), La Rata (the rat), The Tooth and many more." While the "rundown," added the writer, sounded like a roll call at San Quentin, most of those nicknames now belonged to "fellows who . . . own highly respected places in San Antonio society."[52]

The players' nicknames did not seem so unique to a coach who himself had carried with him the tag of "Nemo" since his early years when newspapers extolled his athletic achievements. None of his players remembers knowing the origin of the name. It was not until Herrera's induction into the Texas Hall of Fame that a newspaper opined that he had been named after a cartoon strip character, although the newspaper got it wrong when it dated the character as popular in the post–World War I era.[53] "Little Nemo in Slumberland" was a comic strip created by pioneering cartoonist Winsor McCay. It ran in the *New York Herald* from 1905 to 1911. Later the prolific artist, who is said to have drawn over one million cartoons, would move his comic strip to the *New York American* and rename it "In the World of Wonderful Dreams."[54] That comic strip would run for four years until an unappreciative William Randolph Hearst turned McCay into an editorial cartoonist and put an end to Little Nemo.[55]

At a time when comic and cartoon strips were about "rambunctious young brats who wreaked havoc on the adult world," Little Nemo was a much darker cartoon about a boy who when asleep awoke in a fantasy land of jungles, slaves, imps, large butterflies, kings, and queens. One reviewer described the cartoon as being as much an "architectural fantasy as fairy tale."[56] Little Nemo wore his hair unkempt, spoke in a "quaint and stilted language," and seemed to always have a faraway look. More than anything else, Little Nemo seemed not always to fit his surroundings. His nemesis-turned-friend Flip—a green-faced character who dressed like a minstrel, always carried a cigar in his mouth, and was sometimes referred to as "boy" by Nemo—was often the instigator of the dream adventures. The cartoon is laden with complex symbolisms that connote racial tensions of the period.

Given that the cartoon ended its run by Herrera's fifteenth birthday, if the cartoon indeed was the source of his nickname, he likely received the name in his early middle school years or even before. Was it his faraway look, his sometimes ruffled hair, his quiet but curious demeanor, or something else that reflected the character of Little Nemo? We can say that he must have liked his nickname or found something telling about it. One does not move from one stage of life and across wide distances and have a youthful nickname follow unless one repeats it and makes sure others become familiar with it. Why else would they have known him as Nemo in Georgetown, Beaumont, probably Mexico, and then San Antonio again? It became so common to refer to him as Nemo that sports writers came to substitute it for his first name.

There is, however, another version to how Herrera got his nickname that his son says came from Nemo himself. This version reveals how Mexican Herrera's early life really was. It also underscores the transformation that Mexicans experienced in an Anglo world. Charles Herrera, his youngest son, says his father was actually known as Guillermo, which is the Spanish translation of William. As would be the case in the Mexican familial world in which he grew up, he came to be known as Memo, a shortening of Guillermo. As a batboy for the San Antonio Bronchos semi-pro team in San Antonio, the name was changed to Nemo because few of the English tongues in the dugout could repeat the Spanish nickname.[57] In an alumni profile, Herrera confirmed the naming this way: "While I was the batboy for the San Antonio Bronchos in 1911–1913 one of the players tagged me "Nemo" because he didn't like the name Memo, which is short for Guillermo in Spanish. It stuck."[58] The name change was a common occurrence in the Southwest, where whites rarely bothered to learn a Mexican's name and simply called him or her by the English name closest to the original. So Antonio became Tony; Roberto, Robert; Sara, Sarah, and so forth.

Regardless of what Herrera would say nearly fifty-three years after his naming, the Memo of the Mexican family became in the minds of his Anglo classmates, team partners, teachers, and the not-interested-in-digging-for-the-truth sportswriters the Nemo of the cartoon strip. No matter how Herrera's nickname came to be, he was Nemo in the public world of the sports pages of Texas newspapers. Like many Mexicans in his era—and even mine, I might add—Herrera lost the Spanish-sounding name his family and his community had bestowed upon him because English tongues could not pronounce it and some Anglo ears did not like it. And like many Mexicans whose careers and marriage choices caused them to leave behind their Mexican world, Herrera simply adjusted. It was much easier for him, as it has been for Mexicans of every era, to simply accept the linguistic transformation of the name rather than spend time correcting friends, neighbors, and colleagues. This acquiescence came in exchange for an opportunity to pursue a career, a degree, or peace of mind.

In Herrera's case it was the price to be paid for participating in the sports world that he loved and in the game of basketball, which was in his time an effective sport for those who saw immigrants and ethnic young men as being in need of integration into the American social fabric. How better to teach them to be American than to teach them the game of basketball, where they would learn teamwork, rules, skills, and hard work? Basketball taught individuality—the dribbling, shooting, rebounding—but within the context of a group. It was also in those small groups, after a hearty game, that counselors and coaches taught the young men values and morals. Sports was the great social and cultural school for those who often dropped out or who had no structured home environment and grew up with little knowledge of how American society worked. Given how his boys remember him, Nemo Herrera was imbued with all those notions of building character and citizenship.

In his scrapbook he proudly pasted "The Coaches Code," which went well with the notions of building character and teaching American values:

> My first consideration shall be the welfare of the boys. My leadership shall . . . contribute to cleaner living, better health habits and a true respect for the rules of play [and] authority of officials. . . . My objective shall be to win if possible, to lose if necessary, but at all times to have the conduct of all contribute to a fuller understanding and a keener appreciation of fair play. I shall teach that Good Sportsmanship is Good Citizenship and as such is essential to individuals, communities, state and nation. (Unknown author)

Being outside the home environment—where so much time was spent trying to survive or to keep the family from dysfunction—coaches and teachers like Herrera had the time and luxury to teach these young men to navigate a society most of them did not always understand. Said one sports columnist years after Herrera had retired, "[He] was far more than a coach. He knew more about his boys than did their parents for it was to Nemo that they carried their big problems. Those who crossed swords with the law . . . always dialed the coach's number when given a chance for that one phone call."[59] Herrera loved to do the job handed to him by the school and society. He felt he could understand his boys better than others. "I didn't have anything either," he would tell one reporter. "I was poor, they were poor, but everything I did was for those kids."[60] He understood that they had so little that to find the next meal was, as he described it, a "monumental challenge," and for them the "the Depression was all the time."[61]

Herrera's concern for his players, however, was structured within the context of teaching them basketball. Herrera was a father figure to his players, but like many fathers of the 1930s and 1940s, his was a tough love. One reporter described him as someone who "coached them . . . counseled and sometimes beat the hell out of them if they needed it."[62] This was an exaggeration on the reporter's part, but one to emphasize the point that Herrera would do anything for his "kids." The tough love came only after he first befriended them and made them feel welcome. Both Jesse and Carlos remember him as the "friendliest guy you could imagine." Carlos remembers being able to kid with Herrera before and after practice. Herrera tried to get to know the players on a personal level, providing them advice and pointing out when they were making mistakes. He even visited them when they were sick at home. This was so rare—that a teacher visit a student at home—that sometimes the family would not let him in. He explained, "They thought I was the police."[63]

Carlos remembers having a steady girlfriend but being fascinated by a senior girl who seemed to share the attraction. He was tempted to seek out the girl and dump his Anita. Herrera, who kept close watch on his players, called him in one day and said, "She's a senior. She's going out soon. You better stick to Anita." Carlos did and ended up marrying his high school sweetheart. To others Herrera gave advice and even pointed the way toward a career or college. Aside from visiting them at home or advising them in the hallways, Herrera sometimes dropped by the local drugstore to see what his players were doing. Later, when some of them went to war, he went to see them off at the train station or drove them to the army depot, partly because none of them had cars but, more important, to provide them with moral support in what was the most important step they would be taking as young adults.[64] Having that kind of relationship with his players allowed Herrera to be stern with his boys. Carlos once goofed off during practice, and Herrera took the paddle to him. Immediately after making his point, Herrera smiled and told him, "Come on, come on, you're still alive. Get in there," and gave out a laugh.[65]

On the court, "He meant business." He took no lip from his players, ran them until their tongues hung out, and then ran them some more. "Come on, come on," he would say, and sometimes let out something to the effect of "You serious?" when the players did not perform at the level he wanted. Lack of full commitment got them a "kick in the butt once in a while."[66] His demeanor in practice was serious, and he did not hesitate to scream at his players, but his boys never perceived him as verbally or physically abusive. Aside from the aforementioned paddling, none of his players remembers him as being mean.

Paddling was a common form of punishment in Texas schools and a practice that continued up until the late 1960s and possibly the 1970s at Lanier. Having been the victim of several paddlings during my time in high school, I can testify that they tended to be more embarrassing—to some probably humiliating—than painful. Moreover, paddlings were no less physical than what most Mexican American youth were accustomed to at home.

Although abuse, in some instances worse than others, occurred, Lanier graduates rarely found paddling to be traumatic. In a survey of Lanier 1969 graduates, one interviewee found that "humiliation was the hardest [part] to deal with," while others believed that recipients "deserved it," an indication that paddling was nothing uncommon. Interestingly, two remember being paddled by coaches, and in both cases the coaches were Mexican American. One remembers the coach letting him choose the paddle with which to be punished, and he remembers having chosen the one that ended up being the most painful. He did not believe, however, the paddling to be abusive. Interestingly, that same coach—who happened to be my art teacher—was almost as successful in coaching track and cross-country as Herrera was in coaching basketball. His teams would dominate those sports in the district and city competitions for nearly five years in the 1960s.[67]

Nicolas Rodríguez and Benjamin Dominguez both remember a ritual that had become common among Lanier coaches by the 1960s and may well have come from earlier coaches like Herrera. When a group of students misbehaved in gym class or during basketball practice, the coaches would get a paddle and make the boys—rarely girls—form a circle. Each student had to paddle the person to their right or left, then pass up the paddle to the next person until the paddle arrived at the starting point. Then the paddling would proceed in the opposite direction. According to Rodríguez, the "paddle was a small baseball bat cut down the middle to about 12 inches from the handle." Benjamin remembers that the "strength" of the paddling had to "meet the coach's approval." After such sessions, everyone went to the showers with a "red streak across their butt."[68]

There were, however, worse things than being paddled by the coaches or teachers. Said one student, "I would rather get paddled at school than have my parents come to school to talk to the dean of boys or the principal because I knew I would get it worst [*sic*] when I [got] back home." This was a common sentiment from students who knew that their parents did not like to be humiliated by having to come to the principal's office, a place where many of them felt treated like children because they could not understand the language or simply did not have fluency. Being scolded for your child's behavior was just one more "experience" with whites or Anglos that Mexicans did not want. Every one of my Lanier '69 respondents confirmed that their parents were "strict disciplinarians" who paddled them and their siblings, made them kneel down in a corner, locked them in a room if there were any extras, pinched them, or pulled their ears. And one knew better than to run from them because parents rarely gave up. While some admitted to being more afraid of their parents than their teachers, there were a few teachers with long-held reputations of being a "witch" or, as one student so poetically put it, of being "potty trained at gunpoint."[69]

David Rodríguez, all-state player for Lanier, remembered misbehaving and being sent to the vice principal's office, where he was given three swats with a thick paddle. "It stung like hell," he recalled sixty-plus years later. Though students would often get the choice of being paddled or having their parents come to the office, David's father was summoned to the school, anyway. When the vice principal told him about the three swats, David's father replied, "Is that all you're going to give him? I'll take care of him when we get home." Dad had a razor strap, and David remembers that he "never [misbehaved] again."[70]

Being paddled by Herrera, which happened rarely, was probably to most players less painful than being made to "duckwalk," an excruciating exercise meant to strengthen the ligaments in their ankles and keep the players from turning or spraining their ankles. The son of one of the players remembered learning that "the coach really drove them hard and he knew the reason why."[71] That reason was that they were always going to give size advantage to the teams they played. "I never had any tall kids," Herrera would tell a magazine writer.[72] He also understood that there were a number of players, like Ramiro Bernal, who had lost their fathers to disease or to abandonment and needed a male role model. But most of all, his players needed discipline and the will to sacrifice their bodies and minds to pain, exhaustion, and verbal tongue-lashings. If they could not be taller or faster or better shooters, they were going to be in better condition and play the game more intensely until the final buzzer. Herrera remembered that his practices and exercises made them "fast little Mexican kids and they just worried the opponents to death."[73] More important, they learned how tough it was to be an adult with goals and ambitions.

Herrera knew, according Ramiro Bernal's son, that he "had good players, he didn't have great players . . . but he taught them how to play together." Bernal, a coach himself at Lanier who took a small, all-Mexican team to the state finals in 2002, believed that it was Herrera's ability to make them play as a team, as a cohesive unit that brought him the success. "If your guys work together all the time that takes the place of talent a lot. I think you can get a lot further when you have guys playing together than if you get five great players who don't play together," he added sixty-seven years after his father played.[74] While most players and contemporary sports writers might agree with much of what Bernal said, there would be some question about his assessment that Herrera had no "great players," but that is a later part of the story.

Herrera's "specialty was to always [be] on the go. From the start of the game until the end . . . you've got to keep moving, keep moving. . . . That was his . . . plan," said Rivera, one of Herrera's favorite players.[75] The coach did not believe in playing a slow-down game or anything that resembled a zone. The idea, drilled into the players' heads in every practice, was to use quickness and speed to beat the other team down the court, find the open shot, or simply tire opposing players for easy layups. Most players they faced were not into fast breaks, long passes, or quick dribbling. Back then, the speedsters were in football and track, not necessarily in basketball. Typical basketball winning was based on methodical half-court passing, low-post play, and sharp stand-up shooting. This was a difficult combination to beat if a team was short and had no great shooters, and from the newspaper accounts it does not seem that Herrera ever had a team full of great shooters. It was their ability to get to the basket, to steal balls, to get trash points, and to tire their opponents that made them successful. And all of that started with the hard practices in the gym.

During the games Herrera transformed into a stoic man. He said his piece in the locker room before the game, and he was more than willing to correct or chew out the players after the game or during half-time, but otherwise he kept his cool. Carlos and his brother Jesse remember him as "pretty quiet" during the games while he paced the out-of-bounds line. They don't remember him arguing with the referees much. It was not acceptable back then, and it had the potential to backfire with referees who were mostly volunteers or low-paid officials. It is quite possible that Herrera also understood the dynamics of race relations in the sports world of Texas. His teams were always respected, and few journalists ever said anything negative about them, but that was so because Herrera's teams were disciplined, quiet, and rarely scuffled with opposing teams. Mexicans had to be civil in order for them to be given the license that Anglo teams, some possibly much more aggressive and less clean, got.

The world of Texas basketball might have been small compared to that of football and baseball, but it was still governed by the same social rules that the major sports were. Players were supposed to behave on the court, be respectful to authority, play clean, and show character in adversity. The court was simply another place in which the young men were to reveal the morals and values they were taught in church and at home. No one would ever question Herrera's ability to teach that to his boys.

CHAPTER TWO

Mexicans Can Play, but Not Everyone Is Pleased

ON SEPTEMBER 10, 1929, THE *SAN ANTONIO LIGHT* REported that Wright Riley, former coach at Brackenridge High School, would take over senior coaching duties at Sidney Lanier Vocational School.[1] This meant an immediate demotion for Herrera, who had served one year as the head coach of all the school's sports and saw a second-year promotion to senior coach as a real possibility. Instead, he found himself lucky to have a job. In his demotion, he replaced Lyons McCall, the junior high coach, who resigned that summer to go into the dry goods business. Had McCall not chosen a different career path, Herrera would most likely have been left unemployed.

His luck at retaining a job, however, did not mean he would run any of the high school sports as he sought. In addition to Riley's arrival, two other developments served to bump Herrera down the coaching ladder in his second year at Lanier. First, Jack Tolar, who had coached the Lanier football team prior to Herrera's arrival, decided to return after a couple of years away coaching an independent team. His return moved Herrera to an assistant coaching position in football while making him also the head man of the junior high basketball team.[2]

The district's conversion of Sidney Lanier into both a junior high and a high school in the fall of 1929 was to have elevated Herrera to a senior coach with a raise in pay. However, unbeknownst to the superintendent, Riley, who had been released from his coaching duties at Brackenridge High School, had signed a contract stipulating that he would be a "senior coach." This combined with the hiring of Claude Kellum, a popular local ex–football player and successful coach, to create a situation in which there were four senior coaches for three high schools. The superintendent found himself in a quandary but promised that the district would meet its obligation to Riley.[3] The solution was found in giving him the new Sidney Lanier job.

Riley, often called "Toady" or the "midget head coach" for being quite small, came to Lanier with good credentials. For three years he had been a successful head coach at the city's premier sports school, Brackenridge High School. His football teams were the best in the city and sometimes in the region. One of them once fought for the city championship and attracted a crowd of ten thousand people for a game against traditional rival Main High School in 1926. The following year, he fielded what he called a "super eleven" team with a large number of returning starters plus a player from Oklahoma whom he described as the greatest athlete he had ever seen in high school.[4] From what little is written about Riley, he comes across as a colorful fellow with a ready quote for any reporter that got near him.

While it seems that coaches moved positions repeatedly, it is odd that after such successful seasons he was released as Brackenridge coach. The original article announcing the move mentioned that Riley had been tabbed to go back to the junior high system in which, said the paper, "he achieved success." The announcement was made in August, but the official appointment of his replacement, Claude Kellum, did not come until almost a month later. This gap indicates some behind-the-scenes maneuvering. Perhaps Riley lobbied hard to keep his job at Brackenridge and, when that failed, pressured the district to give him the only other position available, which was the Lanier coaching job.[5]

Without school newspaper copies and no yearbook until years after Riley left Lanier, it is hard to piece together what he did as coach of the Voks. A couple of articles allude to him having won district or city titles in 1931, 1932, and 1933, but no newspaper articles were found that detail those triumphs.[6] Sports coverage in the San Antonio papers in the 1930s proved sporadic. Big games were often announced, but the scores or even the outcome did not necessarily make it to the newspaper's pages the next day. No pictures survive of that era, and little is known of the players. What we do know is that Riley was determined not to be sent into a pit of sports mediocrity. He told the newspaper that he "would immediately begin a campaign to put the senior division of the West Side school, where the student body is almost wholly composed of Mexicans, on an equal basis athletically, with that of Main Avenue and Brackenridge." Riley also set out to upgrade the facilities and asked for a practice field, a clubhouse with showers, tackling dummies, and other equipment that would allow him to field teams that could compete for championships.[7]

It is not likely that Riley received much of what he requested, given that only four years after he was hired Lanier parents were demanding better facilities for their children's education. Still, his energetic demeanor may have helped to at least make conscious the situation at Lanier. What we know of Lanier sports during his time comes from a few available local newspaper articles, and they clearly point out that Riley did not arrive at a school that lacked a sports tradition. As a junior high, Lanier had actually competed successfully in both basketball and football, winning games and championships. In 1925, the Voks were Class A junior high champions in both basketball and football; in 1929, they were rated the best junior high basketball team in the district; in 1928, they won the district track championships; and throughout the first five years of Lanier High School's existence, the Lanier boys were competitive in every sport.[8] Riley must have known this, and so his comments about putting Lanier sports at the level of other schools was an indication that he understood that "Mexican achievements" rarely left a lasting impression on the Anglo community. Of course, it could also have been a way to downplay Lanier's successes before his arrival.

So well established were the Voks as sportsmen that in one newspaper account of a football matchup the Voks were categorized as the "heavy team" with big linemen, strong backs, and speedy defensive backs.[9] No doubt there were very few schools available to play at the time, and some of the bigger and possibly stronger schools in the area were just outside the school district's boundaries, but this does not diminish the success of the Lanier boys. These boys came to school and sports a bit more mature and more seasoned given the hard work that some were engaged in when they helped their parents in the agricultural fields, the pecan-shelling home shops, and other places where they could accompany them. These boys also learned from an early age to be independent and often self-reliant. The life of a Mexican boy in the San Antonio of the 1930s was a difficult one, and while this difficulty hampered some aspects of their social and educational life, it helped them in those activities that required physical stamina and maturity. While some were intimidated by what they saw as Anglo dominance of the public space, once taught the fundamentals and freed to participate in sport and play, they responded with a confidence that other, more sheltered children lacked.

Participating in organized sports in the local community centers also prepared them for the football field and the basketball court. The Progressive Era had brought a concern with masculinity and moral uplift that was unparalleled in American history. Combining with Progressive lessons and instruction on citizenship were religious lessons from a Protestant movement concerned with building a "Muscular Christianity." While diverging in reasons for this emphasis on masculinity and moral uplift, both the Progressive Movement reformers and the religious clergy placed a lot of effort in building young men who could withstand the rigors of life and who resisted the feminization of modern society. While these efforts were usually reserved for young Anglo-Saxon boys, and while many mainline Protestant groups had softened the masculine aspect of the uplift by the 1930s, they retained many of the character-building aspects of the ideology and continued to use sports to assimilate youth of the different ethnic groups into American society.[10]

The emphasis on sports, discipline, and self-reliance helped those who chose to become active in school athletics. We do not know how many students at Lanier participated in community center activities, but as noted earlier, many community centers, modeled after the Eastern and Midwestern settlement houses, placed emphasis on getting the Mexican boys of the West Side involved in sports. Many of the Lanier players who constituted the winning teams in the 1940s first acquired their skills through the efforts of such facilities. It was there where they first played, learned fundamentals, were taught team play, and had a chance to travel around some parts of the city to play. It is also there where they engaged in their first competition with boys not of their race or ethnic background.

Lanier's athletic accomplishments, however, were not limited to players who participated in football, basketball, or track. Some Lanierites proved more than capable of competing with their Anglo counterparts in nontraditional and nonteam sports. Case in point is the story of Manuel Gonzales, Humberto Ramirez, and Bernie Gonzalez. The three were golfers, and they all made it to the finals of the citywide junior golf tournament sponsored by the *San Antonio Light* newspaper. Manuel and Humberto teed up against each other for the singles championship, and Bernie matched up against another junior high student for the championship of the "second flight" division. At the end of the tournament, Manuel won first, Humberto was a close runner-up, and Bernie won his division. All three won most of their matches, handily revealing that Mexican boys could, if given the chance and the training, compete with boys from the East and North Side schools in not only team sports but also individual ones.[11] That they did it in a sport not common among Mexican Americans or even white working-class youth only made it more amazing. They probably did it with borrowed equipment.

For their first game or two, the football team wore mismatched jerseys, hand-me-down helmets, and whatever padding they could acquire. But through the efforts of the Latin American City League, neighborhood residents raised $8,200 to buy uniforms, pads, and helmets to make the boys more presentable. It was important for the community residents to have their boys look good, especially when they went outside the confines of the barrio. Led by legal and educational reformer Manuel C. Gonzalez, the league used the occasion of the money's delivery to the school to call a meeting with the parents to encourage them to get their children to school on time and to have them there every day.[12] For the league, education was of utmost importance, reflecting a new emphasis by Mexican American reformers to educate the barrio's children and make them good civic neighbors.[13]

When Riley took over Lanier's senior sports, the school got an experienced coach used to winning—but one with a chip on his shoulder. Riley knew that most people saw him as the coach who had been removed from the top high school in the city and relegated to coaching Mexicans. He set out to prove that he could win even in a school with no senior sports history. One of the first articles about Lanier to appear after Riley took over mentioned that his 1931 basketball team had won district and bi-district play to get into the state playoffs and came to the state meet with an "impressive record." "After a ragged start," said the newspaper, they captured the city title and then beat Bloomington High School to advance to state. "The competitive going in district and bi-district play," continued the article, "has not been telling on Sidney Lanier. Although its five is generally of small stature, it possesses a fast, aggressive and sharp-breaking offensive. Its players are all Mexican boys."[14] The last comment revealed that the sports writer was as surprised as anyone that Mexican kids could compete in a sport not viewed as natural in the barrio.

It was to the misfortune of the Lanier five that they opened the state meet against Denton High School, which had won the state meet the year before and fielded another strong team. No article could be found detailing that match, but we know that Lanier lost, 35–25, to the defending champions, who then lost to the eventual state champions, Athens.[15]

While very little of significance is available on Riley's teams, there is enough to note that he produced Lanier's first basketball star. Anastacio Farias, renamed "Stacey" by sportswriters who could not or did not choose to pronounce his "difficult" name, was a three-time all-city selection as a five-foot-eleven center while leading his team to three city championships. Sportswriter W. R. Beaumier of the *San Antonio Express* called Farias "one of the greatest centers ever produced in local high school cage circles . . . he stands head and shoulders above the other centers." Another sportswriter added, "With Farias . . . the Voks have a king-pin around which to revolve and when once started will find them a mighty difficult team to halt." Farias led the city in scoring during his final two years as a Vok.[16] It seems, however, that Farias was not the sole star in those Riley teams. In 1931, three other teammates, Jesse Santos, Ike Mendoza, and a young man identified only as "Sanchez," made the all-city selection along with Farias. All three would join him the following year to again win the city championship. Santos joined Farias in 1931 as a repeat performer on the all-star team.[17]

Farias's talents were not limited to basketball, as he played football, where he was also selected to the all-city team as, ironically, a center. He was also a star baseball player in the city leagues. While Farias did not play high school basketball for Herrera, his son remembers him always talking about "Nemo," whom he considered a great cage coach and for whom he played in the Lanier junior high squad. "He liked Riley," recalls his son George, "but he thought Herrera had been the one to teach him to play basketball well."[18] Herrera was as successful coaching in the junior high school level as he would be as a varsity coach. In a picture in the *San Antonio Light*, Herrera is pictured with a broom under a heading "'Nemo' in Clean Sweep." Next to the picture are two other pictures showing two of his three teams that won district titles in the A, B, and C junior high school classifications.[19] It is likely that Farias's bond with Herrera solidified when he played football for him when Nemo was helping out with football duties. Farias would be one of the first graduates of Sidney Lanier High School, receiving a commercial certificate from the vocational division. Though he did not receive a "high school diploma"—Lanier had only those two categories for graduates—he was offered a scholarship to Southwestern University in Georgetown, Texas. He declined the scholarship to help provide for his family.[20] Farias would go on to play city league basketball—and baseball—in his hometown of Laredo and be selected numerous times to the all-city teams.[21]

The year Farias left, we read about the Lanier football team, this one led by now-head football coach Nemo Herrera. On October 26, 1932, the Voks met the Edison High School Iron Men for the District 24 championship in the northern half of the class B football league. In the Edison Bears the Voks met a team that had not lost in two years and had outscored its opponents 124 points to zero. Lanier came to the game with its best record in school history. While not considered to be in the same league as Edison, Lanier had won some grudging respect. Said a reporter for the *San Antonio Light*, "Herrera has a smart team, virtually all Mexican, from the West Side, and they have romped through some stiff competition unscathed. They haven't demonstrated the scoring power of Joe Ward's Edison aggregation, although they are capable defensively and well-grounded in football fundamentals."[22] The newspaper sang the praises of Edison's quick backs and capable quarterback but warned the team to be on "their toes watching for Lanier's wicked pass attack and some tricky backfield stuff."[23]

Coach Herrera proved to be a good football coach and managed the Lanier teams for several years before being replaced. At the end of his coaching career at Lanier, he again took his place on the gridiron, fielding competitive teams. Interestingly, a number of his football players would be basketball players. Herrera liked his players tough, but he did not always like his basketball players to play football. Those who had particular skills that went beyond athleticism he kept glued to the basketball court and away from the distraction of the football field. And yet one of his finest basketball players would be team captain and quarterback for the Voks. Herrera had the knack for knowing who belonged where, and he had no compunction in telling someone to take off one uniform and concentrate on living up to the other one.

In 1933, Riley decided that he wanted to concentrate on football and let Herrera head the senior basketball team. There is no explanation for this except that maybe, in spite of his success in basketball, Riley was determined to regain his reputation as a football coach. Whatever the reason, his giving up basketball allowed Herrera to inherit a winning program, and he soon found his team one of the favorites for the city basketball title along with Brackenridge, which was the team to beat for most of Herrera's tenure at Lanier. It is probable that Herrera had assisted Riley in coaching or at least was familiar with the style of play the Voks used to compete against much taller opponents. Being just as short as Riley, Herrera had learned to be aggressive as a player, and he knew his players would have to play a similar style. Given Riley's fast-paced approach to basketball, Lanier players did not see a great transformation under their new coach, except possibly in intensity. If Riley was intense and aggressive, Herrera was even more so.

In early 1933, Lanier faced the Thomas Jefferson High School Mustangs. In that game, the Voks started off hot, but in the fourth quarter, "their breath became a little shorter, their legs tightened and their shots became a little more careless." They lost 34–27. "The seemingly perfectly-conditioned Ponnies [*sic*] pulled their usual 'iron man' finish to snatch the game away from the West Siders," said one local newspaper.[24] The game proved exciting from the start and revealed some of the characteristics of the Lanier team that became common during its more successful years. While Jefferson started out in the lead, the Voks came back, "led by Rodríguez, Escobedo and Sánchez" to take a one-point lead at halftime. They extended that lead to four shortly after the second half began but then tired, and "Jefferson's Roy Smith and Carl Dietzel 'giant point-snatchers' got going." Jefferson's guards "fed them the ball" and the postmen used their height advantage over the Lanierites to push the Mustangs to the lead while those swift guards kept the Lanier attack stymied. The boys from Lanier nevertheless impressed the fans as Sánchez and Mendoza played "sensationally," Escobedo "roped in some timely shots," and Rodríguez "looked good under [the] post."[25]

The paper makes no mention of Herrera's reaction to the difficult loss to Jefferson, but he certainly was anything but happy that it was the "perfectly conditioned" Mustangs and not his players who ran up and down the court contesting every pass, fighting for every rebound, and driving to the basket around a tired defender. Herrera believed in tenacity and outlasting opponents. In fairness to the Voks, however, the Mustangs might have been well conditioned, but they also had a height advantage that allowed them to set up plays, to get the ball inside over the outstretched but shorter arms, and to score on the inside without expending too much energy. The Voks simply had to run as fast as they could to get to the basket before the taller players got into position to block the basket and force them to take long shots.

That same year, the newspapers mentioned the Voks as having lost to Central Catholic High School, whose Buttons were the hottest-scoring players in the city, averaging 45 points a game over a twelve-game early schedule. The Buttons' only loss had been to Brackenridge, but they had managed only a two-point victory over the Voks. On the same sports page, the Voks were mentioned as the next opponents of the Randolph Kaydets who had a "good club." The Kaydets were part of a military league in the city and were the second non–high school team Lanier played in one week, the other being the Texas Christian University Horned Frogs several days earlier. It was not uncommon during the 1930s for high school teams to play nonscholastic clubs and college teams and sometimes even beat them.[26]

The Lanier gym, while quite small in comparison to most others in the city, was used for games in the numerous city leagues popular back then. A gym in the West Side of San Antonio, along with those in the other parts of the city, kept former high school and college players playing the game they loved. The Alamo League, with colorful team names such as the Stockyard Brahmas, Post Office Tigers, and the Nationals, provided competitive games for residents who could not get enough hoops through their high school teams. There was a unit described as the "Junior Voks," but the designation is not clear, and so it might have described a group of former players from Lanier or just the name of a local team that had taken the mascot of the West Side's only high school. By the mid-thirties, the Lanier Voks were forging a reputation as a team or set of teams capable of competing in the city's basketball wars. Teams back then also had fans that followed them closely and young boys who sought to emulate the antics of their favorite players.

Meanwhile, Riley kept Lanier's football team in the news. Toady, according to the local newspaper, had his "wise boys" waiting to play that "one game . . . [the] experienced youngsters are said to have in them."[27] The words "clever" (also used in the article) and "wise" implied that the boys from Lanier were "outsmarting" their opponents rather than physically or athletically outplaying them. It is ironic that Mexican boys who were often seen as not as intelligent or smart in school or public affairs were now perceived as clever or wise on the gridiron. In fact, Mexican children were often seen as "retarded," and educational policy tended to be geared toward meeting the needs of those who could not compete with other, mostly white children.

Most of these children were expected to be good with their hands, to learn enough to do the jobs that were available to Mexicans, and occasionally to excel enough in school to attend trade school or possibly even college. Wisdom and cleverness were simply not characteristics ascribed to Mexican students in most activities in which they were engaged.[28]

Seeing the Voks as more physically talented, however, ran counter to the white population's image of the strength of white masculinity and prowess, which was fundamental for the psyche of American white males. Religious fundamentalism and Progressive politics and educational views reinforced these notions of the importance of the body. Progressives believed that a healthy mind went along with a good education and social skills to make individuals, but particularly immigrant and ethnic communities, more American. The concern with a healthy body revealed the ambiguity that Progressives felt about, on the one hand, those who were on the bottom rung of society and, on the other hand, those who were becoming "soft" in a modernizing society where consumption and leisure were becoming more common even among working-class men and women. For religious fundamentalists, Christians needed to be muscular, able to withstand physically as well as spiritually the trials of the world. Men, and to some extent women, could not serve Christ and their religion if they were weak and lacked discipline or strong Christian character. In their own way, proponents of Muscular Christianity saw it as a way to strip away both the ethnic and class distinctions of Americans and make them middle-class Americans, if not always in terms of social status, at least in terms of their national perceptions.

For many whites already nervous about black muscularity, any challenge to white manhood was a threat. It is quite possible, though the literature does not deal much with it, that Progressives and white fundamentalist Christians, most of them southerners, reacted to this black muscularity with their own efforts to become muscular physically, emotionally, in foreign policy, and in play and sport. The fact that immigrants were coming from countries where there were no notions of muscularity meant that they needed to "learn" the new American concepts of physicality. Industrialization had also stripped many of these immigrants and other working-class Americans of their strength and self-esteem. The American proletariat, rather than being built up, was being demoralized and marginalized both physically and economically. But because capitalism was seen as God's economic system, Christianity had no alternative economic or social philosophy. So the only way for them to counter this devaluation of man was to make him and his offspring hyperconcerned with muscularity. Of course, the reality was that this muscularity was middle-class-focused, required leisure time and stable economics, and necessitated a progression of both body and soul that was out of the reach of most working-class individuals whose time and money was in short supply.[29]

Perhaps the terms "wise" and "clever" implied that, since Mexican youth were not supposed to be as muscular or athletic as Anglos, they could not simply overpower or outmuscle their white counterparts and had to use tricks or other kinds of maneuvers to win.[30] It is, however, unfair to put words or thoughts into the mind of the writer of "Mustangs Ride High." Quite possibly the shorter and less physically imposing Mexican players were seen as wise or clever in using whatever tricks they could to get around the bigger players. No doubt some sportswriters were being complimentary by using such terms, but in doing so they were creating a category outside of muscularity and physical talent and encasing Mexican basketball players with skills that were often useless in the outside world or that tended to reinforce the stereotypes of them as shifty, conniving, and treacherous. But what sportswriters and others saw as "tricky" was actually a different way of being talented and athletic, one adjusted to their own circumstances as shorter players. Only after the team began to win state playoff contests would they come to be seen as talented, though the words "physically talented" were rarely used to describe them.

There was, however, always the possibility that the Lanier boys were using another trick to get their victories. By 1935, there were rumblings about Lanier using ineligible players, and the first formal complaint came shortly before the Voks played Alamo Heights for the District 35-B football title. At the time, the Lanier team stood undefeated (with one tie with nearby Floresville) and was the favorite for the championship. W. P. Sylvester, principal of Edison High School, made the accusation and headed the committee investigating whether Lanier "might" be using a composite of junior and senior high players in their teams, which would violate Texas University Interscholastic League rules and would make Lanier ineligible for the championship.[31]

Principal Dick Brewer of Lanier quickly responded with an internal investigation and informed the committee that if there were problems with any of the players, "he would forfeit all [the] games" Lanier had played.[32] Brewer, who became a strong advocate for his West Side "children" over the thirty-two years he served as principal, pointed out to the district committee that Lanier was the "only institution of its kind in Texas, in that it [was] neither a junior or senior school, but a junior-senior school with no relation whatever to the system used in the other San Antonio schools."[33]

The crux of the complaint was that Lanier was using eighth-grade players in its varsity team. The complaint, while legitimate, seems to have been more out of prejudicial feelings than out of any concern over harm done to the other boys playing the game. After all, Lanier was not being accused of using older boys for an unfair advantage; rather, Lanier was being accused of using younger ones. In addition, the situation should have come as no surprise to the other schools. Claude Kellum, director of athletics for the district, presented the committee a letter from the Interscholastic League acknowledging Lanier's payment of dues for "Class B" participation (for schools of 350–500 students). Said Kellum, "if the team [is] ineligible it [has] been so for several years." He added that he believed that the league knew about the situation and had not considered it a problem.

Brewer's quick response succeeded in defusing a potential embarrassment for the school. He explained that being a vocational school required adjusting the circumstances of each particular boy's situation. Older boys were often advanced from junior high to high school and given credits. This was done to provide the boy "practical education when it was determined he would not be staying long" in school. Brewer asked the committee to "take time to understand" the situation that confronted his school. His job was to educate and prepare the West Side youth for the city's industries, and that effort had to take into consideration that many of them did not graduate or did not advance enough in their junior high studies to make it to high school without a little push from the administration.

Superintendent of Alamo Heights G. W. Gotke moved to table the motion to investigate Lanier. "There is a time and place for this sort of matter," said Gotke, "and it isn't now, before a championship is to be decided." His motion passed.[34]

Though nothing came of the accusation, it served as a reminder of the difficulties that Lanier faced because of its unique structure. No doubt the participation in sports was an effort to Americanize the Mexican youth and to make the school as "normal" as possible, but because it was both a junior and senior high and because Mexican boys did not always follow the same track as other high school boys, there was always the danger of being seen as not following the rules. Being different created both advantages and disadvantages for the Lanier students. It could, and often did, excuse them from having to be judged with the same standards as other students in San Antonio, but it also meant that by being different they were considered inferior and were often under suspicion when they competed well or surpassed expectations. They walked a fine line in being both part of the system and different within it. Principal Dick Brewer served as the most important navigator of the Lanier ship in white waters. And he would be called upon to do this on numerous occasions.

By 1936, the Lanier Voks were again seen as threats to win the district and city basketball titles. Just before a game with the defending city champions, Thomas Jefferson High School, an article described the Voks as "perched high" as they had beaten Brackenridge earlier in the season. "The Voks are more polished, and can handle the ball much better than the Mustangs," the article said.[35] The Lanier boys were no doubt influenced by the style that Herrera had developed in his own career as a player. As a small and sometimes "midget" forward, Nemo had learned the value of good ball handling, quick moves to the basket, and accurate shooting. Nothing much is known about the boys that Herrera had that year except their names: Max Torres and Edward Peña as forwards, Ventura Trejo at center, Jesse Galindo and Anthony Rodríguez as guards, Frank Casanova as crack guard, and the sixth player off the bench.[36] Incidentally, the Junior Voks were still in the race for the title in the Latin American League. That team roster lists last names similar to some of those in the Lanier team, but it is difficult to tell whether they were relatives or whether some of the high school players were moonlighting.[37] That seems unlikely, but the scant sports coverage of both teams makes it impossible to tell.

The 1937 basketball season is similarly thinly documented, but in January 1938, we first read about Tony Cardona scoring fourteen points to lead the Voks to a resounding 58–17 victory in a practice game against Alamo Heights.[38] One month later, Cardona led Lanier with twelve points in another rout, this time against Fox Tech, the school that became the Voks' ultimate rival until 2010 when Tech discontinued its sports programs.[39] In spite of Cardona's heroic play, which landed him on the all-city squad, Lanier was able to salvage only a 5–4 record and came out third in the city championship series. The 1938–1939 season began with a last-second victory against Central Catholic High School, 25–23. That year's team featured another star player who would come into his own, John Jesse Saldaña, who, according to his obituary, went on to be an all-city player. There is, however, no record of Saldaña in any of the newspaper clippings of the era, though there was another player with the same surname who proved to be a standout that year.[40]

But before the Lanier fans could come to appreciate the talents of this team, their attention was focused on the football squad that occupied first place in District 42-B and was the defending champion. On November 13, they read about their team needing a victory against the third-place Alamo Heights Mules in order to clinch the title. The Voks had a bruising running attack led by quarterback David "Dave" Romero that gave them a sweep of their first four games. While heavily favored, they knew the Alamo Heights passing attack could prove a potential obstacle. Alamo Heights came into the game with two very close losses, one to Edison, 6–0, and one to Fredericksburg, 12–0, and both of those teams had given Lanier all it could handle. The year before, when Lanier also seemed a cinch to clinch the title, the Mules pulled an upset, and it took the Voks a playoff game to win the title.[41] If they lost, they would fall into a tie with their old nemesis, the Edison Bears.[42]

Unfortunately, the Edison Bears, or at least their school administrators, were up to their old tricks. Just before this very important game, they again filed a protest to the District 42-B board of directors alleging that Romero was ineligible to play and had been throughout the season. F. S. Bakley, superintendent of the Alamo Heights Independent School District and, according to the local newspaper, an "Edison official," declared in a statement that Romero had been nineteen years of age when he entered Lanier at the beginning of the fall term. If that were true, Romero would have been ineligible according to Texas Interscholastic League rules, which prohibited any student from playing high school sports if he turned nineteen before he entered school. Lanier stood to forfeit all of its games, thus giving Edison, whose only loss had come to the Voks, the title.[43]

These allegations of wrongdoing were the second in less than five years and were leveled by the same school, indicating that Edison officials were not yet convinced that Lanier could be so good in their sports without violating the rules. Edison was what would have been known in the barrios of San Antonio as a "real white school," meaning that not only were most of its students white but that the school itself reinforced a constructed dichotomy that divided the two schools not only by geography and ethnicity but by perceptions of fairness, honesty, and integrity. Mexican boys were not to be trusted to corroborate their signed statements, and their word provided no assurance. This allegation of wrongdoing might well have sought to disparage the name of the man who stood vigilant over his school and who had already debunked one previous charge of ineligibility. This accusation added a more insidious element to a heated feud among white and brown boys. It might seem unfair to say that Edison officials were being malicious until one learns how they went about getting their "evidence" about Romero's eligibility.

Upon hearing the allegations, Principal Brewer submitted a statement in which he charged Edison officials with trying to intimidate Romero's mother into giving them information that might compromise his eligibility. According to the statement, Romero's mother had been approached by Edison administrators accompanied by a federal immigration official who threatened to "take her to headquarters" and pressured her to make a statement concerning her son's age. The frantic mother called Brewer, but the Lanier principal was unable to find out—likely because of a language barrier between them—whether she had said anything that could incriminate the boy. But Brewer was confident that the school had done nothing wrong, and he told the board of directors that the actions of Edison officials were grossly inappropriate and that the matter needed to be settled properly, through a fair process and not through intimidation. "Whenever they are ready to call the board meeting we are ready," he wrote.[44]

Brewer had two important things riding on the board's decision. First, his mission was to Americanize and integrate the boys and girls of Lanier into the white world in which they would live for the rest of their lives, and he saw any effort to treat them as somehow less than good civic citizens as a threat to that process. He also had his own integrity to defend. After all, Mexican students were not the ones who had to make sure that all documents were in order and that they met all eligibility requirements to participate in extracurricular activities. To say the student had lied was not to put the whole blame on the child or his family but to indict the school officials for negligence. It is also possible that Brewer detected some kind of animosity among other school officials for his work at Lanier. If they did not initially, most would come to know that Brewer did not want to teach or administer anywhere else. He would serve as Lanier's principal until the day he died while on official business for the school. He would marry a Lanier teacher, and his children fondly remembered that dinnertime at home usually meant talking about Lanier.[45]

When the board of directors for the district met at a local YMCA, Edison officials produced a birth certificate "fulfilling," in the words of a newspaper writer, the conditions of ineligibility they had alleged. The newspaper article does not mention where they got the certificate or whether it was legitimate. But whatever the effect of their evidence, it proved fleeting, as Brewer countered with two documents showing "David Romero to be only 18 and that the certificate that Edison had produced was one of David's deceased brother who was born a year earlier." Upon seeing the evidence, the board of directors "threw out" the protest and declared Romero to be eligible to play the following day.[46]

With the allegations disproved, Lanier had dodged yet another bullet, but the incident served as a reminder that their winning ways remained suspect. And there lay the key to the high reputation that the coming championship teams were to garner. It would be built on the ability of the school teams to comport themselves well on the fields and courts and to remain above reproach in the way they fulfilled their athletic obligations.

Two days after the decision, Lanier beat the Alamo Heights Mules 13–7 in a defensive battle. The Voks managed twelve first downs to the Mules' two, but Lanier's scores came in the first two quarters, and they were held scoreless for the rest of the game, penetrating the Mules' twenty-yard line only twice. The powerful Vok running attack, led by running back Alfonso Rodríguez, showed occasional flashes of their season-long dominance of the striped field. Lanier's defensive backfield and line stymied Alamo Heights's strong passing attack, and the Mules scored only when a substitute defensive back intercepted a pass as Lanier threatened to score again in the waning minutes of the last quarter. Monte Frazier snatched the wayward pass at his twenty-five yard and hightailed seventy-five yards faster than a speeding Mule for his team's only score.[47] With that hard-fought victory, Lanier had its second district title and proved that the Voks not only could put the ball in the basket with efficiency but could also dominate in what was America's second most popular game by the 1930s and the one sport that would dominate the state of Texas even up to the twenty-first century.

Although Nemo Herrera had pretty much become a basketball coach, he was still helping out with the football team. The newspaper article highlighting the coming game named him and Dub Norton as the coaches planning strategy for the big game. The reality is that Herrera, who had coached the junior high teams before becoming the senior coach, helped out before the basketball season began. He carried the burden of both sports for a couple of years until he was joined in 1935 by Dub Norton, a former Alamo Heights Mule and graduate of Baylor University. Norton took over the gridiron duties and found himself just as successful as Herrera, winning three straight district football titles and going on to bi-district play, where his teams lost but represented themselves and their school well.

Some of Norton's boys, like Alfonso Rodríguez, Erasmo Hernández, Indalecio Canamar, Arthur Morín, Joe Gonzales, Frank Casanova, David Romero, and Matías Muñoz, became local heroes for their exploits on the gridiron. With a few exceptions, they were undersized players who had simply learned to run faster, hit harder, and outlast their opponents on the football field. In Norton they had a young coach who himself had been a high school athlete, who lettered in all the sports he played, and who had gone on to receive all-conference honors in college as a guard. In his first coaching job, he had taken Malakoff High School to a regional title in football.[48] In Herrera and Norton, Lanier had a talented duo who knew how to coach, had themselves been successful athletes, and could inspire their players with good instruction and personal memories.

In nine years since initiating its senior sports program, Lanier had found success frequently and in doing so developed a tremendous pride among its West Side followers, who at times during those years had little for which to cheer. San Antonio through the late 1920s and most of the 1930s was an extremely segregated society and one that often showed blatant hostility toward its Mexican and Mexican American residents. Yet during those times, there was also a steady growth in the numbers of Mexican Americans who were getting an education, finding professional or skilled jobs, and taking an interest in civic responsibilities. These were augmented by a group of rich, or at least educated, exiles who kept coming across the border to escape the continuing conflicts in Mexico, whose revolution had not yet been fully consolidated. These two groups viewed their futures differently: the exiles yearned to return to Mexico and thus sought to enhance Mexican culture within the San Antonio community, while the middle class had begun casting its lot with American society and sought to Americanize their community in order to gain rights of citizenship. At the same time, these two groups often came together to confront discrimination and to develop the strong ethnic pride that each saw as serving its own vision of the community.

Sidney Lanier High School played a crucial role in the vision of both groups, even if most of their children did not attend the West Side school. The fact that it served as the only school in the West Side and one that had been specifically established for Mexican children gave it a greater importance than any other school in San Antonio. In the 1930s, many Mexicans and Mexican Americans in rural areas attended "Mexican schools," one- or two-room, poorly constructed buildings with no running water or inside toilets. These were often situated at the edge of the town where even the paved roads did not reach. For those students who attended school with Anglo students, their experience was one of segregation within the school itself, either through special courses or simply by the attitudes of white students and teachers. Usually those who went to integrated schools were few in numbers and rarely lasted the full school cycle. They often left either to work in the migrant fields or small factories to help out the family or because they were pushed out by the hostility within the school.

Lanier, however, represented something new for Mexican Americans. Yes, it was still segregated, and the curriculum was geared toward making the students good workers for the city's industries and not for college, but it was their school, within their community's boundaries. And within the school, all the club, student council, sports teams, and other positions were available to them, giving them a chance to excel at least within their own Mexican world. As a graduate of Lanier High School, I, too, can fondly remember being a member of the state quarterfinalist debate team, the best actor in the senior play, and having numerous friends who were student council presidents, students seen as most likely to succeed, or football, track, and basketball stars. Within our own world, we were somebody important, and we were also important to the community around us. The people, some graduates of the school and others parents or simply neighbors, took pride in coming to the carnivals, the theater productions, and the sporting events.

Whenever one of us made it into the newspapers for something good we had done, a good portion of the community rejoiced along with our families. Lanier had such a positive impact on many of us and also our parents because few of them had ever had such an important institution within their midst. Those who were recent immigrants had never had a school that big and that "good" back in Mexico. Those who were more established residents could remember back before Lanier existed, when they didn't have a high school to attend or a team to cheer to victory so close to home. It is then no surprise that the community threw a celebration for the 1938 football team at the Tapicla Mexican Restaurant. The newspaper announcing the honoring of the team spared only four lines on the event, but it is reasonable to say that for the parents, neighbors, and the larger Mexican community, it was a much more important event than advertised.[49]

Lanier came to fill a need in the barrios of the West Side, and residents were appreciative even when not all things seemed right at the school or with the teachers and administrators. Since many parents in the 1930s and even in the 1960s had not attended high school, much of what happened at Lanier was new to them, and they tended to give school administrators the benefit of the doubt. Most of the students came to school with the parental instruction to behave, listen to the teacher, and, more important, not get in trouble and involve the family in a discussion with the principal. Mexican parents understood the asymmetric relationship they had with whites, and their hope was that their children could educate themselves enough to be able to balance out the relationship. Language and labor skills, they knew, were of utmost importance in changing the dynamics of their and their children's lives.

When the school began offering vocational training, most Mexican parents must have rejoiced—that would be the appropriate word—because their children were now preparing to find more stable and permanent jobs. Instability, unemployment, and underemployment kept the community where it was, and language and labor skills were necessary to break the cycle of poverty. Like most other people, Mexicans and Mexican Americans saw upward mobility as an individual pursuit within the context of group uplift. That is, most Mexican Americans understood that the community could and would progress if the individuals within it could find better jobs and if their children stayed in school.

We have no record of what the Mexican population around Sidney Lanier thought when the school opened its vocational section in the fall of 1924 for its first full year, but we do know that the first 125 slots were filled quickly. At the time, school officials stated that 50 percent of the students who graduated from junior high the previous year would soon enroll in one of the seven trades to be taught at the school. The other 50 percent of the students would enroll in one of the high schools in the city. That may have been, however, a very optimistic outlook since few Mexican students went on to high school in another part of the city since no public transportation existed in the immediate area.[50] It was more likely—a fact the school officials did not want to admit—that students not participating in the school's vocational program would simply go into the workforce. Most Mexican Americans in those years simply did not advance from elementary school to junior high school, let alone to an outside high school.

School and city officials promoted Lanier to the community and the rest of San Antonio as the only "public school of its kind in the United States." Whether it was or not, Lanier did offer an array of trades taught by "men who have experience in these trades and have made their living with them." These instructors taught auto mechanic and machine shop, printing, sheet metal welding, auto painting, auto top and seat covering, woodworking, and commercial art. The spring before the school's official opening, one hundred boys had participated, and already "some were placed in jobs," according to Principal J. O. Loflin.[51] This new experiment in the West Side no doubt had as its stimuli the need for workers with vocational skills for the city's growing factories and manufacturing outlets that were peppering the city by the mid-1920s. The other important reason for the program was to keep the Mexican and Mexican American students in some kind of schooling as few were likely to go on to a traditional high school. At the same time, there was a strong belief that most Mexicans had an aptitude for some vocational trade. They "were good with their hands."[52]

The vocational program consisted of three hours of trade courses and three hours of academics—often related drawing, mathematic, and English instruction. Students were given credit for apprenticeship training for the hours spent learning a trade. Students still in junior high were given a chance to try out for the trades that they might seek to pursue after graduation. Not only did this expose them to a potential area of study, but it also served to keep the students in junior high by making it a prerequisite that they graduate from the eighth grade in order to qualify for vocational training. While the school "is in the Mexican district and is primarily for Mexican students, boys of any nationality are welcome," said the school officials.[53] There is little to indicate that any significant number of non-Mexican youth took advantage of the offer.

Yet in spite of their efforts to create a place to educate the youth of the West Side, school district administrators were rarely able to stay ahead of the growth of the student population. By the late 1930s, Mexican and Mexican American parents were sending their children to school in greater numbers. At the beginning of January 1939, the school experienced a four-hundred-student jump in its enrollment, which only exacerbated the problem of the previous year, prompting one assistant superintendent to say, "Theoretically speaking, the students are hanging out the window at each school." This she declared after Lanier's efforts to send students to other junior highs proved futile since those West Side schools were also completely full.[54] The school administration then suggested renting space in a nearby building one block from the school that had once housed a pecan-shelling factory. The school officials pushed the issue because their forty classrooms, built for thirty-five students each, were now serving an average of forty-three students. The rest of the school building was also swamped by the increase of students.[55]

One newspaper article pointed out that students were studying "in corners, others were holding landscape classes . . . in the school cafeteria" and that the school had created "traffic policemen" to direct the flow of students from one class to another.[56] "Changing classes takes 10 minutes," wrote one reporter, "three times as long as normal." He added that the auditorium, library, cafeteria, and even the janitor rooms were being used as teaching space. In one classroom, eighty students, seated two per chair, attended music instruction. The cramped spaces not only disrupted attentiveness but also skewed educational policy at Lanier. The school responded to the mass of brown bodies by creating "intelligence sections" that grouped students by intelligence levels. This simply meant defining students by their grade-point averages and congregating those who were doing well in one section so they could continue learning quickly while forcing slower students to remain with other slow students, thus compounding their learning problems. It was a problem, said the newspaper, created by teaching 1,500 students in a building designed for 1,200.[57] Another article described the school with 1,877 students in a space capable of serving 1,400.[58]

The school board, pressured by the growing numbers at Lanier and by Principal Brewer's insistence that he needed space, finally approved the request to rent the nearby former pecan-shelling factory building for $50 a month. The board also approved $1,000 to convert the new rental into four classrooms (still short of the eight needed). Brewer accepted the half-hearted effort and hoped to have a bond passed for a new building within two or three years. The board debated raising the tax rate that had remained stagnant for several years but decided against it, hoping to handle the overcrowding and the need for improvements through available internal funds. They also simply transferred four teachers from Lanier's "elementary division" to the new building instead of hiring new ones, meaning that the space problems were compounded by a shortage of teachers for the "old" classrooms.[59]

Nearly five years after a massive 1934 school protest at Lanier, the school board had again promised to do something but ended up making cosmetic adjustments that moved students around and created some extra space but did not deal with the fact that Lanier needed new buildings. The school's growth rebutted the notion that Mexican and Mexican American parents did not believe in educating their children. Interestingly, when district officials discussed the issue of overcrowding they noted that most of the increase in student enrollment had occurred on the West Side while the North Side had actually seen a decrease in enrollment in its elementary schools.[60]

Overcrowding was also in the minds of state accreditation officials, who had put Lanier and three other San Antonio high schools on a list of "warned schools" because of numerous issues but particularly, in the case of Lanier and the new Technical and Vocational High School (Fox Tech), for overcrowded conditions. A report by the Texas Committee on Classified and Accredited Schools noted that the biggest problem facing these schools was the "overcrowded condition existing in some of the academic departments."[61] The committee was particularly concerned about the pupil-teacher ratio in three English classes in the vocational school, given that language skill acquisition remained one of the most important responsibilities the trade schools performed. The committee, however, did take note that the "training in citizenship through self-governance was a . . . 'splendid' feature" at Sidney Lanier. It also approved or at least noted that Lanier had employed an attendance teacher. Keeping students in school and teaching them to be good Americans seemed to be the biggest concern for district and state educators. While the report described major facilities improvements and curriculum development in other high schools, it was silent on any improvements to Lanier.[62]

Within two weeks of the outcry over the lack of facilities, education officials proudly announced one student increase they were happy about. Two new units of the ROTC were established, one at Luther Burbank High School and the other at Lanier. Increases in unit strength were also approved for Brackenridge and Jefferson High Schools. In ten years, ROTC participation had grown from 300 to 1,400 cadets. L. W. Fox, director of the district's Vocational Education, praised the growth as a "gain" for the youth of San Antonio. Besides promoting better personal appearance and discipline, said Fox, ROTC also promoted patriotism and greater physical fitness. He continued, "ROTC is ambition stimulating. I don't think there is any influence in our high schools today that contributes more to character."[63] For San Antonio's white educators and politicians, vocational skills, patriotism, and "moral character" were the best ways to assimilate Mexicans into the larger landscape.

Most of the boys playing in the basketball team, at least in the first years after Lanier became an official vocational junior-senior high school, were in the vocational program. In the later years many of them were in the more traditional academic program, and some of the players went on to college, some through the G.I. Bill and others with athletic scholarships. Lanier, like the sports teams it fielded, was a work in progress when it came to academics. Surely it did not lead with any innovations but rather seems to have simply provided training for skills that fit the local economy. When it occasionally sent a young man or woman to college, it was mostly through the individual efforts of the student.

CHAPTER THREE

Lanier Makes Its Run at State and Finds Its First Stars

LANIER ENDED THE 1938 CALENDAR YEAR WITH A DRUBbing, 39–26, at the hands of the International Clubmen of the Commercial League of San Antonio.[1] In the early years of Texas basketball, teams of all classifications played against each other. As mentioned earlier, Lanier occasionally played university or college teams as well as military cagers. No record exists of the rosters of the Commercial League teams, but there were familiar names in the box scores of these city league units. The team that beat Lanier had a fellow by the name of Trejo who played center. This may have been Ventura Trejo, "the elongated center" who only three years earlier had been the rebounding and scoring leader for the Voks. There was also a Flores and a Hernández, and since few other teams at the time produced Mexican players and most of the league's players had high school or college ball experience, it is reasonable to assume that most of these Spanish-surnamed players were ex-Voks.[2]

The Commercial League played competitive ball, and most of its players were at one time or another local basketball heroes who had taken jobs in local industries. The league, like so many others around the state and country, provided former high school and college players a chance to continue in a game they loved. For former Voks of the pre-war years who rarely went to college, the leagues allowed them to remain local basketball heroes until their bodies gave out and they were replaced by newer graduates of area high schools or regional colleges. Herrera himself played for a time in the league, though no record exists as to how long. It is likely that by 1938, when he would be thirty-eight years of age, he had hung up his uniform but not given up his connection to the league. The players he sent his own boys to battle were much stronger and tougher and played against high school boys more confident than his own squad. Playing by different rules, Commercial

League players were also more creative on the court, and Herrera could count on them to teach his boys some dribbling and passing innovations. Playing against the Commercial League teams was like playing street basketball in later years, when even college and professional players went to pickup games to learn new tricks.

Lanier players were good because they had grown up playing basketball in the community centers, in the local churches and community leagues, on the playground, and often against each other whenever and wherever they could find a space and a basket. Tony Rivera, all-state forward, remembers that after school hours they sometimes played alumni.[3] This provided Lanier players a measuring stick as to whether the program had matured to enable current players to match up against former legends and stars. Herrera played his team against all kinds of competition because he wanted the current Voks to gain confidence to play anyone at any time. Playing older players who were ad-libbing on the court gave his players a larger arsenal to use in a system that had them running, finding the open man, passing, or driving for a layup or a clean shot. This on-court savvy allowed multiple possibilities for a team that relied not on set plays but on finding the open man for a quick score.

An earlier victory against Alamo Heights had raised hopes, but the defeat at the hands of the Clubmen showed the Voks that they still had their work cut out for them. The Commercial League players may have been older and tougher, but they were not necessarily the best opponents the Voks would face that year. It was not uncommon, as the Voks themselves would prove, for a high school team to beat city league teams or even college teams. Despite the loss, however, most coaches and sportswriters believed that in '39 the Voks would finally "forsake their role of perennial runners-up in the city cage race and step forth as full-fledged champions."[4] Sportswriter Ed Elmendorf pointed out that "even Coach Nemo Herrera" would be surprised if he did not contend at the top of the pack given his five second- and one third-place finishes in his first six years. The coaches of other schools agreed that Lanier had the goods, starting with the fact that it had the largest squad in the city with fifteen players who took turns playing on a regular basis. "This helps a lot," wrote Elmendorf, "for it's part of Nemo's design to send a stream of substitutes into any game with the object of wearing the opposition down."[5] Aside from the ability to send in multiple waves of players, Herrera had developed at "least four players . . . who are fine long-range basket tossers" led by all-city "crack shot" Tony Cardona. Elmendorf continued, "Herrera believes in keeping the hoop hot with field goals and attempted field goals. His boys shoot for the basket whenever the darn thing gets in the way."[6]

This running and shooting had no particular formula, as the players were instructed to pass the ball around, look for seams in the defense, and take a shot when they were in the clear. Opposing coaches saw the Voks as the "fastest-breaking team" in the city, a squad that did not know how to slow down, choosing instead to outrun and outmaneuver the "enemy" and "seldom allowing him to get 'set' to stop the play." In a typical Lanier formation—if there was anything typical about the Voks—Raul Hernández, the only tall player on the team, positioned himself on the foul line near the basket. Joe Martínez, forward, stood deep in the court to the right with Jesse Saldaña, guard, a few paces behind him. Mariano Medina, the other guard, played directly in front of the foul circle, and Cardona, the "sharp shooter," roamed on the left side of the circle. This spacing allowed the Lanier guards and Cardona to "cut into the circle and shoot." Using no set plays, the players were simply to "meet" the ball at all times and look for the open shot, or if no shot became available they would pass off to an open man.[7]

Elmendorf describes the action this way: "Suppose that Hernández backs over into the corner behind him and gets his hands on the ball. That's a signal for both Saldaña and Martínez to move across the court toward him, but not to get the basket behind them. This is on the theory that it's easier to pass to a man coming toward you than to throw to one stationary or going away."[8] This cutting across the lane was preferred over using screens to get a man open. While using them on occasions, the Voks liked better to "depend on speed and shiftiness to get the defense out of position and break the ball into the clear." Beating the man instead of relying on a screen allowed the dribbler to contend with only one man instead of clogging up the passing lanes with other bodies: the defender, the screener, and anyone else moving in to pick him up. It also left the four other Lanier players open for a pass since they would all be moving toward a position to shoot, and no one would be out of range because of screening. Herrera wanted everyone to be ready to receive a pass and shoot or drive toward the basket, and this put the pressure on the dribbler to spurt around his defender.

By 1939 Herrera decided to have all his players "crash the boards" for rebounds to make up for what Elmendorf called the "small size of his material," hoping that numbers under the rim would make up for the inches they gave up to opposing players. Quickness and numbers were Herrera's only options to compete under the boards. If the ball bounced to the opposing team's players, then he expected the Voks' speed and hustle to make up the distance to their basket and catch up to what they expected to be a slower white player. This strategy of a collective lunge for the rebound gave the other team an advantage on fast breaks. Herrera knew the gamble often worked only adequately, but he needed rebounds and more than one shot at a time. If the Lanier players were held to one shot every time they entered the opposing team's side of the court, his players were not likely to shoot a percentage high enough to win the game. In case of a fast break, he simply trusted his players to fly after the rebounder at full speed and protect their side of the court. That was what all the hard practices and leg-strengthening exercises were about: outrunning or catching up to the opposing player.

On the defensive side of the game, the Lanier Voks had gone to a man-to-man defense to make it more difficult for the opposing players to set up plays or get into scoring position. The pressure was meant to force teams with less capable dribblers to pass the ball crosscourt, thus allowing the Voks a chance to steal the ball and set off on a fast break. But a simple man-to-man worked only so well against good dribbling teams or those that passed well. So Herrera resorted to a "shifting man-to-man" defense, which allowed any player that broke away from his defender to be picked up by another, thus maintaining defensive pressure no matter where the ball went. This defensive scheme was difficult to teach, admitted Herrera, but "it's nice when it works."[9]

The shifting man-to-man was particularly effective against teams that passed the ball well and on those that used screens to allow players to get a clear shot. When screens were first introduced, they were effective because the usual man-to-man defensive efforts were thwarted when the player guarding the ball dribbler had to go around the screening player, thus allowing the shooter a clear shot or a space in which to drive to the basket. But by switching off from one offensive player to another, they kept the ball guarded at all times and allowed the defensive player left behind to pick up the screener, thus preventing any man from being open at any time. The "stick-to-itiveness," as Elmendorf described it, was meant to apply pressure at all times and eventually wear down the opposing players by challenging them mentally and physically throughout the game. The tension would eventually force them into a turnover, and those would multiply throughout the game and increase the pressure on the dribblers to a point that some simply chose to pass the ball as soon as they got it and thus disrupt any plays the coach had designed for them. The Voks' large squad enabled them to maintain this pressure. It also enabled Herrera to choose a starting five that matched up with the competition.

This matching up to the competition meant that stars like Cardona did not always start. In the first game of the new year, Tony came off the bench to score six points as the Voks defeated a talented Central Catholic team. But it was fellow substitute Joe Treviño who scored a free throw and a field goal in the last minute of play to secure the win. In all, the substitutes scored fifteen points off the bench. This strategy was useful in tournaments when a team played three or four games in three days, as was the case in the San Antonio Invitational Basketball Tournament, which pitted five local teams against six Houston teams and a couple of other area quintets. The Houston cagers came in as heavy favorites, as one or another Houston team had won the tournament three years in a row. Jefferson Davis High School of Houston arrived as the '37 champion of the San Antonio tournament and as the winner of the Humble Tournament only days before, while Houston's John Reagan High School returned as tournament-defending champion and the previous year's state semifinalist after falling one point shy of the eventual champion, Dallas's Woodrow Wilson High School.[10]

Reagan turned out to be the Voks' first opponent in the tournament, while the Brackenridge Eagles, the last San Antonio team to win the tournament, took on Sam Houston High School, another powerhouse from the bayou city. The first day, however, turned out to be unlucky for the returning champions, as Brackenridge lost in sudden death, 23–25. Two Houston teams also fell, with San Jacinto High School, the '36 champ, losing and Lanier beating Reagan 19–13. Cardona was too good to be coming off the bench, and he again led Lanier with eight points, while Hernández, the center, added six. Jesse Saldaña added three points in a low-scoring affair that was tight through the first half, which ended with an 8–7 lead for Reagan before Lanier's waves of players finally wore the Bulldogs down and broke the game open.[11] Following that impressive victory, the Voks disposed of Colmesneil High School, which was considered a dark horse in the tournament. Unfortunately, no score exists for that game.[12]

The two victories put Lanier in the semifinals against Jeff Davis, which quickly proved to be the class of the tournament. The smaller Voks came out with no fear and played the taller Davis boys to a 12–12 tie at the half. The tight game continued during the second half as the Voks fired up the shots and kept the ball moving around, looking for the open spot, while the Davis team methodically and patiently played its game, which revolved around using its height for inside baskets. In the one picture available of tournament play, Davis's Kelley is seen jumping high with outstretched arms as he garners a rebound at a height too tall for Lanier's Joe Riojas. In the same shot, Mariano Medina looks undersized against three taller Davis players surrounding the basket.[13] In this picture, Herrera's strategy of sending all his players to the boards did not seem to materialize, and even if it had, the Davis height advantage clearly proved too much. Cardona with nine and Hernández, Saldaña, and Medina, each with four, kept the game even for most of the night, but eventually Davis proved too strong, and the Panthers moved into the final game with a 31–27 victory. They would then go on to win the tournament title with a hard-fought 23–20 victory over Houston's Lamar Redheads.

No doubt that a semifinal loss dampened the spirits of the players who had been praised so highly just a day before. But looking back, the players and Herrera could see the talent and tenacity of this squad, even if the city sportswriters did not believe that any of the San Antonio schools could "do much outside the local district."[14] Lanier nonetheless shook off the criticism and walloped the Harlandale High School Indians of the Bexar County League, 47–13, in a practice game at the home gym where West Side residents could see their Voks play. Cardona again shone with twelve points, followed by Hernández with five. In the page reporting the game, two pictures of Nemo Herrera and his boys appear. In one he is seen taping the ankle of Raul Hernández, who is in street clothes but wearing his letterman's jacket. Herrera is wearing a white shirt and tie and has a slight smile on his face. While no doubt the picture was posed, it seems clear that the coach and his player had a connection, given how the player looks at him with smiling admiration written all over his face. The second picture has Herrera with Mariano Medina and Oswald Rodríguez sitting next to him while Joe Martínez takes a piece of paper out of a hat. The caption reads, "Herrera . . . has so many good boys in his squad he picks the starting lineup by lot."[15]

As if to prove the point, Herrera used ten players to defeat the defending city champions and the tallest team in the area, the Jefferson Mustangs. The Voks beat the Mustangs 34–24 in a game one writer called "a contest between the Voks' speed and the Mustang height, with the little Mexican lads having all the better of it."[16] Another sportswriter said, "The little Mexicans spotted the North Siders nearly a half-foot apiece in height, and then spent the night running rings around them, darting in and out like a bunch of *mosquitoes* [author's emphasis] to take the ball right out of their hands time and again."[17] The game was played at the Lanier gym, where Herrera's boys had "a habit of being hot." The hometown crowd saw their boys running at full speed, but they were also treated to a change of strategy when the Mustangs made a run at the Voks in the second quarter. Herrera shifted to a zone defense that frustrated the Jefferson players, who ended up throwing the ball away on numerous occasions. While the Mustangs threw the ball away, the two Saldaña boys, Billy and Jesse; the center, Raul Hernández; and Tony Cardona were scoring at will. Tony again led the team as he "ran under and around his larger opponents to take scoring honors with 14 points."[18] Hernandez would add nine.

The defeat of Jefferson in the first week of city play solidified Lanier's status as one of the favorites for the city title. Brackenridge, which won the consolation bracket in the San Antonio Invitational Tournament, also triumphed in its first city game and placed itself among the favorites, with only Burbank and Fox Tech, the newest schools in the city, being counted out. Jefferson, the defending champion, still had much to prove after the defeat by

Lanier, but it did have the best big man in the city in Roscoe Morris, whose brilliant play brought the Mustangs back from a horrendous abyss in the first half that doomed them for the game. Helping Herrera's boys hold onto the favorite spot was the addition (or possibly the return) of Joe Treviño, a six-foot-two big man who possessed "one of the best eyes in the game." Treviño's addition came just in time as Jesús Saldaña and Zaragoza Gonzales ended their eligibility. The big man's entrance into the team must have been anticipated because one sportswriter mused that Herrera would have "gladly add[ed] half of the remainder of the squad to get Treviño."[19] Interestingly, Treviño had played at least one game at the beginning of the season but then became ineligible. Unfortunately, no information is available on why he was ineligible.

Herrera knew better than to dream of how far his team would get in the state playoffs because he had been in this situation before, only to lose out at the end. In 1936, his team began the city series with a strong win over Jefferson and a sluggish but impressive victory over the Brackenridge Eagles. At the time, the Eagles also had a dominating center, Jack Krauss, on whom they counted for the big rebounds and the inside shots. In their meeting, Lanier had taken a script from Houston San Jacinto, which had beaten the Eagles in the San Antonio Invitational by crowding, surrounding, and double-teaming the big fellow. With not much scoring power from the other players, the Eagles continually looked to Krauss to "break clear for crisp shots under the basket." But Ventura Trejo, Lanier's "elongated man," hung on him like a "Maypole" with a little help from one or two other teammates. Attempts to pass the ball to the big man ended up putting the ball in the hands of the Voks several times.[20] That victory, wrote a sportswriter, "justifies a round of Paul Revering through the city league with the message—'the Voks are coming.'"[21] But all that jubilation went for naught as Lanier ended up second in the city series that year.

In the hype before the clash with Brackenridge, the Voks again were declared the favorites as the headlines in the *San Antonio Light* declared, "Other High Teams Rally Forces to Stop Lanier's Runaway." If "Herrera's lithe Mexican boys" with their "everlasting speed" could give the same dose of medicine to the Brackenridge Eagles as they did to the Mustangs, then they had clear sailing ahead. Undoubtedly this was hyperbole since the season had just started and each team had to play each of the others twice. But the hype continued two days later as the Lanier quintet unleashed an unmerciful 44–23 pounding of the Burbank Bulldogs, which set the city's season high score. In that contest, Billy Saldaña came into his own by pouring in a personal-best fifteen points and establishing the fact that Lanier had more than a two-man offense in Cardona and Hernández (Treviño had yet to come back). For his part, Cardona, described as Nemo Herrera's "pride and joy," scored ten points, though he played little in the second half, as Lanier entered the last period leading 22–10.[22]

The day of the Brackenridge game, however, was marred by a stinging denunciation by Lanier's principal, R. H. Brewer, of Los Angeles Heights School Board President D. G. Hays. As a representative of the district and, by extension, of Edison High School, the district's major program, Hays had released a statement announcing that the Edison Bears would no longer play the Voks in football "because people here think Lanier boys are too old to be playing against us."[23] Hays then added that he had "thought so" himself for several years. His protest, said the *San Antonio Light*, rekindled the feud that now had manifested itself several times since the first objection to Lanier's participation arose several years earlier. Each time, the school board had ruled in favor of Lanier, although the Edison school officials had argued that it was too difficult to know for sure the age of the boys. Thus the perception of wrongdoing persisted among some, and the suspicions grew with each Lanier victory, especially those over Edison and Alamo Heights, the latter one of the more exclusive schools in the city. Whether the superintendent spoke for other schools in his district or even other schools in San Antonio is unknown since Edison was the only school singled out as not wanting to play the Voks again. While no other school publicly agreed with the charge, it is not difficult to assume that some white residents found themselves incredulous that "Mexican lads" could be so good on the court or football field.

Brewer took Hays's statement as a "slur on my reputation and that of the faculty of Lanier school" and declared in his own reply that articles in the daily papers had left an impression that the school administration was being dishonest in its record keeping. As principal, he continued, he would be disloyal to the faculty and the student body if he left the allegations unchallenged. He expressed regrets over the conflict, as his policy had always been that "it is the duty of those whose responsibility it is to teach and train students for citizenship to foster and aid good will toward their neighbors." Then he tore into Hays, whom he accused of having never taken up the invitation to see the Lanier records even though he and other Edison officials had been invited to do so. Brewer pointed out that those accusing the school of improper record keeping were using records from the Catholic Church, U.S. Immigration Office, city health department, and the players' elementary and junior high schools but had never looked at the records at Lanier, which under Interscholastic League rules were the official documents used to determine eligibility. Those were the documents that the district's committee had used to make its decision on the Lanier players' eligibility during the prior dispute.

"Lanier, I can say for a fact, can show more early documentary evidence on the ages of its athletes than can Edison," said Brewer. Then the young but tough-minded principal took some not-so-veiled shots at the Edison officials. After first expressing his respect for those who lived in the Los Angeles Heights district—including some of his own teachers—he then declared that he would never think to question Edison school officials' integrity as these officials were now doing to Lanier. He added that his school had no "misunderstanding [with] other schools which competed" against them. Why weren't others joining the protest, and why was it that even the superintendent of the Los Angeles Heights School District or that of South San Antonio School District or the principals of Burbank and Alamo Heights High Schools had not found merit in Edison's protest when they served in the district's investigating committee? "It is hard for me to understand how a man . . . well trained scientifically and technically . . . will jump to conclusions without first making a thorough examination and investigation of the case," said Brewer. He then dug the rhetorical knife deeper when he declared, "We have nothing to hide and when we take a licking we come home and forget it and prepare for the next time."[24]

Brewer well understood that Hays and those who supported his stand were out on a limb, taking a chance that the larger community would see them as whiners for a sports program in decline. For the two previous years, Lanier had won the district title, and the Edison Bears, who once dominated the district with their "Iron Men," had been relegated to bridesmaids by a vocational school from an ethnic community with a short history of playing the sport. If Hays expected support from others in his district, disappointment quickly set in. When P. S. Eackeley, superintendent of schools in Los Angeles Heights, was questioned on the matter, he responded, "I'm not making any remarks whatsoever." Coach Joe Ward of the Edison Bears was even more elusive, "Don't ask me. I'm just working here." Claude Kellum, who directed all athletic sports for the city's public schools, admitted that Edison could play or not play whomever they wanted, but failure to play Lanier would result in an Edison forfeit. This meant that for any chance of winning the district title, Edison would have to play a perfect season, while Lanier could afford to lose once since they now had the tie-breaker advantage.

Being isolated did not do anything to weaken the resolve of Hays and his school board. Being called out in public by Brewer only made it harder for Hays to back down. When asked to respond to Brewer's statement, Hays smugly remarked, "It would sound good at a pep rally."[25] He then added that he could not understand "the fuss" over Edison's unwillingness to play Lanier again. He reminded those who cared to listen that in earlier years no one had found reason to complain when three other schools had stopped playing

Lanier, though he failed to mention that in leaving the district those schools were under no obligation to do so. In Edison's case, they were staying in the district but choosing whom to play, which would have put them in a special category and opened up a Pandora's box for the district schedulers. Hays left open the possibility that another board could change the decision in the future, but he made it clear that only a complete "round about face" by the present board would have Edison playing Lanier the next season.

Hays's hard line and the use of other records by Edison and Alamo Heights officials showed the length to which these school officials and their supporters were willing to go to prove that Lanier students cheated. The earlier charges had been that Lanier was using eighth graders to play in their varsity teams, but that probably backfired—at least with some football fans who found it ridiculous to hear that Edison High School was protesting the use of younger players as an unfair advantage. This time, Lanier's detractors were determined to prove that the Mexican players were too old to compete. The spying on Lanier players revealed a deep-rooted suspicion that Mexicans simply did not play fair, and that suspicion fed off the old stereotype that Mexicans were treacherous backstabbers who sought to circumvent the rules. These perceptions had been used for decades to question the integrity of the Mexican population and as a way to underscore their "inability" to play by American rules.

To believe otherwise was to accept that Mexicans could maintain their ethnic identity, culture, and social-religious ways and still succeed in the American games of football and basketball. American sports' triumph and the legends that made those victories possible were canonized with a virtuous, follow-the-rule, oh-shucks character that exhibited a not totally unique American perception of itself that was particular to whites in the United States. No school had a monopoly on these young men, and even among these Christian boys, some were more equal than others. One school was expected to come out on top in the struggle between community heroes, but the victory of white young men of great moral character over "others" allowed the perpetuation of the myth among the larger community. Everyone recognized that the myth was simply that, a sports fable maintained more by repetition than reality, but its constant perpetuation allowed some white Americans to feel good about themselves at a time of economic hardship.

No matter the words of praise for the young lads, accusations such as these reminded the Mexican community that the world beyond the basketball court, the football field, and the sportswriters' cubicles rested on a different set of standards. They could be praised and might even be the darlings for a time, but every praise and every triumph rested on a fragile foundation, and always there lurked some potential challenge to their status. For the most part, Lanier athletes, isolated within the gridiron or basketball court and seen only through the prism of winners, found an appreciative audience and one or two sportswriters who admired their play and sought to place them in a space that defied the traditional view. An action like Hays's, however, reminded them of what they forgot in the heat of battle and while their bodies strained and twisted and gave what didn't seem givable: they were different and always under suspicion.

Lanier's status as a full-fledged public high school protected the players from the harsh realities of a being a small minority within a larger Anglo world as in some schools or even of being part of a one-shack, one-teacher Texas "Mexican school," but it could not protect them from the larger society. As one player remembered years later, "We could go to the state tournament but we could not swim at Woodlawn Lake."[26] Once the players were out of uniform and back on the segregated streets and businesses of San Antonio, not much differentiated them from the mass of Mexican youth who were often harassed by police officers and treated with little respect by business owners or by the white citizens with whom they shared the sidewalk. I will deal later on with how they were treated on the court, but for now I can say that the difference there was the possibility of payback with an on-court win or even a well-placed forearm, something not always possible on the outside.

Yet being at Lanier provided these athletes a paternalistic umbrella that often came to their defense if for no other reason than that any questioning of the behavior of the boys of Lanier directly questioned the work of those assigned to teach and make good Americans of them. This is visible in Brewer's ferocious rebuttal to Hays's accusation of impropriety. Lanier's Anglo administrators and teachers knew that their colleagues did not always appreciate their work and even questioned its effectiveness. To maintain their professional integrity and justify their effort, they could either wink in concurrence of the criticism or they could defiantly defend their efforts. Either they felt their work important or felt themselves good teachers in spite of the quality of students. My own experience at Lanier taught me that all the above feelings were present among the teachers I came to meet there. Over time their views and feelings changed, with some converting to the mission of Lanier. Others simply became used to the work. In a discussion of our favorite and least favorite teachers, I found my fellow classmates had developed a "horror" list in 2010 which tended to be longer than the "most favorite" one.

Brewer himself was a contradictory fellow who defended his boys and girls against maligning by anyone outside the school but often treated his students as wards who needed very strict oversight. Jesse Camacho, a starting forward in 1940, remembers Brewer as being unfriendly and as someone who thought that with few exceptions Lanier students were incapable of going to college. Under Brewer's tutelage, vocational training at Lanier grew and became the main medium for educating the West Side children. When a course-scheduling glitch disrupted my plans in my sophomore year, I was channeled into a commercial art class without any regard to whether I had talent or whether I even really wanted the course. The class turned out to be a great experience, but the preemptory placement into vocational over academic courses could well have been disastrous for my desire go to college if I had not left the class the following year.

By my time, Lanier's principal was Brewer's protégé Fidel Tafolla, who would be only a bit more committed than his predecessor to a college education for his students. In fairness, these men and the teachers they often recruited were individuals who knew the West Side youth and sought simply to do with them what had been done in the past: place them in a vocational program that would allow them to find a job and become contributing members of their community. Because of the traditional way of educating Mexican American students and the way that tradition was maintained at places like Lanier, educators were often correct to believe that most students were vocationally inclined. The self-fulfilling prophecy continued to play out at Lanier even after I left.

It is impossible to know how much students at Lanier knew about Hays's accusations or Brewer's response, but if they knew it must have only been a distraction, though an annoying one. Most students, or at least those who were basketball fans, concentrated on the upcoming game with Brackenridge and its first-place implications. The Eagles stepped into a hostile arena to do what one sportswriter said people believed could not be done. Driving to the West Side transported them into a world few knew or understood. Entering into the Lanier gym must have been an intimidating experience, as it was always packed with vociferous students whose cheering soon took the form of one loud voice that mingled with the whistling, booing, and jeering with which the Lanier fans showered the opposing teams. They did it, however, within boundaries, as they knew that their teachers and administrators were vigilant about their behavior, and anything that went beyond the bounds of civility and respect could easily get them reprimanded or expelled. During my own tenure there, Lanier was known as the strictest school in the city and one with the best-behaved student body. The troublemakers had all been pushed out. Back in the late 1930s, most of those had probably never even made it to school.

As intimidating as the noise could be, the overcrowding was what could rattle an opposing team. One reporter wrote that the players taking the ball from out of bounds literally had to "beg someone's pardon" in order to find room to throw the ball into play. Several hundred fans, mostly from Lanier, came to cheer and to see the battle that most believed would decide the title race.[27] Both teams were high scorers, though they differed in how they put the ball into the basket, with the taller—by four to five inches per man—Eagles relying on easy baskets from right under the rim and Herrera's Voks looking to shoot from afar or drive in for layups. Brackenridge came in with an "iron man" five against Lanier's large herd, but in the end it became a game of five versus six as Herrera kept his starters in when he realized that the Eagles came to steal one away from home. And the Eagles came out looking not only for a victory but a sizeable one as they took a 17–11 lead by halftime with a bruising inside game.

Lanier had managed to contain an equally tall Jefferson quintet with a tenacious zone that had Voks clinging to the tall Mustang center, but the Eagles' overall height advantage allowed them to throw the ball over the heads of their shorter opponents and neutralize the zone's effectiveness. When the ball did not go over the Voks' heads for a pass, it went into the basket from the hands of sharpshooting Ray Lackey, the Eagles' lanky forward and the previous year's captain. This was his second-to-last game for his team, and he made the most of it.[28] By the middle of the third period, the visiting team had built a 21–12 lead. They then held on for dear life as the Voks found the range and cut the lead to "21–18, 23–20, 25–23, and 27–25" with Cardona heaving shots from a distance. But Cardona's final mid-court lob missed the basket, and the Voks fell 28–26 in a thriller that had fans and bench players on the edge of their seats. "They said it couldn't be done—that you couldn't beat the Lanier Voks in their own gym," wrote Bill Michaelis, "but the Brackenridge Eagles did it."[29] And they did it by going up for the rebound and coming down with it "three-fourths of the time." Michaelis noted that the four or five inches had been the difference between winning and losing, and so had been the Eagles' refusal to be "baffled by the zone defense that had crumbled the Jefferson attack only a week before."[30]

Lanier expected to keep its home-court advantage, and the Voks seemed ready to move swiftly past the pack, but the one weakness that had always hovered in the background—their lack of height—surfaced at the wrong moment. The team's fortunes rested on their sharpshooting and their ability to drive to the basket. When the rim became elusive and the tall Eagles successfully hunkered down inside the paint and spread their wing-sized arms, it became difficult to score. Lanier's only option was to keep the score low and try to steal some errant passes and then beat their opponents to the basket. Against a good team—and Brackenridge was much better than it had shown in the San Antonio Invitational—the margin for error was so much smaller. The Eagles, unlike the Mustangs the week before, made fewer mistakes with the ball and then found a way to break both the full-court press and the zone defense. Herrera also learned a valuable lesson that eventually all coaches learn: having a deep bench works well against weaker teams and even some talented ones, but in the big games and particularly the tight ones, it all comes down to the top five or six players to maintain a rhythm. Any substitution that even slightly diminishes the talent or efficiency in the court can cost a victory. One other point to underscore is that Treviño had not played as he was not yet eligible—though the box scores seem to indicate that a Treviño had played in an earlier game—and the height and scoring abilities he later exhibited might have made a difference.

The Lanier fans who crowded the out-of-bounds line and whose hooting and cheering nearly brought the Voks back left deeply disappointed. It must have stung that their so-much-praised team had once again fallen to their crosstown rival in an important game. For the last six years, Brackenridge and Jefferson had traded off important victories over their beloved Voks, and it must have occurred to many a dejected West Side fan that this was "déjà vu all over again." No doubt that for some fans it was just a game, nothing over which to spend the night fretting, but for others it was more than just a competition. Lanierites believed that the rest of the city seemed always to be assessing or evaluating them, and the influence their victories or successes held over public perceptions were fragile. They knew that others viewed their successes as sporadic or based on some violation of the rules of eligibility. Every period at the top of the summit seemed to be followed by a precipitous fall.

Was it a flaw in the character or a fatalist notion that social scientists would write about in the preceding decade that best described Mexican Americans? No, it was more a conditioning that had rooted itself in the barrio's psyche and that expressed itself by an uncertainty of success. I remember in my own high school experience how often we were disappointed. In the one year that our football team stood in first place, a popular radio show came to our school to promote our last game against a tough but beatable foe. It was the first time in two decades that anyone had taken notice of Lanier football, and we were all proud, but few of us, except for the cockiest, were sure we would win district. Unfortunately, we were clobbered that night by more than thirty points, and all the uncertainties of who we were came crashing down on us. There were tears of fan disappointment, but those simply disguised the deeper and more profound pain that we felt as also-rans who could not beat the Anglo schools when it really counted. It was especially bitter to hear the opposing cheerleaders and fans sing the songs that became our battle cry for the season and this important game. They, of course, sang it to mock us and tell us that we had been aspiring beyond our reach.

Our self-esteem or sense of peoplehood did not rest on our sports successes or failures, but we knew our place in the city's pecking order often depended on how we were perceived by the larger society. Like the Mexican Americans of the late 1930s, we also knew they were looking at us, and while a victory or defeat did not really attract that much attention in the more affluent neighborhoods, it did add to the overall perceptions of the West Side school. We may have overstated the value of each individual struggle, but we were sure that the collective activities did formulate a view about us that revealed itself in certain moments. We hungered for success simply because that is the way we knew American society functioned. It honored the victor but often disdained the loser.[31] And in our case, there was rarely ever a "moral victory"; that was reserved for the boys on the other side of the railroad tracks that not only divided us from the rest of the city but that also isolated us in the poorer and browner side of town.

For us in 1969, as I am sure it was for those in 1939, any defeat in whatever endeavor just became part of the larger narrative of our constant losses. Whether it was the Battle of San Jacinto, the U.S.-Mexico War, or even the Alamo, where Anglo Texans had managed to turn a rout into a moral victory, we were always losing, and they were always winning. We lost not only in the battlefields, the football fields, and the basketball courts, but also in the job promotions, politics, beauty pageants, and, more important, in the upper-mobility battle. We were separate but unequal and always the uninvited. Yet while defeat was hard to take, it did not fully dominate our lives because we were part of a larger community that was supportive. In spite of the difficulties at school and on the other side of the tracks, our community provided a full range of activities and spaces in which we could grow, work, fall in love, and debate our futures and those of other Mexican Americans in San Antonio. Our festivals, stores, churches, parks, *boticas* (pharmacies), eateries, theaters, and particularly our families were all part of what helped us to survive and sometimes to prosper. Each generation built on this and added its own unique aspect on how to survive Anglo indifference or hostility.

Whatever disappointment the fans felt—and surely the players did, too—the Voks quickly jumped back into form. In their next game, they beat Fox Tech 35–21 and then followed that up with a trashing of the Kerrville Tivy Antlers. The Lanier players got back into form by racing to a 26–6 halftime lead against the Antlers and then tightening their defense even more in the second half to finish with a 46–9 victory over a hapless rural opponent. Without doubt Lanier's shifting man-to-man defense caused the Antlers to commit numerous turnovers and errant passes, which led to fast-break opportunities. If the Antlers crossed the mid-court line, they were met with a smothering zone defense that clogged the area under the basket and forced them to shoot from the outside, and they proved not to be too efficient there.[32] Against lesser teams, the Voks could be overpowering. Though they had lost Jesse Saldaña, they were starting to find the rhythm as a running team.

Playing his first game back, Joe Treviño scored nine points right behind Cardona's ten. "The Voks are . . . strengthened for they have a new comer entering their ranks," said the *San Antonio Light*. "He is Joe Treviño who is over six feet and two inches. Ineligibility prevented him from playing in the first half (season) but now that he can play the Voks have the team that they have been waiting for all year."[33] No picture exists of Treviño in a high school uniform except for mug shots, but a picture of him after high school shows him to be a man among children, with broad shoulders, a wide torso, big arms, and massive legs. He was the most imposing player to don a Lanier uniform up to that time. With Raul Hernández and Treviño the Voks finally had the height to go with their speed and sharpshooting—though this advantage proved to be less imposing in the following game, as the Jefferson Mustangs, all but eliminated from the title chase, gave the Voks a tough game and only succumbed at the end by two points. This time Billy Saldaña led the scoring with fifteen and Cardona followed with eleven.[34] In spite of the closeness of the game, the Voks' shooting impressed one reporter, who wrote, "It didn't take the Voks long to get percolating and when they did it was swish, swish! Points and more points."[35] The swishing climbed to a new level when two days later they set a new scoring mark for the year by beating the Burbank Bulldogs 53–25. Led by Saldaña and Hernández, they quickly built a fourteen-point halftime lead and then outscored the hapless Bulldogs by another fourteen in the last two quarters.[36]

All these victories were a tune-up for the much-anticipated return match against the Eagles, who now had the role of favorites after their close victory at the Lanier gym. With the game at a neutral venue—the Jefferson High School gym—the possibilities for an Eagle sweep were substantial, and a sure victory seemed almost a given when the Brackenridge quintet, "playing the defensive game of their lives" and offensively led by Milton Crain, took an 8–1 lead and held Lanier to a single free throw for most of the first half. With one minute and five seconds left before the half, both teams exploded for a combined ten points, but only those by Lanier counted, as the Eagle scores were waved off for infractions.

Treviño, Saldaña, and Cardona each hit a bucket in succession to cut the lead to 8–7 by the sound of the first half buzzer. Then they came out with a surge with Hernández hitting the first goal of the second half, followed by Treviño with a free throw and a bucket, and then Cardona flipping in another score. The Voks soon had a 19–11 lead, all of their points coming in a nine-minute stretch starting with one minute left in the first half and ending in the third quarter. Then they went scoreless in the fourth quarter. This would have been disastrous if the Voks had not themselves played the "defensive game of their lives," holding the Eagles to nine points for the full second half and thus squeezing out a 19–17 victory. In that period, the hero for the Voks was small Mariano Medina, who shadowed, stripped, and smothered Brackenridge scoring leader Billy Dreiss and held him to two foul shots for the game to stymie a furious Eagle comeback. In two games, the evenly matched squads ended with forty-three points apiece and left their fans and other city basketball aficionados salivating for the rubber match.[37]

Treviño gave Lanier what it expected from him as he led the team with seven points against Brackenridge and then followed it up with sixteen as the Voks again ran past the Burbank Bulldogs, this time 47–25.[38] The sixteen points were the most by a Lanier player for the year and one of the highest totals in the school's history. This could not have come at a better time. Herrera now had three and sometimes four players who could lead the team in scoring. Saldaña had showed that he could have a big game, Hernández was steady in his point making, and Cardona was the scoring leader and the one player with the potential to score at any time. Treviño added another dimension by not only how much he was capable of scoring but also by being able to do it under the basket, a place that had often proven a barren spot for the Voks. Herrera also found that his boys—especially Mariano Medina—could play inspired defense when called upon.

On the day of the rubber match, sportswriters seemed split on the favorite for the third meeting. "There isn't any favorite for tonight's ball game any way you look at it," wrote one. He pointed out that the Eagles were the best defensive team, keeping opposing teams to sixteen points per contest, while the Voks outscored their opponents through the efforts of their "tricky little forwards" Billy Saldaña and Tony Cardona. With both teams having won a thriller and neither one having a point advantage on the other, the writer added, "You can't ask for anything much more even than this."[39] He admitted, however, that this might change if Brackenridge's Billy Dreiss did not play, as he had been sick for most of the week and had missed the previous game. When Dreiss seemed likely not to play, the afternoon edition pointed to the Voks as the favorites. "Under ordinary conditions," wrote another sports reporter, "the Eagles' smooth-working outfit would be favored slightly . . . but . . . not with Billy Dreiss, Eagle forward and as classy a cager as the city boasts, still abed with an attack of the flu."[40] His spot would be taken over by an all-city tackle in the football team who was deemed "far from being that good on the cage court." Unlike the Voks, the Eagles had depended on their starting five to play the whole game with an occasional sub stepping in to give them a breather.

Herrera now seemed perched to finally win the city title that had eluded him for six years. "Often a runner-up but never a champ—that's Herrera's trouble," said the writer. "But Friday night at Brackenridge Gym, it appears that the song is likely to have a different ending for once."[41] The song did end differently, but only after another classic struggle between the two schools that saw their series end with a two-point advantage for Lanier after three fiercely contested games. Few details are available on the game as most writers focused on the events that occurred after, but it seems that Brackenridge led the game in its final minutes. At about four minutes left, Alonso Rodríguez entered the game for Joe Treviño and became the game's first hero when he hit the shot that tied the score with less than thirty seconds left. No one hit a basket in the last seconds, and the game ended 24–24.[42] The teams went into overtime, where the rules of the game back then mandated that the first team to score won the game. Carlos Camacho, who was on that team, remembers the Eagles being the first to try to score, but when they missed the ball went to Lanier and into Cardona's hands, who dribbled to the other side of the court and dropped in the two-pointer for Lanier's win.[43] Before anything more than an instantaneous player celebration could happen, "a fist of an unknown Brackenridge supporter landed on [Cardona's] head." Immediately, according to the newspaper account, "students swarmed onto the court and the fistic battle was on."[44]

Swinging fists and elbows, pushing, kicks, and some hair-pulling spread across the floor, onto the stands, and even outside the gym as students and fans from both schools released their pent-up emotion against the nearest body of the opposite team. Three extremely close games as well as the racial tensions that always seemed to surround Anglo-Mexican interactions created a battle that school officials and more mature fans could not contain, and thus a call went out to the police department. As soon as the officers arrived, they saw "approximately 100 students" fighting outside the gym and throwing rocks at each other. Groups of sixty or more Eagle students were also congregated in adjacent corners trying to block the Lanier supporters from leaving the area while the Lanier students and fans sought to fight their way out. The police, with the help of school officials and other adults, finally dispersed the crowds, and several squad cars escorted automobiles full of Lanier fans out of the vicinity, though not before many of them received bruises from "flying fists and rocks."[45] The Lanier bus carrying the players had to be escorted by eight police cars as scattered rocks rained toward it.[46]

On the other side, an all-city backfield Brackenridge player was stabbed in the chest, but his ribs protected him from a serious injury from the one-inch deep and quarter-inch wide knife wound. Treated at the local hospital, he was released quickly. From the sketchy newspaper accounts, he was the only one to go to the hospital, and no other injuries were reported.[47] It is possible, however, that there were others who might have been hit by a rock or received multiple punches but who simply took care of injuries with home remedies. Many fans, unless seriously injured, would have avoided the clinics and hospitals owing to cost of treatment during the height of the Depression. Whatever the actual count of the injured, there is no doubt that both sides had gone into it with passion and a desire to unload the emotions that had built throughout the season. It was probably only after a few hours had passed and the adrenaline had stopped flowing through their bodies that they felt the impact of the blows.

The fact that both newspapers carried only short articles on the mêlée seems to acknowledge that the Brackenridge fans were the instigators and the ones that caused police the greatest headache. No arrests were made, school officials were not penalized or reprimanded in any way, and the story was soon dropped. Had the action occurred in the Lanier gym, it is hard to believe that the police would have reacted with such restraint. Mexican riots were not tolerated, as would be seen only a few years later when Mexican American youth engaged in numerous street fights in Los Angeles with military personnel who attacked them. This would lead to tens if not hundreds of arrests of Mexican youth but none of the white participants in the fights.[48] The overreaction of the Eagle fans was simply a part of a "free-for-all" caused by a "bitterly contested basket ball game," according to the newspaper accounts.[49] Yet the game itself was simply a manifestation of the racial animosity that brewed at the time. Yes, no doubt the game had heightened emotions, and it was for all practical purposes a game to determine the city championship and the chance to go to state, but there had been other important and close-played games without riots. Only when the Mexicans went from perennial runners-up to champs did the emotions boil over.

Tony Cardona remembers the incident slightly differently. He remembers Joe Treviño tipping the ball to Billy Saldaña, who fired a pass to him while he was in a full gallop. Upon receiving the ball, he dribbled past the last player and hit the shot. He remembers that as the players went onto the court in celebration, he bumped into an Eagle player who immediately pushed him, but before he could react, he felt the punch in the back of the head. It was not a hard shot, but before he could turn around and see who did it—he was sure it was an adult fan—Coach Dub Norton quickly took him by the arm and escorted him out of the gymnasium just as the stands emptied. He doesn't really know why he was taken to a car outside the gym and told to stay quiet. While the mêlée raged inside, he was lying on the car floor, listening as people rushed by the car, probably Brackenridge fans looking for someone to fight.[50]

Tony, many years later, could not say the fight had anything to do with being Mexican. He had grown up in a mixed neighborhood with German American neighbors and, in fact, credited one of the boys of that family with teaching him how to play basketball. He argued that he never confronted discrimination in the basketball games. He had gone on to a successful career in the meat-selling business; married the 1940 Lanier valedictorian, Rebecca Jimenez; and lived a good life. But while he did not remember discrimination, his wife recalls hearing from her friends about the racial problems at the games and in places outside of the barrio. A studious, light-skinned, and tall young woman, she moved to the West Side when her grandfather died and the family lost its economic stability. She quickly learned to stay away from places that might be problematic. She was one Lanierite for whom English was the language at home. Though her father had been born in Coahuila, Mexico, he was quite light complected and learned English, possibly from his American-born wife.[51]

Interestingly, Tony would later retell a story that indicated that he, too, was a victim of discrimination, though he never used the term. He remembers that after the season ended, Coach Norton took him to Austin and the University of Texas to meet Jack Grey, then basketball coach of the Longhorns. Cardona did not say what Grey told him, but clearly no scholarship was offered. Several years later, when the war began, Tony was sent to Corpus Christi, Texas, to the naval base there. Upon arriving, he tried out for the naval basketball team. In the second or third week—he doesn't remember for sure which—the coach approached him and said, "When you get out would you mind coming down to the University of Texas to play?" The coach was the same Jack Grey who had turned him down earlier. "I said, 'Will never happen,'" chuckles Cardona. He told the story with all its implied biases but never used the word discrimination, as if to avoid contradicting his assertion that he never faced it.[52]

The reaction of some white San Antonians to what was just a game underscored the challenges that Mexican Americans confronted when they ventured into arenas outside the confines of the West Side. Both Camacho brothers as well as Tony Rivera (whom I talk about soon) remembered vividly that Coach Herrera always prepared them for the abuse they would encounter outside their own gym. "He told us not to listen to the crowd," remembered both Jesse and Carlos at the same time, "just to win."[53] Rivera vividly recalled opposing players and fans engaging in name calling and verbal abuse and also remembers Herrera stressing to his players that a win was the best way to get back at those whose behavior was inappropriate.[54] Given the situation in which they found themselves, it was surely the safest way to respond. Winning also made others accustomed to seeing Lanier in a different light. Herrera developed a good relationship with sportswriters because he was a gentleman and because he neither boasted nor whined after a game, and that is what he taught his boys.

Herrera's boys had to learn to play the game right, and that meant being gracious as both winners and losers. For Mexican boys, such sportsmanship was the one way that they could navigate a white world that saw itself as accommodating to gracious winners and losers but that expressed hostility to those it saw as not playing by the rules. Despite the fact that there were white players and coaches who broke protocol and behaved in ways unbecoming of sportsmen, within their large numbers those who did behave appropriately always represented the true example of American sports. For those not yet considered part of the mainstream, it was of paramount importance for them to play by the rules; since they had yet to prove to the dominant culture that they understood American sportsmanship and their role within it, they were given little room to deviate from the norm. What the Brackenridge community did was disturbing, but had the riot occurred at the Lanier gym, it would have been seen as savage, and it is not likely that the police would have been so forgiving or the newspapers so tempered in their coverage.

Seventy-two years later, another good Lanier basketball team found out how it felt to be considered outside the mainstream of American sports. Though not as highly touted as the 1939 team, this band of small Mexicans had caught fire after finishing fourth in their district and had gone on to beat the best teams in San Antonio in their category. They reached the 2011 state quarterfinals and met a team from Austin. This game also turned into a very competitive contest, and while there were no fistfights at the end, the taunting began early and never let up as scores of students of Cedar Peak High School began chanting, "USA, USA, USA," inferring that this was a game between nationalities and not just schools. They also shouted, "Arizona, Arizona, Arizona," which was a reference to the state that had only recently passed stringent anti-immigration bills that targeted all Mexicans as potentially undocumented. Finally, they shouted, "This is not soccer, this is not soccer," implying that the Lanier team did not really play the all-American game of basketball but some presumed foreign sport.[55] Little did any of them know or acknowledge that soccer is the fastest growing sport in the United States. But their behavior did acknowledge that for some whites Mexicans still are not real Americans; they are foreigners who have yet to learn the American way of sports.

The Lanier fans of 2011 were stunned, and so were the Mexican American administrators and board members. The Cedar Park officials were embarrassed since they prided themselves in their efforts to make their mostly white student body sensitive to multicultural students. Everyone sought to point out the peculiarity of this event because it served no one's interest to underscore the prevalence of such actions. Surely Mexican Americans wanted to see things as having progressed to such a point that they were no longer seen as foreign, while white school officials sought to remind people that in their schools prejudices had been all but eliminated. If this were not so, then sports' promise of bringing together all of the nation's youth has failed today, as it did when the 1939 Lanier Voks were first making their way through the state playoffs.

To say that these occurrences of racially based taunting are infrequent does not mean that white racism toward Mexicans and Latinos has diminished to a rarity but only that discrimination against them has always been of a different character than that toward African Americans. Mexican American sports victories back in 1939 could be acceptable and even praised, as they often are today, but they were so because they were seen as rare and unthreatening to the sports power structure envisioned by those who followed sports in San Antonio and elsewhere. When the victories became more common and runs toward championships more certain, then what prejudices lurked beneath the surface rose into the public space. In this, sports relationships are no different than labor relationships, where Mexican and Latino workers are seen as hardworking and dedicated until they are seen as a threat to the "American" labor force or to the social structure of this country. Thus Mexican and Mexican American acceptability is still, in some quarters, conditional.

The Lanier run toward the title, however, was anything but conditional as they closed out the season with a 53–28 whipping of the Fox Tech Buffaloes and "formally clinched the City High School Series basketball race," ending the Voks' six-year drought in a sport they had not only learned but were now dominating. In this game, Treviño again proved to be the most dominant player, scoring a season, personal, and school record of twenty-four points and prompting one sportswriter to say that he "came very near defeating the Buffs by himself."[56] That performance by Treviño and the Voks quickly earned them the favorite's role in the district meet.[57] Seven other teams from the surrounding area, along with South San Antonio, the Bexar County champion, made up the competition, but none were considered to have faced as tough a schedule as had the Voks. The "goal-hawking" Lanier quintet started off hot by beating La Vernia High School 53–13 as they "made merry at the expense of the slow Lavernia boys" by moving the ball around with accurate passes that led to open shots through most of the game. Even the second stringers, known as the "pointless wonders," scored at will as "the Mexican boys were as hot as the St. Mary's Gym was cold." Cardona led all the scorers with fifteen points.[58]

The Voks followed their first playoff victory with a 49–28 pounding of

Christine Medina, with Joe Treviño scoring twenty points. They then won the finals of the District 22 championships with a closer-than-expected 34–28 victory over a stubborn and highly motivated South San Antonio squad.[59] This time, lanky Raul Hernández led the Voks with eleven points, underscoring the team's ability to produce a different scorer in every game. In the three games, Cardona, Hernández, and Treviño had each stepped up in turn to lead the team in points scored. It must have dawned on those who followed the Voks that Saldaña also lurked in the lineup, ready to do his own damage. The team's forty-five points per game offensive average, along with its ability to keep opposing teams to twenty-three points a game, distinguished it as the team to beat, this time in the regional playoffs to be held in San Marcos.[60] But whatever notions of invincibility may have arisen in the fans' minds soon came to an end as the Voks lost to the St. Anthony's Yellowjackets, the unbeaten winners of the city's Academic League Championship. The defeat came in a warm-up game in the same gym where the Voks had won the district crown. There they were scorched by "Tiny Tim" Fanning, who might have been as short as any of the Lanier players but who bested their dribbling skills and sharpshooting accuracy. The Voks lost by only two points, but Fanning's twenty-four points revealed them to be still vulnerable in their defense against a player who could break their full-court press and penetrate their shifting zone.[61]

Still, "Herrera's lithe Mexican lads" were picked as the best of the lot that came together at San Marcos. With Hernández and Saldaña at forward, Treviño at center, and Cardona and Medina at guard, Herrera had a squad that could run, shoot, and play tenacious defense. Cardona and Saldaña had ended up one-two in the city scoring race. Coming off the bench in particularly strong fashion were Alfonso Rodríguez and Joe Martínez, the latter whom one of the Camacho brothers called the best player on next year's team.[62] At the same time, some wondered which team would show up: the one that had roared through the district championships, or the one that had barely beaten South San Antonio and lost to St. Anthony's. Said one reporter, "If they are hitting their shots they should walk right through to the state tournament next week in Austin, but if the Voks go into one of their relapses it will go hard with [*sic*] them."[63]

The Voks seemed intent on proving both assessments true as they barely escaped with a 23–20 first-round victory over Shiner in a double-overtime thriller. They then followed up this close contest with a "red-hot rally" in the final period of their title game to put the Austin Maroons away 25–20 to win the regional title behind Treviño's twelve points and Cardona's eight.[64] The victory put them in the State School Basketball Tournament in Austin with a first-round matchup against the Gilmer Buckeyes, who were rated as the "real dark horses" in the tournament just behind Abilene and Livingston.[65] In this tournament, the Voks were not considered to be even close to the same class as the upper-echelon squads, given what one sportswriter called their "hot and cold proposition—when they're hot, they're pretty good, but when they're off they can be mighty, mighty bad," as they had been in the regional series. These "Mexicans" were capable of having beaten those teams hands down, wrote the reporter, but now they were "kissing their 'chicken coop' gym goodbye for the rest of the season." A gym whose court and backboards, said the newspaper, the Mexican boys "know better than their frijoles and tortillas."[66] It was a gym where the Lanier fans yelled them on—"and how they do yell"—to victory.

Herrera, conscious of such criticism, decided to take his team to Austin early to practice in the larger gym. His team had not "choked up" in the regionals. "It was the backboards that had them off," he told the reporter. "They were about the same color as the walls behind and the kids just couldn't get the range. That's one reason we are trying to get them one day of practice in Austin."[67] Herrera also planned to "tighten their man-to-man defense" to adjust to the larger court and practice breaking the same type of full-court pressure that he expected to get from the other teams. But the early practice proved a disaster as Alfonso Rodríguez, one of the heroes of the city championship game, broke his left wrist when he fell to the floor after leaping to block a shot by Tony Cardona. While not the starting guard, and without having played in the regional tournament, Alfonso Rodríguez was nonetheless considered the first guard off the bench, and his injury left only the rarely used Oswald Rodríguez as backup to Cardona and Medina, who played tenacious defense and handled the ball in the very fast-breaking offense. Herrera called Alfonso Rodríguez "our sixth man—and very valuable" and lamented his loss at such an important time. To make things worse, Lanier was placed in what most considered the tournament's toughest bracket.[68]

One sportswriter predicted that the first engagement for the "speedy, tireless Mexican youth" in the state tournament would be their last, as they faced a "tall, well-disciplined" squad in the Gilmer Buckeyes. Another argued that the Voks were "somewhat removed from the favorite's role they occupied before the accident."[69] The last comment seems to have been a San Antonio writer's hyperbole because few considered the Voks in the same league with the perennial powerhouses in the tournament. For his part, Herrera expressed quiet confidence in his team's ability to contest every game. "We'll just play our usual game, and if the boys are 'right' we'll give 'em some trouble," he told one reporter. "This Gilmer team is probably tall, but we're used to that now."[70] And play their game they did, as the Voks' "fast breaking quint" raced to a 24–10 lead at half time and then withstood a furious Gilmer rally—that had the Buckeyes within six points—to win 40–32 and advance to the semifinals against Abilene High School. Treviño led with twelve points, followed by Cardona with eleven and Hernández with eight. Saldaña added five points, and the rarely used Richard Cardenas put in two field goals, thus providing Lanier a balanced attack that hit the Buckeyes from every angle on the floor and rattled the much taller players until the final quarter of the game.[71]

In the next game, the Voks collided with Abilene High School, a tournament co-favorite and the Voks' toughest match since the city finals against Brackenridge. The Panhandle quintet had pushed back a tough Kingsville Brahma team 32–28 in the quarterfinals and seemed on-target to meet the other favorite team. Treviño, however, came up with another tremendous game, scoring nineteen points and controlling the boards against the taller Abilene players to keep the Voks close. Then in overtime he swished in the last shot to send Lanier to a 33–31 win and their first state finals. The improbable had happened, and the Voks now stood ready for the last game. These short, speedy Mexicans had reached the pinnacle of the high school basketball world in Texas, and they had done it with a fast-paced offensive game, a tenacious man-to-man press, and a shifting zone that often baffled taller teams and smothered slower ones. Ironically, in the path of these "little Mexicans" stood a nearly all-Indian team from Livingston, Texas.

Nine thousand fans came to see the final game, and it must have dawned on them that this was a different final from those they had witnessed in the past. No tall, white, methodical team stood ready to battle another similar squad for state basketball supremacy; instead, a team with one tall Mexican amid a number of small ones faced a mostly Indian team with strong boys but no massive timbers in the middle. Livingston had been in the tournament the year before and now stood ready to take the next step in its basketball rise, while the Lanier Voks were trying to make history in their first try. Both teams brought with them an outstanding ball-dribbling shooter and an explosive big man: Cardona and Treviño for the Voks and Foster Bullock and Alex Weatherford for the Lions. Both teams had beaten some impressive opponents to get to the finals, with Livingston outlasting Mount Vernon, a powerful one-loss team, and then shading an explosive El Paso Bowie High School all-Mexican team that would take third in the state. Lanier beat two teams favored over them in Gilmer and Abilene, both of storied basketball glory. All the ingredients were there for a classic matchup, and neither team disappointed.

"It was a stormy, smashing game that concluded two days of spectacular play," is the way one sportswriter described it. He continued, "The tricky dribbling and passing of two swarthy guards, Capt. Tony Cardona of the all-Mexican Lanier team and Foster Bullock, Livingston's full-blooded Alabama Indian, helped make the championship game the most sensational of seven thrilling clashes during the two-day tournament."[72] Both teams came out raining baskets and pushing the ball hard down the court, with Saldaña and Cardona dribbling, passing, and scoring for the Voks and Bullock and Harmon Walters, all-state forward, setting up their teammates for scores and occasionally putting up the ball themselves. The Lions jumped out to a lead as their shots fell through the basket, while Lanier missed too many in the first half though they continued to shoot at a faster rate than did the Livingston quintet. At the end of the first half, the Lions led 18–11. They then upped the lead through the third quarter, entering the final period with a 28–20 lead, but Lanier rallied to make it a game.

After having been held scoreless in the first half, Treviño came alive under the boards, putting back loose balls, making turnaround shots, and laying up the crisp passes from Saldaña, Cardona, Medina, and Hernández. It was a performance that more than matched the one Treviño had against Abilene when he scored more than half his team's points and dominated the middle. Facing Weatherford, who also led his team in points, Treviño showed why he and not the big boy from Livingston would be the center of the all-state team. His efforts allowed the Voks to outscore the Lions in the fourth quarter and set up last-minute heroics for both teams. With less than a minute left, Saldaña got the ball and moved toward the basket, where he was fouled. With less than thirty seconds, he went to the foul line for two shots, and he put one in to tie the game but missed the other. The Livingston guards quickly moved the ball toward the Voks' basket and found Weatherford, who swirled away from Treviño and his teammates and "fired a one-handed shot through the hoop." With less than ten seconds left, he sealed the game for the Lions and ended Lanier's chances of a state title.[73]

It was a bittersweet moment for Herrera and his crew. The team's stars had stepped up, with Treviño, who scored fourteen, and Cardona, who added ten points, again leading the scoring and Saldaña getting a chance to tie and then take a lead for Lanier. Their rally had been furious, and for a moment, said one journalist, the effort came "near being enough to blow the Lions" out of the game.[74] "We should have won," said Herrera after the game. "The kids played the greatest basket ball game of their lives and I'm proud of them, but luck was against them."[75] The "luck" was simply not making enough of their shots even though they lobbed almost twice as many balls toward the hoops. "My Sunday shooters, Tony Cardona, Billy Saldaña and Joe Martínez—kept firing away, just as I told them to do, and they hit the hoop nearly every time. They wouldn't go through often enough, that was the trouble," lamented Herrera.[76] But he added that there "are no alibis." The Voks had gotten their chance but had fallen short, and Herrera wanted his boys to know how much they had accomplished when there had been those who believed that his squad was not good enough to do much outside the district. To them, he said in the locker room, "You did the best you could. I did not expect to get this far."[77] They had lost the final game, but in his mind and those of the players, there was no doubt which had been the better team for the last half.

CHAPTER FOUR

Sidney Lanier

AN AMERICAN-MEXICAN LANDSCAPE

JESSIE VARGAS LIKED WALKING TO LANIER FROM HER house on Monterrey Street. Along the way she met up with a number of her friends, most of whom lived near the school, a place her boyfriend, the basketball team captain, called the "prison." Like many of her classmates, she "loved her school" because it provided her with everything a hardworking, studious girl might want. Her teachers were kind and caring, the clubs and organizations allowed her to participate in activities she liked, her neighborhood friends all attended the school, and it provided her protection from the hostile world outside.[1] As a member of the pep squad, she enjoyed going to the games and cheering for the boys of Lanier as well as participating in parades, pep rallies, and other school activities. Her love affair with Lanier lasted long past her five years as a student (1937–1942) and through seven years as secretary to Principal Brewer, a position she took shortly after graduation. Her high school beau, Jesse Camacho, became her husband almost thirty-five years after graduation, and their memories of the great Lanier years would occasionally bring a smile to their faces. To Jesse Camacho and Jessie Vargas, Lanier was more than just a high school. It encompassed many of their fondest memories and provided them a head start in life, though they would not always agree on the merits of a Lanier education.

The 1940 yearbook, *Los Recuerdos* (The Memories), the first hardcover one in the school's history, provides us the first real glimpse of life on the Lanier campus, as well as of the administrators and faculty. In the front page of the yearbook, we see R. H. Brewer, a serious-looking man with penetrating eyes, and quickly understand why he often won the battles that he waged publicly in defense of his beloved Lanier.[2] He would be a presence at Lanier for thirty-two years, and during that time the school had a ferocious protector. Brewer was born in the small town of Alvin, Texas, on June 20, 1894, and attended Caldwell High School, where he played football and baseball. He later attended Southwestern University, where he met Nemo Herrera and played baseball on the university team with him. He received his master's degree at the University of Texas in 1926 but by then had already worked for three years with the San Antonio school system as director of athletics. He served there until 1932, when at age thirty-six he became the second principal of Sidney Lanier.[3]

The yearbook staff wrote of Brewer, "The dynamic personality of Mr. Brewer is felt in his community, city, and state because his greatest endeavor is to serve his fellow man . . . as a principal he is fair and just; as a friend, true and sincere. No one's problem is ever too trivial for consideration and he seems to live consistently by the school's motto in everything he attempts: 'Do it because it is right.'"[4] At the time, Brewer, a World War I veteran, was state chairman of the American Legion's Committee on Americanism and assistant chairman of the City Civilian Defense Committee. He also served in several committees that provided the school district with leadership recommendations on bettering the San Antonio public schools. A civic-minded individual, Brewer believed in the same type of paternalism common to many white progressive educators of his time. He cared deeply about his students, as we have seen and will see later, but he also believed that they confronted such challenges that they were often incapable of being more than wards of the school system, to be trained to survive economically and become good citizens.

Also pictured in the yearbook is F. L. Tafolla, vice principal and one of the few Mexican American educators to hold such a position in pre-war Texas. A tough-looking man with a quick smile, Tafolla was known for his rigid discipline and his paddling of wayward boys and girls. Jessie remembers feeling uncomfortable about the paddling out in the open where everyone could see.[5] By the time I came to school, Tafolla, who succeeded Brewer, seemed a friendly old man, but it took me no time to find out that he ran a tight ship, and though he had delegated the paddling to his subordinates, he could still deliver a stinging rebuke. Most of us developed a love/hate relationship with him as we found him friendly, humorous, and just as committed to the school as Brewer. But we also knew him as someone who could humiliate our parents, lecturing them like children whenever we misbehaved.

I remember my first encounter with Tafolla when I was, I believe, a sophomore. I had a new and rather naïve young teacher who heard me say a word in Spanish to a classmate. Speaking this "foreign language" was against the rules in Texas up until about the 1970s, and it was so when Jessie went to school. Most teachers, though surely not all, would let a word pass with a stern warning, but this teacher, from up north and unaccustomed to the idiosyncrasies of Texas public schools, decided that I had so violated the rule that she sent me to the principal's office. It was the first time I had ever set foot there. Quickly, I was told to bring my parents to his office the following day, when Tafolla proceeded to lecture them about how I would never learn English if I kept speaking Spanish. Ironically, he spoke in Spanish to my parents, neither of whom spoke English. Needless to say, my parents were humiliated, and I paid the price at home. The incident did not, however, deter me from continuing to speak Spanish when no teachers or tattletales were around to hear. While my classmates and I were bombarded with Americanization, we were still too barrio to forget our mother tongue or the slang we picked up on the streets. Besides, speaking Spanish was to us and generations of Lanierites before and after a way to affirm our difference from the status quo and unsophisticatedly express our Mexicanness. Ironically, the existence of Lanier simply reaffirmed our cultural identity and made it possible for Mexican students to continue to be connected to the West Side of San Antonio. Lanier was in Jessie's time, my time, and even today a contradiction of purposes, and much of the loyalty to the school was based on the cross purposes it served in the barrio.

Tafolla, however, was doing only what he had seen Brewer and countless other educators do: to try with whatever method worked to make us Americans but, more important, to keep us from being Mexican. There were other methods, some more enticing, to get us to become American. Spearheading the softer approach was the other person pictured along with Brewer and Tafolla, Miss Belle Woodall, dean of girls. A soft-spoken, religious woman, she so impressed the students of her time that the Class of '41 dedicated the yearbook to her. "There is a member of the faculty of Sidney Lanier School who is never too busy to give thoughtful consideration and wise counsel to anyone who may bring a problem to her. That member is our Dean of Girls, Miss Belle Woodall," read the dedication. "Her high idealism, her gracious and sympathetic manner, her fine sportsmanship and her untiring enthusiasm have been an inspiration to all."[6] She was still there when I arrived at Lanier, but I do not remember much about her. Yet fifty years later, two former cheerleaders and classmates of mine remembered her and said much the same thing about her as did the Class of '41.[7]

By using the carrot-and-stick approach, the Lanier administrators created a campus in which students learned discipline, skills, manners, and how to navigate the contours of American society. Paternalism mingled with a sincere—if often only among a few—concern for the welfare of students that most administrators and faculty knew were going to spend most of their lives confined to the West Side of town, where educational and economic opportunities were limited. Lanier's administrators sought to make its students productive citizens who understood their place in a white society. Even Jessie, who loved the school and the administrators, admitted that she never heard any of them talk to students about going to college or about making something of themselves beyond vocational workers, secretaries, factory workers, or housewives. Much of the early Lanier education, as was mine in the 1960s, was about preventing us from becoming delinquents, welfare cases, and a burden to society while maintaining the docility that the largely white staff interpreted our shyness and good manners to be. The shyness and the drilled-in behavior of respect that our parents taught us made things easier for our educators and may well have reinforced the notion that they were doing something good for the poor Mexican American students who attended Lanier. And they were doing it without having to challenge the segregationist and discriminatory practices in the larger society of San Antonio.

While it is possible that some, or maybe the majority, of teachers did not want to be at Lanier, there were those who enjoyed the fact that the students were well behaved and demanded so little of them and that their parents were not intrusive or demanding but quite the opposite, very appreciative. The problems of Mexican American urban schools were still a few decades away in San Antonio. Jessie remembers most of the students at Lanier as being rather shy and as often simply bowing their heads when addressed by a teacher or other adult.[8] No doubt they were taught such behavior by protective parents who believed that staying out of trouble and obeying the teacher was as important as acquiring a trade or learning to read and write. Most parents wanted their children to be better off than themselves. There were also, by this time, educational reformers who insisted that Mexican Americans stay in school, learn their rights, and become contributing members of society. The whole concept of citizenship became important to the generation of Mexican Americans who were coming of age during this time period. From the early years of their advocacy, these reformers believed in the fundamental value of an education and often saw the lack of one as the main impediment to their integration, sometimes to the point of blaming their own people for not working hard enough to get one.

Whatever their intent, the administration and faculty nonetheless exposed Lanier students to an American cultural world that differed greatly from the one they found in the poor neighborhoods and federal housing projects in which many lived. While some of these activities were not unique to American society, they were new to working-class young people from Mexico or to their parents, who never went to school or participated in school activities either because they dropped out of school in the elementary grades or because they attended the infamous "Mexican schools," where they were segregated, crowded into classrooms with students of varied grades, and taught by one teacher for most of their school years. Lanier, while also segregated, provided many more activities and facilities, and that made it better than the Mexican schools and the ones in which students were segregated within the same school or even the same classroom. With the court-mandated integration of Mexican Americans in the late 1940s, in-school segregation became more common and would lead to sustained litigation by Mexican Americans who sought equality in the school system.[9] Lanier never confronted that type of litigation because all the students were Mexican American, and so they participated in all aspects of student activities.

Encouraging their participation in clubs and organizations proved to be one way to Americanize the students. Being a member of a club or team was something uncommon in the barrio except in some religious community centers, but even there few actual clubs existed for youth with particular interests. Other than playing in athletic teams sponsored by such centers—which in itself was a part of the mission of Americanization—teenagers had few outlets for their creativity or places in which to mature socially. Dances in the barrio were the only organized places to hang out, although sporting events for adults and those teenagers capable of holding their own against the older men of the barrio were sometimes available. For young women in the barrio, there were even fewer outlets for their interests outside of family gatherings, where women might congregate to talk about their interests. For many working-class women, this usually meant talking about the home, religious institutions, or marriage. American society thus offered more space for those young men and women who had interests beyond those found in the barrio.

One of the most prominent clubs at Lanier was the Royal Blue Collegiates, founded in 1932. According to *Los Recuerdos*, the Collegiates Club was organized by students who desired to have a social club in school. No doubt its sponsor, a Miss Jessie Shane, had an important hand in developing the bylaws, which promoted the learning of "good form in social activities" through parties, picnics, and the "annual dance for the benefit of the school."[10] Restricted to students from the school's high school division, the club's principal aim was to promote school spirit and "a spirit of good fellowship among the club members." These aims reflected a desire by educators to prepare students for the outside world. They were also fundamental in contributing to the process of Americanization as seen in the development of Mexican American middle-class organizations and advocacy groups, which took many of their procedures and social activities directly from those they learned in high school, complete with *Robert's Rules of Order*, formal dances, and the selection of a queen of something or other. While no doubt influenced by the *mutualistas* (mutual aid societies) of the immigrant communities and the clubs of the Mexican elite exiles of the Mexican Revolution, these social and advocacy clubs, which began forming in the 1930s and 1940s, were very much pro-American and quite high schoolish.

Besides the Collegiates, there was the Stamp Club, established in 1934, which promoted a way for students to get along, focused them on a "common interest," and taught them parliamentary procedures for conducting a meeting. "As to stamp collecting," said the yearbook, "the students find great pleasure and enjoyment besides [gathering] a great deal of valuable information about people and their ways of life all over the world."[11] Given, added the yearbook, that participants could honor their national heroes, admire great inventions, and "contribute greatly in helping charitable causes through special issues of stamps," the student could explore much about other societies and find that the information would prove useful years later. There was also the possibility that they could "run across a rare stamp" that would bring them a small fortune. Between 1935 and 1941, the Stamp Club members collected, studied, classified, and catalogued thousands of stamps and then exhibited them to other students and the community. The annual exhibits also invited collectors from the community to exhibit their stamps. In 1941, the Stamp Club set up an "Aid to Britain" campaign to send "used stamps and duplicates" from the student body for the entertainment of British troops engaged in the early years of World War II in Europe.[12]

"A thing of beauty is a joy forever" was the motto of the Symphonian Club, founded in 1928 and named after the poet Sidney Lanier's "The Symphony," which was a protest against the rising commercialism of his times and a lament over the conditions of the poor, whose work hours and horrible living conditions prevented them from seeing the beauty of nature and the arts.[13] The purpose of the club was to make students "useful to the school," promote participation in all "recognized student activities," and to help the students cultivate an "appreciation for beauty and worthwhile things."[14] In 1940, the members started a bulletin that was named after another of Lanier's poems, "The Chattahoochee," and which dealt mostly with the goings-on among the club's members. In 1941, they sponsored a Christmas party and an April Fool's activity. They also held a formal Valentine's dance at the gymnasium that "netted the club a good sum" of money, which was donated to the general school fund.[15] The members also drew up a constitution and bylaws and started a history of the club's activities.

The 1940 yearbook did not mention it, but the school also had a glee club for "students who love music" with special attention given to those "talented students who show promising possibilities."[16] The club actually started in 1923, before Lanier became a combined junior/senior high school, and for a number of years, only boys participated. But by 1941, and possibly sooner, girls were included in the singing club and even became officers within it.[17] Before the integration, however, a mixed chorus, also founded in 1923, provided an opportunity for students of both sexes to learn "worth-while music" that led to the development of "an exalted conception of human relations." Several of the students later "entered the musical profession."[18] The activities of both clubs, which were still around in the 1940s, included studying famous composers' contribution to the musical world and learning some of their songs. During the year, they sang musical numbers for Open House Day, the Father's Night Program, and for PTA meetings. And by the end of the year, they serenaded the student body and "friends" with some help from the school orchestra in observance of Music Week.[19]

The orchestra was also quite busy that year, as it played at a one-act play contest, a Pan-American stage show, and at numerous elementary schools in the area, as well as during the graduation services of the both the junior high and high school. The orchestra played overtures, waltzes, marches, and other kinds of music. The requirements for making the orchestra, particularly the Senior Orchestra, were steep. Interested students faced a number of challenging musical tests and had to prove themselves over two semesters and pass the physical qualifications that included having "properly formed teeth, lips and fingers" in order to play the brass, reed, and string instruments. Those who made it got to play at important events and locations in the community and city, including the San Pedro Playhouse and the city's exclusive country club. Graduating seniors received white wool sweaters decorated with blue lyres, something akin to an athlete's letterman's attire. Musically talented students also had an opportunity to participate in the Sidney Lanier band, which not only played at football games, rallies, and pep squad exhibitions, but also at the Armistice Day Parade, Open House Concert on campus, Color Day Parade, convention meetings at hotels, band concerts, the Army Prize Fight at the Municipal Auditorium, the Fat Stock Show, the Battle of Flowers Parade, the River Carnival, and other places where they were requested.[20]

Accompanying the band and orchestra at most events were the Blue Jackets, the school's pep squad, which came to number as many as one hundred girls in blue-and-white military-like uniforms. They performed dance routines and were the mainstay of student support at Lanier football and basketball games. Sometimes they performed at college games, as they did in 1940 when the Wildcats of Villanova came to play the Baylor Bears at Alamo Stadium. They also took part in the annual memorial service at Milan Square for the heroes of the Alamo and other famous Texans. Ironically, in participating in the latter activity, they provided cover for those who argued that the Texas Revolution had never been about racial issues but only about fighting for freedom. Accompanying the Blue Jackets were the ROTC Sponsors, which was a group of Lanier co-eds who accompanied each officer in the school's ROTC program to the different activities required of the cadets. They also "took part in the Pilgrimage to the Alamo."[21]

Rounding out the organizations that promoted Americanization were the Student Council, National Honor Society, and the Hi-Y Club. Big events for the Student Council included the promotion of a Speak English Campaign as well as a Vacation Time Exhibit, which must have been quite interesting given that most Lanier students were too poor to travel for vacation except to visit relatives in Mexico or to work the fields in El Norte in the late spring and summer.

The Hi-Y club, an all-boys version of the YMCA, sought to promote "high standards of Christian character." Its motto: "Clean speech, clean sports, clean scholarship, and clean living." The use of the term "clean" could be interpreted to reveal a particular concern for hygiene and whiteness, as Mexicans were often perceived to be filthy and dark. One way to make these boys "clean and Christian" was to have them engage in recreational activities that were deemed more American than cockfighting, boxing, wrestling, and other activities in which barrio residents participated. The Hi-Y boys met on Monday nights at Lanier and then went swimming or played ping-pong, basketball, or other games in the gymnasium. They also read in the library and participated in Bible reading and "devotional exercises" to gain spiritual direction in their lives.[22] No other club description captured the essence of Americanization more than that of the Hi-Y Club, and probably no club attracted more hard-core students, who had made a decision to integrate into American society.

For the National Honor Society, "members [were] selected on the basis of scholarship, leadership, character and service."[23] This, too, emphasized the limitations of the Mexican students, as white Texans had often seen Mexicans as incapable of being trusted or becoming leaders. No doubt many of Lanier's teachers were interested in preparing their students to be good Americans, but the interest in making them American was complicated by the belief that most of the students would never really become part of the mainstream. Even in the National Honor Society, as Jessie and her future brother-in-law Carlos Camacho remembered years later, no discussion about going to college or "going places" ever took place.[24] In many ways, the Mexican American students of Lanier were being prepared to live a middle-class life while never leaving the life of a working-class person. It was a disingenuous way—though not always intentionally so—of making them American culturally while keeping them Mexican economically and socially.

Lanier students were teased with Americanism, and the most ambitious and studious of them bought into the notion of their acceptance and upward mobility. This hope was particularly enticing to those who were raised in poverty and who were only too conscious of their parents' struggles. They wanted something other than the poverty of their parents, other than always being on the outside looking in. The American promise, or whatever they understood of it, was for those who could participate and were equipped to take advantage of the opportunities before them. There were many, of course, who understood what awaited them, and they simply enjoyed their lives in the present. Others, however, dreamed of something much more important. This can be seen by the number of organizations and clubs to which they belonged and the leadership positions in which they served. They were natural leaders who quickly rose in the hierarchy of the clubs and school organizations and were recognized by peers for their intelligence and work ethic.

This leadership, however, went to those more willing or anxious to accommodate to American values. Without doubt some wanted to be seen as American and not Mexican, although those were, at the time, probably the minority. The others simply saw themselves as Americans either because they were born in this country or because they had lived here long enough not to know any other place. The American dream was theirs, too, and they did not differentiate themselves, at least in terms of worth and merit, from other Americans. They understood the barriers that confronted them outside the barrio, but those had to do with the people beyond the West Side and not necessarily with the country in which they lived. Like other immigrants, they saw American society as fundamentally good even while so many of their white neighbors were not. This, of course, applied mostly to those who were able and willing to go to an American high school. Thousands of other Mexican American youth did not attend school or did not last long enough in school to come to believe in the American dream. The Lanier students were different just by the fact that they attended a high school that was their own, at least in terms of its location, and that schooled mostly Mexican young people like themselves. The fact that it also served as a gathering place for the people of the West Side resonated with many of the students and their parents.

The Class of '69 attended Lanier at a time when desegregation was at its highest point, and yet we were spared the turmoil that accompanied the process. It was also a time of tremendous social conflict and protests that would ultimately come to Lanier, but always there was safety and familiarity. When we took to protesting the conditions of the school, we did so, not because we did not like the institute or because we wanted to be like the North Side schools, but rather because we believed the barrio and its children deserved better. We liked that Lanier was located in the barrio, that it served the Mexican children of the West Side, and that many of our parents and relatives—

though none of mine—had attended the school. We wanted the youth of the West Side to keep attending Lanier, but we also wanted them to be better prepared for college and to have a sense of pride in their heritage. Lanier was as much a part of the heritage of the barrios, or the "Latin quarter," as anything else because it reflected the reality of the Mexican experience in San Antonio. We lived, celebrated, and ate like Mexicans, but our lives were not untouched by Americanism, and throughout the twentieth century all barrio kids who went to Lanier would confront the duality of their heritage.

Administrators like Brewer and Tafolla were not blind to such conflicts. They understood that in spite of efforts to stamp out the Mexican presence in San Antonio it only grew. Mexican culture was a part of the city and one that was often promoted to attract tourists. One could say that, without the Mexican presence, there was no Texan culture because it depended so much on the Mexican contrast. People did not come to the Alamo City to taste cowboy food or hear hillbillies play their instruments, nor did industry relocate there because of cheap white labor (although there were many unemployed whites back then) or because Texas was close to major cities in the United States. San Antonio's proximity to the border meant an abundance of labor, markets across the border, Mexican shoppers—even back then—and a bicultural setting created both by popular working-class lifestyles and by the more sophisticated taste of the Mexican exile elites. All this made San Antonio both an American and a Mexican town. Of course, the setting itself served as a cover for the miserable existence of the barrios in the West Side, where poverty, illiteracy, alcoholism, and dysfunctional families were apparent characteristics.[25]

Brewer understood that the students' ability to progress in school depended on self-esteem and in their ability to see themselves as part of the society in which they lived. Successful students also had to believe they brought something with them that they could contribute to their nation, even though there was nothing new about them since most were born in the United States and had lived here all their lives. Still, they were Mexican American, and that often meant being seen as foreigners outside of the West Side of San Antonio. In an article titled "Latin American Pupils Learn Americanism via Mexico Route," the reporter begins, "The best in Mexican life is good Americanism. This idea, expressed in 1001 ways is shaping a new kind of education in San Antonio." The reporter went on to add that the new curriculum at Sidney Lanier was "made to order" for the nearly 1,500 students who attended, and it was designed "to overcome a mass inferiority complex and to make the boys and girls proud of their Mexican ancestry."[26]

"The Mexican people have been browbeaten [for] 1,000 years," Brewer was quoted as saying. "They have developed an inferiority complex . . . [and]

people with an inferiority complex don't make good citizens and we decided to try to overcome it."[27] The way to overcome this complex, according to the article's take on Brewer's philosophy, was to pick out the "best qualities" of those he referred to as "Latin Americans." These qualities were the "uncanny skill" in making beautiful things from clay, their love of colors, "the . . . grace of their native dances," and the "picturesque" nature of their costumes. In other words, Mexicans were good with their hands, loved variety in their colors, and danced well. Long before multiculturalist educators came on the scene, Brewer was promoting the notion of using the children's culture to find their niche in American society. Nothing was said about their intelligence, work ethic, commitment to family, or religious values. They were artisans and dancers, not thinkers and builders, and this would set the foundation, influential until the present, for how Mexican Americans would be educated and for what skills and talents they would be recognized.

But as Brewer soon found out, West Siders were Mexicans through their experiences in American society and not necessarily through their knowledge of or connection to their ancestral land. If Brewer or anyone else had expected them to put on a costume and do the *Jarabe Tapatío*, Mexico's national dance, they were soon disappointed. The Mexican American kids were more likely to want to do the Lambeth Walk, the dance craze among American youth at the time. So, like Indian educators would do in the reservations, Brewer set out to teach the Mexican youth their dances, songs, and culture. With the help of his personal secretary, Mrs. Rosa Elida Cardenas, he established Las Mejicanitas (the little Mexican girls) in 1933 as a group of dancers from Lanier who performed at local civic clubs, school festivals, conventions, and other schools throughout the city and South Texas area. They danced the Sandunga, which told of what happened to a village when a bundle of baby clothing from a shipwreck washed ashore. Or they danced the Chiapaneca, the story of a Mexican girl's adventures on her way to market. We do not know whether Mrs. Cardenas was a professional dance instructor or a former dancer, but by the pictures and the snippets in the yearbook, we can surmise that she committed herself fully to the task. She designed the costumes and taught the dance steps and no doubt the history of each dance.[28] There would be many like her in the barrios of San Antonio who sought to teach their sons and daughters to keep their culture alive.

The 1940 yearbook editors had this to say about Las Mejicanitas: "It is the hope of the school that this club will continue to exist for it reveals the talent and the heritage that is found among students of Mexican extraction."[29] Another organization founded in 1935 to promote Mexican heritage was Los Trovadores, "the most colorful and popular organizations at Lanier," which evolved from a suggestion from Brewer shortly after coming to the school.

The intent of the club was to get the boys to sing popular Mexican songs accompanied by string instruments. Brewer again found someone to carry his dream forward. Ralph Cardenas, a clerk in the main office and the husband of the girls' dance instructor, became the sponsor and taught the boys how to sing and play the instruments. Almost instantly, Los Trovadores became a hit in the school and throughout the city, playing for local civic clubs and in school festivals and in other activities to which they were invited. The success of Los Trovadores also led to the formation of singing groups in the barrio and the rest of the city, including a double male quartet and a large Mexican chorus, this one formed by a Professor F. Hernandez.[30] Said the yearbook, "Thus we find the Lanier Trovadores not only introduced to San Antonio audiences a different type of entertainment but also in revealing the talent and quality of the heritage of our fathers served as an inspiration that gave birth to other such musical organizations in our city."[31]

To his credit, Brewer did not believe that just singing and dancing popular Mexican tunes would change the lives of the students, no matter the impact on ethnic pride. "All the pride in the national background won't help unless we can do something for them economically," he told the reporter. To that end, he established the Department of Mexican Arts and Crafts. There students learned leatherwork, metal craft, clay modeling, drawing, and design. All students were required to take those classes for one semester, and the ones who showed talent and promise in them were encouraged to continue their training. The hyperbolic reporter added, "Here the Latin American students are taught the age-old ways to beauty of form, line and form learned 1,000 years ago by the Mayans and Aztec Indians, later modified by the Spanish casics [caciques] of the Conquistadores."[32] The end product of their work, added Brewer, was neither Mexican nor American but rather something akin to the language they spoke outside the classroom or what he termed the "San Antonio style."

The school could not escape this biculturalism, and it seemed to permeate so many of the activities and organizations that were sponsored. The school newspaper, first published on March 5, 1924, was named *El Nopal*, or the cactus, by Miss Mena Harrell, with the approval of the faculty and the principal. She believed that the name "fitted well because of the surroundings and the community in which the school is located."[33] According to the 1940 yearbook, the purpose of *El Nopal* was "to bring about a closer relationship between the school and the home" by letting both students and parents know about the activities in the school.[34] The school offered four journalism courses to prepare the students for writing in the school newspaper, and those who excelled in their second year received a journalism pin. No copies of the school newspaper of those years are available, at least not beyond individual copies, and so it is hard to know whether it covered the activities of the surrounding community and how it might have treated racial or ethnic issues, such as athletic eligibility or conflicts in sports contests. It is quite possible that those stories would have been left out of the newspaper by administrators who sought to downplay racial conflicts.

Similarly, the memories that the school staff, faculty, and administrators wanted to promote in the school yearbook, *Los Recuerdos*, were not the ones that most Mexican students brought with them. Rather, they attempted to create among the students an image of themselves as American. But they understood that these new memories had to come in transitional phases, and this required making the students' heritage part of that past. Students in Spanish classes performed Spanish plays, and there were always several instructors teaching the language. And in spite of the Spanish-language ban in the school, most students on recess or off campus spoke Spanish to discuss the Mexican dances, conjunto music, or the Spanish-language movies at the Zaragoza and Guadalupe Theaters only blocks from the school. Most of the students spoke as much or more Spanish than English, although by then there were already a few who were becoming bilingual illiterates, unable to speak or write either language well, a result of the school's effort to strip them of the Spanish language while doing a poor job of teaching them English, as Jesse Camacho would attest.[35]

Whatever the intent of making Spanish available through Las Mejicanitas and Los Trovadores, two groups in which language was key to what they did, or in making Mexican culture so much a part of the school day, the results was that students were reminded that they were different—but that the difference was not inherently bad. After all, why would the school promote something that it considered inappropriate or unfitting of Americans? It must have dawned on one or two of the brighter students that much of what they were learning and how they were being constructed as American citizens was contradictory. They would have seen this same incongruence in the city festivals and the community's promotion of Spanish culture even as it treated its Mexicans and Mexican Americans as second-class citizens. Some may have perceived the naming of the school newspaper and yearbook as condescending, but it is likely that most simply saw it as natural. After all, *nopales* (cacti) were common in the barrio yards and lots and even in the barrio kitchens. And everyone had *recuerdos* (remembrances) in the barrio since hopes were sometimes less prevalent than memories during hard economic times. The students, more than their teachers and leaders, understood that their bicultural experience and their San Antonio style differentiated them from Anglo counterparts in the North Side schools.[36]

Brewer recognized earlier than most Anglo educators the bicultural and bilingual lifestyle that Mexican Americans lived. While Spanish may not have been permitted on campus, the emphasis on Mexican crafts and culture was seen as a way to motivate Lanierites to finish school and learn a skill or trade. The San Antonio style of which Brewer spoke represented the hybridization of two cultures and reflected the asymmetric relationship that they shared. By the 1940s, Anglo culture in San Antonio was reflected in the private parties and within the elite organizations of the city as well as in the business approach of the powerful and influential. Yet Anglo culture, except for the rodeos, German festivals, and Texas historical commemorations, had all but subsided. In San Antonio as well as in many other places in Texas, culture had become "Spanish," a much-exaggerated colonial style that still depended on Mexican song, dance, and food to provide it substance. For many Texans, their region had gone from being Spanish to being Texan and then American, with the Mexican period a minor speed bump in the historical process. But the reality was that Mexican culture, with a few remnants from the Spanish era, was the only significant folkway for the Lone Star State.

The Mexican exiled elite had their high-society balls, newspapers, and commemorative festivals reminiscent of an older Mexico, but it was the "chili queens" and the mom-and-pop stores and restaurants that captured the imagination (and taste buds) of most tourists to Texas. The mariachis were yet to be developed and popularized by a Mexico City radio station, and so Trovadores-type music groups were more common, as was the growing accordion and *bajo sexto* instruments of working-class groups and their conjunto music. The elite Mexicans' ways and the Texan interpretation of Spanish culture may have served as a foundation for the biculturalism of San Antonio, but it was the growing Mexican population with its festivals, food vendors, dances, marketplaces, and daily chatter that really drove the city's culture. The *mutualistas*, mutual aid societies, many with names of Mexican revolutionary heroes or pre-conquest Indian warriors, were the core sponsors of many of these events, as they fought hard to maintain a sense of identity within the Mexican populations. While not advocacy groups per se, they were often the only organizations to which a Mexican could turn in case of legal or social challenges. The Catholic parishes that dotted the West Side and stretched into the downtown area were also promoters of Mexican culture, even if only by the sheer number of their parishioners who were deeply devoted to the religion of their motherland. The great number of Mexicans served as the backdrop for whatever biculturalism existed in the city since more of them knew English than their counterparts knew Spanish.

People like Brewer understood these dynamics better than most, as did politicians like Maury Maverick, who used a coalition of liberals, unionists, and Mexican Americans to bring progressive politics to this bastion of conservatism. Brewer, more conservative, sought to use whatever mechanisms he could to educate the children of the West Side. Paternalistic and at times doubtful of the intellect of the Mexican "kids" in his school, he nonetheless saw them as his charge. He understood their limitations but saw those at Lanier as capable of pushing higher the ceiling that often held them down. He had shy, reverent, and for the most part, obedient students, and his heart must have ached to see so many of them drop out and so many other young people in the barrio without any skill or hope for the future. The Progressive Era had ended at about the start of his tenure at Lanier, but some of its views still affected educators and social reformers who believed that immigrants and their offspring could be made American by teaching them American ways, providing them skills, and encouraging them to become participants in the nation's activities. But unlike other reformers on the East Coast and the country's Midwest, Brewer realized that these immigrants were not going to disappear or "become" white as other immigrants had.[37] Whatever his views of Mexican culture or his faith in his Mexican boys and girls, he seemed committed to them. When his wife died several years after he did, one of their children would remember that talk at the dinner table always revolved around Lanier.[38]

The mixing of Americanism with Mexicanism at Lanier provided students a little of both worlds and, in some ways, the best part of each. They were learning skills, gaining familiarity with American society that was often out of limits to many, and yet still (by implication if not by practice) validating aspects of their culture. This meant that the school could not, or more likely would not, engage in grossly discriminatory practices. The school provided a sanctuary from a more hostile outside world, and within that world, teachers and administrators could work out their own issues about working at an all-Mexican school. These barrio outsiders saw the best and the brightest of the West Side, and while some might not have always felt at home with the majority of their students, they did find their favorites. Those who gave themselves to their profession eventually accommodated and served as best they could. This did not mean that all prejudices were eliminated or that teachers served all the students, only that eventually a semblance of normality settled in. With the strict environment and with most troublemakers quickly removed—and there is almost nothing written to suggest that Lanier confronted many troubled youth at this time—Lanier could be a good environment for any dedicated teacher.

My own experience at Lanier supports the claim that prejudices or discrimination were not really an issue. There were insensitive teachers and one or two who didn't think that most of us would amount to much, but rarely did that lead to open condemnation of us as a student body. Having Brewer and then Tafolla lead the school made it difficult for teachers or other administrators to openly show prejudice or discrimination. What we often confronted was condescension, paternalism, and individual prejudices over our language deficiencies, poor writing and reading skills, clothing, and supposed hygiene problems, but only on rare occasions were these issues racialized publicly. Having administrators committed to their Mexican students, being surrounded by miles and miles of barrio residents, as well as being looked down upon by some of their peers for working at Lanier made many of the teachers more adaptable. Having basically good kids around them—and we were still pretty conservative and respectful students even in the 1960s—made it even easier. Their greatest challenge would be our difficulty in learning, and this at times led to lowered expectations and indifference toward our education.

This Lanier "style" provided a more positive environment for Mexican American youth than did the rest of San Antonio society and allowed them to grow up in a more normal way. This, of course, applied only to those students who conformed to the American high school model. Not all students adjusted because of very deficient language skills, because they had to work, or because they or their parents simply did not see education as important. For those who fit the model, however, Lanier extended their youth, provided leadership opportunities, opened cultural space to forge an identity, and offered athletic exploits in with which to develop fond memories. Looking at the yearbooks reveals that Lanier's students were engaging in the same rituals as other San Antonians and were doing so without the conflicts that Mexicans in Anglo schools confronted. They were creating their own space and finding their own sense of Americanism. While Mexican American reformers were charging that the segregation of Mexican Americans in their own schools was discriminatory, one teacher defended the system this way: "Nevertheless, it is true that where there is a large percent of Mexicans, it is to the advantage . . . to maintain separate schools for them; because first, teachers, textbooks, and methods can be selected with a view of meeting the needs of the children, and second, the Mexican children will be freer and happier and will attend during a larger period of years."[39]

Such comments often represented a rationalization of the isolation of Mexican students and at best wishful thinking by those educators who actually believed that most teachers affirmed the educability of the ethnic child. Some elements of truth, however, were hidden within those rationalizations. In pre-1960s America, and surely many years after, attending school with white students rarely proved a pleasant experience for students of color and particularly for Mexican Americans. Mexican students from elite families and those who were what the writer Richard Rodriguez calls the "scholarship child" eventually found opportunities often lacking in segregated schools, but for the most part, these pupils, even the bright ones, confronted discrimination and racial hostility from not only white classmates but often the teachers.[40] The experience of Fidel, a fieldworker, in the early 1950s was often a more common occurrence. When Texas schools were officially desegregated for Mexican Americans in 1948, Fidel was transferred (along with a number of other Mexican children) to a predominantly Anglo school. As he entered the classroom, the teacher told him to "sit in the back and shut up," which he did for the time he spent in school. He never learned to read, write, or speak English.[41] Other students dropped out or graduated with few skills.

Desegregation, if it had been proposed in the 1940s, would have been close to impossible socially, demographically, and geographically for Lanier. The social reasons we can already assume, but geography and demography merit explanation. There were too many Mexican students who came from the surrounding areas, and there were no predominantly Anglo schools within easy busing distance. The cost to the school district of busing Mexican students to Anglo schools would have been prohibitive, and given that most educators still saw Mexican children as mostly future skilled and semiskilled workers, vocational curriculums would have had to be enhanced at the Anglo schools within a strapped school district with too many students and too few tax dollars. Desegregating Lanier never became an option even during the heyday of busing and desegregation. I went to a segregated school, and forty years later, I would come to do research in a school just as segregated as the one I attended. Had Lanier been an inner-city school with feeder elementary and junior schools from different areas of the city, desegregation might have been possible, but given that Lanier was located in the middle of the West Side, across the tracks from the rest of the city, desegregation was never a serious option.

Lanierites and their teachers and administrators, then, had no option but to make space within the West Side and convince themselves that Lanier offered a path forward. In the late 1930s, what Lanier offered was simply a promise of things to come, though mostly to the most prepared, the hardest workers, and those who had something to offer to a society that was not going to "lift their boats" simply because they claimed citizenship or a love of country. When the Class of '69 graduated, we did so with many dreams and a few more possibilities, many of which were self-constructed. Only a few had more than that, and it was no different in the early 1940s. Yet a least for a short time, they dreamed of bigger things, as we see in captions that accompanied the section on graduating seniors in the first Lanier yearbook.

According to the yearbook, Joan Adame, the ever smiling "Mejicanita," was going to gain fame as an entertainer; Richard Bustamante would became a famous artist; Mercedes Cantu, a "prosperous" secretary; and Ramiro Cardenas would have to think hard and long to "make up his mind whether to outshine Bing Crosby or become another Pasteur." But Roque Garza gave him a run for the best vocal chords in school. Lupe Blacarte, "so quiet, so serene," would surely be a great lady, while Jimmy Casiano was sure to head Standard Oil Company, and Elma Cueva would be an indispensable nurse in some hospital. Daniel Castañeda and Cristóbal Encina were going to make many gardens and landscapes beautiful, and they might just end up working for William Booker, president of the landscapers club and one heck of a singer as president of the Glee Club. If not, they could work with Dante Barron, who was going to be an "asset to any sheet metal shop he wishes to work in." Of course he might be working for friend and classmate Guadalupe Martínez, president of the Sheet Metal Club. Oscar Enriques was likely to be the boss of all of them, given that he was the president of the Lanier Leaders' Club and someone whose "friendliness is so comforting." Mary Falcon might have something to say about that, given that she was a leader herself as lieutenant colonel of the ROTC Sponsors and a very popular young woman. The "beautiful" Ethel Casillas was likely to leave the business world to her classmates and set out for Hollywood for a screen test. If she couldn't act, she surely could sing given her experience with Las Mejicanitas. There she might run into Mejicanita companion and just as "pretty" Augustina Franks, whose "glamour" career began with a second place in the Interscholastic Play Contest and as duchess of the Texas A&I University Lantana Festival in 1939.[42]

In California or maybe New York, the two beauties might run into Irene Garza, first-place winner of the "What I Like about My Town" essay contest, or possibly Concepción Hernández, playing in the U.S. Open as the next Helen Wills. She might, however, have to get past Bertha Rodríguez, another "whizz at tennis." Rosa Venegas, Daniel Rivera, Jesse Rabago, Olivia Martínez, Ernest Herrera, Frank Gonzalez, Pieter Koster, and Bennie Alvarado, all former colleagues in *El Nopal*, just might end up covering their exploits. In writing sports, they were likely to take orders from Antonio Hernández, he who played with the '39 state runner-up team and the one person who is "of the most likely to succeed." But even he would be taking assignments from Magadalena Cavazos, who had "a mind of her own" and was an award-winning journalist with *El Nopal*. Mariano Medina's tenacious defensive skills on the basketball court would come in handy, and he might just become a policeman given his tenure as TD (traffic director) chief and his "one in a million" personality. Ralph Parada, a yell leader, would cheer all the Lanierites on, while to Lorenzo Mora, the class poet, would fall the obligation to write the final chapter on the Class of '40.

The Class of '41 was sure to have a "radio announcer" in Jesse Rodríguez and a doctor in Alfred Hernández.[43] Richard Zamora, Petra Hernández, and

Josephine Martínez would be successful in business, while Joshua Grijalva was to be a good shepherd "who will give his life for his sheep"—probably a pastor, a social worker, or a father of many. Jesse Camacho, a man of many offices, would "win friends and influence people" (he ended up being a successful pharmacist). Carlos, his brother, "was born to command," though he became a trailblazer by rising higher in the civil service hierarchy of the local air base than any Mexican American before him. Maria Virginia Sánchez could possibly join Ethel Casillas and Augustina Franks in Hollywood because she had "the temperament of a real actress." But then José A. Rodríguez "ought to be in pictures" as well, maybe playing the part of Napoleon. Manuel Almaguer was to be a "statesman, actor, financier," or whatever he chose because "he's good at all." José (Joe) María Riojas was likely to settle for "room and plenty of air"—after all, they called him "Alitas" (Wings) because of his ability to fly into the air for the rebound when playing with the basketball team.[44] Blas Herrera was an "ambassador of good will, tall and dignified," so politics or the Foreign Service was not beyond reach.[45]

Susie Jimenez could look toward a career as a chef, given that she well understood that "civilized man cannot live without cooks." Delfino Aguirre was a lover of poetry, and Zulema Salinas was a "beautiful dreamer of dreams," so something in the arts awaited. For Victor Forestello Jr., a military commission was quite possible given his rare combination: "the gift to lead as well as the power to command."[46] Charles Flores was sure to be a florist, and Leopoldo Gonzales would invent "quips, and cranks and wiles" long after he left school, while Angelita Villarreal was the consummate librarian with her encyclopedic mind. Esperanza Cox would make beautiful dresses, while Mike Sulaica sculpted masterpieces. Alicia López could well be the editor of the *San Antonio Light*, running reporters ragged with her "driving power" but keeping readers engaged with her "winsome personality" writing. Frank Barboza was going to take on the likes of Joe Louis and Rocky Marciano and after beating them both "live in ease."[47] That ease would probably be made easier by Luis Alonzo's "fine furniture." And his fame would be extended by journalist "of note" Marie Espinoza.[48] He might even get to be a cartoon on the sports pages if Cecilio Maldonado got his hands on a pencil and paper, while Frank Leyva might decorate his home for a price and Catalina Orona teach his children.

All of this, of course, was conjecture during graduation season, when dreams soar, everyone is a friend, and hope for a better life abounds. Lanier students, despite the Depression and the possibility of war in Europe, had dreams and hopes, and given their isolation in their own segregated world, they could not see why such dreams could not come true. With few exceptions, we don't really know what happened to these students, but given the statistics it is likely that most simply blended into the barrio until the war sent them spiraling toward another future, some to the grave. The yearbook's musings of hope and success give some glimpses of the realities for the Lanier students. They would be good homemakers, good friends, hard workers, and fun to be around. Some would be their family's "greatest worry," others would ask you to "lend [them] a dime," and still others would be "loyal to Lanier" as good alumni who continued to attend the games, participate in school carnivals, and send their kids to this bastion of West Side education. In terms of higher education and professional accomplishments, these cream-of-the-crop Lanier students would rank far below their counterparts in the North Side of San Antonio and other white students throughout the state and nation. But in the West Side, they represented a stable group of individuals who came to dominate the businesses, shops, and skilled professions necessary to maintain that area as an active community. Historian Richard García described these San Antonians as a "lower middle class that had skills, aspirations, a work ethic, and a hunger for success."[49] When my family moved to the West Side of San Antonio, I came to know many of these former Lanier students.

As the Class of '69 neared graduation, our commercial art teacher, one of the most popular and hip teachers in the school, mocked in a friendly way all the crying that occurred during graduation. He told those of us who listened that with college on the horizon and with all the possibilities of a good profession there was nothing to cry about and nothing to tie us to our high school. Our reaction—which we didn't share with him—was that he wasn't a Lanier graduate and did not understand the context of life in the barrio. Deep within our minds, we knew that for many of our classmates this was the end of the education line. No doubt our class produced more college students, possibly many more, than previous classes, but we knew that the overwhelming number of us would never enter the doors of a college or university. Things were changing for Lanier graduates, but not enough to make any other institutional experience—except for maybe those who made the military a career—so significant. Lanier graduates of the 1940s and earlier likely spent five to six years at the school. Many found their spouses there, though not always the one they dated as students. (Or like Jessie Vargas, some came to rediscover them thirty years later.) Many got their vocational skills there, and a lucky few discovered their passions. Friendships were forged, and so was an identity.

Historian Mario T. García argues that Mexicans in the United States began developing an identity in the 1930s that would tie them together as a community. While being victims of discrimination, working similar jobs, and living in the same neighborhoods provided them a point of reference, it was not until they began speaking English, adapting to American ways, and becoming concerned about the everyday issues they confronted in American society that they began to fully create an identity for themselves that spoke to their present circumstances. Although García writes about only one segment of the community—those who were American citizens or had been long-time residents—this was the more dominant segment by the 1940s. World War II served as a watershed event for Mexican American integration into the broader society, but it was so because many had already been exposed to the good and the bad of American society. Those who fully took advantage of their military experience were those who had best utilized their public school experience to learn the language, understand American culture, and gain employment skills. More important, they came to identify themselves as citizens. As part of the San Antonio Council of Parents and Teachers "Youth Marches On" radio series of 1939, Lanier's student council president, a female student, along with another student dialogued a program titled "Latin-America Speaks" that explained how the public schools were "assisting the Mexican children to become good citizens." Lanier's thirty-five-piece orchestra and the all-boys Glee Club provided entertainment for the series.[50]

Many Lanier graduates who served in the military had already served in ROTC units, and a good number had held leadership positions. Lanier's ROTC was established in January 1939 with about 120 students opting to be part of the new organization in school. They got their uniforms from the military units in the area, and the students were subsequently tested to select cadet officers.[51] By 1941, just months before the attack on Pearl Harbor, Lanier had four companies of ROTC cadets, with each company picture showing between thirty and fifty members. Another picture showed twenty cadet officers.[52]

A Girl Reserve club had also been organized in May of that year and was functional by the fall semester.[53] The Girl Reserves had been established by the YWCA in 1918 to promote patriotic fervor among women and girls near the end of World War I. It was one of the few female organizations open to women of color.[54] The members held conferences, set up lectures, did service, and committed themselves to being good patriots. There were even Girl Reserve chapters set up in the Japanese internment camps during World War II.[55] Their motto was "I will do my best to honor God, my country and my community, to help other girls and to be in all ways a loyal true member of the Girl Reserves." Fashioned in some ways after the Boy Scouts of America, the Girl Reserves sought to make young women into model citizens by instilling in them those middle-class values so much lauded during this period of time:

Gracious in manner.
Impartial in judgment.
Ready for service.
Loyal to friends.
Reaching toward the best.
Earnest in purpose.
Seeing the beautiful.
Eager for knowledge.
Reverent to God.
Victorious over self.
Ever dependable.
Sincere at all times.[56]

With twenty-eight members, the Girl Reserves Club of Lanier was dedicated to building "a fellowship of girls devoted to realizing in their lives the ideals of personal and social living." In 1942, one of the club's major projects was to knit items for the Red Cross, most likely for the soldiers or their families. None of these organizations provided any kind of feminist education or even a notion of equality, but they did offer girls activities, challenges, and positions of leadership that the barrio did not. It was thus attractive to many and facilitated their own Americanization process.

While there were few Mexican Americans in the military before Pearl Harbor, a sizeable number had served in World War I, including many of the early leaders of organizations such as the League of United Latin American Citizens (LULAC). With war in Europe escalating and tensions with Japan growing, many Americans were beginning to doubt that the nation could stay out of war. It is hard to imagine that Mexican Americans thought any differently, and many Lanier students may have taken ROTC to prepare for their future participation in the conflict. I know that many of the Class of '69 did just that. While the war in Vietnam was only a police action when we entered Lanier in the seventh grade, by the time we were seniors, there was no doubt in our mind that if we did not go to college or have influential parents to keep us out, we were all going to war. Similarly, most of the male students of the Classes of 1940–1942 were learning about Europe and Asia and were wondering where they would be heading if war broke out between the United States and the Axis powers.

Kino Rodríguez poses for a picture as if shooting in the old Lanier gym, known as the "chicken coop." (Photograph courtesy of David Rodríguez.)

Three Lanier teachers pose for a picture in front of the school's front entrance. The three were part of a group of young teachers hired by R. H. Brewer to help assimilate his Mexican American students. (Photograph courtesy of David Rodríguez.)

Frank Rodríguez, one of three all-state players in the 1945 championship team, looks at the camera as he dribbles during practice. (Photograph courtesy of David Rodríguez.)

Opposite page, top: The 1935 Sidney Lanier football team, coached by Nemo Herrera, which won the district championship. Herrera was also a successful football coach and inspired great loyalty from his players, though they were never able to win a state title. (Photograph courtesy of Charles Herrera.)

Opposite page, bottom: The 1945 Lanier state basketball champions. Front row (left to right): *David Flores, Raul Gonzalez, David Rodríguez (behind trophy), Kino Rodríguez, Frank Rodríguez. Back row* (left to right): *William "Nemo" Herrera (standing), Joe Contreras, Joe Calderon, Ruben Rodríguez, Raul San Miguel, Ramiro Gonzalez, Teddy Castellano, Gilbert Bernal (manager). (Photograph is from the William Herrera scrapbook, source unknown.)*

District champions of
1935
Sidney Lanier's "VOKS"
MORIN

State Champ
1945

Principal R. H. Brewer, pictured sometime in the 1940s. He was principal of Sidney Lanier High School for over thirty-five years and a fierce defender of his Lanierites. (Photograph courtesy of Charles Herrera.)

Fidel Tafolla was assistant principal under Principal Brewer and later became principal of Sidney Lanier High School. He was one of the few Mexican American educators in the state to serve at that level. (Photograph courtesy of Charles Herrera.)

Opposite page, top: The 1943 state championship team. Front row (left to right): *Walter Kelley, David Rodríguez, Tony Rivera, Ramiro Bernal, and Henry Escobedo. Back row* (left to right): *Coach Nemo Herrera, Manuel Gonzalez, Refugio Olivares, Frank Rodríguez, Richard Reyes, Raul Gonzalez, and Bruno Herrera (manager). (Photograph is from the William Herrera scrapbook, source unknown.)*

Opposite page, bottom: The state championship team of 1943. Front row (left to right): *Henry Escobedo, Refugio Olivares, George Reyna, Coach Nemo Herrera, Manuel Gonzalez, Ramiro Bernal, Frank Rodríguez. Back row* (left to right): *Tony Rivera, David Rodríguez, Bruno Herrera (manager), Raul Gonzalez, Richard Reyes. Not pictured: Walter Kelley. (Photograph is from the William Herrera scrapbook, source unknown.)*

4
14
16
11
5
12
8
1943

Lanier

William "Nemo" Herrera sits in front (center) *as the star of the 1918 Brackenridge High School Eagles, who won the city and the South Texas basketball championships during his senior year. (Photograph courtesy of Charles Herrera.)*

This was a spread in the San Antonio Light *for a story about "Nemo" Herrera's basketball system in the West Side of San Antonio, which produced the 1943 state championship team. The player being examined is Joe Bernal.*

(Photograph from a San Antonio Light *photo spread, "From This to This to This.")*

The Brackenridge High School Eagles city championship baseball team of 1918. William "Nemo" Herrera, who played infield, is seated fourth from the left. (Photograph courtesy of Charles Herrera.)

The Comanches Jrs. City basketball champions, in which William "Nemo" Herrera (center, *first row) played point guard and forward. No date available. (Photograph courtesy of Charles Herrera.)*

CHAPTER FIVE

War Comes to the West Side, and Lanierites Respond

SEVENTY YEARS AFTER JESSE CAMACHO MADE LANIER'S varsity basketball team, he lamented that nothing was left over from the state finals team of 1939 when he joined the team in 1940. After all, Cardona, Treviño, and Medina had graduated or were no longer eligible to play, and that was a threesome hard to replace. But it was not completely accurate to say that Nemo had no talent, at least not in the beginning.[1] The *San Antonio Express* could not disagree more with Camacho's assessment when it declared, "Nemo Herrera has another of his fast-breaking clubs that runs opponents dizzy in the course of the night's work, more than making up for their deficit in size."[2] After one sloppy and easy win by the Voks, the paper reported the Voks' passing as leaving a "good deal to be desired," though they were still the "best of the lot." And they solidified that view with a hard-fought defensive struggle in their "very loud" home court against the San Marcos Rattlers, who the semester before had won the San Antonio Invitational Basketball Tournament and were rated as one of the top teams in the region. The Rattlers would in fact go on to win the state title.[3]

Leading the game for the Voks were Billy Saldaña with eleven points and Joe Martinez with four. They got help on the boards from Raul Hernández, center and tallest player on the team. Those three had gained tremendous experience in their run toward second place in the state the year before. Against San Marcos, they trailed 7–6 at halftime, spurted to a 13–7 lead in the third, got tied 15–15 in the final quarter, but were saved by a mid-court shot by Martinez and a Saldaña one-handed shot from near the out-of-bound line.[4] This would be the only blemish in the San Marcos Rattlers' great season. The Voks then went on to win four other games to top the city series league with a 5–0 record on January 23. Only four days earlier, they had beaten the other favorite in the league, their nemesis Brackenridge.[5] But around this time is when Camacho's point became obvious. The *San Antonio Express* agreed when it declared early in the season, "The first four games Lanier [should] have a 'capable and scrappy club' but after mid-season it [will] remain only a scrappy team." The reason was that by midseason both Saldaña and Hernández had played the allowable eight semesters of basketball and were thus no longer eligible. They played their last game against Brackenridge and led the team to victory.[6]

Those early victories, especially the one over San Marcos, revealed that the Voks were experienced, talented in the starting five, and had good bench support. They may have been, if not as individually talented as the 1939 team, as good in playing team ball. Hernández had been the starter before Treviño took over. Both Carlos and Jesse Camacho said that most of the team and even the coach were surprised at how Treviño had caught fire as Lanier's big center in the state playoffs and become the hero he did. "He was not very impressive before the playoffs," remembers Jesse, though he admits that Treviño had a few good games during the season. Nemo, according to Carlos, called Treviño "Goofus" because he reminded him of the Disney character Goofy, who was not particularly coordinated. It may also have been because he had not a serious bone in his body and was always playing around.[7] Hernández, who now replaced him, had been a blue-collar player with shades of talent that remained valuable throughout the run in the state playoffs.

Saldaña, however, had shown the previous season that he was a talented ball handler who could periodically take over a game. His clutch shooting during the tournament revealed a confidence that only grew when he became the star of the team for the first part of the season. That confidence, according to Jessie Vargas Camacho, also revealed itself in his "flirting" with the girls at Lanier. Adding Joe Martínez to that duo of steadiness and confidence provided the Voks three players who could score and play defense and who knew well how Herrera coached the game.

The Voks won one more game, this time led by Martínez, sophomore Gilbert Carrasco, and Jessie's brother, Carlos, all of whom proved to be capable players. But the loss of Hernández's height and jumping ability and Saldaña's shooting and driving proved too much for the Voks. Their first game after the duo left, they beat an improving but still mediocre Burbank team 31–30 to end the first round of the race.[8] By the end of the second round, the Voks had lost twice to Jefferson, once to the Brackenridge Eagles, and twice to the up-and-coming Fox Tech Buffaloes.[9] In their last game of the season, already locked into third place, the Voks met the Brackenridge Eagles and were heavy underdogs. Nemo, smarting from a season that could have been better, declared, "I'm not saying that we are going to beat them, but I guarantee that we'll make plenty of points. If they make more than that, there's nothing we can do about it."[10] Unfortunately, the Voks did not put up enough points and lost their last game. It was a very disappointing season made worse by an inconsistency uncharacteristic of Herrera's teams.

Both Jessie and Carlos remember their most frustrating game and one that underscored how young and inexperienced the team was even by the end of the season. They led Fox Tech in their second game by one point. All they needed was to run the time out to win, something not common to Nemo's teams, who usually ran and ran until the buzzer sounded. With a one-point lead, the Voks began the slow-down with clear instructions from Herrera to hold the ball until time ran out. Unfortunately, the ball went to Santos Belton, a young but talented athlete who would see better days on the court. This was not, however, to be one of those days. To the amazement of his teammates and total shock of Nemo, he took a shot. He missed, and the Buffaloes got the ball and hurled a long, desperate shot that went in and sent the Voks down to defeat. It was the first time in almost a decade that Lanier had come out lower than second and the first time during that era that they lost to a team like Fox Tech that did not finish in either first or second—and to do it twice.[11] Herrera, who usually said little during games and was not one to get angry with the players, at least not in public, was livid. He let Santos know about his displeasure and kept him in the doghouse for a while. But he had faith in the young man with the big ears, tired eyes, droopy cheeks, and slumping shoulders. Herrera saw something in him, possibly that one day that young man would also be pacing the sidelines and directing young players. He trusted Santos Belton enough to get him into the starting lineup for most of the rest of his high school career.

Belton would be my science teacher some twenty-seven years later, and I often found his dry humor disconcerting, given that in my junior year, I was still far from sophisticated enough to fully interact with my teachers. He made jokes, and those who knew him from sports got the punch line. The rest of us just stood there with blank faces. He always had a tired look on his face, perhaps a reflection of his displeasure in having to teach science to a group of Mexican American kids who rarely understood. He tolerated more than liked us, and he spoke to inspire more than to instruct, which revealed his coach's demeanor. Having grown up during a time when Mexican kids had to aspire and dream to simply escape their surroundings, he often spoke in platitudes, urging us to go beyond ourselves. When the student protests erupted in 1968, like many of the other Mexican American teachers, he was nowhere to be found. Belton reflected much of his generation's approach to life: work hard, learn the system, stay out of trouble, and respect authority. It was the Nemo Herrera way, and it worked for many of that generation. But for a new generation, it would be a lesson to relearn in another context.

I know, though, that many of us would have loved to have heard the story of Santos's ill-fated shot to remind him of past sins when he got a bit tough with us for making stupid mistakes.

The Santos Belton I knew was not, however, the Belton that others knew. Richard Menchaca, one of Lanier's greatest track stars at the 880 yards, called him "my guardian angel" in a memoir that he dedicated to the man who saved him from reform school and a life of poverty. In that memoir, Belton comes alive as a caring, dedicated track coach who knew how to inspire young men, show patience in their difficult moments, and focus on building character as much as if not more than winning track meets.[12] From the memoir we get the sense that his runners were as enamored of him as Herrera's own boys were of him. There is the Herrera approach to hard work, the willingness to listen, and drive to go out of his way to help his boys. In Herrera's case it was lending them money and getting them out of jail, and in Belton's case it was picking up a troubled youth to practice early in the morning because he had to work after school. And it was about rushing Menchaca from work to the track meets and then back to the Piggy Wiggly grocery store so the young man could contribute to the family's finances. Yet he was also a man who hated to lose and put his heart and soul into preparing his boys for competition.

Back to the story: no document or newspaper article is available to tell us how Herrera felt about his worst season since taking over as head coach at Lanier, but given his character and competitiveness, it is easy to surmise that he was not only disappointed but frustrated. The player eligibility issues were something he could not control, but he had believed that even without Saldaña and Hernández, he could put a good team on the court and be quite competitive. He had even told the local newspaper that his team was capable of beating "a couple of good clubs" after the two players left.[13] Joe Martínez was a good player, maybe even a very good one, Jesse Camacho was experienced, and Carrasco, though quite young, had already shown some talent in practice. Herrera tried throughout the season a number of lineups, and when things went bad, he sent out all of his players, but none of the combinations ever worked well. He simply had no height, too little experience, and no two players as talented as Cardona and Treviño. Oswaldo Rodríguez and Benny Alvarez had done their best to replace, respectively, Hernández and Saldaña, but they lacked the experience and overall talent to bring about the same results.[14]

Like all successful basketball coaches with a particular philosophy or strategy, Herrera believed he could work, practice, instruct, and train players with varying degrees of talent to function smoothly as a team and to win. No doubt that Nemo could get much out of his players and probably made a few stars out of simply good players, but he could not make miracles with middling players any more than any other coach. His teams, when they lacked real talent, were likely to beat the mediocre teams and on a good night give the better ones a run for their money, but they could not beat the much more disciplined, taller, and skilled teams. And on a bad day, his Voks could lose to lesser teams such as the Fox Tech Buffaloes, who despite beating the Voks twice could not overtake them for third place. Nemo's teams, even when talented, usually battled the obstacles of lack of height and the occasional bad shooting night.

When his teams were not as talented, they struggled mightily. One reason is that teams in the early 1940s were not particularly great at shooting on the run. Most shooters were stand-up shooters who needed to find a spot, set up, and shoot. Herrera's teams were supposed to continually run and shoot, and that often required the player to quickly find his spot or to drive or fire the ball on the run. Shooting ability became even more important in a team that ran so much and played full-court pressure because players needed to be able to shoot even when they were nearly exhausted, a feat at which only a few select players excelled. His smaller teams, which often confronted fierce taunting, unfriendly crowds, and sometimes hostile opposing players, also needed swagger because confidence meant a lot on the court. But that came only through victories. Tony Rivera remembered that Herrera asked the players to confront the hostility by whipping the opposing teams.[15] That counsel worked when his teams were talented enough to win despite the odds, but when they were not, the loss of confidence was precipitous.

Soon, however, Herrera would no longer have to worry about finding one of those talented players that all teams need to compete beyond the local level. In 1941, Tony Rivera entered Nemo's life, beginning a new era for the Lanier basketball program that led the Voks to greater heights than ever before. Rivera remembers that as a young boy he crossed the street in front of his house to get to school, and every afternoon he crossed a couple more to get to where many of the other Lanier greats got their skills: the community center courts and the local Boys Club, where he played numerous past and future Lanier players. "I would . . . go home, have something to eat, and then go to the Boys Club. That's where I used to hang out all the time, and that's where I started playing basketball," said Rivera years later. "They had all kinds of things going on." But he admitted that he went mostly for one thing, and that was to play basketball, a game he picked up at the age of six.[16] At the Boys Club, he was coached by a former Lanier athlete who ran the Club's sports program and no doubt told him about the school's storied basketball program from the days of Wright Riley to Nemo Herrera.[17] Rivera eventually worked at the Boys Club while still playing for Lanier.

Rivera was not tall—possibly five-foot-eleven—and not particularly fast, but he knew how to handle the ball, and he could shoot with both hands. In fact, he was one of the few players in the state who could. "I was always the high scorer . . . because I learned to shoot with my left hand. . . . I was the only guy that shot ambidexter [*sic*]."[18] Rivera was the prototype of the new basketball player, someone who could improvise, fire from the right or left side, drive right or drive left, or simply shoot over his man. He became a scorer at a time when much of the point making was shared. He later credited Herrera's approach to the game with helping him develop as a player because all the running and the "keep moving, keep moving, [and] keep moving" philosophy allowed him to find open spots throughout the court.[19] Herrera's training also enabled him to still have legs at the end of the game when most opponents guarding him were exhausted.

Rivera remembers going to watch Tony Cardona as well as other Lanier players in the years before he started for the Voks. These players were already providing a new way of approaching high school basketball with their quickness and their court play, which tended to be more like the way the black schools were playing (African American students were also segregated in San Antonio at this time and were developing similar styles of playing basketball). Another thing that Rivera believes helped him were the community tournaments that the school sponsored. Students, teachers, and alumni flocked to these events that were not only competitive but also allowed fans to see former players and students. These games brought back many old stars as well as those who were starting for city teams in the Commercial and the Spanish American Leagues, which sported a very entertaining and fiercely competitive style of play. "It was a lot fun," remembered Rivera, "and at the same time we picked up a lot of experience playing [against] . . . the older guys."[20] No pictures or articles remain of that era, given that most issues of the school's *El Nopal* were not archived, but one could imagine the competitive contests where the present Voks attempted to show the old guys they were keeping the Lanier traditional alive and improving on it.

The third-place finish the year before, while not comforting to Herrera and the Lanier faithful, did not really damage the team's reputation among many of its opponents. The Voks were still seen as a powerful force. When they went to play the Tivy Antlers in nearby Kerrville at the start of the 1941 season, they were hailed as world-beaters. "The name of Lanier in basketball circles is something akin to the reputation of the Amarillo Sandies in football," declared a writer for the *Kerrville Mountain Sun*. The Sandies had won the state title in the just-concluded season. "Only last year," continued the writer, "Lanier was nudged out of the race by the state champions San Marcos Cagers in an overtime tilt by a single point."[21] This overwrought hyperbole was also inaccurate, as Lanier had not gone to the playoffs the year before, but it did reveal the respect that the program had garnered over the last few years and particularly through their second-place finish in the state playoffs.

The newspaper quoted the Tivy coach as saying that the Kerrville fans were in for a "revelation . . . in so far as the visitors' ability to play the game as it should be played." He proved right, as the Voks beat the Antlers 45–30. The paper reported that the "San Antonians swished the ball through the meshes in a brilliant display of shooting accuracy" along with "a fine court game."[22] Leading the attack were Rivera with twelve points; the player-in-the-doghouse, Santos Belton, with seven; Alvarado Gutiérrez, who tried to fill Saldaña's shoes the season before; and Carlos Camacho, who was getting his first real chance to play consistently.

Rivera continued to lead the Voks as they got into the middle part of their season, though things were much rougher than expected. Fox Tech, which had now become a strong rival, put up a fight but succumbed by a score of 31–28. It was sweet revenge for the two defeats they had pinned on the Voks the season before. In that game, "Little Tony Rivera peppered the basket like a machine gun the last half for 11 points" after having been held scoreless the first half.[23] The next nine days, however, did not prove a bright time for the Voks. They lost to both Jefferson, which led the league, and Brackenridge to fall to third place, as they prepared for a rematch with the Tivy Antlers.[24] In their own court and in front of a loud home crowd, the Voks were barely able to squeeze out a 31–28 victory over an inspired Kerrville quintet. Center Benny Gutiérrez led the team with fifteen points, while Carrasco added seven, providing the Voks a lift while Rivera had an off night in front of the home crowd.[25] The victory proved that, even on a bad night, the Voks could win against good competition, as the Antlers went on to win their own district crown and enter the state playoffs.[26]

Yet the young team proved inconsistent, as they lost almost as many as they won in the city series, including another loss to crosstown rival Fox Tech, this one by 31–17. This occurred even though they had taken the top two teams in the city into overtime, beating Jefferson by two points and losing to Brackenridge in a squeaker.[27] Still quite young, Rivera proved inconsistent, as did the other Voks. Yet Herrera could not help but be hopeful for the coming season. Rivera returned with a year under his belt and another strenuous preseason to prepare him to take leadership of the team. Herrera knew that in Rivera he had an exceptional player who simply needed seasoning to become one the greatest players ever at Lanier. Also returning were Gilbert Carrasco, who would be team captain; Santos Belton, a fine though inconsistent baller; Noe Cueva; and Joe Del Toro, who was also a good football player.[28] Carrasco, Belton, and Del Toro, along with Rivera, had the most game experience, but joining them were young players who were to make names for themselves over the next couple of years. These included Henry Escobedo and Ramiro Bernal, two guards to be remembered for years, as well as Walter Kelley, a tenacious forward who had his moments. This was material that Herrera knew could bring him some important victories and maybe a return to the state playoffs.

But the return to the playoffs and the beginning of the impressive runs for state titles and accolades momentarily took a step back to a momentous event that changed the lives of not only the students of Lanier but also the whole community of San Antonio and the nation. Carlos Camacho heard about it while he was at the theater with his girlfriend. Jessie Vargas was out riding with her family when President Franklin D. Roosevelt came on the radio to declare that the Japanese had launched a massive strike against American forces at Pearl Harbor. It was particularly devastating news for the Vargas family, as their son Richard was stationed in Hawaii. In less than a day, they found out that their oldest son had become the first Lanierite to lose his life for his country.[29] In the first few days following the attack, casualty lists were printed in the local newspapers, but none of them carried the name of Richard Vargas or any other Mexican American. Yet Mexican Americans were some of the first to respond to their nation's call for volunteers.

Albert Peña, who became one of the most famous civil rights reformers to come out of San Antonio, rallied his friends and high school mates and led them to the recruiting station to join the armed forces.[30] Throughout the Southwest, Mexican Americans joined to fight against "tyranny" and against those who had attacked the nation. They came to fight in spite of the fact that so many came from communities where racism, discrimination, and segregation prevailed. Felix Longoria, who died in the Philippines, came from Three Rivers, Texas, where the cemetery in which his father worked was divided between "Whites" and "Mexicans" and where a wake for his body could not be held in the town's only funeral home. This would launch the civil rights movement in Texas in 1948.[31] Hector P. García, a future civil rights icon and the person who would get Longoria buried in Arlington Cemetery, would join the army after leaving his medical internship in Nebraska; he had been advised not to apply for internships in his home state of Texas because he was Mexican.[32] Thousands of others left their segregated barrios and Mexican schools, their fieldwork and factory jobs to fight for a country that saw them as second-class citizens but happily greeted them as a military force.

The day after the attack on Pearl Harbor, a large rally, or "ceremony," was held at Lanier. Administrators, teachers, and even some students gave patriotic speeches and called for unity and a willingness to defend the homeland.

No newspaper article or other written account documents the event, but Jessie Vargas Camacho remembers everyone being in shock, some in tears, all of them bound by a feeling of pride in their country.[33] That scene was replayed in many communities across the Southwest and even in the Midwest where Mexicanos lived. Almost from the beginning, there was little debate about what young Mexican American men were supposed to do. A huge divide existed between what many Mexican Americans saw as discrimination in their communities and what they saw as their obligations to the nation in which they were born or where they now resided. What is surprisingly missing from the history of Mexican Americans is evidence of any divide, or even major discussion, between those who believed that they should serve and those who might have resented the fact that they were being asked to potentially give their lives for a country that seemed not to want them.

Within the barrio were two currents, one represented by the emerging Mexican American middle class and the other by the leaders of the immigrant community. While immigrant leaders stressed their Mexican ancestry and sought to bring pride to their heritage, the middle-class advocates stressed in their newspapers and in their functions the necessity of being good citizens and exemplary representatives of their race. The larger Mexican community thus could find something legitimate in both arguments. Most understood and embraced their origins while they sought to find their place in American society. Immigrant leaders helped them in educating their children culturally so they could function within family and community, while the middle class assisted them in educating their children socially and politically so they could navigate American society. Mexican families often took their children to Mexican patriotic festivals and stressed speaking Spanish at home and with relatives while emphasizing attending school and learning English. An uneven process that tended to tilt to one side or another among the different Mexican families in San Antonio, it nonetheless served to create a bilingual environment in which those who chose to could take advantage of those two strains within their community.

At Lanier those two currents coexisted. The culturally Mexican aspect revealed itself in groups like Los Trovadores and Las Mejicanitas as well as in the drawings in the yearbook and newspaper. The more integrationist aspect manifested itself in clubs, yearbook musings and descriptions of the seniors, and participation in sports. Within the school were those who spoke more Spanish than English, and vice versa. And there were those who were capable of participating in both Los Trovadores and the Glee Club, acting in English plays in school and dancing with Las Mejicanitas for Anglo audiences throughout the city. Jesse and Carlos Camacho, Tony Rivera, Joe Treviño, and future star David Rodríguez, as well as other Vok players, could star in the all-American game of basketball in San Antonio and throughout Texas while also playing in Latin American leagues and even in tournaments in Mexico, where they were both lauded for their skills and despised for being *pochos* (Mexicans who had abandoned their native land).[34]

My own experience and that of many of my classmates more than twenty years later reflected this bilingual experience. While a member of the debate team, a club with the ultimate need for English-speaking skills, I was sent to the office for speaking Spanish in class. My friend Homer García was the most English-articulate student in the whole school, and yet as a leader in the student protest of 1969, he sought the legitimization of Spanish as a spoken language in school and the end of the punishment associated with speaking it. We spoke English while we waited to dance to Mexican music at school dances, and we spoke Spanish to our parents at home while we waited for our favorite English-language television program to start. We may have been as oblivious to the ongoing integration debates, as were our counterparts in the 1940s, but we were not immune to their effects. Growing up San Antonio and attending Lanier High School put us at the center of those debates. For us, Vietnam and the civil rights movement made us reaffirm our ethnicity as Mexicans, while World War II and its Americanization programs made Lanier students of the 1940s affirm their citizenship as Americans.

The schooling that students in the United States received became a point of concern as the nation reacted to war. Politicians, as well as educators, wondered if American students knew their country's history well enough to engender a passion to defend it. They also worried whether these same students were in sufficient physical shape to respond well to the stresses and demands of combat and whether they had the science and math background to function in both the defense industries and in what would be a more technology-dependent military. Within one year of Pearl Harbor, schools began emphasizing math, science, first aid, safety, and physical education.[35] Schools also increased their offerings in social sciences by 65 percent and in both home economics and commercial subjects by 34 percent. Interestingly, foreign language did not receive as much attention, though soldiers would be fighting in foreign lands and military intelligence would need capable translators and decoders.[36] American soldiers would stand out for their unwillingness to learn much about the countries in which they fought or the cultures they were sent to defend.

According to educational historian Phillip W. Perdew, there seemed to be three purposes to the changes in the educational curriculum at the high school level: "to serve immediate needs such as purchase of war stamps and bonds; to prepare young men, primarily, and young women, to some extent, to serve their country more effectively in the military services, or industry . . . ; and . . . to fulfill a long-time need for better health, safety, and physical fitness, and a continuing need for improvement in American history teaching."[37] The latter concern arose after a *New York Times* survey revealed that among seven thousand students from thirty-six colleges, misinformation and misunderstanding of American history were rampant. This led to a national debate on the emphasis in colleges and public schools of American history and the quality of the instruction. National organizations dedicated to the study of history and social studies launched an investigation into the problem of student deficiencies in history and found that although sufficient school time was allotted to the study of American history, the quality of teaching and the amount of resource material were poor. The report led some states to add the study of American history to high school graduation requirements.[38]

Unfortunately for American students, none of the changes sought to remedy the ignorance that most students had about the world or the place of the United States within that world. No time was given nor resource materials developed to help students understand the causes of "the world's plight," or the nation's aims in fighting the Axis Powers, or even what might be a reasonable outcome of war.[39] The government's Victory Corps program, developed by the Office of Education, mostly emphasized physical preparation for war and training specific to waging it. It sought to militarize high schools by recommending uniforms, insignias, and military training for all students. While some schools and some public figures nationally rejected this militarization, many school districts increased physical education, and many also established ROTC programs.[40] One other course of study that grew in leaps and bounds during this time was preflight aeronautics. In California, 60 percent of high schools established this distinct course shortly after the beginning of the war, and many of the other 40 percent provided some kind of preflight aeronautics in their traditional science courses.[41]

Lanier did not remain immune to the changes in public education, though it is possible that, given its vocational orientation and its emphasis on Americanizing students, it was already poised to address the new concerns. The Wartime Commission of the Office of Education promoted math and science but also stressed practical skills such as "food preparation, clothing design, conservation or nutrition," courses already offered at the West Side school.[42] Lanier also added aeronautics to its curriculum and, unlike many other schools in the country, increased its foreign language offerings, the latter mostly due to President Roosevelt's Good Neighbor Policy. The Good Neighbor Policy came out of the Office of the Coordinator for Inter-American Affairs, which promoted American ideals and "democratic principles" to Latin American nations while informing American citizens about the language, culture, and history of those southern neighbors. All of this was intended to develop better relations with nations to the south in order to keep them in the Allied sphere.[43]

Mexican American activists and reformers quickly took advantage of this effort to reach out to them and their countries of origin to advocate for more jobs, better education, and an expansion of the space in which to practice their rights of citizenship. Carlos Castañeda, a historian at the University of Texas and member of the Mexican American intelligentsia developing at this time, had begun even before the war a complimentary history of Mexican Americans in Texas and used the forums that the war gave him to promote this view to a larger audience. In his writings and lectures, he proclaimed a neo-Turnerian view of the early Mexican colonization of Texas and the rest of the Southwest. In this "new" interpretation, Mexicans were every bit as democratic and individualistic as were Americans, and surely just as Christian. He also saw Mexicans as more Spanish than Indian and as natural Americans who could be counted on to defend freedom and promote American values. Castañeda did not downplay Anglo discrimination or hostility and did not acquiesce to a fully Anglo-American view of the history of the Southwest or the Mexicans within it, but like the emerging Mexican American middle and skilled class, he saw no alternative to integration within American society. Mexicans were here, and that is where they were going to stay, and so it behooved them to adjust, gain full citizenship, and make the most of the opportunities.[44]

Lanier students fit quite well into this new historical interpretation because the school itself had been established to promote Americanism, though admittedly it was supposed to build in students an allegiance to their nation while preparing them to become the skilled and semi-skilled labor needed for San Antonio's burgeoning industries. What no one had foreseen was the emergence of such a forceful and committed educator as Principal Richard Brewer and the faculty and staff that he put together. Brewer came to Lanier to make a school that responded to the needs of West Side residents, whom he saw as victims of Anglo hostility and their own heritage of failure. He recruited and oriented many young teachers toward his vision of creating a well-trained, if not educated, student population that would bring credit to their side of town and slowly integrate into the larger society. Lanier had a greater purpose than just teaching students the ABCs. Many teachers, whether they believed fully in his vision or not, spent most of their working lives at Lanier. It was then easy for them to grasp the notions of a school focused on the war effort because this was a mission with a purpose not so different from the one they were already engaged in. It is quite possible that ethnic and minority schools were able to grasp their new role more quickly than many predominantly white schools.

Few could have imagined also that there were enough Mexican American students from the poor barrios around the school who yearned to do something that distinguished them from the mass of their people whose lives seemed destined for poverty and marginalization. The school offered them opportunities to do things they knew their parents and neighbors did not and often could not do. When the war came, these students were ready to do their part. They may not have been the majority of students or of West Side residents, but they were enough and had the advantage of being part of a wave of patriotism that was sweeping the nation. The fact that there was still cohesion within their community allowed them to have an influence on it. Rita Gomez, a Lanier student at the time, remembers, "You could talk to your neighbor . . . you knew the people on the block."[45] This meant that the patriotic fervor that the students took with them was likely to reverberate beyond their homes. Given that the students were the windows by which most of their parents and other adults understood the Anglo world, what part of Americana they brought home became part of the hybrid culture and philosophy of the neighborhood.

When the war became the main topic of discussion both among their elites as well as their children, West Side residents became anxious to know more about the conflict. The fact that the community's men were donning uniforms, traveling to foreign lands to fight, and dying only made it more imperative to get every bit of information that came, even if it came from one of their children's social studies class or a school announcement. The war also created within the students a desire to formulate an independent identity that allowed them not only the opportunity to navigate the larger world but to ground them to who they were. Given that youth were to carry a large part of the war effort through their participation in scrap metal drives, victory gardens, stamp and bond buying and selling, and of course, military service, it became easy to develop a sense of themselves that transcended the boundaries of the West Side.

The editors of *Los Recuerdos*, conscious that their lives were to be encompassed by a world at war that required not only a commitment to sacrifice but a willingness to be actors in the conflict, called Lanier students to be part of something bigger—a new generation of young people called to defend the world from tyranny:

> To youth—the youth of the Americas—we dedicate this volume of *Los Recuerdos*. From the icy borders of the Dominion of Canada on

> the north to the tip of Argentina on the south, we see the youth of today—courageous in their heart, sturdy in their body, undaunted in spirit—bearing the torch of liberty in a common interest against a common foe that threatens our democratic way of life.[46]

This sort of hyperpatriotism was intended to motivate students to overlook the circumstances of poverty, isolation, and political marginalization in which they found themselves in the West Side. This patriotism served two roles for Mexican American elite students and adults. By elites, I mean those who had learned to navigate the openings that American society provided them. They were far from economically secure, and they had little influence beyond their own neighborhoods and communities, but they had elevated their status beyond that of their fellow residents or students. They thus saw the world in terms of possibilities rather than in terms of hierarchies or even available opportunities.

The war thus provided them an opportunity because the call for sacrifice extended to them as it did to every other American. Inside a military uniform, as part of the committees to gather scrap metals and other materials, with their money that bought stamps and bonds, and in every other instance in support of America's war effort, there was no color, no national origin, and no ethnicity—at least so they told themselves. It was important for the West Side elites to "feel equal." The world of Lanier gave them the environment in which to let their minds marvel at the greatness of American society and its democratic institutions. Interestingly, Texas history was not a subject taught at Lanier high school at the beginning of World War II.[47] Whether by design or not, its absence from the classroom spared Mexican American students from having to face the usually humiliating lectures and discussions of Anglo-Texan underdog heroes fighting against dastardly and often cowardly Mexican soldiers.

In my own time at Lanier, I do not remember having to take Texas history, but I do remember classmates who talked about the dreaded Alamo lectures of an old Anglo teacher whose passion for the great heroes of the Texas Revolution often led her to tears. In contrast, her voice would rise, and a scowl would come across her face when she talked about Santa Anna and those "Mexicans" who killed Texans at the Alamo and Goliad. Except for the clueless students or the self-haters, most of the Mexican students hated that part of "their" American history, and they often advised their fellow classmates to avoid that teacher if they could.[48] Again, whether by design or not, most Lanier students were not presented with those kinds of "histories." The great problem for us was the fact that we did not come into history at all except as the backdrop to the great American migration to the West and Southwest.

And like our 1940s counterparts, we also did not get courses in German, Latin, commercial geography, physics, or chemistry, at least not until some of those courses became available because of the school protests of 1968.

Two other elements in Lanier of the 1940s helped create an environment of Americanism that became easy to tap into for the war effort. One was the vocational training courses available for Lanier students. The 1942 *Los Recuerdos* provides a much more expansive picture of the role of those courses in the institution. While the first two yearbooks mentioned the vocational shops collectively, the 1942 book provided a page for each shop and at least several paragraphs to describe the activities and the students. Interestingly, the shops functioned in part like clubs, as each one of them had a president, vice president, and secretary, while some others had a reporter and a monitor, and still others had a foreman and an assistant foreman. The club-like approach made it possible to keep the students interested in the vocational activities beyond the classroom and involved in extracurricular functions outside of school. Students were not only being educated but, more important, being trained to work in the shops and industries around the city and state. This type of cohesion was particularly important during time of war, as most of the young men would be expected to be part of a team or military unit.

The club environment and structure may have also been the result of collective and familial tendencies of the young men and women, who came from the nearby barrios whose residents knew each other and were often related and whose neighborhoods were deeply and widely connected. It was easy to see that these young people enjoyed working alongside each other and functioned well as a group, a dynamic that was appealing particularly to the teachers with the time to spearhead extracurricular activities and the experienced shop instructors who often came from close-knit shops themselves. These young men and young women were a throwback to a more collective America, which was beginning to disappear even in the early 1940s. Twenty-plus years later, Lanier teachers still appreciated how easy it was to get us to participate in collective efforts and how much we enjoyed being around each other. While many of the North Side schools were confronting much more individualistic and self-centered student populations, we at Lanier were still quite familial and group oriented. It was easier to mold us into club members and our vocational shops into large extended families. Vocational students in my generation were usually the closest knit among the students, along with athletes and ROTC members.

Vocational teachers who wanted to do more than teach had a very attentive group of students. In the 1940s, Miss Virginia Worthington got the Vocational Arts and Crafts Shop students into something native to their culture—mural painting—and soon had them using their talents to spruce up the cafeteria and the gymnasium. We have no surviving pictures of these murals, but if they followed the mural tradition of Mexico and the southwest, they might have depicted some aspects of their community, their history, and an occasional hero. It would have been quite interesting to see how these Mexican youth saw their own community, what they were developing as a historical narrative, and who their heroes were. By then, Mexico's great muralists, like David Siqueiros, Diego Rivera, and José Clemente Orozco, were already internationally known, and it would have been difficult to teach this art style without at least a mention of these great artists. This would have added to the Mexican youths' pride in their heritage or at least created an acknowledgement that their people had a history.[49]

After a time, and consistent with Brewer's desire to get jobs for graduating students, the art shop became more geared toward the making of jewelry and leather goods. The students were given leeway in developing their own designs for the jewelry, leather, and metal products that they produced. While most of the end products were usually for personal use and for gifts to family members, there were those that were sold during periodic sales at the art shop. "The students are taking a great interest in their work," said the yearbook, "not only for the work itself but because the training . . . will assist them in finding positions when they graduate from high school."[50] It is not likely that there was much future in designing leather goods or jewelry, but the experience of creating and selling their products provided the students a chance to understand, if only partially, the American marketplace.

Lanier also had a three-year auto mechanics program in what was described as "one of the best equipped shops in the San Antonio schools." Beginning students in the program were in the morning class, while the more experienced students took the afternoon course, both of which were three hours long. During 1942, the afternoon class, with an occasional help from the morning group, repaired and fixed a hundred cars belonging to both students and faculty. The fact that the nation was in the midst of a war did not escape the school administration. "The experience and training received by the students in this shop fit perfectly into that demanded of mechanics by the National Defense Program," boasted the school yearbook. "The graduates will have no difficulty in getting jobs," it added.[51] The school could also brag about their students in the Body and Fender Repair Shop, who were taught welding, brazing, soldering, solder wiping, metal work filing and grinding, and body repairing and aligning. They, too, were prepared to do their bit in the military or, more particularly, the defense industry with such skills.

Male students whose interests were not in cars and mechanics could take Mill Shop to prepare to be mill workers as well as cabinetmakers and furniture repairmen. Eleven machines allowed the boys to take their one hour of theory each day and put it into practice by repairing old furniture and making new. In 1942, the shop graduated its biggest class, with eight young men receiving their certification. Tony Rivera was one basketball player who took opportunity to learn a vocational skill and served as the secretary to the Paint and Trim Shop, where he learned to paint vehicles, patch fenders, and make car tops. But the shop's work went beyond cars, as students painted and upholstered furniture, finished desks and tables, and even painted scenery for the auditorium. The equipment was as up-to-date as anyone could boast in the San Antonio schools, which again reflected Brewer's constant effort to get the best that he could for his students.

One other shop for male students was the Print Shop, which served to feed the voracious appetite for an industry that expanded during the war years. The students in the shop printed office forms, grade cards, registration cards, permanent records, absent coupons, and game tickets. And of course, they printed *El Nopal.* Students also had responsibility for the yearbook, which was a large undertaking and prepared them for more complicated jobs once out of school. Except for auto mechanics, none of the shops had as much impact as the Print Shop on the future jobs of students from Lanier. Print shops were as common in the barrio when I grew up as were mechanic shops. Eventually, photography and commercial art shops were added as complementary training for future print workers. With the print explosion that came after World War II, many Lanier students were prepared to take jobs.

The 1942 yearbook reveals only one vocational shop exclusively for female students: the Vocational Dressmaking Shop. The purpose of this shop was "to prepare girls for entrance into the dressmaking trade, to teach skill in cutting, fitting and styling for individuals," as well as to "develop personality and improve personal appearance" in order to make dressmaking "more interesting and profitable."[52] Each year the girls in the shop made the uniforms for the Blue Jackets and the drum majors. They designed and sewed the costumes for the school plays as well as the outfits for Las Mejicanitas. They also made "hundreds of garments for the British Relief and the American Red Cross," thus tying them directly to the war effort. Of course, the girls occasionally used their skills to make their wedding dresses and formal wear for graduation and other social functions. At the end of the year, they sponsored a fashion show where they modeled their own designs. Said the yearbook, "The girls in the dressmaking department have the advantage over the other girls in the school because they learn how to buy economically and appropriately, how to meet the public, how to be tolerant, and how to be self-reliant."[53]

This last part well reflects what the school sought to do with the students of Lanier. By teaching them middle-class values and providing them with skills, Lanier was seeking to integrate students into the larger society while maintaining the social structure as it was. The only thing better than having a skilled and loyal workforce was having one that had also been inculcated with middle-class notions of civility and proper behavior. These behavioral lessons were intended to make graduates a docile workforce that understood its place and did not engage in strikes and union activity. Already, city leaders and educators had seen what unassimilated and unskilled Mexican pecan workers could do when awakened to their economic and social situation by union and socialist activists. Vocational training at Lanier was supposed to make skilled workers who could make more money but who were also conscious of the products of their efforts and thus took pride in their work. This pride, along with notions of civility, would make them less likely to undermine the authority of their bosses.

The value of the vocational shop experience has received little attention in history books that deal with racial and ethnic groups, and what little attention it has received has mostly been negative. In the case of Lanier students, it would be easy to assume that these young people were being simply channeled into vocational jobs and away from universities and professional careers. Perceived this way, there is little value in what Lanier students learned. But life and societies are much more complicated than this, and groups do not always conform to the goals of society or their educational systems. Lanier students entering the shops for the first time saw brand-new machines and work space that was comfortable by their age's standards. Within these shops, they were sharing space and learning skills with classmates and neighbors, and they were choosing leaders, competing to be the best, and learning skills that had actual application in their lives. The vocational enhancement at Lanier surpassed anything they, their parents, or other barrio residents had ever experienced or could experience out in the larger society. Their skills were not only good for the larger industries in the city, but they fed a large growth in the self-employment of the barrio.

Skills learned in shop could be used to establish businesses and create independent, self-employed people, thus providing Mexican Americans a way out of jobs in which they earned low wages, were treated badly, and brought little status or dignity to the West Side. Barrio residents had been a community of unskilled and semi-skilled workers who rarely understood the language, knew business practices, or had any hopes for the future. Most Mexican and Mexican American business and labor opportunities consisted of hole-in-the-wall eateries, hauling services, tedious assembly-line work, crop picking, or some form of rudimentary landscaping service. Interestingly, Lanier offered a landscaping training course, though it seemed intended more for students seeking after-school jobs and for those who had no interest or proclivity for more skilled work.

Given the bleak career outlook for many West Side residents, it is not at all difficult to understand what fundamental changes this skill enhancement brought to the barrio and to individual Lanier students. By the time I came to school, these vocational courses and the workers they produced were so common and so successful that we rebelled against them as the only promoted option. Our fear was not only that we were not being prepared for college but that too many of our fellow students were being attracted to training that had, in our minds, an immediate payback but not a long-term benefit.

Even in the 1940s, some students did not like vocational training as the only option. Historian Julio Noboa interviewed a number of students who believed that they were being herded toward vocational training and given no option of going to college. Jesse Camacho remembers not "learning anything" in mill shop.[54] Most of those who complained about vocational training, however, were those who either chose to go to college, like Camacho, or those who did not take vocational training and did not see much of worth in the education they received at Lanier. Those who found jobs in postwar industries, started their own businesses, became independent contractors/workers, or used that training to have a stable military career saw things differently. And it is they who moved their community toward an embracement of American citizenship. Because they possessed skills and jobs that provided them a greater sense of worth, many became strong supporters of reform after World War II, promoting Mexican Americans as a community ready and able to participate fully in American society. They were those who would vote, join organizations, and establish chapters of the League of United Latin American Citizens (LULAC), the American GI Forum, and other organizations that advocated on behalf of the nation's barrios.

It was the Lanierites and other graduates who were "herded" into vocational training who helped to create an infrastructure of work and employment in the Mexican barrios of the city. Many of them looked inward when they were not hired by Anglo companies or industries, and while some left their skills behind and simply got the jobs they could, others started their own businesses catering to their community, and each small pop-and-mom shop that opened led to the opening of others. While Chicano scholars often speak of internal community building as something that occurred in the latter part of the nineteenth century or the early twentieth, the reality is that a second and more significant process of internal community building occurred after the 1930s and particularly in the 1940s and the early postwar years. This is when small shopkeepers, businessmen, and independent contractors came to the barrios and when a small middle class began to grow within its confines.[55]

This middle class, however, was composed mostly of skilled workers and families, rather than professionals. It also contained the children of the exile generation, who often lived on the peripheries of the barrio or in the few integrated neighborhoods of San Antonio. There were still many unemployed and underemployed poor in the West Side, but for a change, there were also skilled workers and high school graduates who spoke the language, could buy or construct their homes—especially after the war—and had a little money to spend. The fact that these numbers were growing at a time when housing was still segregated and most Mexicans kept to the West Side meant that the barrio itself was beginning to flourish in a way it couldn't have when it housed only a few businesses and few residents who understood the larger society and its language. With this growth came orchestras, radio stations, music companies, restaurants, barbershops, and print shops, and all this fed into the development of a more vibrant West Side.

In addition to vocational training, the other school entity that helped create support for the war effort at Lanier was ROTC, which expanded dramatically during the war years and became a permanent fixture of a Lanier education for boys. When I came into high school in the early 1960s, every boy had to take at least one year of ROTC unless granted a waiver. This was, of course, during the draft, and most young men had to do military service. In almost every club picture of the yearbooks of the 1940s and in many of the individual school photos, the boys wore their uniforms. The photo introducing the Clubs—Activities section shows a drum major's hat and an ROTC officer's sword, a reflection of the importance that military symbolism had acquired at the school. As the first club or school organization listed in the yearbook, ROTC was highlighted, showing a Sergeant James H. Vanlandingham as advisor. While there had been an officer in charge of Lanier's military training before, at a time of war, most of those had gone to the front or to training assignments.

In a spirit of egalitarianism, both ROTC officers and Sponsor officers appeared side by side. Rudy Peña headed the boys' unit as lieutenant colonel, while Jessie Vargas held the same position with the Sponsors with a similar rank. Majors Edward Vargas and Adelina Piña were next in command to their respective units, and below them were Captains Henry L. Garza and Bertha Grijalva, as well as Lieutenants Dennis Perez and Mary Louise García. A total of 129 cadets, 15 officers, and 15 Sponsors constituted the ROTC program at Lanier. From those cadets and officers were also constructed the Drill Platoon and the Crack Squad; the former marched in the parades and performed in the flag ceremonies, while the latter was composed of the top shooters in the corps. Among those taking military training were the best to take the court for the Voks: Tony Rivera, Ramiro Bernal, Gilbert Carrasco, and Henry Escobedo.[56]

Drum Major and Captain Thomas Gomez led the ROTC band, which formed another part of the student military units and which created the greatest impact on the assemblies and ceremonies, as they played patriotic songs and represented the school along with the Drill Platoon. Established in 1938, the twenty-eight-member band met during the school's second period to learn and practice songs, often in conjunction with the larger school band, to which all of the cadets also belonged. They played during the Armistice Day Parade in November, at ROTC reviews on Wednesdays, and at an event called Field Night at Alamo Stadium, in which other bands in the city also participated. In each event, they sought to create an environment of patriotism that reminded the students that the nation was at war and that many if not most would be required in some way to sacrifice for the nation. "The members of the band are being taught army tactics once a week," said the yearbook. "This not only gives the students of the band the advantage of exercise, but also prepares them for army life."[57]

But the ROTC band and the other student military units were meant to do more than prepare young men for battle. A second purpose, perhaps just as important, was to create within each student a commitment to support and defend the nation. Few institutions could do a better job than the military, and in the high school, ROTC, with its traditions, pomp, uniforms, command structure, and the respect that it engendered, created a space in which to mold students into citizens. Students could not be good cadets without buying into the narrative that the military promoted. Wearing uniforms, marching in patriotic parades, learning how to fire weapons, and cooperating within a hierarchical structure, the Lanier students would have found it difficult not to feel like true, even first-class, Americans, no matter the circumstances outside the parameters of the barrios of San Antonio. The fact that an "un-American" world existed outside of the West Side made it possible to create a barrio world in which many of these young men could fight for their democratic country and yet come back to fight undemocratic policies at home.

CHAPTER SIX

Adjusting to War and Getting Back to State

THE TRAUMA OF PEARL HARBOR WAS NOT SOMETHING that could easily be ignored, but once the nation settled down to prepare for war and the fear of an immediate Japanese assault on the mainland subsided, there were some things that went back to normal, or as normal as possible. Those still in high school, not having left and enlisted, had more reason than ever to try to both enjoy and benefit from their instruction and extracurricular activities. This seemed especially so for the Class of 1942. In their first senior class meeting after Pearl Harbor, the students in uniform predominated, not in numbers but in the way they stood out from the others. While there were a few smiles in the picture that came of their meeting, most of the students were somber, conscious that the horrendous attack on American soil five weeks earlier had changed their future.[1]

Most were too old to have fathers join the military, but no doubt there were those who had older brothers, possibly an uncle or two, and surely neighbors answering the call to fight. This type of connection to the war effort and an acknowledgement of their future involvement, whether in uniform or in the various support committees, caused many students to jump into extracurricular activities and school functions with greater zeal. This was particularly true for the 120 members of the senior class, many of whom had been together since the sixth grade.[2] The yearbook depicts the seniors and other students very much engaged in school activities, and while not overt, allusions to a nation at war are apparent from the pictures that show Lanierites in all kinds of uniforms, those that show landscape gardeners displaying a "V" for victory, as well as numerous shots of parades, flag ceremonies, and drives for the Red Cross and other entities supporting the war effort. The yearbook also shows many of the typical stand-stare-and-smile pictures so common during that era.

The pictures reveal an American world within a segregated environment as these students would likely not have been part of similar activities outside the barrio during the beginning of the war. While many students wore uniforms and Mexican Americans served in large numbers, hundreds if not thousands of them were rejected for military duty for reasons as varied as lack of English skills, illnesses, or simple biases.[3] Many would continue to face discrimination even when in uniform. The students in the pictures look quite healthy, yet Mexican Americans in Texas made up most of the one quarter of the nation's infantile deaths that the state contributed to the national average. Mexican American deaths from tuberculosis amounted to an average of 160 per 100,000 cases, which compared horribly to 40 per 100,000 for Anglos and 50 per 100,000 for black Texans.[4] While Lanier produced valedictorians and members of the National Honor Society, the majority of Mexican American young people were either not in school or were dropping out in large numbers. By the end of the 1930s, the age at which most Mexican American children ended their schooling was twelve.[5] The 1942 senior class at Lanier had itself lost twenty of its members within one year.

Many of the student leaders, except for some of the more talented, would find that opportunities for leadership outside Lanier were limited. Even those who continued on to get a higher education found opportunities to lead few and far between. One group of Mexican American reformers found fault in society's unwillingness to provide such young people with sufficient opportunities: "It cannot be emphasized too much that one of the reasons for the neglect of the Mexican American in the Southwest has been that his own leaders have not been his spokesmen." Those who choose to speak for them, continued the reformers, were individuals that have "either not known what the true score is, or it has not suited their . . . ambitions to read the score correctly."[6] The smiles and confident demeanors of the students might have faded had they fully understood what awaited them, though it is probable that most knew that their world would not be that much different from their parents' when they left school. But for the time being, their American world was important and provided them a sense of hope for the future.

These broader concerns were also not the most important thing on the minds of Lanier boys seeking to be part of the basketball team and its growing reputation of producing winners. George Wright, a writer for the *San Antonio Light*, called Sidney Lanier a "basketball high school" with a "system [that] pays off."[7] That "system" was actually the availability of a hard-surface court on the school grounds where boys from the barrio congregated to shoot "wadded-up paper bags, tennis balls, volley balls," and anything else that they could hurl at the basket when a regular ball was not available. "The boys look forward to the day when they'll realize the big ambition—to toss in a few goals in the Lanier gym," wrote Wright.[8] Augmenting the number of players who came from those early-morning and late-afternoon pick-up games were those who came from the intramural leagues within the school in which all fourteen homerooms participated and that played twice a week.[9] This allowed younger or less-experienced students to match up against varsity players to test their courtyard skills.

Without doubt the young boys were emulating those Lanier players who had captured the imagination of the barrio. In the collective imagination of the heads dripping with sweat under the hot sun and humid air were Cardona, Treviño, Saldaña, Martínez, Hernández, and Rivera driving to the basket, shooting from afar, grabbing the high rebound, or stripping the ball from an opposing player. The existence of such heroes allowed youngsters to develop particular skills as they emulated and expanded upon their heroes' repertoires. Because most of these youngsters spent as much as five years together in school, and because they played together out on the court or in community centers, they became familiar with each other. Herrera's system filtered out those unlikely to make the team. Before any of them walked into his gym, they were already indoctrinated with the notion of fast dribbling, quick shooting, and tenacious full-court defense. They also came knowing they were going to work hard and that Nemo did not put up with silliness.

Both Walter Kelley and Tony Rivera, a new generation of Lanier players in the war years, learned, as had others in the past, that the soft-spoken Herrera did not tolerate deviation from his system. "He kept you in line," remembered Tony Cardona. He also remembered that Herrera normally took the players aside when correcting them so as not to embarrass them.[10] But by the time of Rivera, Herrera was either more forceful or simply felt more confident being direct with the players. It may also be that Nemo felt confident in getting after Rivera, who remembers a day when he came to practice with knee pads only to have Herrera say in a firm and slightly miffed voice, "take those pads off." Sixty-eight years later, Rivera still did not understand why Herrera made him take off his pads. Revealing the defiance that seemed to characterize his playing days, Rivera half rolled his eyes as if to say, "What do pads have to do with playing good?" But he quickly caught himself and proceeded to explain that Herrera knew what he was doing and was "a great coach."[11]

Kelley, a quieter guy nicknamed "Rough House" because he was all of one hundred pounds, still seemed in awe of Herrera six decades later and proud that the coach had asked him to try out after seeing him play for the junior high team. A defensive specialist, Kelley believed his coach had the right kind of knowledge of the game and knew how to get the most out of his players because he treated them with respect while remaining strict. Herrera's players called him "El Viejo" (old guy). Some of them hung out in a nearby pharmacy where they got malts and shakes and where Herrera occasionally dropped by, saying "You guys probably say, 'Here comes El Viejo.'"[12] Nemo had seen his boys become ambassadors for his system through word of mouth and through their play in the games, in the intramural leagues at school, and in their post–high school days with city leagues, and he was proud of them.

The other part of Lanier's system that Wright pointed to was the number of boys from the same families who played for the Voks. "Whole families of lads come through the neighborhood play and intramural leagues system," he wrote. Lanier would have its Bernals, Camachos, Hernándezes, Rodríguezes, and a host of other brother combinations, as well as others who were like brothers because of their family-like ties on the basketball court.[13] The fact that whole families followed the sport provided continuity as each household that had boys became a feeder unit for Herrera. Former players kept in touch, and whenever they could, they encouraged boys to try out for the team or simply inspired new players by telling stories about Nemo and his boys, how they filled gyms, outplayed bigger white boys, and made their community proud. Beating the "white boys" had nothing to do with race but everything to do with beating the odds and proving that Mexican Americans could compete in an American sport. This we-are-as-good-as-they attitude spoke to a rising sentiment among acculturating Mexican Americans that they had to compete in mainstream activities to prove they were real Americans. It was one more reflection of the bilingual and bicultural world in which they lived. Unlike Mexicans of prior eras, they were not willing to be contained in their segregated barrios and limited to Mexican things.

The system of which Wright spoke was the American way, but it was the American way for the immigrant. It would be immigrant youth—Jewish, Italian, Polish, West African, and Mexican—who took advantage of the community centers, Boys Clubs, sandlot fields, hard-surface basketball courts, and high school sports programs to enter the American mainstream of sports and, at times, dominate it.[14] White Anglo-Saxon Protestants had lost supremacy in the sports arena by the early part of the mid-century, and only the whitening of some of these immigrant groups made it seem otherwise. Before private sports lessons, camps, and little leagues became a mainstay in youth sports, athletes became skilled on the street, the musty gym, or the open lot. These were the spaces of the immigrant community and its offshoot, the poor white families that had spread out to small communities and large outer suburbs.[15] African Americans, though slightly different, also followed much of this path toward athletic prowess. The Mexican community brought with them a knowledge of—if not a specific experience with—American sports as Mexico had quite early in the twentieth century become obsessed with American recreational activities. One of the distinguishing features of pre-1950s baseball, basketball, and to a limited extent, football was the fluidity of sports competition between Mexican Americans and Mexicans, as they both traveled across the border numerous times. Joe Treviño, Jesse and Carlos Camacho, David Rodríguez, Tony Rivera, and others would play in Mexican tournaments after they left Lanier.[16] They also played in what had become in great part Mexican leagues—the city basketball leagues.

All the parts of Herrera's system worked only because of what happened once the boys entered the Lanier gym and gave themselves completely to his torturous practices. Raul Zuniga remembers his uncle Lazaro Moreno, who played in the 1942 team, telling him how the gym doors closed promptly at 3:45 P.M. and a marathon of fundamentals would commence. For the time they were confined to the gym, Herrera's boys practiced passing the ball, playing full-court defense, dribbling, and shooting.[17] All of this came after they had duckwalked and run to exhaustion. Once drilled in the skills of basketball and once their legs could barely hold them up, they practiced free throws, and that exercise ended only when every one of the players had hit 80 percent of their shots. "This was every day," Zuniga recalls his uncle telling him. "[Nemo] knew they had to play a perfect game to win"—because of the referees.[18]

It is difficult to prove, but it is quite possible that by the 1940s Herrera's innocent—possibly naïve—view of fair play and honest refereeing had evolved into a more complex view of how race affected the game of basketball. Surely his players knew that basketball in 1940s Texas was not simply a game in which two teams met on the court and were allowed to play. Most of the scores reflected the abilities of one team over another, but in the close games, the refereeing made a difference, if not in determining who won, then surely in the way teams chose to play and how coaches designed game schemes. In today's professional and college basketball games, referees are known for the way they make calls and in how loose or tight they allow the game to be played. Back then, most referees performed their duties out of the love of the game and often relied on the knowledge they had acquired as players. Too often, they harbored the same biases of the communities in which they lived.

In an e-mail to a former Lanierite, Joe Bernal, a member of the 1944 state semifinal team, confided that a friend and former president of the Southwest Basketball Officials Association had told him that the Lanier Voks always played five against seven. "The opposition," wrote his friend, "was five high school opponents and two refs."[19] The revelation surprised even Bernal, who had gone on to serve in the Texas legislature and was known as one of the top civil rights advocates Texas has produced. Bernal was anything but naïve about how white Texans treated Mexicans, but sometimes it was hard to know to what lengths white officials would go to make Lanier's games difficult to win. Jesse Camacho did not remember referees treating the Voks any differently than they did the white players, but players like Bernal and Rivera did. At the same time, while Camacho saw no bad fans or hostile opposing players, his future wife, Jessie, saw tremendous hostility in the fans and even the players when she went to the games as a member of the pep squad. The calls didn't have to be flagrantly wrong to shift the momentum of the game, they simply had to lean one way or another.

Without doubt, World War II would complicate matters even more because, as patriotism rose, so did intolerance for those who were different or did not conform to the norms of who was an "American." However, unlike the Italians, Germans, and particularly Japanese Americans, who were targeted as potential enemies of the state, Mexicans were not part of the conflict. Thus their mistreatment was often more nuanced, though not always subtle or private. The Lanier players saw this mistreatment more often while playing at rural schools or working-class schools in the city. At Jefferson, the city's elite high school, they often encountered hard-fighting opponents but rarely racial hostilities. "The elites seemed not to be as prejudiced," recalled Bernal years later. "But those schools like Harlandale, Hot Wells, and Brackenridge were difficult to play."[20] Edison High School, Lanier's longtime nemesis, was often one of the most hostile places in which to play, if not the single most hostile. The players and fans reflected the same disdain that the administrators had toward Lanier. David Rodríguez also remembered the hostility in those schools. He recalled that he would go downtown with some of his teammates and that they would say hi and even chat with players from Jefferson and the "other schools," possibly the Catholic schools, but such rarely was the case with students from the outskirts of town or from the white working class.[21]

The working-class hostility reflected fears among some white San Antonians that in the Depression economy and during a war they were confronted with a growing population that had set its roots in the city and was beginning to compete for unskilled, semi-skilled, and occasionally skilled positions created by the war effort. National leaders' promotion of patriotism and unity during these years did not seem to extend beyond the intragroup parameters established before the hostilities. Most European ethnic Americans, with the exception of those whose countries were waging war against the United States, found integration and assimilation mostly a done deal by the start of the war, and whatever vestiges of resistance remained were soon swept away by an interethnic patriotic wave that rose among white Americans. While patriotism increased among Mexican Americans, African Americans, Native Americans, and even Asian Americans, its exuberance did not transcend the rigid racial lines, with but a few exceptions and in a few exceptional communities.

One reason wartime patriotism did little to further racial integration may well have been that while these racial groups saw their service in the war as exceptional or particularly praiseworthy because of the circumstances in which they found themselves, most whites saw it as simply a matter of duty for everyone. Americans of color had nothing on their white counterparts, as members of both groups were joining the military in high numbers and making the ultimate sacrifice. Not acknowledging the unfair treatment of racial minorities made it easy to not recognize how exceptional their response to the war effort was. To accept that there was something special about minorities' service was to acknowledge that whites had cheapened their own service by fighting against a racially based system that they often duplicated at home. No doubt whites rarely fully engaged in reflection on their own biases or racial prejudices, but only the most ignorant would completely miss the contradictions of American participation in the war. The reminder made many whites uncomfortable, and so the war remained for many a retaliation for Pearl Harbor and for German aggression rather than a fight to end the racism of Fascism, Nazism, and Japanese imperialism.

The team that represented Lanier in the second year of the war was young but talented and, with a couple of exceptions, the team that would win state. No one doubted who the team leader and captain should be. Tony Rivera had put together the kind of sophomore season that most juniors and seniors would have loved for themselves. He provided the firepower and offensive diversity that broke down most defenses. By his junior year, he could shoot a hook shot with either hand and do it with a twist that made it difficult to stop. Rather than hook the ball with his outstretched hand in front of his body, he shot with his arm parallel to his head, forcing the opposing player to go through Rivera's body to block the shot. Sometimes the ball left Rivera's hand while his arm was actually behind his head. Walter Kelley remembers that when Lanier had the ball, Rivera would often cross the court, quickly position himself within few feet of the basket, and call for the ball.[22] David Rodríguez recalls Rivera running slightly behind the basket and shooting those hook shots to clear the backboard and fall through the net.[23] When those shots were not available, Rivera had no problem putting the ball on the floor and driving to the basket to score on layups, one-handed running shots, or free throws as opposing players fouled him in desperation to stop him.

Rivera, years later, remembered that his favorite shot was a complicated maneuver that left his hands at about waist height as the ball spun all the way up until it hit the basket. None of the interviewed players mentioned this move, but Rivera, seventy years later and by that time suffering from a mild case of dementia, vividly described its use: "I would drive down the out-of-bounds line and then jump slightly backward and let go of the ball," he said. Because he seemed to be going out of play, the opposing players would be caught flat-footed as he released the spinning ball.[24] While proud of his accomplishments, Rivera, jokester but the undisputed leader of the team, preferred to talk about his teammates. He found few weaknesses in them, giving Herrera full credit for having made them team players.

In 1942 and the following year, there was no one, in Rivera's mind, who played as well or was as valuable to the team as Henry Escobedo.[25] Escobedo was the ultimate athlete, as he became the team captain in both football, where he played quarterback, and in basketball, where he directed the team as point guard. Kelley remembered him as a player who could deliver the ball to the inside as well as anyone, though Kelley admitted that, as a one-hundred-pound forward not known for his scoring, he rarely got the ball from Escobedo. Rivera also praised Escobedo's passing, acknowledging that when Henry had the ball, all eyes had to be on him because "he could take your head off with his passes."[26] Escobedo's favorite targets were Rivera and the big men who could score inside. Escobedo was a *picado*, a Spanish term meaning that he would often hold the ball for himself or pass only to those he trusted. He was sparing with his assists but was not beyond going continually to a player on a hot streak. While he would not be team captain until the following year, Escobedo looked anything but a follower.[27] He was muscular and had narrow eyes that let everyone know he was watching them and that he would tolerate no nonsense when he directed the team. Interestingly, Henry was one player who had no nickname, although at times he was called "Scooby," as a take on his name.[28]

Assisting Escobedo in the backcourt was Ramiro Bernal, another quick, good-dribbling, and accurate shooter who passed the ball around to those not lucky enough to be on Escobedo's radar. Both Tony and Walter liked the way Bernal played and often found that when he brought the ball down it tended to move around a lot more. He complemented Escobedo, and this gave the team multiple scoring possibilities, which confused opposing defenses. Bernal also offered a contrast to the more serious-looking and quieter point guard. In his high school senior will and testament, Bernal facetiously chose to pass on his "good looks" to a fellow student.[29] Others of his teammates considered Bernal a real ladies' man, though by nature he was quiet and appropriate in his behavior. His son, Rudy Bernal, who at the writing of this book had been the Lanier coach for nearly twenty-eight years, remembers his father as a quiet man who provided suggestions and advice but never sought to impose his will.[30] It was his commitment and discipline that spoke for him and was the one thing that people remembered of him most.

Other players would not engrave their names in Lanier folklore but nonetheless formed part of an impressive group of young men. Joe Del Toro was one well remembered by teammates. Kelley said of him years later, "He was good," and he meant it as more than just a routine compliment; the words revealed true admiration.[31] Rivera remembered Joe as a good outside shooter. "He would kill you" from the perimeter, said Rivera. While other players were accurate, what made Del Toro stand out was that he had a glass eye, making him rather unique as a basketball player where zeroing in on the basket requires good vision. Tony remembers playing against Del Toro in practice and at the Boys Club and using one of his hands to obstruct Del Toro's good eye. He laughed as he remembered, but his voice revealed a profound respect for a teammate that could easily have been sidelined for what today would be considered a handicap. Del Toro was such a determined athlete that he also played football, which made Rivera a bit envious since Herrera did not let him play football even though he tried out for the team. Rivera remembers running into Herrera one day while dressed for football and the coach firmly telling him to take off the uniform and "concentrate on basketball."[32]

Rivera remembered Richard Reyes as a good substitute, though a rather quiet player. And Manuel Gonzalez, or "Mosco" (Fly), "was a pretty good shot."[33] "Skinny and light," Gonzalez loved to get his hands on the ball. "He was *picado* (ball hog) like me," remembered Tony Rivera.[34] Then there was "Shy," or Lazaro Moreno. A less talented player, Moreno tried to imitate the style of other more talented players, but Rivera took him aside and in his often humorous but pointed way told him, "Play your own game." Moreno took the advice and became a good support player who could be called upon when the top shooters could not find the basket.[35] All of these young but talented players were captained by Gilbert Carrasco, a veteran of the 1941 team and the one person who, along with Rivera, made the team dangerous though inconsistent. Carrasco had befriended Rivera and some of the others at the Boys Club and thus felt comfortable leading them, though he occasionally allowed Rivera to calm the team when things did not go well.

Rivera's leadership proved particularly valuable when the Voks played teams that were blatantly hostile to the "Mexican kids" from Lanier. Rivera recalled that white players, particularly those from rural schools, taunted them and would deliver an extra hardy push from behind or a smack on the hands and arms. "They were trying to throw us off our game by making us mad," recalled Rivera years later. While he was the one player who spoke more openly about the discrimination that occurred, he also believed himself to be one of the best in dealing with it. He knew he could outplay any player in the city, and he took to heart Herrera's admonition that the best way to respond was to beat the taunting players. "We respected each other," he would say about the Lanier team, which tried to be as egalitarian and democratic as possible in its work on the court. "But I had more experience and so [I] told the guys to keep it cool. I'd call a time out and tell the guys that they [opposing players] were trying to get them mad so they wouldn't play as well."[36] That usually was enough to get them back in rhythm.

That rhythm made the Voks one of the favorites in the San Antonio Invitational Basketball Tournament, which kicked off the season for most of the area schools. The other pregame favorites were Jefferson High School of San Antonio and two Houston schools, Lamar and Reagan.[37] The tournament was a brutal two-day affair. The winner would be the best conditioned team with a very solid bench or the team that could slow the pace and use its big men to score. Lanier had the conditioning, but its bench was still unproven, and they made it only to the quarterfinals. They were beaten, 23–22, by the Milby High Buffaloes, who proved the surprise of the tournament by beating Lanier and another tournament favorite, Lamar, in one day. The Vok/Buffalo affair proved an exciting, back-and-forth game that remained undecided until the last minute, though the bigger factor turned out to be free throws. Lanier had gotten to the free throw line often but missed twelve shots in an uncharacteristic performance by a team that practiced their free throw shooting constantly.[38]

Rivera came ready to play and scored fifteen of the team's twenty-two points, but he found little support from his teammates, as Santos Belton scored four points and team captain Gilbert Carrasco scored only two. Future all-stater but first-year player Escobedo was not even in the lineup, and Walter Kelley was a no-show in terms of performance, as were Ramiro Bernal and Del Toro. A fellow by the name of Zartalan and a Juan Rodríguez, who did not appear in the team's end-of-school yearbook picture, were credited as having played as well.[39] While disappointing, this early outing revealed the Voks as a team that could hang tough against strong competition but whose nucleus had not yet come together. It also proved that the Voks were ready to make a run for the city title and the state playoffs, though it might have caused Herrera concern that the Jefferson Mustangs won the tournament title in a relatively easy win over a very tired Milby squad. While Jefferson and Lanier were now in different districts, and Jefferson was playing in the larger Class AA division, the two schools would meet several times in the fight to claim the title of city's best.

Whatever the doubts about the Voks' ability to win the city title, there was no doubt that they were the heavy favorites to win the newly created District 28-A title. In an early assessment of the district race, one reporter argued,

"Going to the wire, Lanier looks like an easy winner with the other teams playing for second place."[40] South San Antonio High School had been an early co-favorite after winning its own tournament, but that moment of glory quickly faded after fellow–district school Edison defeated them a couple of days after they copped their tournament's crown.[41] The Voks did not disappoint when they walloped the Alamo Heights Mules, 41–21, in their first district game. Said one reporter, "Lanier's easy licking of the Heights Mules . . . indicates more than ever that the Voks are the team to beat." He then added that the Vok bench had been cleared early and even then the West Side quintet's second and third stringers never lost control of the game or looked sloppy. Gilbert Carrasco affirmed that his strong play the year before had not been a fluke, as he tied Rivera for top scoring honors with eight points.[42]

But even before starting district play, the Voks were already collecting wins. In their first nondistrict game following the tournament, they beat Central Catholic High, which was becoming one of the powerhouses in San Antonio basketball. This despite the fact that Central Catholic did not play in any of the major districts but in something called the Academic League, an organization formed for the city's private institutions. The Voks showed their versatility as Joe Del Toro led the scoring with seven points, while Rivera and Carrasco both added six.[43] The Voks then followed with a victory over the Brackenridge Eagles in a tough overtime game that ended with the Voks on 22–18. In the low-scoring win, Rivera scored eight, Kelley five, Bernal four, and Escobedo three. This victory kept Lanier tied with the Jefferson Mustangs for the city series championship.[44] This series allowed some of the schools within the city limits, who by now were playing in different districts and different classifications, to compete against each other to decide which of the city basketball teams was the best.

The Voks' impressive win over the Alamo Heights Mules, coupled with their earlier wins and the close game against San Antonio tournament finalist Milby, got the Voks rated as the third best team in the Houston Junior Chamber of Commerce High School Basketball Tournament behind defending state champions El Paso and undefeated Livingston.[45] Herrera's teams had never won a basketball invitational, but he must have sensed that this tournament was winnable. The loss in the San Antonio tournament had been a winnable game, and their two subsequent wins had given Herrera a chance to see the kind talent that he had. Winning this tournament, as with the previous one, depended on good conditioning and a good bench because it, too, was a two-day affair in which a team could end up playing three games in one day.

Herrera's confidence no doubt was bolstered by the encouraging words that he read in Harold Scherwitz's column, "Sportlights." Scherwitz was not just any sportswriter, but the sports editor of the *San Antonio Light* and one of the most respected sports analysts in the region. In his column, titled "Why Herrera's Teams Are Always Favorites," Scherwitz told his readers that he was under obligation to recognize merit "whenever the opportunity" arose, and so he tipped his imaginary glass to "William Herrera, known as Nemo." He continued,

> The Lanier High School team coached by Nemo Herrera didn't win the local high school basketball tournament just concluded—in fact, it didn't come close—but it's a good team, nevertheless, as Nemo's teams usually are, and it is established as a matter of course as one of the favorites in the Houston tournament set for Friday and Saturday. In fact, it seems any team Herrera coaches can count on being established a pre-tournament favorite wherever it goes, because the Lanier brand of basketball *or the man who produces* it has pupils or ardent admirers scattered everywhere.[46]

Scherwitz pointed to Holly Brock, head of the Houston Junior Chamber of Commerce Invitational Basketball Tournament and successful insurance businessman, as one of those admirers. Brock, one of the "all-time basketball greats of the University of Texas," began his roundball career at Beaumont High School just at the time that Herrera became a rookie coach there. Said Schweritz, Brock "steps right up and says that Herrera taught him more basketball than any coach under whom he ever played. You can see why Lanier . . . would be established as one of the favorites to win the Houston tournament."[47] Brock's statement spoke to the fact that Herrera was not simply a run-and-gun coach that tried to use physical traits to overwhelm teams. He sought to teach fundamentals and then to expand from there. David Rodríguez remembered that at the start of every season Herrera would begin with fundamentals. "He'd start drilling in us in dribbling, passing, and learning defense. He'd say that most players could shoot the ball but few played defense," recalled the future all-stater.[48] Soundness in play made Herrera's players capable of controlling as well as running the floor. For those who were talented, fast, tall, or simply ball-savvy, he expected—and got—an expansion of their range and skill. He made average boys into capable players and good players into stars.

Scherwitz pointed out that Herrera lacked height. In fact, he called him "a shorty" and likewise described Brock as such, but, he added, "Many of the Mexican boys Nemo coaches . . . are not skyscrapers that some coaches consider necessary to basketball success. But Herrera knew how to overcome the handicap of [being a] shorty on the basketball court, and he knows how to impart that knowledge to his pupils. In other words, he gets the most of out of his material. That's the answer to success in a lot of lines."[49] What Herrera taught Brock and many of his own players was that lack of size was not an excuse for not playing or excelling. Lack of height simply meant that you needed to learn to play fast, dribble well, shoot accurately, and play tenacious defense. Herrera did not spend much time telling his players that they had to overcome obstacles. He instead spent the time getting them to learn to do what they were capable of doing. When he had tall players—quite rarely—he taught them to play big, and when he had short players, he taught them to play fast. Like he did when he confronted discrimination, he responded by preparing his players and then telling them to win. Overcoming a lack of height was like overcoming on-court prejudices. You won, and if you didn't, there were no excuses.

Unfortunately for the Voks, the tournament turned out to be a disappointment, as they lost in the first round to the Huntington Red Devils, 30–25. They started the game missing most of their shots and could not overcome the Red Devils' rebounding advantage under the boards. The Voks, however, did not go down easy, as they rallied in the second half "with Rivera showing the way" to take a 23–22 lead at the end of the third quarter. But the Red Devils tightened their defense and kept Rivera away from the basket, and the Voks—or better said, Carrasco—were able to score only one bucket in the last quarter, while Huntington scored four to pull away with three minutes left in the game. Rivera again led the team with twelve points, and Carrasco added eight, but the rest of the Voks failed to score in double figures.[50] Herrera's most dastardly nemesis, lack of height and periodic poor shooting, proved too big a hurdle for the Voks to overcome. While their defense worked to hold down the Red Devil scoring at the start of the game, it got progressively porous by the end.

The loss prompted one sportswriter to declare, "Lanier just didn't have enough height or aggressiveness in the early stages against Huntington." The reason for the early intimidation came from facing a team with four six-footers whose outstretched arms made their zone defense look even more impenetrable.[51] That the Red Devils played it well and could swoop up any missed ball gave them a leg up on the Voks. While pressure and quick movement to the basket could at times neutralize the Red Devils' size advantage, it was hard to sustain. It was particularly difficult when only two players scored consistently. Lanier had a bench of hard-charging players who knew their fundamentals, but it had yet to develop a third go-to guy who could pick up the slack. A different player could step up on a given night, but none was a consistent third scorer.

It must have been particularly disappointing for Herrera to have received such praise, be a co-favorite in the tournament, have one of his former students watching, and not get past the first round. But the reality must have sunk in that although his team was talented, had good players, and at stretches of time could play with most teams they confronted, they still lacked experience, and Rivera, as a junior, was still short of becoming the leader they needed. Carrasco was a consistent player, one who could step up at any given moment, but he could push his players only so far. Herrera also had no really physical player, as he had earlier in Joe Treviño, who could dominate the middle and intimidate opposing players. Three years removed from his state finalist team, Herrera had a team with many of the elements for success but without a take-charge point guard, senior leadership, or sufficient instinct for finishing off a team when they had them down.

Still, the tournament gave the Voks three games in which to work out some of their deficiencies. After their loss to the Red Devils, the Lanier players had little time to rest, as they entered the consolation round and faced a small but scrappy Robstown team that took them to the wire. Trailing by one point with fifteen seconds left, Santos Belton stole the ball. Once Belton was on the gallop with the dribble, it must have dawned on Herrera and the rest of the Voks that no one was going to catch this fellow who had shown his great speed in track and field competitions. Belton laid the ball up, and Lanier was on to the next round.[52] It was redemption for Belton, who periodically made his coach want to pull his hair out. Belton was a likeable fellow, and all his teammates remember "Orejas" (ears) fondly, but all of them also had their story to tell of his on-court antics. His theatrics were accentuated by the lost look on his face and his extra-large ears. His appearance did not always reveal the top athlete that he was, and it would be easy to mistake him for a student lost in the hallways. Rivera remembers once when Herrera told the team to hold the ball, but once it got to Belton's hands, he let it go. Herrera quickly called a time-out and between clenched teeth said, "I told you guys to hold the ball. Santos, do you know what hold the ball means?"[53]

When Belton, years later, became my science teacher, we all knew him as the coach of a series of mediocre teams. He had a dry humor but found a way of endearing himself to those who worked with him. He had his own style of coaching, and his mostly losing teams could never have been confused with Nemo's, as they were slow, zone-playing teams that rarely pressed or ran. But knowing Belton provides me a glimpse of Herrera and the generation in which he grew up. When the Lanier protests occurred in 1968, most of us looked to our Mexican American teachers for support. I cannot say specifically what Belton thought of the protests as I did not have him for a teacher during that time, but I do remember that no teacher came to our defense, and to my knowledge, none—except an Anglo drafting teacher—ever privately said, "right on."

Belton came from a generation that, while feisty and demanding of its rights, shied away from cultural issues—while we wanted to speak Spanish and learn our history. Belton's generation sought to be good Americans, not different Americans—we were starting to call ourselves Chicanos and promote our own identity by the late 1960s. Herrera had also faced a major controversy while at Lanier in the protests of 1934, when parents demanded that the school district provide better facilities for their children. What research has been done on that protest reveals that, as in 1968, no teachers became involved in support of the students or the parents. With hardly any, if any, exceptions, the few Mexican teachers—and there were a few more when I was going to school—of both eras had nothing much to say. It is understandable that they feared for their jobs, but to my generation of militant Lanierites, it was not a good excuse.

Herrera never got involved in issues outside of the ball court or school grounds, and his players admit that he rarely touched on the subject of discrimination or even what it meant to be Mexican in American society. His and Mary Leona's children grew up without their paternal grandparents. The children only met one of their cousins from that side of the family when he came to a player-sponsored memorial to Herrera and introduced himself.[54] Herrera did not live in the barrios of San Antonio—though Cardona remembers him living a couple of blocks from the school for at least two or three years—and did not belong to any of the Mexican American civic, religious, or cultural organizations that were so prevalent then. It is doubtful that Herrera would have sent his boys to Lanier, and Belton did not, either.

Yet both coach and student were committed to Lanier and willing to spend their lives teaching Mexican kids and helping them to progress in life. David Rodríguez, whose exploits are discussed in later chapters, remembers Herrera taking him aside and telling him to drop his mill shop class and start taking courses to prepare for college. Herrera then helped Rodríguez get into junior college when he came out of the service.[55] And all of the players remember Mary Leona Herrera as one of the staunchest supporters of the Lanier Voks and as someone who rarely missed a game and whose voice could be heard from the stands either praising the team effort or pointing out something the referee might have missed.[56] Except for his first year in coaching and until later in his sixties, Herrera never coached anyone but Mexican kids, and his son Charles remembers him taking the family to Mexico each summer to supplant his meager teaching salary by umpiring in the country's professional baseball leagues.[57] There is no doubt that Herrera knew who he was and felt comfortable within a Mexican American sphere, but he simply lived a more complicated life, as did many who married outside the barrio and practiced their profession in an Anglo world. Lanier, despite its Mexicanness, was still an Anglo world, and teachers and students learned to navigate the contradictions of an Anglo institution in the barrio.

Back at the tournament, the next opponent for Lanier, Sam Houston High School, turned out to be tougher than the first two teams they faced, and the Voks fell, 34–26. No details exist on the game, so it is hard to know what occurred, though it is possible that both lack of height and sporadic shooting hurt the Voks again. Luckily for the Voks, league play gave them a chance to regain their winning ways. Facing the Edison Bears in the Golden Jubilee Game, the Voks came out "smoking." "Starting good," said the *San Antonio Express*, "and ending better[,] the Voks led 18–10 at the half and then turned on the steam." They clubbed the Bears, 34–15, and dropped them from first place, where they were after beating South San and a couple of other mediocre teams. Rivera led the Voks with nine points.[58] The proceeds from the game went to the Naismith Foundation, which was trying to erect a monument to the game's founder. Three days later, the Voks started to really turn up the heat on the rest of the league teams by beating Hot Wells, 67–13, for their fourth consecutive win. This time Rivera scored fifteen points, and the rest of the scoring was spread out among the team.[59]

The Voks followed the Bear victory with a game against the second-place Burbank Bulldogs, who were on a short winning streak themselves. "Usually such a pairing would make a close game certain," wrote a sportswriter for the *San Antonio Light*, "but the Voks have been whipping previous rivals with such soundness that their steady shelling from every part of the court is expected to leave the Bulldogs wondering how many men Nemo Herrera had on the floor." He added that the Voks had been averaging nearly fifty points a game in the last few district contests.[60]

One week later, the Voks had attained six straight victories and took a break from district play to meet the Central Catholic High School Buttons on the road. By this time, Central Catholic had established a basketball tradition that would stretch into the 1960s and make them one of the premier teams in the city. In a hard-fought game, the Voks proved that they could start off strong and defend. Going into the fourth quarter, they led, 24–17, getting balanced scoring from Rivera, Carrasco, and Belton, who had turned into the second-leading scorer on the team. But then the Voks went cold. Central Catholic threw at them a tough zone that clamped down on the smaller Lanier players. They smothered Rivera inside and challenged the other players to beat them with long-range shooting. Then they began chipping away at the lead with well-placed shots until they tied the score with twenty seconds left. They got a free throw, and Lawrence Jordan hit the shot to send the score to 25–24, and the tough Button defense proved capable of holding the desperate Voks one more time. In all, the Buttons scored eight points at the end while holding the Voks scoreless. Again, the Voks' lack of killer instinct left them stunned and bewildered.[61] It was particularly disappointing since they had beaten Central Catholic earlier in the season.

But back in district play, the Voks again proved to be a quality team. On January 30, 1942, they faced their former co-favorites, the South San Bobcats. By this time, however, none of the teams in the district were seen as capable of beating the Voks. Said one reporter, "Unless there is an upset of earthquake proportions, the Sidney Lanier High School Voks [*sic*] fast, tricky and dead-eye picks from any spot within firing range, will all but tuck away the district 28-A basketball championship."[62] They had already beaten the Bobcats earlier by a score of 45–17. By the time they faced them again, the Voks were the only unbeaten team in the city in Interscholastic League play and had won eight straight district games. No score is available for the South San game, but a few days later, the Voks again walloped the Edison Bears, 34–11, with Rivera hitting for sixteen points. By this time, Lanier was rarely beating Edison in football but was enjoying its dominance in basketball. Before Fox Tech High School became Lanier's eternal rivals, Edison was the team that it looked forward to beating. The Voks followed the Bear victory with a second thrashing of Burbank, 36–20, after trailing 14–12 at halftime. Rivera scored ten, Belton eight, and Carrasco seven.[63]

By the end of February, the Voks had won twelve consecutive district games and the district title. With title in hand, the Voks met the San Marcos Rattlers for the bi-district crown. The Rattlers, 27-A title champs, were still smarting from the loss they suffered to the Voks the year they won the state title. But the thought of revenge dissipated as the Voks limited the Rattlers to eighteen total points on their way to a twenty-point victory in the Rattler gym. The Voks were now firing on all cylinders and had found greater diversity in their scoring. Belton had established himself as a consistent scorer, and Carrasco had become the dependable third option. Ramiro Bernal and Henry Escobedo were now consistent as backups for Carrasco and Belton. With the bi-district title, Lanier entered the regional tournament as favorites against Lampasas High School, which had needed two games to win their own bi-district title and were seen as having little chance of winning their region.[64]

The Lampasas Badgers, however, did not come into the game intimidated. The Badgers quickly took a lead in the first quarter, 9–8, and then extended the lead to 17–13 by halftime. In the nip-and-tuck first two quarters, the teams exchanged leads frequently. In the second half, the Badgers took firmer control and lost the lead only twice. In the third quarter, Lanier tied them 20–20, but Badger Fieldon Berry hit a field goal to put his team ahead until near the end of the game, when Escobedo sunk two free throws to make the score 32–31 in Lampasas's favor. After the Badgers failed to score on their next possession, Rivera took the ball and scored one of his classic shots to put the Voks in the lead with only minutes left. But the Badgers responded with a field goal of their own, and then their star, Willerson Yeary, the game's leading scorer, hit a free throw to give his team a 35–33 lead and a potential win against favored Lanier.[65]

With less than three minutes left, Rivera took matters into his own hands, taking the ball, dribbling, and moving until he saw a path to the basket. He did not score, but he drew the foul. At this point of the game, Rivera had fourteen points, and the game was in his hands to tie. It must have dawned on him that this is what he had practiced for in that old federal housing basketball court where he had spent hours imagining, as young boys do, of being where he was at that moment: the game on his shoulders, and the ball in his hands. The game had been tougher than expected, and yet the Voks could still salvage a win over a team they were supposed to beat. Rivera lobbed the ball toward the basket, and while we do not know if it went in and out, or rolled around the rim, or whether it was simply a brick, we do know that he missed the first shot. At that moment, the game strategy changed. The Voks now needed Rivera to make his second shot and then force a turnover. Or maybe their strategy was for him to miss and hope for a rebound to tie the score. We don't know the Voks' strategy, but we do know that the second ball did not go through the net, and the Voks went back on defense empty-handed. Their clutch player had missed or played the odds and not delivered. The Badgers did not give the Voks another shot, as they kept the ball moving and away from Lanier's desperate hands, and they ran out the time to win the first game of the regional playoffs. They now had home-court advantage as the teams headed to Lampasas for the second game.[66]

"Lanier's players' main trouble rested in their inability to sink field goals," wrote the *Express* reporter. Rivera had scored, but Belton had only three points, Carrasco had been nonexistent, Escobedo had scored only on free throws. Del Toro had worked hard under the baskets and come up with five points, but center Juan Rodríguez had been held to two points. In contrast, Badger center Yeary had taken command of the rebounds on both sides of the court and outscored every other player in the game. The players were disappointed, and Herrera might have worried about having to go to an unfriendly gym with a crowd and an opposing team that smelled blood and the opportunity to upset the region's favorite team. Complicating things was the fact that Lampasas was one of those towns where most Mexicans passed through but rarely stopped. Even those who lived in the area usually went to town only to buy food and other necessities because they knew they were not welcome. Not winning at home always brought complications, and Herrera must have thought about the racial temperature even if he did not articulate the concerns to his players. The yearbook makes mention of an "unpleasant farewell" when the team played in the regional tournament.[67] There is no way to know exactly what this refers to, but some players remembered rough moments in that community.

Whatever Herrera did to prepare his team for the second game worked out well. The Voks came out smoking and took a relatively easy 33–21 victory in the Badgers' gym. While the newspapers in San Antonio did not cover the second game, they do describe Lanier's third-game win. "The Voks were never headed last night," wrote the *Express*, "behind the fine all-around play of Juan Rodríguez, [the] full 32-minute center for Lanier." Rodríguez turned in a "neat floor game" while scoring four field goals and two free throws to lead all scorers.[68] The *San Antonio Light* reporter added a bit more flair to his reporting and pointed out that "tall Juan Rodríguez, who seldom finds his name among the high scorers, and George Reyna, a tiny substitute forward, got together . . . to sack away the Region 7 . . . championship."[69] Reyna was the second-leading scorer with eight crucial points, followed by Rivera with seven. While the two straight victories were relatively easy, they were not pretty, and the Voks had to depend on their bench players and their unheralded starters.

Said one reporter, "Herrera looks for his boys to show better form than in the Lampasas series, for he feels sure his guards, Santos Belton and Gilbert Carrasco, can't continue to miss their shots as they did then. Belton failed to count a field goal in the Lampasas tilts and Carrasco, the team's best long-range gunner, got only four."[70] He pointed out that Rivera had also been off in the series, particularly in the last two games, but even in the first game, when he had scored fourteen but missed the crucial shots at the end. It may have been for this reason that instead of heading out early to have his boys practice on the tournament court in Austin, Herrera chose to keep his players close to home, using the court at nearby St. Mary's University to practice. He knew that his players had to be ready because they were scheduled to play one of the state favorites, Aransas Pass.[71]

In spite of the Lampasas series, Herrera felt his boys' physical and mental condition was such that they were ready for "lots of hard basketball." They had to be because the Aransas Pass quintet came into the semifinals having won twenty-one out of twenty-three games during the season. Lanier came in with a 19–4 record, though the *Corpus Christi Caller* pointed out that the Voks had mostly lost against Class AA teams.[72] "One man told me Aransas

Pass is about the hottest team Texas has ever seen," said Herrera. "But that kind of talk isn't scaring us. The boys are in the same frame of mind as my 1939 team which went to the state finals, and I think we have a chance."[73] It did not appear, however, that the Voks were prepared for what hit them in the first half as the Panthers ran past them to a 24–11 halftime lead.[74] Given how Aransas Pass had marched through the last half of their season, few fans in the stands could have given Lanier much chance of coming back to make the game close or much less to beat the team from the Coastal Bend. A thirteen-point lead by a team that ran just as much as the Voks did seemed insurmountable.

The lead, however, was in danger as soon as the Voks came out in the second half with a determined Rivera and a focused Carrasco. Rivera put on a scoring show that led one reporter to declare that the Lanier star "became the gallery's favorite with his sparking play."[75] Rivera had the ability to excite the fans with his style of play and with the confidence he brought to the court. No one else had the flashiness or the skill to put a team on his back and carry them for a full half. Initially, it was a basket-for-basket match as "the pair of South Texas teams brought cheers time and again with fast-breaking, alert play which kept them racing up and down the court."[76] Rivera scored from each side of the basket as he normally did, and when he did not, Carrasco picked up the slack with his long-range shooting. There is no record of what points either of the two scored in each half, but their twenty-eight combined points were exactly the number needed in the second half to overcome the Aransas Pass lead and take the Voks to a convincing 39–31 victory. The intense running, shooting, and man-to-man defense eventually tired the Panthers, who found themselves "short of replacements" to relieve the exhausted starters. Rivera hit for twenty points, breaking his slump from the Lampasas series, while Carrasco added ten and proved that the team captain was going to be critical for this run at the state title.[77] Like Treviño and Cardona of the 1939 team, Rivera and Carrasco seemed capable of taking their team to the finals.

Now marked as a favorite with their victory over the highly touted Panthers, Herrera and his players would have been justified in momentarily thinking forward to the team they would face after the semifinals. The Van High School Vandals were actually hotter than the Aransas Pass team had been, having won twenty-nine out of thirty games and coming into finals—they won earlier in the day—averaging fifty-three points a game in the tournament. Led by "a group of six-footers," they loomed as the team to beat. Unfortunately, the Nederland Bulldogs were just as intent on getting to the finals, and things ended sooner for the Voks than expected. With a team that produced two all-state players in the tournament, the Bulldogs matched the

Voks basket for basket and even tied the running Voks 20–20 at halftime. Though not as flashy or intimidating a player as Rivera, Nederland's Areigh Duff, a slight and less-than-imposing forward, hit key baskets to take his crew to a three-point lead with only two minutes left in the game. It was only the second time that Nederland had been able to take the lead from the Voks, whose steady play seemed capable of getting them to the finals. A Lanier miss, however, gave the Bulldogs the ball, and they never gave it back.[78]

This time the Rivera-Carrasco duo could not perform heroics. Carrasco had remained consistent, but Rivera could not climb to the heights of the Aransas Pass contest. His eleven points were simply not enough. Carrasco's eight were important, but with Belton continuing his slump with only two points and no one else hitting for more than four, the Voks simply could not score enough to win. They would have the same trouble scoring in the third-place game. Rivera scored only six points, but Carrasco's eleven points allowed them to squeak by Elkhart, 34–32, in overtime and end what most would describe as a very good season. While meaningless to the Voks' third-place finish, it was not pleasant for the Lanier players to see the Van Vandals end a near-perfect season with a 35–27 win over the Nederland Bulldogs.[79]

CHAPTER SEVEN

The Voks Finally Make It to the Top

HERRERA MUST HAVE CRINGED WHEN HE READ THE *Los Recuerdos* yearbook sports editor describe the 1942 basketball season as having "started . . . with a bang and ended . . . with a bing."[1] It would have been particularly annoying given that the team finished third at state and had their best player named to the all-state team. This had been the school's best team since the 1939 state finals, but for at least one yearbook writer, it had simply not been enough. Maybe the writer had expected more from the team, or maybe he was wondering whether the returning starters and some impressive upcoming players were going to make the '43 season a better one. Whatever the reason, clearly there was disappointment in how the season ended.

To make things worse for a coach trying to forget the way the season ended, the yearbook mentioned without explanation an "unpleasant farewell" when the team played for the bi-district title in San Marcos. "[It] did not discourage the hard fighting team," said the yearbook.[2] The exact nature of that "unpleasant farewell" can only be speculated, but several players mentioned difficulties in playing in communities like San Marcos. Fans taunted, opposing players talked trash, and there was always the possibility of violence in communities like those where Mexicans were mostly low-paid laborers or longtime residents who had made a niche for themselves by avoiding conflict with their white neighbors. As in many other rural communities surrounding San Antonio, Mexicans were not seen as winners or heroes. It would not be the last time something unpleasant occurred at that regional-play hub of Central Texas.

Yet no matter the yearbook's mocking description of the season, the disappointment of losing to a team they should have beaten, or even the repeated incidents of hostility toward his players, Herrera felt confident about the upcoming season. Tony Rivera, by most accounts the best player in the state, returned for his final season. Knowing the young man's pride and tenacity, the middle-aged coach was sure that redemption would be on his mind. Tony loved the accolades and respect he got from his teammates, sportswriters, and even a few opposing players, but he was also a proud young man who could not bear to be praised when he was not performing. The last two games in the state tournament had disappointed him. Herrera knew that his star forward would be out in the Boys Club gym or even in the abandoned federal housing basketball court working on his game and imaging the critical plays that would come his way in his senior year. He would replay over and over his mistakes and the missed free throws. He needed no motivation to be ready.

The loss of Carrasco and Belton meant that new players would have to step in at the guard positions, but Herrera felt pretty confident with Henry Escobedo and Ramiro Bernal, who were a duo as good as any he had had in the past, with the exception of Tony Cardona and Joe Martínez in 1939. That tandem had been better shooters, but Escobar and Bernal were going to be better floor managers, capable of getting the ball to the open players and taking it to the basket when given an open lane. Walter Kelley, with his rebounding and defensive skills, was back, and George Reyna, who played critical minutes in the state tournament, rounded out the five returning starters. Joining them were Refugio Olivares, Richard Reyes, Frank Hernández and the Gonzalez young men, Manuel and Raul. Those five came from a Class B team that had a history of engaging in competitive games and winning against squads from the larger schools.[3]

These new players came in with great anticipation since they knew that Herrera believed in an open system where every season meant the potential of a new starting five. Everyone's job was on the line, and no one, not even the all-state forward, could expect their spot to be secured until after the practices were done.[4] They also knew they had been scouted by the coach not only during their past season but also during the homeroom tournament held every September through October on campus. This was a time—much more formalized than when it first started—when all the students who loved the game got a chance to play against classmates. Even the varsity players looked forward to playing in those games, though only one of them could play per homeroom. One player remembered, "At noon everyone would take their tortillas, lunches, and whatever [they ate] to the gym and watch the homerooms play."[5] Students chanted and cheered for their homeroom boys, playfully mocked opponents, flirted, or made plans for the rest of the day, but they also watched competitive games where varsity and junior varsity players sought to affirm their superiority and the occasional barrio athlete worked hard to show that he could play with the *batos* (the "guys") on the team. It was not always about making the team as much as showing friends and any girls who paid attention that they could play with the boys of Lanier.

The noon ritual had its athletic purpose, but it also provided students an opportunity to come together, mingle, and feel good about their school. Teachers and administrators knew they had to do whatever they could to make the young people of the barrio want to come to school. This included providing them chances to be with their friends and have the kind of leisure time not available on the outside. School loyalty, often an extension of homeroom or team loyalty, was often the motivator for students to give the institution and its teachers a chance to instruct them and prepare them for a life of hard work and little upward mobility, though still a better life than their parents had. But the idea of fostering group ties was not totally the school's. In fact, the school was at times simply reacting to the kind of familial and communal relationships that the students brought from home.

In some ways, these relationships were not that much different from those of white students in rural areas but that were now being lost or shed by those in the nation's urban centers. Even by the early 1940s, many white families were moving away from the communal, toward a more individualistic lifestyle. Educators saw the economic and social benefits of one paradigm—individualism—but recognized the advantages of the other—communal relationships—in providing a control mechanism for large groups of ethnic students. For the teachers of Lanier, many of whom were young and idealistic, group and team activities were attractive because they provided an esprit de corps that could be utilized to move the students toward an appreciation for their studies.

By the time I came to Lanier, those homeroom games were a thing of the past, but the homeroom camaraderie remained long after my peers and I had left. Today when I reacquaint with some former classmates, the inevitable question comes up: "Whose homeroom were you in?" By my time, homeroom games were replaced with school-wide pep rallies that took almost half the instruction time each game day. The band played, the pep squad and cheerleaders danced and chanted, the coaches and players made predictions, while most of us talked, flirted, planned the rest of the day, and joined in singing and dancing when the fight song began and ended the communal celebration. There we were "scouted" by teachers and administrators who judged our behavior outside the classroom so they could categorize us into good kids, troubled kids, leaders, or followers. In those moments, they probably felt much like their 1940s counterparts, either in how lucky they were to have such a tightknit student body or how much of a burden had been placed upon their shoulders to educate and assimilate such a huge group of students.

In 1943, Nemo would pull up a chair, sit on the bench, or lean against the gym wall and watch the homeroom games. With his quiet demeanor, he might have been invisible to most students, but everyone on the court knew who he was. After every good play, on-court hopefuls shot a glance toward him to see his reaction, though it rarely showed in his stoic face. Making a bad pass, letting go of a poor shot, having the ball stolen, or fumbling the pass made many look anywhere but where the coach stood. Many a dream ended in those noon shootouts, though some lasted until November, when the dreamer failed to receive an invitation to try out for the team.[6] For those who harbored no thoughts of making the team, the experience was more enjoyable, especially if they had gotten off a good play against one of the varsity guys. For the varsity players, this was a time to stay in the minds of their loyal fans, to play with teammates, and to scout out the new kids who might soon be joining them on the practice court. No doubt some of them served as unofficial assistants, volunteering information on good players to the man they called "Chato" (flat face) behind his back.[7]

Herrera already knew those players who had shone on the junior high teams and those in the Class B squad, but he wanted to make sure no player had slipped through the cracks. He might find a player, like Walter Kelley, who had been unsure about whether he was good enough to play on the varsity team. A nod from Herrera was enough to get such a player excited and motivated to work hard on his game. More important, the varsity players, and those seeking to be, were also separating themselves from the rest. While it is possible that some diehard students ended the tournament believing that they were as good as the varsity players, most succumbed to the reality that Herrera's boys represented the best that Lanier and the West Side had to offer. In proving this, both the coach and the players were developing a loyal fan base that knew how to rock that small gymnasium, which some reporters liked to call the "chicken coop."

By scouting out the boys who loved to play, Herrera was simply legitimizing a system that had evolved organically within and around the Lanier campus. If it wasn't the Boys Club, the community centers, or the federal housing complex, it was a basketball court in some park or even in someone's backyard that provided space for the get-togethers among boys to refine skills and show the coach or those who were his eyes and ears that they were capable of being part of the Lanier teams. It was an inspiring landscape for a coach who ate and slept basketball, as Herrera did. His son Charlie remembers his father being consumed by the game. Nemo left home early and often came back late, and while he rarely talked basketball at home, his boys knew what was on the old man's mind when he sat quietly.[8] During the homeroom tournament time, Herrera was on the lookout for anyone who could dribble, shoot, or rebound but who also could hustle after balls, run hard down the court, and refuse to let fatigue affect their game. "He did not tolerate lazy players," remembers his star center, David Rodríguez.[9] Leisurely play was no one's luxury, and his players knew Herrera's willingness to sit any lackadaisical starter and give a bench player an opportunity to shine, as he had with George Reyna in the regional tournament the previous season. "You hustled all the time you were on the floor or you were going to sit," remembered David.[10]

Rivera remembers the coach coming to him during a physical education course and saying in his quiet but firm way, "You keep it up and you'll make the first team." Sure enough, Rivera made the squad as a sophomore.[11] To be recognized as capable of being one of the Lanier boys brought incentive enough to make a boy work harder, even if at times it proved embarrassing. David Rodríguez remembers Herrera coming to him while he was still in junior high and saying, "You're better than your brother Johnny."[12] Juan "Johnny" Rodríguez was the starting center for the '42 team, the star of the Lampasas series, and someone David, the younger brother, considered "really good" and much smarter than he. Herrera, however, could see the difference between the two brothers. Both were tall, though David was more so. They both worked hard and did what their coaches told them, but the younger brother had that intangible quality that appears among truly great players and separates them from others whose physical traits and commitment are often comparable. Herrera understood this as well as anyone, and so he looked for young men who not only could start immediately but who had potential in years to come, as was the case with Tony Rivera and David Rodríguez.

Like his brother before him, David towered over everyone around him. It dawned on many who saw him walk the two miles to school from his home on Pecos Street and Matamoros that this was one of the tallest Mexicans they had ever seen. He would eventually grow to be six-foot-five, though he hovered around six-foot-three in high school. He was a soft-spoken young man who grew up, like many of his teammates, in extreme poverty. There were no electric lights in his home, and his family shared a toilet with others in the neighborhood. They had a wooden stove in a three-room house that grew to four when his father enclosed a back porch. Not until David's junior year was a shower added to the space his family occupied, but no hot water came with it. "We liked to play sports because we could shower at school," he would say years later as he sat in his nice home in El Paso.[13] On Saturdays, they had to bathe in tubs in order to get all the eight children—"who survived the Depression"—cleaned and ready for what few activities the family could afford. And those weren't much, as David's father, Matias, a day laborer who mowed lawns and took any odd jobs he could find, and his wife, Paula, were both illiterate immigrants from the northern states of San Luis Potosí and Coahuila and had few of the skills necessary to make a better life in segregated San Antonio.

David remembers the area around his home and on the road to Lanier as "open space" with periodic clusters of "shanty towns" breaking up the undeveloped area that went from the tracks that separated the West Side from downtown San Antonio to the edges of downtown. The area enclosed by the streets of Matamoros, Monterrey, San Saba, and Pecos, where he lived, had an abundance of brothels and bars where many men would spend their free time drowning and forgetting their frustrations over the lack of good jobs, friendly bosses, and adequate housing. "The center of activity in our neighborhood was La Unión, a union hall where community dances and other Mexican festivities were held," David would recall years later.[14] Through La Unión activities, people tried to bring some sense of community to their lives. Though closer to the rest of the city than those who lived further—or deeper—in the West Side, most of the residents of David's neighborhood felt excluded and distant from the whiter part of town and no more integrated in San Antonio than did residents of other Mexican areas. Except for the churches—both Catholic and Protestant—and some of the *mutualistas*, or mutual aid societies, that had arisen among the postrevolutionary Mexican exiles, there were few institutions for barrio residents.

Like most of the kids in the barrio, David could often be found on the streets playing whatever games his young mind could conjure up. Mexican kids were free to roam the streets, the alleys, and the open backyards of the neighborhood. With almost no car traffic in the area, children could play safely under the watchful eyes of the *vecinas* and *vecinos* (neighbors) who sat outside their homes and talked to each other or told stories of old Mexico to those kids who sat still long enough. David remembers playing "team base," a game in which the kids would try to run around some bases—like baseball—without getting hit with a ball or tagged out by a player standing behind home plate. The streets often served as football fields where the kids chose teams to play or simply tossed the ball to each other, much like kids of all ages do today. But instead of a well-inflated spiral football, theirs were often homemade toss-able creations, usually made of cloth. Occasionally one of the neighborhood boys got a real football, which was a treat for David and his cohort, including his three cousins, Tony, David, and Fernando Hernández, and another cousin, known as "La Bola" (ball), and Joe Contreras, who would later be a teammate.

They were a group of friends that went everywhere together, sometimes even near downtown, where they swam in the San Antonio River, which at the time had a sizeable flow through the city. The river could prove dangerous after a strong rain, but it was available to the boys, something that the most popular swimming spot in the city—Woodlawn Lake—was not because it was located in the glitzier part of town where there were few Mexicans. The boys, along with other friends, also flew homemade kites, which according to David went pretty high, though they were mostly made of newsprint or any other paper material the boys could get their hands on.[15] The kites were put together using sticks, string, and homemade glue. But boys being boys, these contraptions had an added feature that would be scandalous in today's middle-class neighborhoods and surely illegal. Competing for the skies with other kids, kite-makers sought whatever advantage they could, so they would tie old razor blades to the kite's rope to see if they could cut the ropes of other kites and bring them down. Without adult supervision, these boys were quite creative and at times ornery, but most of the time it was simply friendly competition.

When they weren't cutting down other kids' kites, they were playing marbles against each other and with anyone who had a handful or even a pocketful of those shiny little balls. At times, an unofficial tournament would arise as each boy came to challenge the others and then stayed to urge on someone else or hope for their demise after being cleaned out themselves. If it was not marbles, it was a game of "tops." This game involved the flat tops of pint-size milk bottles. One top was placed on the ground, and then two players would stand on opposite sides and each hurl down a top so as to land on the one on the floor. Sometimes the floor would be littered with tops until one player managed to land one on top of another and thus claim all of the ones on the ground. Those who were good at this game would often find their pockets bulging. It was a rather inexpensive game, but one that aroused a passion and usually an audience that would ooh and aah with the ebb and flow of the game.

By the time I got to elementary school, both marbles and tops were games that dominated the recesses of J. T. Brackenridge Elementary, which was two blocks away from Sidney Lanier. Boys and girls, though more the former than the latter, would surround a game of either marbles or tops and spend time cheering for one side or another or simply being entertained. Teachers, always fearful of conflict and fights, did not like those crowd-gathering games but were powerless to do anything about them. For a season, these games would dominate school recesses, and then they would simply fade into the background, only to arise to heights of popularity again the following semester. By my elementary school years, the games had become the domain of the schools, as the streets were full of cars and much more dangerous places in which to play.

David moved his play away from the streets when he discovered the Boys

Club, which opened when he still attended Navarro Elementary School. There a new world of recreation opened to him, though initially one much above his own skill level. He remembers Roy Guerrero, the club manager, closing the doors after hours but opening up the gym for those who wanted to play basketball. A proud graduate of Lanier, Guerrero proved a key part of the unofficial system that fed Herrera's ranks. He taught the boys the game and encouraged them to practice hard and to play often. David, however, did not impress anyone when he first took the court. He remembers, "When they chose teams nobody wanted me."[16] But his height always got him on a team. By the eighth grade, he was already five-foot-ten. Things would change when Tony Rivera took an interest in him and began teaching him how to play. While awkward and uncoordinated when he began, David quickly picked up the game through constant practice and through Rivera's tutelage. And he kept growing, so that by high school he was over six feet tall.

Rivera, as he sat in his recliner in 2011, would chuckle as he remembered David's first exploits on the basketball court. "We use to call him 'Verdura' because he was so green when he started playing." *Verdura* is "vegetable" in Spanish, though it is usually used to refer to the green variety. "Some came to call me 'Verde' (green) or 'Verdie,'" remembers David. The nickname came, however, not only because David's skills were undeveloped, but also because he worked with a man who drove his truck down the street selling vegetables to barrio residents. David also worked at the produce market near his house. There he helped the *verduleros*, or vegetable handlers, unload produce from the trucks and stock it on the shelves for both retail and wholesale buyers.[17] Mexican kids, skilled at finding nicknames that caught the essence of someone's experience, simply combined David's employment experience with his lack of skills on the basketball court to give him a name by which he would be remembered for decades after he left both the school and the vegetable market.

The Boys Club experience allowed David to play with boys who grew up in his neighborhood and to meet others who became teammates. Playing in the gym, he learned the street-smart skills that provided him confidence to make the school teams. The Boys Club played against quintets from Wesley House, the House of Neighborly Service Center, the Mexican Christian Institute, and other centers whose mission was to take Mexican kids off the streets. In those teams, David faced future teammates as well as future rivals from Fox Tech, Burbank, and some of the Catholic schools in the city. Lanier greats like Joe Contreras, Manuel Gonzalez, fellow all-stater Frank Rodríguez, and star football player Bennie Castillo all began as Boys Club teammates.[18] By the time he made the Lanier varsity team, David was already familiar with the type of game that both his teammates and his opponents played.

Though he probably had no other option, coming to Lanier was exactly what David wanted to do. "Lanier was the place all the [barrio] kids wanted to go to," he remembered. He recalled that bystanders at the city parades would cheer at the sight of the school's band and pep squad and ROTC units and proudly say, "Hay viene la garra" (Here comes the rag), a name that had been placed on Lanier as a term of endearment for some or a mild insult for others. I remember once having dinner with two former cheerleaders who bristled when reminded of that nickname for the school. Ironically, the term may well have come from what was then the only other school with a large Mexican student population, Fox Tech. Fox Tech eventually replaced Edison High School as Lanier's most hated rival and became their opponent in the famous Chili Bowl football game that captivated the interest of the Mexican communities of San Antonio until it ended in 2010. But back in the early 1940s, Lanier was the Mexican school where all the young heroes of the barrio went. The fact that his Boys Club teammates all attended Lanier only increased David's pleasure in being a Vok.

The pleasure of coming to Lanier would be just as great on the fan side of the sports equation. There was anticipation for the '43 team, and David was part of the reason. Wrote *El Nopal*'s sports reporter, "If you take a peek in the gymnasium in the afternoon, you will see 'all-state' Tony (Molo) Rivera and David Rodríguez warming up for the coming basketball season. David is about 6 feet tall and played with the Junior 'A' class team last year. He is the brother of our famous star, Juan (Big Indio) who played center for the Voks last year."[19] "Big Indio," according to his little brother, had a sturdy body, played good defense, and could score. "Nemo had a system," remembers David, "everything revolved around the center. The ball went into the center and from there began the execution. [Juan] handled the ball well, and he was a good passer."[20] Juan did not score much, as he took most of the shots inside. But he had proved in the regional tournament against Lampasas that he could score when others did not. On another occasion, the school newspaper predicted that "Nemo is going to have a grand time this season since he has two six-footers; an all-state forward; probably three lettermen and possibly two stars from last year's junior Voks."[21]

When David made varsity in his sophomore year, Coach Herrera was waiting for him. "He told me, 'I want you to jump rope every day.' One summer [his first] he got me into the gym, tied my right hand behind my back, and forced me to use my left hand, and this helped me become a scorer with both hands."[22] This also helped David to use both hands for rebounds and probably helped him to block shots with either hand. Herrera had noticed how Rivera's ambidexterity had made his star forward not only a great scorer, but someone who drew in the defense because he could move to either side for his hook shots. But this kind of dexterity was even more important in a center because the center was the one that often started the attack. Herrera had a "lot of little tricks" that he used to give his players an advantage. He rarely scrimmaged his players, opting instead to practice fundamentals and fast breaks. He kept them running two on three, one on one, two on one, and every other combination he could develop. He placed a rebounding ring on the hoop, and when the shots bounced off, it was David and the forwards' job to rebound the ball, quickly get it to the guards—usually Escobedo but also Bernal—and head off to the races.

Slow-moving centers did not survive at Lanier. The big men had to be able to run the court, catch the ball while moving, pass it, and then set up to receive it if the play did not end with a quick shot or layup. David's constant play at the Boys Club and his tenacity, as well as his slim body, allowed him to keep up with the rest of the players. At the start of his Lanier career, he was barely thicker than a stick, but he soon began to fill in, though never enough to be an imposing presence in the middle. Still, he could jump, and he intimidated opposing players with his ability to block shots. As a sophomore, he was not yet as good as his brother Juan, but by then he was more versatile, and that gave the team a bit more quickness. He also proved that even in his first year, he was a better scorer than his brother. His style of play quickly meshed with the quickness and the push-the-ball-down mentality of Henry Escobedo and Ramiro Bernal, two guards ready to make Lanier basketball history. David would be the baby of the group, but there was no doubt that he quickly added one more fast and well-conditioned body to the squad.

The Voks began their basketball campaign as usual in the South San Antonio Basketball Tournament the week before Christmas. The tournament, facing war shortages and district realignment, had a reduced participation—from sixteen teams to eight. These were the six schools of 28-A district, as well as Central Catholic High School and Fox Tech, the only tournament participant from the City Series, which itself had been reduced to three teams.[23] The Voks gave immediate notice to the league and the city teams that they were going to be an offensive and defensive force on the court by beating the Burbank Bulldogs, 41–11, and then following it up with a 41–13 shellacking of the South San Bobcats.[24]

Rivera led the Voks with eleven points in their victory over the Bulldogs, while David added nine. In the final game, David scored eleven points to lead the Voks to a 27–21 victory over the Central Catholic Buttons, emphatically making the point that his opponents could not simply concentrate on

Rivera.[25] The game was a tougher than expected, and the Voks trailed until the third quarter, when they "went wild and started making points from all angles of the floor."[26]

The tournament win capped the 1942 year, as the teams took off the Christmas holidays. At the start of the season, one newspaper had identified Brackenridge, Jefferson, Lanier, and Edison as the top teams in the city. While praising the other three schools, the newspaper left its biggest accolades for Lanier, describing this Vok team as "another fine goaling outfit under the leadership of Nemo Herrera, one of the town's outstanding cage coaches."[27] Another newspaper tagged "Herrera's speedy Voks" as the favorites for the 28-A district title and co-favorites in the City Series along with the Jefferson Mustangs.[28] The Voks confirmed the favorite's role by beating Class AA Fox Tech 27–16, giving them first place in the City Series. Rivera led the Voks with fourteen points in what was a fairly easy victory.[29] They followed that win with a another game against Central Catholic, and this time the game was not even close, as the Voks, again "making goals from all angles of the court," ran away with a 39–15 victory. The Voks used a brand of ball hawking to force the Buttons to shoot from afar, only to see their ball rarely enter the basket.[30] The next game presented a bigger challenge, as the Voks met the Brackenridge Eagles, their most difficult opponent throughout Herrera's tenure.

This matchup seemed to favor the Voks, who had five wins under their belt while the Brackenridge Eagles had yet to play a game. Still, Coach "Red" Forehand's quintet had been preparing for their first game since the latter part of the 1942 year. The veteran coach forsook tournament play in order to work on fundamentals with the team. The Eagles, who had normally perched at the top of the city basketball world, had found themselves out of the top for the last couple of years, losing to either the Jefferson Mustangs or the Lanier Voks. Hoping to build on the success of the past, Forehand called upon some of his former stars to come and work with the team.[31] Some of these former players had participated in very tight games against the Voks and been part of some heartbreaking losses either in the last minutes of play or in overtime. It would not be hard to imagine former players letting the current Brackenridge roster know of the Voks' quickness, the difficulty of playing in the Lanier gym, and how most of their games would be bitterly fought until the last seconds of the game. No matter which team was the favorite, the outcome could not easily be predicted before the game.

The Voks-Eagles game turned out as each coach expected and how fans had come to anticipate: close and low scoring. But Lanier led all the way, though never by more than four points. The Eagle defense had prepared well and found a way to slow the Voks and force them to shoot from the outside.

They used eight players to Lanier's six, and their tall players were able to shut down David completely in regulation and hold Rivera to seven points for the game. What they could not do was hit their free throws, missing all five of the opportunities they got. Had they hit at least one, they would have upset the Voks. Instead, they depended on a long shot to tie the score, 18–18, with less than thirty seconds to play. Unable to break the tie in regulation, the Voks settled for the win in overtime. By 1943, overtime had gone from being decided by the first goal scored to today's specific time period. David, as he proudly scribbled on his scrapbook, scored the only field goal in the overtime period, and Ramiro Bernal and Tony Rivera each added a free throw to lead Lanier to a 22–18 victory. Rivera had been quite effective with his "left-handed push shot" outside the foul circle.[32]

Fresh from their two City Series victories as well as the South San Antonio Tournament, the Voks turned their sights on the district race as prohibitive favorites. In first place was a Burbank team they had trounced by thirty points in the South San tournament. The only other team given much of a chance was the South San Bobcats, and the Voks had beaten them by twenty-eight points. Only Hot Wells, undefeated in league play and second in the district, remained an unknown in terms of their ability to compete with the Voks. They were led by one of the few Mexican players in the city not on the Lanier roster, Albert Martínez, who played center for the Hot Wells Blue Devils. The young man was the leading scorer in the second week of play of the new year. He scored thirty-nine points, three more than Rivera, who trailed with thirty-six.[33] At the start of the third week of the season, Martínez led his team with eight points to beat first-place Burbank to take over the top spot in the district. Lanier went on to beat South San, 34–18, in its first league game the same week.[34]

The value of this victory went further than the score. Rivera scored ten points and David only four, but Walter Kelley and Escobedo broke out of their slumps. Neither had played much of a role in the heavy scoring that the Voks had achieved in the first part of the season. Besides Rivera and David Rodríguez, only Bernal had scored his consistent four or five points. In the South San game, Kelley scored six points, and Escobedo scored eight, providing the Voks a balanced attack. George Reyna, the first man off the bench, scored three.[35] None of the players had gone on a scoring spree, but then few players, not even Rivera, scored in the twenties during the 1940s, when games were usually balanced scoring affairs.

The balanced attack came at the right time for the Voks, as the Hot Wells Blue Devils invaded the Lanier gym in a game for first place that pitted speed against height. The visitors sought their fourth straight district win, while the Voks went after their third. With only a third of the district race behind them, the Voks and the Blue Devils had already distanced themselves from the rest.[36] Unfortunately for Hot Wells, their only feature that compared favorably with Lanier was their undefeated record in district play. The similarities ended there, as the Voks came into to their gymnasium ready to prove that the district crown belonged to them and no one else. By 1943, Lanier's gym had become even more intimidating, as the Voks played with great confidence. Their fans expected a win regardless of the opponent, and they used their lungs at full capacity all through the game. When opposing teams walked in, they usually did so "tight or scared" recalls David. The Mexican opposing players, especially those from schools like Hot Wells, where few other Mexican Americans attended, probably felt particularly uncomfortable. Most, though not all, belonged to more affluent families and had not grown up in the barrio.

"We use to think that they were better off economically than we and wondered if they thought they were better than us," said David as he remembered playing Martínez. Beating the Blue Devils was particularly satisfying, though in actuality the Lanier players saw the opposing Mexican American players as little different from their white teammates. White players facing Lanier probably felt uncomfortable or isolated since rarely did any fans from their school come to see them play at the Lanier gym. Most whites in San Antonio feared or at least felt out of place going to the West Side and coming into a gym so jam-packed with Mexicans. David admits that many of the Lanier players felt that the white fans that came were those who considered the West Siders the "scum of the earth."[37] Lanier's players did not harbor resentment and often avoided saying anything that indicated that they were acutely conscious of discrimination, but all of them acknowledged when interviewed that white hostility existed and that they enjoyed beating their opponents at home, where Lanier fans could cheer them on.

The Voks, anxious to prove they were still the team to beat, quickly jumped on the Blue Devils, hitting some quick baskets and playing a tenacious defense that forced the Hot Wells quintet to take wild shots. At the end of the first half, the Blue Devils had scored no points and would score only eight all night as the Voks won easily, 37–8, in a game that had no rallies, no ties, and no excitement for the visiting team. The Vok faithful went wild cheering for their team, feeling quite confident that the district race was a foregone conclusion.[38] David came into the game ready to play the Hot Wells big man, and the matchup proved no contest. Whatever skills David continued to develop as an offensive player, they were more than complemented by his defensive skills. He believed that every rebound belonged to him, and he loved to block shots. Playing defense was not only a skill that Herrera taught, it was a state of mind for the coach. He practiced defense continually, believing that when players defended well, scoring opportunities followed.

On the offensive side, Rivera affirmed his status as the top player in the city and in the district. He hit four goals in the first half and then followed that up with five more in the second half to lead all scorers with eighteen points. The total gave him the lead in the district scoring race with forty-one, two points ahead of George Duncan of Hot Wells. Rivera's hook shots, drives, and stand-up shots were rarely contested, as the quick Voks' ball movement as well as their steals and fast breaks confused the Blue Devils, whose height proved of little use. The Devils' free throw shooting did not help their cause, as they missed eleven of those. The Voks were no better, missing nine, but their shots from the court were accurate. Ramiro Bernal scored six points, followed by Escobedo and Kelley with five each. David scored only two points, but his defense stood out as he held Hot Wells' high-scoring Martínez to no points.[39] In fact, David did not allow the Blue Devil center to even put the ball in the air, as he smothered him with a tight defense and intimidated him with his shot blocking.[40] The battle of the two tall Mexican American centers never materialized. The Voks' quickness, their agility inside, and their accurate shooting proved too much.

The easy victories over their district opponents worried Herrera. Even before they demolished Hot Wells, he had the team working hard to correct what he saw as their deficiencies. In a photo published in a local newspaper, Herrera and Rivera held up a sign apparently meant to keep the team from complacency. It showed a big headline that said "Score," and under it was "Lanier 10, Edison 89." The newspaper writer did not buy Herrera's skepticism. He wrote, "Don't look now but our dauntless Captain Nemo Herrera in his land-going sub, the good ship 'Sidney Lanier' is all set to fire a flock of torpedoes into the ancient freighter known as 'Thomas A. Edison' [high school] . . . and without warning, too . . . the meany!"[41] It pointed out that one of those "torpedoes" was Tony Rivera, who "is going fairly good in games to date." The reporter predicted that the Edison Bears' ship was going to "be sunk without a trace under a landslide of baskets." But Nemo, fearing overconfidence, stressed that he had no real sharpshooter on the team and was not completely satisfied with the team's performance so far. "Nobody pays him any attention," rebutted the reporter.[42]

While not even Herrera could make the case for a tough time in the district race, he knew the City Series would be a tougher race. The Voks had beaten the two bottom teams, Burbank and Fox Tech, and even the third-place Brackenridge Eagles, but the Jefferson Mustangs loomed large, not only because of their size but also because they had a veteran team that had dominated the series for the last couple of years. In addition, they had a "cage maestro" for a coach in Dean H. H. Hamilton. "If Herrera wins, he stays where he is, which is at the top," wrote "Jedge" Winkle. "But if Hamilton wins, he pushes Señor Herrera out in the cold." Calling both teams "goaling machines," Winkle predicted a packed gym for "this demonstration of mechanical skill."[43] The matchup, as it had in previous years, came down to height versus speed, and this time height won out. Jefferson had a good team, and they proved it by going into the Lanier gym and beating the Voks in front of their fans. Unfortunately, no article or clipping exists that tells the story of the game or even the final score.

The Voks quickly shook off defeat and went on a rampage in the district race while continuing to dominate every other team in the City Series. Several days after losing to Jefferson, on January 25, the Voks smothered the Fox Tech Buffs, 46–5, in what one sportswriter called the "slowest" game of the season.[44] The Voks then followed that victory with their second in a row against Brackenridge, 34–28. In the Tech game, David led the scoring with sixteen points, hitting five field goals from around the basket and then going six-for-six from the free throw line, where he was sent by opposing players who tried to get him off his game with physical play. His ability to shoot with either hand and to slip through the defender to get the rebound and put it back in was too much for those defending him. Nothing worked, and the Tech team's concern with him allowed other Voks to score easily. Herrera saw his "Little Indio"—as some Lanierites began calling David, in contrast to his big brother, "Big Indio"—as a center capable of taking his team far into the playoffs. Rivera and Kelley added eight points each, while Bernal had seven. Gilbert Gonzalez, one of another brother duo (with Manuel) for the Voks, also chipped in seven points against the Fox Tech Buffaloes.[45]

In the game against the Eagles, Rivera hit a season high of eighteen points, David hit for six, and so did Escobedo, as the team continued to find scoring balance.[46] Several times Rivera's heroics brought the Voks from behind and then kept them ahead as the Eagles, who had beaten the only team (Jefferson) that had beaten Lanier, sought to take over first place in the City Series with a win. After the close victory over Brackenridge, the Voks then beat the South San Bobcats, 32–20, but this time Escobedo proved that he could carry the team, scoring twelve points to lead all scorers in the game, while Rivera added nine.[47] Escobedo and Bernal were becoming outside threats, and this meant that at any time one of the five players on the court could pick up the slack if Rivera or David was not on top of his game. Carrasco's sharpshooting was not there, but the guard duo of Escobedo and Bernal more than made up for his deficiency.

The Voks followed the Eagle victory with a comfortable 38–30 win over an improved Edison Bears team and just about locked up the district title. In this game, Rivera scored sixteen points from one side of the foul line while David added twelve from inside the key, where he also dominated the boards.[48] Both players were benefiting from Escobedo's passes, which seemed to only get faster and more accurate."[49] The serious-looking guard was coming into his own both in scoring and pushing the ball down the court quickly. Ramiro Bernal was passing the ball to the other side, where Kelley and the Gonzalez brothers (Gilbert and Manuel) were adding their points to the total. Escobedo and Bernal could not have been more different, not only in personality but in the way and to whom they distributed the ball, but they complemented each other and provided a balance that the team had not seen at the guard positions since Tony Cardona and Joe Martínez played together. But in this case, notwithstanding Cardona's scoring talent, the guard tandem was much more balanced. While Escobedo would develop, much like Rivera, into the type of player who could put the team on his shoulders and will it to win, Bernal offered a smoother and more integrating type of play. He involved more players in the action, and his easy demeanor fostered trust and confidence from the other players, especially those who were not the go-to guys but who were as anxious to contribute.[50]

With the kind of play they got from the starters and the bench players, the Voks put the finishing touches on the district race with another shellacking of the Hot Wells Blue Devils, 45–17. David again shut out Martínez.[51] Rivera led the team with thirteen points, while David scored six, but surprisingly, two bench players, Gilbert Gonzalez and newcomer Frank Rodríguez (he had not shown up in either the team pictures or previous box scores), had eight and six, respectively.[52] With the exception of the "close" game against the Edison Bears, the Voks had marched through the district schedule without much of a test. Unfortunately, they had not been as successful in the City Series. While they had beaten Brackenridge (who beat Jefferson), they were not able to use their speed and quickness effectively against the taller Mustangs. Without the "sharpshooter" that Herrera lamented not having, they failed to crack the tough Jefferson defense and lost their second straight game to the Series leader, 32–24, ending up in second place, one game behind Jefferson.[53] Still, going into the playoffs they could claim a victory over every 1-A school they played and, except for Jefferson, could make the same claim against the 2-A schools.

There are no results for Lanier's battle with the champions of Districts 25, 26, and 27 for a chance to play in the state playoffs, but an article mentions that their performance was nothing to brag about. Said the *San Antonio Light*, "Those who saw the Voks in action in last week's Region 7 tournament, in which they played their worst basket ball of the season can't see them as state champions."[54] Herrera's players, while averaging thirty-four points a game for the season and allowing only twenty-one, were terrible free throw shooters throughout the season, missing 183 free shots and making only 174, for a .487 average. Rivera, the top shooter, made only 59 percent of his free tosses, while averaging twelve points a game. In 1943 it was not uncommon for the Voks to miss as many as nine or ten free throws in a game. Rivera, who had missed two crucial free shots in the waning moments of their playoff run the year before, had proved that no matter how much a player practiced their free throws in practice, the game situation was totally different.[55] Perhaps all the exertion with their run-and-gun style and their full-court pressure defense made it hard for the Voks to be steady when they were on the free throw line. Or simply they were just not a good team at hitting the free shots.

The *San Antonio Light* writer quickly added, however, that Herrera's teams were unpredictable and cited the 1939 team that "went to Austin unheralded and then lost out in the finals by a two-point margin."[56] In addition to having played poorly in the regional tournament, the Voks were seen as being "thin" or, as the reporter put it, the most "under-manned team ever to receive such high billing."[57] That "high billing" referred to the Voks' being picked as one of the favorites to win the state title in Class A. This favorable nod came because they were one of only three teams that had been in the previous year's tournament—the others being Lakeview and Aransas Pass—and the only one to have made it past the first round.[58] "Coach Nemo Herrera . . . will have enough players at Austin to load his Gregory gymnasium bench but the boys he is counting on to bring home the championship can be counted on one hand with an extra finger thrown in," said the article. Those five boys were Tony Rivera, Walter "Rough House" Kelley, Manuel Gonzalez (sometimes spelled "Gonzales"), David Rodríguez, Ramiro Bernal, and Henry Escobedo. The bench, the article continued, only played because many of the games—particularly those in the district—were "fairly easy." When the going got tough, Herrera always went back to the six, or at least that is how the article's author explained it.

This analysis, however, misunderstood the way basketball is played. Most teams use five players and substitute only when a player gets into foul trouble or is exhausted. Sometimes a bench player is inserted who brings something to the game that can exploit a weakness of the other team. Usually those coming off the bench are the sixth and possibly the seventh player. Rarely does a coach go any deeper in his bench. Some teams play platoon basketball and use two or three combinations, especially at the high school level where skill and talent are only so plentiful. The analysis also misunderstood the way Herrera coached. His was a zero-based style in which every player had to earn time and their starting spot in every game, every practice, and every season. Herrera saw his bench players not as substitutes but as starters who were simply not in the game. As mentioned earlier, he had no qualms about benching a starter or even starting a bench player when either the starter was not performing or the bencher had proven either in practice or a prior game that he was doing better. Every player on the team went into the game knowing that he could be inserted at any moment. While true to a lesser extent for most teams, this philosophy was particularly applicable to Herrera's teams.

One reason it applied so well to Nemo's quintets was the fact that most of the players on the team were quite talented for their respective competition. The players on the 1943 team were either returnees from the state third-place team of 1942 or champions from the Alamo League for B teams—mostly junior varsity players—in San Antonio. Most had come from winning teams in every stage of competition at Lanier or from the community center leagues. The reporter seemed to understand at least this when he wrote, "Fans often wonder how Herrera's Lanier teams can go at such speed for a full game, often without substitution. But it is the kind of basket ball they have played since coming inside Herrera's orbit in junior high school and a five-minute rest usually seems like a holiday to them."[59] The constant running, which came to be emulated in the unofficial feeder system supplying Herrera's teams, gave Lanier a wealth of conditioned players. But the boys' winning attitude also came from being winners at all levels. Every year saw a championship team coming out of Lanier, whether it was at the junior high level, in the Alamo League, or in varsity competition.

Interestingly, while Manuel "Mosco" Gonzalez had been singled out in this article, it was actually his brother, Raul, who had the hot hand during the last few games of the season. At the same time, Frank Rodríguez, who would be named all-state later in his career, made the jump from the junior varsity, which was in the thick of its own championship run, to add strength to the team. George Reyna, who had been a hero in the previous year's regional tournament, was one player who could come off the bench and keep the Vok five's rhythm intact. Refugio Olivares and Richard Reyes were not to be heard of much during that season, but being on the team usually meant they were good, considering that the B team would win the city championship again and most of those players, two-time city champs, had battled for a spot on the varsity. Herrera knew he was lucky to have such a strong starting five, but his confidence in the team was based as much on his bench's ability to perform when called upon. They were sound fundamentally, and every day they were placed in real game-time situations against some of the top players in the city and state.

The Voks came into the Class A tournament as co-favorites along with Anson High School and Sabine High School, but according to one newspaper, they were "rated weaker than the 1942 team." At the same time, "Tony Rivera and company can burn the netting at a fearful pace."[60] The first team to face the Voks' running style was the quintet from Lakeview, which like Lanier, was a throwback from the previous year. The Voks fell behind early in the game but soon found their range, especially Rivera, and quickly "made a race track of things" in defeating Lakeview, 48–31. This time, Rivera came to play, and he hit shots from his favorite spot as well as from other parts of the court as he tallied twenty-eight points, the highest one-game total of his career.[61] He hit twelve field goals and four free throws. Hitting from the inside allowed the guards uncontested shots from the outside as well as driving lanes. Bernal added eight points and Escobedo six, as Lanier became the only one of the three favorites to survive the first round.[62] The game, the last of the first night, drew a good crowd in spite of what sportswriter Harold Ratliff called the "difficulties of transportation and other wartime stringencies."[63] All twenty-four teams invited to the three classifications of the tournament attended, and many of their fans had also made the trip. That was not the case with most Lanier fans, who found it difficult to travel the ninety miles to Austin.

Next up for the Voks were the Mount Vernon Tigers, who proved to be even less of a challenge, falling to the "speedy Mexicans," who scored at will, this time not allowing themselves to fall behind or the opponent to hang around. The Voks galloped to a 14–2 lead in the first quarter, raised that to 26–8 in the second, continued on to 33–16 in the third, and then ended the fourth outscoring the Tigers, 14–9, for a resounding 47–25 victory. Rivera again came to play, chipping in fifteen points, but this time he had more help. David tossed in eight points, as did Manuel Gonzalez, while Bernal added seven and Escobedo four.[64] The Vok big men, led by David Rodríguez, dominated the inside play, and the guards continued to improve. Undoubtedly the best game of the year for the Voks, it came at the right time and made them the heavy favorites in the finals, where they faced the French High School Buffaloes of Beaumont for the Class A title. The Buffaloes had struggled in both their games, coming from behind twice in order to make it to the finals. The hometown newspaper called the Voks "heavy favorites" who breezed through the tournament.[65]

Walter Kelley remembered sixty-eight years later that the team entered the last game confident of winning. It had been an "easy run" according to Kelley, and the boys were reserved and not overly nervous.[66] They had the seen their opponents play and saw nothing to cause them worry. The Voks were faster, had a better bench than the sportswriters had given them credit for, and had a sophomore center that was as good a big man as any in the tournament. David Rodríguez was facing Herbert Beal of French, who would be selected the state's top center. Escobedo would face Jerry Parrish, who also made the all-state team. But even those players did not really concern the Voks because they had been taught to play their game. Lanier counted on the players to work together, so they worried little about their opponents' abilities, having already faced top-caliber players in the City Series. Besides, with so little time between games, it was hard to develop new strategies for each opponent.

We have no record of how Herrera felt the night before the big game, but given his intensity and passion, it is likely that he was nervous and anxious. While always presenting a calm and stable demeanor, Herrera was a winner and someone who constantly motivated himself and his players. His scrapbook is full of sayings, poems, and proverbs calling him to rise above himself. He was a winner as a player in high school and college, in minor league baseball, and in his two basketball coaching jobs. More important, Herrera knew what it meant to be at this level, one game away from being crowned the state's best. He also knew what it was to have a game slip away and for a team to fall from the top to become a memory held only by its own fans and a few sports enthusiasts checking the score. Few remembered second-place teams or, even worse, runner-up coaches. In Herrera's mind, he knew which had been the better team that March back in 1939, who had led in the critical moments, but also whose defense had failed to stop a simple turn-around shot by a center that was not as tall or as physically imposing as his all-state monster of a postman. Herrera had placed more players that year on the all-state team than the eventual champs. But none of that mattered after that one ill-fated game that lost him the championships. Now, after fifteen years of coaching, Herrera knew he had a team capable of winning it all, and while he knew his team would not necessarily be the crowd's favorite, he knew that most coaches and sportswriters believed that the title was his to take. French players had no chance of winning unless they played above their heads and the Lanier team played below its talent level.

Herrera never publicly made much about his boys being Mexican and being discriminated against. While others would speak of the "disadvantages" of his team, Herrera always spoke about effort and taking advantage of opportunities. His boys knew enough about the hardships of life and how they were judged unfairly because of the color of their skin. He knew what it was to not be served at restaurants on the road and how at small venues, especially among working-class white opponents, the hostilities were right below the surface, if not above it. In spite of all their wins, the boys of Lanier had never been fully at the top. Oh, they had won city and district titles; they were one of the dominant teams in the region, and this meant something to the players and the community. But a state title surpassed anything they had yet achieved. Another second-place finish would confirm in the minds of many that Herrera's "speedy Mexican boys" did not have the mettle to be champions. It is impossible to know if Herrera recognized it, but there were probably a good number of people out there who did—this would be the first all-Mexican team to win a state title in *anything* in the state of Texas and probably in the entire Southwest. (Kelley may have been part white, but as far as the team and coach were concerned, he was as Mexican as anyone else at Lanier.) To win it in a big man's game would be unprecedented and would be celebrated by every Mexican and Mexican American that had ever been called names, pushed around, or denied food at a restaurant, a haircut at a barbershop, or a seat at a public gathering. This would be an all-Mexican triumph.

In the end, this game proved no more difficult than the previous two, with Lanier taking a 30–18 victory. The Voks quickly jumped on the Buffaloes and never trailed. This time, Rivera did not disappoint, nor did he depend on his teammates to carry the game. After a dismal final game the previous year, Rivera came much more prepared and almost singlehandedly outscored the Buffaloes.[67] Rivera hit for sixteen points, bringing his tournament, three-game total to fifty-nine points, or 19.3 points a game, the highest among all the scorers. The Associated Press writer, calling the Voks "ball-handling wizards," described the game this way: "Tony Rivera, speedy little forward led the rim-crashing with seven field goals and two free throws . . . and his mates proved too good at controlling the ball for the scrapping Buffaloes although French held Lanier to its closest victory of the tournament."[68] The Voks started off the game with a 9–2 run, but the Buffaloes closed it to 12–8, and the Voks built the lead back to 18–8 by halftime. In the final quarter, Herrera called for a tighter defense that held the Beaumont team to only three points after having scored just seven in the third.[69]

At the sound of the last buzzer, no spontaneous celebration erupted as had happened when the Voks won the city title in 1939. Nor was there a riot, as the French team quietly walked off the floor knowing they had been bested by a much better squad. A few scattered claps and cheers went up from the few Lanierites that had followed their team, from other Mexican fans that had been able to scrape up a ticket, and from a few white fans that recognized a great high school team when they saw one. But waiting at the sidelines was a jubilant Herrera. He shook their hands, patted them on the back, and probably said a few "Good jobs" or "Well dones." Kelley remembers the coach as the one most excited with the victory. History had been made, and in a dominating fashion. Topping off the amazing run for the Voks was seeing two of their players picked for the all-state team. Escobedo's court leadership, ball control, and precise passing with an occasional score had so impressed the sportswriters that he was picked, along with French's Parrish, to be the starting guard on the all-state team. Rivera, the tournament's best player, repeated as an all-state selection and capped off a great career at Lanier.[70] His name would now be placed alongside that of Tony Cardona as one of the greatest players to ever don a Vok uniform.

CHAPTER EIGHT

On the Summit Looking Up

The iconic, majestic door on the north side of Sidney Lanier High School is the first thing that readers of the 1943 *Los Recuerdos* yearbook see. In that regard, the 1943 edition is not much different from its predecessors. This door would be the symbol of Lanier up until the school was razed and replaced in the 1990s. What is different in the 1943 yearbook is the prominence the north door takes as a symbol of learning and assimilation. The first page is titled "Open Doors on the North" and has two pictures, both framed by trees and shrubbery that make the entrance into a threshold of a garden. Margaret E. Sangster's poem underlines the first picture and pleads for God to keep the heart able to "respond to beauty" and "to never let [the Lanierite] grow too old to see the waking loveliness of early April." The second caption, under an even more majestic-looking garden surrounding the door, boasts of "Wide open and unguarded . . . gates / . . . that lead to an enchanted land / . . . [where] it is written, Toil shall have its wage, / And Honor honor, and the humblest man / Stand level with the highest in the law." The quote from Thomas Bailey Aldrich continues, "Of such a land have men in dungeons dreamed, / And with the vision brightening in their eyes / Gone smiling to the fagot and the sword."[1]

The second page of the yearbook shows a larger angle of the door that even my generation of Lanierites would remember fondly as the school's main entrance. It pictures several students entering or moving toward the door. Almost completely inside is a young woman in uniform, probably from the pep squad. Behind her is a young cadet with books resting on his right hip, and behind him is another cadet, hand in hand with a young woman in a white dress. Behind her are other young men and women. Below the picture is the caption "Our Open Door of Opportunity" and the words of an "Author Unknown": "The threshold 'neath my feet shall be Humility; / The roof—the very sky itself—Infinity. / Give me wide walls to build my house of life." The next two pages of the yearbook also depict doors, culminating with a plea to those who educate that they teach "the ways of life [and] wisdom we need to conquer prejudice and tolerance with which to master strife." There is a further solicitation for "rules that have been proven fair . . . courage . . . to face what lies before [and] guidance in a world now dark. Oh, hold a light beside the open door!"[2]

Who chose the poems is unclear. Whether it was a teacher anxious to instill love and patriotism for a country at war or a wide-eyed student desirous to see beyond both the confines of the barrio and the treatment of Mexicans outside of it, we'll never know. But it is clear the image presented on these pages was a sharp contrast to the reality of Lanierites or of most Mexicans in the West Side of San Antonio. The layout of four pages constructed a narrative of learning, preparation, and happiness that supposedly lay inside that large complex whose doors were open to all those in "search after truth." What the pictures did not reveal nor the words express was that those doors were entrances to a gated community that kept out those not "anointed" by registration, and once inside, no one could leave without the appropriate permission. This "prison," as Jesse Camacho would remember it, was as much about keeping in as it was about keeping out, though it worked well on both counts.

Even before the advent of major gang activity, when most of the barrio was safe and quiet, prison-like fences were erected around the Lanier grounds. Few could accuse the Lanier students in those days of misbehaving or being rowdy. Thus, the gates were not a response to a hostile world trying to get in, but rather a reaction to having so many Mexicans just outside the school grounds. Mexican Americans at Lanier were caged in to protect them from their own neighborhoods lest they remain difficult to socialize into an Anglo world, a place they were expected to know and understand but that remained outside the grasp of their daily interaction. Segregated by the complex itself, they learned to be "American" but also to respect boundaries. There they would see only Anglo teachers, supervisors, and counselors. Authority was race-specific with a few exceptions, and those exceptions were carefully chosen. In fact, those exceptions were what made the construction of a segregated system possible because they implied that all things were possible in American society.

Forty-plus years after leaving Lanier, I am still amazed by both the audacity and the cynicism with which we were taught—or, better yet, instructed—to overlook or to look beyond the limitations that were set for us and even to ignore the low expectations that educators, politicians, and community leaders in San Antonio had for us. At the same time, we were expected to believe that the American dream actually applied to us. In our innocence, we Lanier students—of the 1940s and 1960s—believed these promises. At least for a short time, we accepted that in the world of Lanier principles of Americanism did apply, but it never escaped us that they did not help much beyond the railroad tracks and bridges that both separated us from and connected us to the larger Anglo world. Nonetheless, we internalized those concepts and ideals. We tried to apply them in our small world, and we spoke as if we could easily apply them in the outside world. Eventually, for some of us, they did apply, but not without a struggle.

There is no doubt that some of the Lanierites of the 1940s understood the contradictions of their school, but it was in understanding the duality of their lives in segregated San Antonio that they found ways to live their American lives in the Mexicanized—but not Mexican—world of Lanier. Even more than those of us in the 1960s who knew that war awaited many of us after graduation, the Lanier students of the 1940s were conscious that whatever their feelings about the immediate world around them, there was something much bigger beyond the campus that required their attention. In Humphrey Bogart's words, their lives amounted to less than a "hill of beans" in a world at war.[3] Those Mexican American organizations and reformists who did not support the war effort soon faded from sight, while many other reformers and organizations decided that the logical thing to do was to actively support the war and to tone down—but not silence—their critique of American society.

Voices like those of the leftist National Spanish-Speaking Congress, which declared, "We are children of the United States. . . . We will defend her," became the dominant views in the barrio.[4] The impulse for wartime solidarity led Mexican American intellectual Carlos Castañeda to proclaim that Mexican and American history were complementary to each other and to praise the Texas army at the Battle of San Jacinto as a force for "freedom and democracy" while condemning the Mexican army as standing for "tyranny and dictatorship."[5] The patriotic pitch rose to such an extent that most reformers pushed hard for Mexican Americans to join the armed forces, not only to show their loyalty to the nation, but as a way to gain their rights. If they participated, they would be recognized, and if they gave the ultimate sacrifice, their families and communities would be rewarded by a grateful nation. In the end, the "grateful" part would prove mostly unfounded. But what did come out of the war effort was a sense of pride and confidence among Mexican American veterans to fight the enemies at home as they had done the enemies abroad.[6]

Most Lanierites did not think much about those complex issues. They simply understood that many in the West Side of San Antonio were joining the armed forces, and some were being killed in foreign lands. This was enough to get them to participate wholeheartedly in the defense of their country and the organizations and activities that supported the war effort. They did so with such tenacity that others quickly noticed. "With Jefferson High School and Brackenridge ROTC enrollment considerably declined we should not have been able to show an increase" in overall ROTC enrollment, said Colonel C. M. Tuteur, the head of the school district's ROTC program, "if it had not been for the wonderful enthusiasm in Lanier Senior High School. The Mexican boys in that school have gone all out for military training. They are making splendid cadets."[7] Tuteur emphasized the need for the training and shared a letter with the *San Antonio Light* from a sailor who wrote his principal that his unit had had to learn from an ROTC graduate to "hit the ground" properly since they had not learned it in navy basic training. By this time, the cadet program had gone from simply marching and drilling with dummy rifles to practicing with live ammo and talking about actual combat strategies.[8]

The young cadets were not the only ones involved in the war effort. Students throughout the school district were raising funds for a myriad of military needs. Lanier students joined wholeheartedly the "Buy Jeeps" campaign by buying war bonds and stamps. The response from students was overwhelming, and within two days enough money was raised to buy two jeeps. The school devoted a full edition of its newspaper to promote the sale of both stamps and war bonds, while the art students drew cartoons of the jeeps bought.[9] Less than a week later, the San Antonio school population had sold enough war bonds and stamps to buy 170 jeeps, with the students from Lanier buying $4,603.25 worth of bonds and stamps.[10] While this number paled in comparison to that of the two largest schools, it was significant given that most of Lanier's students were poor and that any money used to support the war effort was a sizeable chunk of the family budget. Still, during the "Victory Drive, more than 95 percent of the student body participated in buying war bonds and stamps. The yearbook proudly quoted students who asked each other things like, "Let's see your stamp book" and "I'm about ready to turn my book in for a bond."[11]

Aside from the buying of war bonds and stamps, Lanier students were imbued with a support-the-war patriotism that subsumed almost all other activities. A section of the yearbook titled "A Song of Victory" pictures eleven students entering the school building through one of the side doors, some carrying donations such as books, blueprints, a model plane, and scraps—two tires, newspapers, and metal. The eleven are clearly part of a longer line of donating students.[12] The yearbook introduces the reader to a student council committee named for General Douglas MacArthur. The committee's purpose was to coordinate the school's participation in the "Schools at War" program. It organized the scrap metal drives, which according to the yearbook brought in 123,000 pounds of metal. The committee encouraged Lanier students to take an oath to become members of the Texas Junior Rangers for one week in October so they could collect metal scraps. The students were also able to collect 7,850 pounds of rubber by the end of the week. They then kept collecting and gathered another 7,000 pounds of metal, which included "old jalopies, small keys, huge boilers, children's toys, kitchen stoves, and Civil War muskets. The collection was dumped in front of the school where the vocational shop boys sorted, broke it up and helped hauled it away. All the collecting brought $657.43, which was used to set up an emergency first-aid unit in the home economics department at the school.[13]

The committee also sponsored a Victory Poster Contest to spur interest in the war bond drive. The winning entry depicted an American soldier with his rifle raised high above his head as he stood over a German military shirt with a swastika on it. In the committee's Scrap Metal Guessing Contest, in which students tried to guess how much scrap was actually collected, a student by the name of Consuelo Blancarte won first prize. To spur even more participation and a greater commitment to the war effort, the committee changed the annual Color Day festival to Victory Day, where they got more than a one thousand students to buy bonds and stamps.[14] The pep rallies, the buying of pom-poms and caps, and the other activities that had preceded games and that had been tradition since 1933 "gave way to seriousness of purpose as students invested in the securities that provide our boys with lead and steel [for] the battle field." The committee followed the successful Victory Day activities with a two-week Anniversary Day campaign, which began on December 7 and raised an additional $2,500 through bond and stamp sales. Not limiting themselves to students, the committee wrote to every resident in the surrounding community encouraging them to save tin cans in order to donate the copper to the war effort.[15]

Every one of Lanier's vocational shops became involved in one form or another in the war pitch. The mill shop set a goal of building 210 model planes for the armed forces so that its spotters could identify enemy and friendly airplanes. The models were also to be used in civilian defense classes so that regular citizens could distinguish among an English Spitfire, the Hurricane, the Mosquito Bomber, the American P-38 or P-40, the Flying Fortress, and the German Stuka or Messerschimdt. The models required "ultra-precision" and were time-consuming. The building of model planes took up most of the class time for the semester, and some of the boys who had few evening activities stayed into the night to finish the models. Since this was not a typical curriculum of the mill shop, the advisor Mr. Vicentini asked members of the student body who had experience in working with model toys to volunteer to help.[16]

Assisting the mill shop was the paint and trim shop, which painted the model planes made by the mill boys as well as model planes by other shops in the San Antonio school district. "When finished," wrote the yearbook staff, "the three hundred fifty model planes will be used by the army to train pilots and spotters for our National Defense Plan."[17] The yearbook pointed out the great need for operators of electric sewing machines to repair parachutes and other army equipment; the boys in the paint and trim shop were acquiring those skills. It also mentioned that two shop graduates, Henry Flores and Joe Perez, were now "enthusiastic employers in the paint shop at Camp Stanley," an army camp near San Antonio. Students in the body and fender class also expected to find work in the manufacturing of automobiles, trucks, tanks, and other heavy equipment used by the military. Already, the yearbook noted, some students who had enrolled the year before were now "employed in national defense and in military service."[18]

The other vocational shops were not to be left behind in their support of the war effort. The auto mechanic shop morning class proudly announced that many of its ex-students were now employed in the armed forces of the United States and could be "found in every continent executing the knowledge they learned at Lanier." The afternoon class boasted that "ninety percent of Lanier ex–auto mechanics are serving the United States Government as airplane and auto mechanics, welders and radio men."[19] The yearbook listed twenty-four students who were working in the civilian defense plant at Duncan Field, Texas. Interestingly, on that list was Henry Escobedo, though it is unclear whether this was the Voks' point guard or another student of the same name. It is possible that Escobedo worked part-time, on weekends, or during the summer in the defense plant.[20] The yearbook section on the print shop mentioned that "several graduates" were working with printing departments of the "different training fields" of the government, while the section on the art shop trumpeted that its students were getting "theory and actual practice to enable them to do many jobs in war plants."[21]

The art shop included women, but none of the others did. The one shop exclusively for women, vocational dressmaking, was also involved in the war effort, though less directly. The yearbook excerpt on the dressmakers did not reference the war explicitly but pointed out that "due to the trend of world conditions" the young women were learning valuable skills to "conserve and renovate old or partly worn garments." These skills were practiced in the making of the school's Junior Women's Army Corps (WAC) uniforms and the mass production of "one thousand garments for the American Red

Cross."[22] The yearbook pointed out that the dressmaking course was unique in the state, as schools offered little for women in terms of vocational training aside from a few home economics classes. "The general objectives," read the section, "are the study of the wise expenditures of the family income, the development of an appreciation of the artistic, economic, and hygienic values involved in the selection of clothing." A more specific objective was to "train the girls in a trade so that they may be self-supporting."[23] Not mentioned is the fact that, with those skills, most of the young women would be recruited to work in the city's garment sweatshops, which at the time were plentiful and among the few venues for "skilled" jobs available to the women in San Antonio. While this was difficult work, it was much better than working in a pecan shelling factory or as a domestic worker.

For the first time, the 1943 yearbook also carried a list of former Lanierites serving in the armed forces. The "First Victory Honor Roll" listed 274 names, likely an incomplete tally as it included only those whose whereabouts were known to the school.[24] For example, two prominent players from the '39 team who had joined the armed forces, Tony Cardona and Joe Treviño, are not on the list. Five names stand out, those of Bertha Adame, Josephine Bratton, Hortense Mata, Mary Orona, and Eunice Cueva, the only clearly identifiable women on the list. The list also includes a few gender-neutral names that perhaps raise Lanier's total of enlisted women to nine. No historical work exists on Mexican American women in the armed forces, and so it is almost impossible to know how many served and how many Lanier females participated in the war effort in uniform.

Another list that is incomplete is the one in a section titled, "In Memoriam," which listed three names: Rudy Cortez, who died on November 2, 1942; Ramiro Gallegos, who died January 17, 1943; and Henry Laas, who gave his life for his country on February 8, 1943. Jessie Vargas's brother Richard, who died in combat, did not make the list. One account has it that 550 Lanier students served or were serving in the nation's armed forces by 1944. By 1948, forty-four ex-Lanierites were known to have given their lives for "the peace and freedom of the world."[25] Others, like Carlos Camacho, served in the war effort as civilians, working in various jobs in which the government felt best to recruit or "draft them" but not put them in uniform. While many did not fight, wear the uniform, or work in defense-related industries, very few remained untouched by the war.

By the end of the 1943–1944 school year, another two ex-Lanierites had joined the list of those who died. Leonard Araiza and Henry Gomez became another reminder of why all those school activities in support of the war effort mattered. While these activities were fun and often bonded the students, most Lanierites knew that war was not something to celebrate. For the young men close to graduation, the war meant a possible stint on the battlefield with its accompanying risks. For the young women, it meant entering an adult world with fewer men, where women's responsibilities grew as they helped out in areas once reserved for men, where jobs were difficult and intense, and where rationing prevailed. Just as Mexican Americans, no matter their sports victories or war contributions, lived in an American world, women lived in a male world, made more so by the fact that it was the men who went to war. Whatever women's contributions, few of them would be heroes or command the same respect as men. In the 1944 yearbook, a collage of twenty-seven pictures filled a page titled "Uncle Sam's Boys," which asserted, lest anyone forget, that this was a time devoted to the praising and even worshipping of the male warrior, though it is likely that many of the young men would have given up this attention for a safer world.

Still, by 1944 the atmosphere at Lanier seemed more upbeat and optimistic. While the yearbook carried a number of sections directly tied to the support of the war effort, the tone was more celebratory than in previous years, perhaps reflecting the recognition that the Allies were winning the war. Together, the 1943 and 1944 yearbooks carried a total of seven names of those who had died in the war. The final total of forty-four Lanierites who died in the war must reflect both a number who had died in the early years and were later discovered and a number who died after the 1944 yearbook was published.

If there was optimism about what was happening overseas, there were also great expectations for the upcoming basketball season. Herrera had lost some very capable players, starting with Tony Rivera. There simply was no player capable of taking over his spot. And it was difficult to see who would take over Ramiro Bernal's shooting guard spot. Also gone was the dependable defensive specialist Walter Kelley, as well as Manuel Gonzalez, Refugio Olivares, Frank Hernández, and George Reyna, who could be counted to come off the bench and give the Vok starters some much needed rest and an occasional spark. Richard Reyes was also gone, killed shortly after joining the army.[26] But beyond their individual skills as players, those young men had been part of a smooth-functioning basketball machine that played its best ball at game's end. They knew each other and trusted their teammates to be where the ball was going. Every one of them was considered a capable defender. As good as the individual parts were, the team as a whole was even better.

Herrera knew the cupboard was far from empty. He had a good core coming back. It started with Henry Escobedo, point guard, football captain, and all-around iron man. He could score, he could pass, but most important, he could run the team. It had been that command of the court that brought him all-state honors as a junior, something that no other Vok except Tony Rivera had ever achieved. Escobedo did not have Rivera to pass the ball to, but he had David Rodríguez, a defensive specialist inside who was also capable of scoring when needed. In the state final game, Rodríguez had more than held his own against French's all-state center. Another quality player was Raul Gonzalez, who earned the right to be first man off the bench for the state champs. Those three returning players were supplemented with seven players from the Class B team, which had won the city championship in their category. Of particular value were Kino Rodríguez and Frank Rodríguez, who, though unrelated, played like twins connected at birth.[27] Their addition proved to be the most important to the team for the next two years.

The 1943 teams had revealed a maturing of the Herrera farm system and its ability to produce very good basketball players. The 1944 team was set to show the seamless transition of Class B players to varsity and the taking on of leadership by a new set of stars. Escobedo had been a surprise all-state pick the previous year given that the team was composed mostly of scoring guards. Sportswriters, however, saw Escobedo's court management, passing ability, and leadership as critical to the team's success. In 1944, Escobedo was ready to be the main team leader and star. His football career over, he took the reins of the basketball team with a tenacity rarely seen in the school's history. Most players remember being friends with each other and allowing leaders to develop as the need arose. Rivera himself was a natural leader, and he led both by example and by providing timely advice and encouragement, as most others in the past had. Escobedo was different in the way he ran the team, especially with Rivera gone. As long as Tony played, he was the acknowledged team leader and Escobedo the quiet floor manager who fed the ball to him. But with Rivera gone, Henry became the "big dog," and he had the self-confidence to mold the team his way.[28]

Being a returning all-state player gave Escobedo a commanding presence, especially among the younger players. The veterans on the team had great respect for him because they knew that few players had as good a grasp of the game as he did. With Rivera gone, the Lanier game needed to diversify. Since he was an excellent dribbler with both hands, could drill the pass between defenders, and had an eye for the open man, Escobedo immediately became a dangerous field marshal on the court.[29] That Herrera had great confidence in him only made him more valuable to the team. In the 1940s, coaches did not huddle with their teams as they would do in later years. During timeouts, only the captain of the team could go over to the sideline; he would talk to the coach and then relay the message to the players. Not since Cardona did Herrera have a team captain who was as talented and as much of a take-charge guy as Escobedo. This meant that when the team captain relayed the message, no one had to look at the top player to see if he affirmed the play. The Lanier teams were disciplined, and they did what their coach told them, but having someone like Escobedo relay the message made it easier to have confidence in the instructions.

For his part, Escobedo was used to calling the plays. He had been the starting quarterback for the Voks for two years. While normally quiet, he knew when to crack jokes and play around with his teammates to put them at ease. One way he did this was to sing. According to David Rodríguez, Escobedo had a good voice and loved to imitate Billy Eckstine, who at the time was a big-time entertainer with the Count Basie Band.[30] Escobedo thought of himself as a good singer, as shown by his senior "Last Will and Testament" in which he wrote that he wanted to "will my singing voice, which gave Sinatra so much competition," to a buddy of his on the football team.[31] His demeanor, then, of a quiet, strong leader who could joke and play around with his teammates yet called them to be serious and disciplined, to carry out their assignments, to look for the open shot, and to handle a pass that could—in Rivera's words—take your head off gave him the gravitas to be the undisputed leader of the team.

Almost immediately, Herrera's boys sent the signal that the rest of the city had better be ready for an even better Vok team. Before their first game in the South San tournament, which opened the city schools' basketball season, most sports pundits believed the Voks would be the team to beat. One sportswriter described them as a "threat to the state crown again this year."[32] The newspaper acknowledged that only Escobedo and David Rodríguez returned as starters, but it expected Joe Bernal and Frank Rodríguez, both substitutes in 1943 to "shine this season," while Kino Rodríguez, the star of the Class B team champions, would "give a good account of himself."[33] The team did not disappoint in the three-day tournament, taking the first game 43–9 over Edison and following that with a 38–6 whipping of the tournament hosts. The Voks then capped their run with a 21–12 victory over Central Catholic. No individual scores are available for the first game, but in the semi-final game, David scored twelve points and Escobedo seven, while in the champion game, Escobedo scored ten points to lead the team and be named the outstanding player in the tournament.[34] It is, however, unclear whether Escobedo received a trophy or was simply cited as the best player in the first tournament of the year.

The tournament final was the last game for Lanier in 1943, and play would not resume until January 4, when the Voks met the Burbank Bulldogs in the first game of the District 28-A race, where the Voks were undefeated since the league's inception. Playing possibly their best-ever game as a basketball squad, the Voks blasted the Bulldogs out of the Brackenridge gym by a score of 50–2. Early in the game, Jerry Mangum of Burbank hit two free throws, and that ended the scoring for his team. The Lanier team's defense continued to dominate as it kept its opponent under ten points for the third time in four games. David scored sixteen points, and Escobedo dropped in thirteen while "playing a nice floor game."[35] Two days later, the Voks again stymied any kind of offense and held the Hot Wells Blue Devil quintet to eight points while scoring thirty-six, with David leading the way with eleven points and Kino Rodríguez adding ten. Escobedo "played his usual bang-up floor game."[36] The Voks followed that up with victories over South San (35–15) and Edison (41–13), where Escobedo again got rave reviews for his floor game and his "feed" of David Rodríguez (eleven points) and Raul Gonzalez (twelve points), the latter a shooting guard/forward who proved to be the second best scorer in the team by the end of the season.[37]

The most significant blemish on the Voks' record the previous year had been their inability to win the city series championship against the Jefferson Mustangs. Their matchup early in 1944 was billed as "the hottest of the season for high school courts." It pitted the Voks' "fast-breaking" offense and their "tight" man-to-man defense against the height and sharpshooting of the Jefferson five. The key man in the contest, everybody agreed, was Escobedo, whom one paper called "the fanciest ball handler" in the city.[38] "It has been his sharp passing to his mates that has played a large part in the Voks scoring sprees to date," said one sportswriter. The Mustangs had to slow down the game, dominate the boards, and shoot effectively, or they would have their "ears pinned back" by the speedy Voks. For Lanier, they had to make their shots count, or they would get dominated on the boards on both sides of the court.[39]

The game, however, did not turn out as expected, or at least was not as close as some thought it would be. While Jefferson's height and "snappy passing" kept them even in first the quarter as they tied Lanier 8–8, Lanier's tight defense became tighter as the game went along. It became so tight that for one seventeen-minute stretch the Mustangs were unable to score a point. Billy Hovel, the scoring ace for Jefferson, found himself "blanketed" by Escobedo and could score only in the waning minutes of the game when it did not matter much anymore. While disposing of Hovel, Escobedo soon found the range and the space for his quick passes inside. David Rodríguez might not have been the tallest player on the court, but he proved to be the most mobile and the best scorer as he took crisp passes from Escobedo and put them in from beneath against the much taller but slower Mustang big men. When the Mustangs double-teamed David or managed to push him off the blocks, Kino Rodríguez slipped in to the middle and quickly put Escobedo's passes into the basket.[40] The Voks took a 16–9 lead at halftime and went on to win,

30–18, to solidify their place as the top team in the city. Escobedo managed only four points but was singled out as the "sparkplug" of the team and the outstanding "floor man" of the game.[41]

Lanier followed up the Jefferson game with a relatively comfortable victory over the Harlandale Indians, who were the tallest team in the district and also the speediest—next to the Voks. David, who had been averaging twelve points a game, failed to score, but Escobedo and Raul Gonzalez picked up the slack with Kino right behind them. The Voks won, 38–22.[42] This was the highest total they had allowed an opponent in the season and the first time a non-Lanier player led in scoring (the Indian's Tobin Role with thirteen). That glitch in a near-perfect season was soon forgotten as the Voks trounced Burbank 42–10 with Escobedo putting up the highest total of his career with seventeen points. David added eight as he fought to get out of a scoring slump that had kept him averaging four points in his previous two games.[43] He scored only seven in the next game, as Lanier beat the Hot Wells Blue Devils, 40–5. For that game, Escobedo again led the team with twelve points, while Kino Rodríguez and Raul Gonzalez added eight each.[44] But three bad games would be David's limit; he came back against the South San Bobcats and dominated the boards and inside play and scored a game-high thirteen points, while teammates Kino and Raul added ten and eleven respectively.[45] The victory over the Bobcats clinched the district title for the Voks and gave them thirty straight wins since the district was first formed in 1942.[46]

The Voks followed their clinch of the district title with a 38–21 defeat of the Edison Bears. Raul Gonzalez led the scoring with twelve points and reaffirmed that he was the next go-to guy after David Rodríguez.[47] One newspaper account described Gonzalez as "the rugged forward who has spelled a large part of the difference for the Voks this season."[48] The amazing thing about Gonzalez was that he had been the top man off the bench as a ninth grader (which was then known as the sophomore year), and now he was outscoring almost everyone, including Escobedo, and doing it when David had an off night. He soon became a prime target for Escobedo's passes. According to one clipping, he had quit football so he "could practice and be in better shape for basketball."[49] David remembers Gonzalez as a "quiet guy" whose nickname was "Repollo," or cabbage, because of his curly hair. At about five-foot-ten, he was a good rebounder and a strong presence inside, thus the reference to being a "rugged forward."[50] Following in his brother's footsteps, Ramiro Gonzalez also played for both the Class B team and periodically for the varsity team. In fact, Raul is not pictured with the '43 team, but he does appear as a member of the Class B team that won the city title.

But the easy victories came to an end, at least for one game, when the Voks faced their old nemesis, the Brackenridge Eagles, at the Jefferson High

School gym. No matter the year, no matter their record, the Eagles were the one team that always gave Lanier all it could handle and had been the team to beat them in the past. None of the players could explain it other than to say that "Brack" had good teams, though David remembers the Eagles as playing harder than normal when they faced the Voks. The Brackenridge boys were from the less-affluent side of town, and they seemed to dislike losing to Mexicans particularly keenly. David remembers that it was rarely a problem for Lanier boys to run into players from Jefferson or the private schools that catered to the more elite youth of the city. But it was a no-brainer to stay away from areas where Brackenridge students congregated. The "poor whites," said David, "were more difficult" to get along with.[51] They were just as difficult on the court, where they pushed, talked trash, and exerted themselves to keep up with the speedier Voks. Even when their best player was out, as was the case on February 7, or when they did not have as good a squad, the Eagles played the Voks tight.

On that night, the Eagles were coming off a 43–36 thriller loss to the Austin Maroons, who were one of the top Class AA teams in the state and had dominated all the San Antonio squads. The Eagles had stayed close in the Maroons game because of their "long-range firing," and they hoped to keep firing away at the Voks. Beating them and then following up with a win over Jefferson, second in the City Series race, would make up for what many of their fans saw as a disappointing season.[52] The only meeting between the teams that season ended in a classic two-point match with Lanier holding onto a 19–17 victory. This time, Escobedo led the team with six points and a "heady direction of offensive play," and the Voks were happy to escape with their unblemished record intact.[53]

With this victory, the Voks proved that they were the masters of everyone that played basketball in the city of San Antonio, having beaten teams from the City Series, the Alamo League, and District 28-A. They would have only one other difficult game, and that was with district foe Harlandale High School, which was taller than the Voks and speedier than most of their opponents. The Harlandale Indians, fighting mostly for pride, even led the Voks at halftime, 11–6, but were unable to hold it. Escobedo led the Voks in this game with nine points, as they took a close, 26–23, victory.[54] The closeness of the game did reveal a slight weakness in the undefeated team: they were susceptible to very tight defensive pressure. This was particularly obvious in the game against Brackenridge, when both David and Escobedo were held in check most of the game by a tenacious man-to-man defense from the Eagles. The Indians had also found a way to slow the game down. No doubt the Voks would have beaten either team nine out of ten times, but the Voks' style of play required them to be in rhythm for the whole game. Once disrupted, the

Voks found it difficult to respond. Herrera's style was hard to contain, but on more than one occasion, his teams had proven that they were not masters of the mid-court offense.

Copping the district crown early allowed the Voks to use the rest of their season games as a warm-up for the regional tournament. They defeated the Central Catholic Buttons twice in eight days, 32–16 and 37–14. Escobedo was "brilliant" in his floor game and led the scorers in the first game, while David "sparked" the team with fourteen points in the second.[55] Raul Gonzalez added eight. In that game, the Vok defense got back to mid-season form, allowing the Buttons only two points in the second half. With that victory, the Voks ended the season with a 18–0 record and set out to get their third regional title in a row. While the previous year, the tournament had been held in San Antonio, in 1944 the three other district champs voted to keep it out of the large city and make Lockhart the host city. The first game for the Voks was against the LaGrange Leopards.[56]

Rather than his usual eight-man traveling squad, Herrera took ten players to the Region VI tournament, with "newbies" Joe Gonzalez and Rudy Aguilar, neither of whom had gotten much playing time. The pair was likely starters in the Class B team, which had not won the title, as it had in 1943, but was still a quality team.[57] As the only unbeaten team, the Voks entered the regional tournament as the favorites. And like the proud young men that they were, they felt confident and possibly even cocky. After all, except for the games against Harlandale and Brackenridge, most of their games had been blowouts. And it was not until the last game of the season that any team scored more than twenty-five points on them. A speedy Texas Military Institute team scored thirty-three points against them, but the even speedier Voks had responded with forty-two.[58] This game had been a tournament warm-up where the players were allowed free rein to run and shoot.

The confidence of the team had risen as the season went along, and David remembers having had to be reminded that Lanier students were not supposed to be braggadocios. It occurred one morning after another lopsided victory over a hapless opponent. Just as David took his seat in Sarah Ware's social studies class, someone from the back of the room shouted out, "How you guys do last night?" David looked back and responded in a cocky tone, "You know that song, 'I Heard You Crying Last Night?' Well, they're singing it right now."[59] Miss Ware, a serious but pleasant-looking woman who more than one player called their favorite teacher, looked at David and, without raising her voice or trying to embarrass him, said, "David, you shouldn't do that. You are better than they are and everyone knows it. You don't have to advertise how good you are. Just show it."[60]

Nearly sixty-four years later, David remembered that admonition. A quiet man with an accomplished teaching and administrative career, he remembered that those words reflected the kind of attitude that Lanier students were meant to have in their dealings with the outside world. Those words were consistent with the life lessons that Coach Herrera taught them. The coach had no problem with his players being confident, but he did not tolerate a braggart attitude, and even less so against an opponent who came to play hard and got motivation from being disrespected. Only two years before, the Voks had been considered the favorites going into the state tournament only to be upset by a team no one believed deserved to be on the same court with them. Yet it was difficult not to be confident. The Voks were undefeated for the season, had not lost in district play in three years, and were averaging thirty-five points a game while allowing only fifteen. They had the best point guard in the state, one of the best big men in the high school basketball scene, and surely, in their estimation, the best coach in the state. They were also the defending state champs.

No doubt that while the Voks got off their traveling truck quietly, did not engage in trash talk, and were often subdued after a victory, they exuded confidence. There was no fear in their eyes at the beginning of a game, and there was no condescension, as might have been demonstrated by players who had earned a victory that they were not so certain at the beginning would be theirs. The fact that they did not overcelebrate or play in-your-face basketball may have been just as difficult for opposing players and fans to take. Being beaten by an all-Mexican team was bad enough; having them do so graciously added salt to the wound. After all, being gracious winners was more the role of the white, Christian young men who played the game for their schools and their communities. Sports for them were supposed to show their adherence to moral values and virtues and distinguish them from those who were different in color, culture, and religion. The brown, Catholic boys might win a game or two or, in the case of Lanier, even win championships, but they were not to be examples of the best of American youth. That they acted confidently and even graciously in winning only stirred the emotions for some white players and fans.

These sometimes raw emotions, however, did little to mitigate the talent and team cohesion that the Voks brought onto the court. The LaGrange Leopards slowed the Lanier quintet a bit and kept them from hitting their full range. They keyed on David and Escobedo, holding them to eight and four points respectively, but they could not find an answer for the Vok defense, which held them to eighteen points. What the Leopards also did not expect was for someone else to take up the slack from the two players they had been told were some of the best in the state. Raul Gonzalez again stepped up and hit four shots and one free throw to lead all scorers with nine points.

The Voks scored twenty-nine to easily win by eleven.[61] The Lampasas Badgers probably thought Raul's play was a fluke because they also concentrated on David and Escobedo, holding the latter to only two points and making sure that the tallest Vok worked hard for his seven points. Raul again found the ball in his hands from accurate passes and rebounds, and he muscled his way to the basket and scored a game-high eleven points to lead Lanier to a 32–24 win and the Region VI title.[62]

Raul would be remembered as the hero of the regional tournament, though the immediate newspaper coverage called Escobedo the "spark" to "both tourney victories." But David and Rivera remembered that it had been one of the Gonzalez boys who had been the hero, though David thought it was Ramiro, Raul's brother, and Rivera remembered it being one of the players off the bench.[63] Interestingly, Raul was not well remembered by his team. Walter Kelley did not remember much about him from the 1943 team, though Raul had some good games for them and was one of only two players brought up from the Class B team to play varsity that year (the other being Kino Rodríguez).[64] David, when asked about Raul specifically, remembered him as a "very quiet guy" and a "steady ball player" whose strength was rebounding.[65] David also remembered Raul's brother Ramiro as a gang leader but someone who never brought "it" to school. Their father was a police detective nicknamed "Güero Polvos," or "light-skin powder," perhaps referring to gunpowder. Ramiro was killed at La Villita, a popular dance spot, by someone described as being "deadly scared" of Ramiro.[66]

One sportswriter discussing Lanier's entry into the state tournament was a bit more conscious of Raul's contributions. He pointed out that the state championship team of the previous year had not had anyone like Raul, battling under the boards and helping out David against the bigger inside men of opposing teams. It was obvious that the writer had not paid much attention to the Lanier run at the title, or he would have known that Raul was there, coming off the bench, scoring points, and helping with the rebounds. Still, he described Raul as an "expert basket-maker and a rugged type fitted for the give and take near the goal."[67] Raul's play in the regional tournament had pushed him into the limelight along with David and Escobedo, but his quiet demeanor and the fact that he was surrounded by a current all-state guard and three future all-state players kept him from ever becoming part of the basketball folklore of Lanier except among diehards who knew every player's name and stats.

The same writer also singled out the "speedy little San Antonio club" as having the most impressive record. "Many observers," he wrote, "rate the 1944 Lanier team a better all-around club than the one that won the state title a year ago." He described every one of the starters as an "expert goaler." Escobedo was a "vastly improved leader and point maker," while David was more valuable than the previous year because of his scoring and his improved defensive skills. "Keno" was a "ball thief" and a "good hand at fast work under the basket," and Frank Rodríguez was a defensive standout who knew how to run the floor. Those four, along with Raul, rounded out the starters. The subs expected to provide valuable service were Joe Bernal and Joe Contreras—David's old childhood friend—who were the first to come off the bench, and Rudy Aguilar, Joe Gonzalez, and Ramiro Gonzales, who were there if Herrera had to reach deeper into the bench. The writer quoted the coach as characterizing Ramiro Gonzales as a "comer."[68]

While the Voks were seen as the favorites, given their record, scoring average, defensive stats, and the fact they were the defending champs, everybody knew their first game might be their toughest. The El Campo Ricebirds also sported an undefeated record at 18–0, fielded much taller players, and scored at a clip of thirty-nine points per game.[69] To prepare for the Ricebirds, Herrera had his team go through offensive drills at the larger St. Mary's University gym. He knew that his team had to adapt, as they had the previous year, to a much larger gym. Defensively, it was much harder to keep an intense man-to-man defense in a gym larger than the one they had at Lanier. Offensively, they had to learn to use the larger spaces so that they could find crevices in the zone defenses or screen and run past their man when the Ricebirds chose to become more aggressive. For three days, the Voks ran through intense drills to match anything that Coach Hoot Masur of El Campo could throw at them. On Thursday, the Voks boarded private cars and rode the one-hour trip to Austin for their 8:30 P.M. game.

The expectations that El Campo could hang with the defending champs lasted only a half, as the Ricebirds made it a game by using their height and slowing the game down enough to trail by only three at halftime, 16–13. Unfortunately for the Ricebirds, the Voks hit their stride in the second half and upped the tempo, forcing the Ricebirds to run up and down the court until their legs and lungs gave out on them. With Escobedo shooting, driving, and finding the open man with his passes, the Voks scored twenty-two points in the second half and then let their tenacious man-to-man defense smother the tired bigger players, holding them to four field goals for the rest of the game. "In addition to his long-range sniping," wrote one sportswriter, "Escobedo fed his teammates with his usual efficiency."[70] Without doubt this was Escobedo's finest hour of the season, and he chose to employ it against the most impressive—record-wise—team they faced. For those who saw him run the court, make crevice-finding passes, and take the ball to the basket when no one was open, no doubt existed as to who was the best player in the state.

In a picture with a caption that read "This'll Be Important," Escobedo was revealed to those who did not know him. He is pictured with the ball between his legs in the form of the old free throw style, his eyes focused on the basket with a seriousness that his teammates knew well. But the Voks were not the only ones that knew what Escobedo was capable of doing. Their next opponent, Mount Vernon, was well aware of how his passes to Rivera, and David had been critical in the thumping they had gotten at the hands of Lanier the year before. Their 47–25 loss was even worse than the score indicated. Lanier had led 14–2 after the first quarter, 26–8 at halftime, and 33–16 at the end of the third quarter. As if to add insult to injury, the Voks added fourteen more to end the game with a twenty-two-point victory. It had been a humiliating defeat that stung even one year later, and most sportswriters and basketball fans expected a similar outcome again for a Mount Vernon team that was actually quite small and had lost to a Class B team twice during the season.

This year, however, brought a different Mount Vernon basketball team. The first difference was the coach. A late hire to straighten out the football team, Milburn "Catfish" Smith was someone who knew basketball and was capable of getting things out of his players that they never knew they had. Catfish Smith had actually been a successful coach before World War II, taking his Carey Plowboys to the state semifinals in 1936 and winning the state title the following year when his team went 50–2.[71] He came to Mount Vernon with a 298–42 career coaching record. The one thing he knew better than how to coach basketball was how to inspire young men to play above their heads, a must for a coach who had spent his career in small, rural schools with few tall players. That ability had come in handy in the first game of the state tournament when his team had come from behind against a much taller and much heralded Throckmorton squad to win 30–28 in double overtime.[72]

In a 2004 novel based on his life, Catfish Smith brings his boys together the day after their win over Throckmorton to talk to them about their next opponent, the defending state champs, Sidney Lanier. He tells them, "They beat Mount Vernon last year, and they think this time will be even easier. But, we've got a surprise for them. We're gonna whip the defending state champs this afternoon, and I'll tell you how we are going to do it." He then proceeds to tell them to play tenacious man-to-man defense, not only on the man with the ball, but on every player on the court. "Press them every minute . . . and they'll make mistakes," he tells them. Then he turns to his smallest but quickest player, Charles Hogan, and says, "You're gonna guard Escobedo. They say he's the best offensive guard in the state. Well, when you shut him down, then I think that'll make you the best defensive guard in the state."[73]

To have a chance to win, the Mount Vernon Tigers had to keep the contest close and make it a defensive struggle, or they knew they would be run off the court by the better-shooting and faster Voks. They managed to cut the court into smaller chunks, as each Tiger kept his man in front of him, and they ran through screens and switched off as needed to keep the pace slower while just as intense. By intermission, the score was only 6–6, but more important, the Voks' third-best player and the hero of the regional and bi-district meets, Raul Gonzalez, had fouled out. No information exists on how the Tigers got him in foul trouble, but it probably had to do with the frustration of being covered by a defensive blanket he had not seen during the season. In the second half, Mount Vernon took the lead, 13–11, going into the final period. Joe Bernal, who made it eleven points for the Voks, followed it up with another shot to tie the score with seven minutes left. But the Tigers came back, and their "brilliant guard," Lollie Loyd, hit a shot. Then teammate J. C. Cannaday followed that up with another basket to give their team a four-point lead with less than five minutes to play.[74]

David, who had been held in check for the whole game with three points, then hit a free throw, and Kino followed it up with another free throw. Then David shook off his defenders and hit a "crisp shot" to tie the game at seventeen all. With twenty seconds left, Cannaday slipped past his man, got a pass, and dribbled to one side of the basket quick enough to set up, let go of the ball, and swished it in with ten seconds to go.[75] The newspaper account ends there, but Joe Bernal, whose goals had brought the Voks back into contention, remembers it well. Escobedo, who had been limited to three free throws by a tenacious man-to-man effort by tiny Hogan, took the ball from one end of the court and raced past everyone, zigzagging as he went—"a one-man show," remembers Bernal—thinking he would score and tie the game. He threw the ball up, said Bernal sixty-seven years later, it went around the rim, and "Henry blows the layup" as the time expires. "Henry was very confident of his abilities," added Bernal as he sat in his home office with his mind back in 1944. "He was a sharp guy. Academically he was also good. He knew he had more ability than the rest of us . . . [and] he didn't care if you liked him."[76] Bernal's voice betrayed no bitterness, just a wistful tone of what-if.

David believed that the Voks didn't take the game seriously. They were confident, especially with the big win over El Campo, and just did not play their game. Bernal doesn't remember anything different about the game. Nobody is alive that heard anything about it from Henry Escobedo, so David and Bernal are the only ones with memories, though they are now mostly faded. But it seems everyone remembers that Coach Herrera was crushed. Raul Zuniga, a sports aficionado and ex-player from the 1950s knows the story: Nemo was so mad that he didn't let the yearbook or anyone take a team picture.[77] "He was so disappointed," recalled Bernal, who for years wanted to ask the coach, "Why were you so pissed off that you didn't want a picture of us?" His "ego was deflated" or he simply "had . . . higher hopes that we had," added Bernal in defense of the man he admired.[78] Kelley remembers how happy the coach had been the previous year; more than the players, he adds. Just as he had greater emotional commitment to winning, he had greater emotional disappointment when it came to losing.

The Voks did not have much time to mourn, as the following day they met Dimmitt to compete for third place. David remembers no letdown, and neither does Bernal, but the Dimmit squad, which had been shellacked by twenty points by the Nacona Indians, 43–23, made a close game against the Voks, who barely won 23–20 over a team few expected to win. This time, Escobedo played a fine game, scoring fourteen points, but was unable to get much production from his big men. David scored only four points and Raul one.[79] It was a good enough performance to get Escobedo back into the all-state team, along with two players from Mount Vernon and one from Dimmitt. The last spot went to Milas Downey, Nacona's high-scoring guard who led his team to an overtime 33–32 victory over the Mount Vernon Tigers.[80] Escobedo being named to the all-state team was no doubt bittersweet for him. As a back-to-back all-stater, he had done what only one other Lanier player had ever done. He had done it by his court play and his leadership. Yes, he had scored well against El Campo, but he had not been a factor in the big games, including the last championship game. His inability to put the team on his shoulders and will them to win certainly contrasted with his confidence, his absolute leadership of the team, and his great court management.

Perhaps this is one reason Escobedo rarely attended the reunions or even the celebrations that would come later. Others would travel hundreds of miles to return, while still others in the area were constant visitors to Lanier and often gathered with old-timers to talk about the old days. But Henry Escobedo rarely did. Maybe a championship while he was the team leader would have made a difference.[81] Not one of his old teammates had a relationship with him, and those who gathered to talk about Lanier lamented their inability to get him out. This says nothing about Escobedo the man, but it does probably say much about how he himself remembered Player #8.

CHAPTER NINE

The Rodríguez Boys Must Be Stopped

THE TRIP TO AUSTIN RESULTED IN DEFEAT FOR THE VOKS, but some Lanierites enjoyed the trip in spite of the outcome. Herbert Kelley, junior class reporter and younger brother of Walter "Rough House" Kelley of the 1943 championship team, hopped on a bus along with two buddies and headed to Austin on the first day of the tournament. Few fans could travel the distance because of lack of money and dependable cars, so what Herbert did was rare for a student back then. David Rodríguez remembered few Lanier fans present when the Voks played out of town or on the far side of San Antonio. Those games were usually played among hostile crowds.[1] The state tournament in 1944 was no different, so Herbert and his friends actually made a sizeable contingent of Lanier fans. The only other fans they met in Austin were Principal Brewer, Vice Principal Tafolla, a teacher or two, a few San Antonio residents who could afford the trip, and possibly one or two risk takers like themselves. The players remember few cheers for them during the three tournament games they played.

Herbert would serve as the sports editor for *El Nopal* and the *Los Recuerdos* the following year, but in the spring of 1944, he was nowhere in the published record of either staff, though it is possible he was taking a journalism class at the time. He was, we know, in both the print and graphic arts clubs. Whatever his connection to the Lanier media, he went to Austin with the intent to write about his experiences. Written for a column—probably for *El Nopal*—titled "Sports Eye," his report was subtitled "Adventures of Three Lanier Students on Trip to Austin as Told by Herbert Kelley."[2] Written in a rather folksy way, the column was more about the travelers than about the team's performance at the tournament. With little money—a common complaint in the column—the travelers "rationed" themselves to twenty-five cents per meal and found the tournament tickets affordable at fifty cents each. At Gregory Gym, they saw four games before their Voks "took the court against El Campo . . . a bang-up game." But all Herbert wrote was ". . . and it was Lanier 34, El Campo 21."[3]

With little money, the three searched until they found a room for rent at a small hotel with a "pretty" lobby. To their surprise, "[we] entered a very small room with one iron bed and two wooden chairs. We began laughing. How stupid we were not to have asked to see the room before renting it! The six bits that each of us paid was far too much. Then we opened one window only to laugh even louder. Not even six inches from the open window was a brick wall!"[4] Having gotten "through the night all right," the three went to the Paramount Theater to watch a movie after breakfast and barely made it to the gym as the game was starting. Herbert records:

> The game was tough. With less than one minute left to play and the Voks behind two points, David Rodriguez sent a beauty through the net to knot up the score at 17 all. (Don't get excited.) Then in less than 30 seconds Mt. Vernon made a basket to defeat us 16–17 [actually 17–19] . . . we were disgusted. Didn't even stay to see the rest of the games. Just left the gym and went to the show again to forget our troubles.[5]

After the show, the fellows and one other young man they met either at the gym or the movies pitched in $1.25 each and got a room at the Capital Hotel, where "most of the boys from Lanier" were staying. This time Herbert and friends had a room with two beds and a window with a view. After settling in, they got a call from "some girls from Austin" and went dancing until midnight. Whether before the dance or after, they met some boys—possibly players—from Mount Vernon and found them to be "swell guys" and got "along very well" with them.

The next morning, Herbert and his friends got up at 11:30 a.m., ate breakfast, and then loafed around until 3:00 p.m., when they took off to the gym to see the Voks play at 4:30 p.m. for third place in the state. "We won that game 22 to 19," wrote Herbert, again giving the wrong score. After the game, the boys "were out of 'lettuce'" and so they went back to the hotel, where they met a friend from whom they borrowed two dollars and another friend who agreed to share his hotel room. The next morning, the young men walked around wondering how they were getting home, met two girls from the previous night's dance, and took them to the movies. After taking the girls home, they met some friends going to San Antonio and hopped a ride home. They "enjoyed the trip," discussing their adventures, likely the movies they saw and possibly even the games they attended.[6]

A few things might be gathered from dissecting Herbert and friends' trip to Austin. First, their story indicates that Lanier students were beginning to move beyond the West Side, even as far as the state capital, about ninety miles away. That they could find hotel rooms, including one where the teams stayed, indicated that segregation was a bit less rigid for high school students and team players. It helped that Lanier was now an almost permanent fixture at the state tournament and that Lanier students were always well—though modestly—dressed and knew how to behave in public. They spoke the language and knew to avoid unpleasant circumstances.

Kelley's trip is notable for its commonness, showing young men behaving much like their contemporaries in the larger society. They had gone to see a game but ended up spending as much time in the movie theaters and going out with girls as they did in the gym. They were not intimidated by the process of navigating a city that was probably new to them. They "got along very well" with the "boys from Mt. Vernon," indicating that they felt at ease talking about what boys talk about. Given what is written about Coach "Catfish" Smith, it is likely that his own boys were well behaved and not given to outbursts of racial prejudice. In fact, Coach Smith had taught racial tolerance by example, threatening to take his team out of the tournament unless an African American man who came with the Mount Vernon squad was allowed entry to the gym. When told the man could enter but would have no place to sit, the coach replied, "that won't be a problem, he'll sit on the bench right beside me."[7]

The experience of Herbert and his friends did not reflect the reality that confronted darker working-class youth who were not articulate in the English language, nor did it mean that all areas of the state capital's society were open to them. It simply underscores that there were crevices and gaps in which well-behaved, English-speaking young men with "smarts and wits" could navigate. The fact that they approached the situation with confidence but not cockiness meant that they could go to places where others could not. Much of what Lanier attempted to do was exactly that. It wanted to create Mexican American citizens who knew how to behave in public, could navigate the spaces available to them, and would be a credit to their race and their school. Said Principal Brewer in the introduction to the 1945 yearbook, "The greatest pleasure that comes to me from my work is that which comes from working with people who know how to and are willing to cooperate with others."[8]

Vice Principal Tafolla agreed with his boss and went even further in describing the kind of students Lanier was producing or at least hoped to produce. In the same issue of the yearbook, he praised the war effort of those students who had shown a willingness to "do their share or assume their responsibility." He added that Lanier placed special emphasis on teaching "spiritual and moral values" as well as academic and vocational skills. "We make a conscious effort to teach that such traits of character, as truthfulness, honesty, loyalty and fair dealing must be practiced," he wrote.[9] Other San Antonio schools could argue that they saw their mission in similar fashion, but the difference was that they saw their students as potential leaders of society. Their students would be the doctors, lawyers, architects, and business leaders of the community. Even those who came from the poorest ranks of white society were expected to receive apprenticeships and become skilled workers with their own businesses or in the highest-paid trades of plumbing, electrical work, and carpentry. None of those trades were taught at Lanier, and Mexican Americans were often excluded from apprenticeships in the unions and in the trade shops of the city where they might get the experience.

Lanier students were being trained to work in the factories, serve in the lower trades, and if lucky, form their own businesses. They would, however, cater to the working-class Mexicans of the West Side, who would undoubtedly pay less for their services. A perusal of the 109 seniors listed in the yearbook reveals that 23 wanted to be nurses; 26 wanted to be secretaries or stenographers; 17 wanted to be welders, auto body and fender workers, millworkers, or woodworkers; 10 wanted to be professionals such as doctors, engineers, lawyers, and pharmacists; and 14 provided no preference. The other 19 "life ambitions" were as diverse as dress designer, writer, photographer, coach or professional athlete, missionary/preacher, and simply "college girl."[10] While the number who wanted to be nurses—all of them women—or pursue another "professional" career might seem impressive for a group of Mexican American senior students, the reality was that few would ever acquire that type of profession. Saying "nurse" for most young women at Lanier was like saying "doctor" or "lawyer" for their Anglo male counterparts at other schools. Those were professions that everybody mentioned when they had yet to settle on a vocation. But nursing was a particularly female ambition given the way that nursing expanded during World War II. During the war, females were the only nurses allowed in the military, and nurses held officer commissions, giving women their only chance to command enlisted men in the armed forces.[11]

Herbert Kelley's dispatch from Austin also touches on the fact that there were well-integrated part-white students at Lanier. In the '44 class, seniors Crystal Quesenberry, Rosie Forrestello—National Honor Society vice president and senior class parliamentarian—and Lucille Ehrlich—student council parliamentarian and representative and senior class secretary—shared the distinction of being part-white/part-Mexican students with Charles Vandervort.[12] As Herbert enjoyed his four-day stay in Austin, back home Vandervort was tending to his duties as Hi-Y Club president, ROTC major, National Honor Society president, and *Los Recuerdos* assistant editor. As the editor in chief of *El Nopal*, Vandervort's was the final voice as to whether to include Herbert's piece. Vandervort had also been junior class president the year before. Joe Bernal, Raul Gonzalez's substitute in the Mount Vernon game, successful civil rights advocate and legislator, and one of the best-known Lanier alumni, would remember Vandervort as a giant and "one of my heroes."[13]

Based on European names and the light complexions seen in the yearbook, Vandervort was in good company as a mixed-ethnicity student at Lanier.[14] The year before, he had Lucille Ehrlich as his secretary and Henry Hue as his sergeant-at-arms in the junior class presidency, while Younger Mapes handled the sports coverage for the yearbook.[15] Another well-integrated student was Lovie Baker, whose nickname was "Güera" or "Blondie" and who was treasurer of the library club, vice president of her homeroom, a member of the Royal Blues, and senior editor of *Los Recuerdos*. She was, however, more likely to be Anglo than of mixed parentage. Elvira Dennis was also a member of the Royal Blues, president of her home room, and a captain in the Junior WAC organization.[16]

In the yearbook's "Last Will and Testament" of the '44 senior class, all the part-white and/or white students seem to have ample social connections with other Lanier students. Lucille Ehrlich willed her "'El Nopal' typing" to Esperanza Moreno, Rosie Forrestello left her "beautiful blue eyes" to Herbert Kelley, Crystal Quesenberry willed her "shyness" to Jesusita Villareal, and Charles Vandervort left his "curls and . . . little black book to John Rodríguez."[17] And following these seniors were juniors Ralph Blakely and Peter Marshall and sophomores Evangeline Hedgebrook, Margaret McCollough, Tony Ramsey, and Johnny Webb. Interestingly, there was also an Asian student named Kin Guan.[18] Some like Vandervort, Baker, Webb, and Forrestello were unmistakably white in appearance, while others were indistinguishable from their fellow classmates except for their names.[19] The latter would not experience high school any differently than their classmates or receive any kind of preferential treatment from their teachers.

From the positions they held in school organizations and from students' recollections, it is clear that these students were treated like any others. Walter Kelley felt comfortable at Lanier and does not remember being singled out for any kind of differential treatment, even though David Rodríguez recalls him as being "pretty white." David remembers most of these "halfers," as he fondly called them, as being just like all the other students at Lanier.[20] A bit incredulous of these tales of seamless integration, I tried to remember my own senior class at Lanier but could not remember any white students except for one young man who sold newspapers on the street corners. He was dirt-poor and seemed a bit slow, but I could not find him in the yearbook. A perusal of the senior, junior, and sophomore class pictures revealed five possibly part-white students in the senior class, five juniors, and four sophomores. I then recalled that one was in my vocational art class, and while we were not close friends, we spoke quite often in class. I realized that, like Lanierites of the 1940s, some of us or maybe most of us too saw our classmates simply as Lanier students and did not equate them with the students at the "Anglo schools." There were, of course, other students who had mixed lineage but Spanish surnames, and they were indistinguishable.

The story of Herbert Kelley and his buddies is also the story of Lanier students living the home-front experience, with little money but a lot of desire to experience the world outside the West Side womb. Few students were as adventurous or daring as Kelley and his friends, so many of their experiences continued to be those that could be constructed on campus. If Lanier students had not been aware before, the war made it obvious that they lived within a larger world and one that demanded their participation. One of the things that truly changed for most young men in the West Side was that military service became a rite of passage whether through personal choice or conscription. Joining *el servicio* became a given for many young men during the war and for many others during peacetime—with the exception of those who went to college, were physically unable, or found a way to get a deferment. The cadet uniform became the default school wear of most boys at Lanier.

By 1945, most Americans knew the war would be won by the Allies, and so the concerns with war began to fade. The few references to the war in the yearbook became celebratory rather than somber, as in the early years. There was an optimism born of the victories overseas and the assumption that things would change even for the residents of the West Side of San Antonio. For the Lanier administration, the war had solidified the claim that vocational education was the way of the present and future for the young men and women from the surrounding barrios. While a few science courses had been offered during the war, especially aeronautics, the vocational curriculum had become well established. Lanier boys and some of the girls were going to be vocational workers, loyal, truthful, honest, fair, unselfish, sacrificing, cooperative, and trustworthy. There was simply nothing in the yearly *Los Recuerdos* message from either Brewer or Tafolla indicating that Lanier's students would be the leaders of tomorrow or the professionals needed to rebuild the nation after the Great Depression and the devastating world war.

Nevertheless, a few students had in mind that they were going to college after high school, and a few teachers were willing to prod students to look at educational options after Lanier. Herrera was one such teacher. He knew where most of these boys would end up if they did not think about some training after high school. He knew that for his boys playing basketball could be a way to go to college. In David Rodríguez's junior year, the coach suggested that he drop his shop class and take courses that would prepare him for the university. David responded by taking summer courses at Brackenridge High School in his junior and senior years in order to get the prerequisites out of the way. David was not one of those Mexican boys who were good with their hands, and his future looked bleak without further education. As early as the 1930s, Herrera had tried to get his boys into college. He got Tony Cardona to attend Trinity College in San Antonio, but Tony got himself in a "jam" and did not pursue his studies.[21] Jessie Camacho, however, did go to college, and so would Escobedo, Belton, and Joe Bernal. There were others who went on to get some kind of post–high school training, either in the service or through apprenticeships.

Beyond motivating his boys to go to college, Herrera spoke to them often of making something of themselves. He knew from his own experience that doing so would require great sacrifice. But his basketball players, especially the good ones, had a particular advantage, not only because they were learning discipline and hard work, but also because they were going out into the larger world and confronting racial hostility, unfair referees, and abusive fans. More important, they were learning how to deal with those challenges as winners. Herrera taught his players to confront obstacles stoically, to focus on the response rather than the difficulty, and to win. Winning was the best way to respond to hostile opponents and taunting fans. Herrera did not believe in wallowing in self-pity or in striking back with the same kind of abuse. The players saw this, and they tried to emulate him. Joe Bernal remembers Herrera as an inspiration because he was Mexican and short yet he was educated, disciplined, and a leader of men.[22] There weren't too many men in the barrio who could claim a college education, a winning record, and respect from Anglo players, teachers, coaches, and sportswriters.

Getting his kids into college, however, was not necessarily the first thought in Coach Nemo Herrera's mind when the time came to prepare for the upcoming '45 season. He was still smarting from the previous season's loss. Nothing made him moodier than losing, except losing to teams he knew his squad could beat. In his mind, his was the best team. He was convinced, as were his players even years later, that they could have won nine of ten games against the Mount Vernon Tigers or the Nacona Indians. Yet the dull pain in the pit of the stomach probably eased when he thought of the players coming back for the 1945 season. He had four starters back: David Rodríguez, Kino Rodríguez, Frank Rodríguez, and Raul Gonzalez. He also had Joe Contreras and Ramiro Gonzalez ready to fight for the last starting spot, as well as some new players from the Class B team that had made a run at the city championship.[23] David had now grown to his full height of six-foot-three, while Frank, Kino, and Raul were proving to be tough defenders, good rebounders, and solid scorers. All Nemo's team lacked was someone who could take command of the team as had Escobedo, who was by then in a tank infantry division in the Philippines.[24]

"The loss of Henry Escobedo from anybody's team leaves a gap that is hard to fill," Herrera told the local paper. Other than Rivera, Lanier had never had a two-time all-state player, and one like Escobedo who had gotten on the coveted all-state team by his handling of the team and running the floor as much as for his scoring. Confident, talented, and suave, Escobedo had been the kind of point guard any coach would have desired. He had been a take-charge guy who could get in someone's face when they were not playing as they should but who led by example and could loosen up his teammates with a joke or by imitating his favorite singers. Without him, the team would have to be led by committee until someone emerged to take the reins and make the Voks his team. That was the job of the point guard or at least one of the Rodríguez boys.

Among the candidates for taking over Escobedo's job as team captain was a handsome fellow with few hard features and so quiet that it was hard to "get a word out of him." In spite of his talents, Frank Rodríguez could not bark orders like Henry, run the floor like him, or take over a game at crucial minutes. At the time, he was seen more as "dependable" than as a very good player.[25] Kino Rodríguez, the other ball-handling forward, who had shown flashes of talent in scoring, had a baby face and looked like he was a freshman in high school, rather than one of the seniors on the team.[26] He was a good shooter, very fast and tough on the boards, but he hardly looked like a team leader. David was the logical choice, but like most of the returning players, he was a quiet young man, still quite skinny, with a less-than-commanding look.[27] No one doubted his talents and his abilities to take over a game, but his style was not as flashy as Rivera's or as hard charging as Escobedo's. There was David Flores, a star of the Class B team, and, of course, the quiet, muscular Raul Gonzalez. Raul was a fighter and sometimes a good scorer, but his personality did not lend itself to leadership. Years after the championship run, while all the interviewed players had good things to say when asked specifically about him, none ever volunteered him as one of the crucial players on either the 1944 or 1945 team.[28] Finally, there were Joe Contreras and Ramiro Gonzalez, but they had yet to prove they were ready to assume a starting spot.

Herrera had always found a good point guard and team leader who stepped up when the previous one left. After all, he was not only teaching basketball, he was also teaching young men how to be leaders, take advantage of all opportunities, and be fighters in life. Young men under his system had a way of stepping up and doing what they had been taught to do. Still, with most of the city teams gunning for the Voks and hoping to end their city and district winning streaks, he had reason for concern. Considering what good players he had coming back, it was surprising that none of the sportswriters saw the Voks as the clear favorites in the city. The press was not oblivious to Lanier's returning talent, but the Voks did lack an all-state player for the first time in three years. While David was considered as good a big man as there was in the city, his less-than-impressive state tournament play did not garner him much press at the start of the season, except to say that he "heads the list of six returning lettermen, four of whom started on last year's team which won third place in the state."[29]

Notwithstanding the tepid press, the Voks got off to a fast start in their first game when they crushed the Central Catholic Buttons 52–27 on December 14, 1944, in Lanier's noisy arena. David Rodríguez left no doubt that, with Escobedo gone, this was his team, and he was stepping up as the go-to player for the Voks. Having improved "100 per cent since last season," according to one writer, David hit "from every angle" on the floor to score twenty-six points to lead all scorers.[30] It was the highest point total for any Lanier player since Rivera's twenty-eight points in the state playoffs in 1943 and the highest season game total recorded for any Lanier player since the school established a varsity basketball program in 1928. Using fully his six-foot-three height and long arms, he shot over smaller players, jumped over taller ones, and left others flat-footed as he pivoted from left to right and vice versa to score with either hand.

While never as thick or muscular as his brother "Indio," by his senior year David had become a physical player who loved to use his elbows when opponents crowded him or push away hands that were grabbing at the ball. He bumped back against his opponents, and then quickly made a move, hooking his arm around the defender and racing past him toward the basket, where he usually hooked the ball in. His best shot was the hook, but he also banged it off the backboard. "That was what the small square above the rim was meant for," he would chuckle years later. He didn't have much trouble going around the taller but slower centers in the city and district leagues. "I went more to my left," he remembered, "because most people thought that as a right hander I would be moving right."[31] His ability to score made the Voks' offense even more dangerous. The offensive plays in Herrera's system always began with the ball going into the center then getting distributed around, or he would take it to the basket. As a presence inside, David was often the recipient of passes by the new starting guard, Joe Contreras, an old neighborhood playmate who loved to drive to the basket, attract defenders, and then dish off to his center or anyone open under the basket.[32]

When he wasn't scoring against the usual six-foot-seven or six-foot-eight centers in the city, David knew how to find his teammates when they positioned themselves for a shot. While the team had no real sharpshooters, it did have people who could score if the ball reached their hands. In the Central Catholic game, Kino and Frank, the other two-thirds of the Rodríguez threesome, combined for fifteen points from both inside and outside the paint, while Joe Contreras added seven with shots from the outside and through strong drives to the basket.[33] The easy victory over the tall Buttons sent a message to the rest of the city teams that even without Escobedo the Voks were going to be real good. The victory made them one of the favorites in the South San tournament that weekend. And victories in the South San Tournament had gotten them started on their run to the state playoffs the two previous years.

Not all sportswriters, however, were convinced of Lanier's skill, and some considered the Voks only co-favorites, along with the host South San Bobcats, who were predicted to give "some first rank opposition" to the defending tourney champs.[34] Another sportswriter saw "no favorite" in the tournament, though he conceded that the Voks were "generally recognized as stronger than last season" when they were undefeated until their championship game.[35] Whether the Voks read and resented the modest expectations is unknown, but they came out "smoking" and ran past the Center Point High School quintet, 49–11, to win their first-round game. The three Rodríguez players were again the top scorers, with David getting eighteen, Kino seven, and Frank nine points. The Bobcats of South San, however, were not to be left behind, as they also won their first game in a rout, 40–13, over Bandera High School.[36] The Bobcats would proceed to win their next two games to make the finals. They beat Edgewood High School of San Antonio 47–16 and Burbank 30–20.[37]

Coming into the finals with a tournament average of scoring 39 points a game and allowing only 16.1, the Bobcats were confident in their abilities, but in Lanier they faced a team that had averaged 47 points a game and were allowing only 15.3 per opponent. And Lanier was a team that had found balanced scoring as Contreras, Raul Gonzalez, and another Rodríguez, Ruben, had all found the range and limited David's need to score to ten and four points in the previous two tournament games.[38] Whatever thoughts the South San players had about winning their own tournament were dashed by halftime, when the Voks built a 23–7 lead and then added another twenty points in the second half while allowing the Bobcats to score only eight more. The 43–15 shellacking was led by Kino, who scored fourteen; David, who added ten; Frank, who chipped in eight; Gonzalez and Contreras, who added four apiece; and newcomer David Flores, who contributed three.[39]

Ten days after completely demolishing the Bobcats, the Voks faced the city's YMCA cagers. The YMCA was part of an adult league made up of many former high school and college players. Leading that team was someone that any hardcore Lanier basketball fan would readily remember. Joe Treviño, the man-among-boys player who had set the standard for Lanier centers, was ready to take on Lanier's newest sensation in the middle spot. David knew that most Lanier fans salivated at the thought of an epic match between the two tallest men to have donned a Vok uniform. David stood at a lean six-foot-three, and Joe was somewhere around six-foot-four and massive in build. It is unclear whether Joe was then an ex-Marine or would be one later, but pictures of the man while he played for the city leagues reveal a wide torso, massive legs, and long, powerful arms. Most fans still remembered him from the 1939 run to the state finals, in which he was the most valuable player, though because of Tony Cardona, not the best player on the team.

"People thought they could beat us," said David in a phone conversation years later. One reason was that the YMCA had a number of former Lanier players. While Joe Treviño manned the center position, there was also Joe Martínez of the 1939 team and Billy Saldaña of the 1940 team. And during a period of time, even Tony Cardona played for the YMCA, as well as another former Lanier player, Melesio Benavides. David remembers Martínez and Benavides and even possibly Saldaña playing in the YMCA-Lanier game, though the box scores do not list them. But notwithstanding the ex-Lanier legends' presence on the team, David remembers the Voks feeling confident against the city leaguers. They were used to beating local army and air force teams and even the St. Mary's University quintet. "We were already exposed to playing older guys," said David.[40] Admittedly though, the younger Voks cherished the thought of taking on some of the past legends of Lanier. No doubt many Lanier fans also found the matchup intriguing.

Tony Rivera recalled playing former Lanier players who periodically came back to Lanier to visit. It was fun, he remembered, to match up against the best and to learn from them. Beating them was an extra bonus. No doubt the ex-players enjoyed the competition as well, if only to remind the fans and to show the newcomers that the Lanier legacy was built on talented players, many of whom were still showing off their skills in the city leagues. That competitiveness from the older players showed at the beginning of the game between the YMCA and the Voks. Almost from the start, David felt the strong push from past legend Joe Treviño, who outweighed him by more than twenty pounds. But the skinny Lanier center pushed back and used his elbows to show the old fellow that he was not about to be moved. The immediate pushback worked, and Treviño backed off. To David's surprise, Treviño did not try to "go through me" toward the basket but settled for moving away and shooting from the outside.[41] While big and muscular, the big ex-Lanierite was not necessarily a very physical player. He had strength going to the basket and gathering rebounds and putting them back in, but he was not one to usually clear out opponents with his massive body. He sought instead to play finesse around the basket.

The big YMCA center managed to score thirteen points to lead his team, but David responded with eighteen. The two other Rodríguezes combined for seventeen more, and Joe Contreras added seven to lead the Lanier Voks to a 51–39 victory. "We wanted to beat them as a team," recalled David, and they did so like a typical Herrera team. They ran and ran and played tenacious man-to-man defense, and by "halfway" the older cagers were breathing hard and losing a step or two to the younger Voks. These older fellows played a lot, but their jobs and familial obligations did not allow them the time to practice as often as they did when they were in high school. More important, the lessons they had learned from Herrera years ago were trumped by those the youngsters were getting from their coach daily. It is likely that "Viejo," "Chato," "Nemo,"—or whichever name his present and former players called him—Herrera enjoyed the contest as much as anyone. Here were his boys giving the fans a good game and accounting themselves well in the sport he loved. That some of them were now stable working men with families must have reaffirmed in his mind that he was doing a good job with the young men of the West Side of town, at least those whose attention he could command in the teams and in his physical education classes.[42]

It was a satisfying victory for the Voks and put to rest the question of how well this team stacked up against its former legends. It might have dawned on some of the Voks that the YMCA team was their future home. Few of them would go to college, and most would stay in town. The city leagues offered a chance to continue to play, win trophies, and keep their name in the city newspapers as those covered the city leagues as often—if not as fully—as they did the high school and college teams. David himself would one day play a few games with the YMCA while on leave from the army—and lead them to a tournament title and garner the most valuable player trophy. He also played with some other ex-Lanier players when he played with the Tomcats Café team after the service.[43] Joe Treviño might have lost this game, but he would tuck many a win under his belt until he retired to concentrate on his career as a sheriff and a firefighter. His wife remembers a "championship" when one of his teams went to Mexico and played in a major tournament.[44]

Many of the ex-players might not have made it to college, but they continued to woo their fans in the city leagues. Their travels to Mexico underscored how fluid the movement of Mexicans and Mexican Americans to and from Mexico was. What the players were doing as a team, individuals and families were doing for personal reasons. Many had relatives in Mexico or went there to get items they could not get in the United States. It is interesting to hear how the players were treated in the former homeland of many of their parents. At times they were hailed as true Mexicans, and at other times they were *pochos* (Anglicized Mexicans) who played the American game well. Jesse Camacho remembers the games in Mexico as being physical, as the Mexican players sought to beat their countrymen from up north. Some of the Lanier players ended up coaching in Mexico for short periods of time. Raul Zuniga, a player who came shortly after the Herrera era, coached in Mexico and knew of a number of ex-Lanierites, both baseball and basketball players, playing for Mexican teams.[45]

After the satisfying victory, the Voks had an opportunity to play in the still-new Municipal Auditorium as part of a doubleheader that matched the Camp Normoyle military team against the Texas A&M University Aggies. At the time, military quintets were a crowd favorite, and most military bases and area army depots sponsored teams that played against other military installations as well as college and city league teams. The auditorium had found "great interest" among the San Antonio populace when it promoted several boxing matches and sought to maintain a fan base by bringing military units to play during the cage season. The quintet from Camp Normoyle, a local depot, was popular in the city, and so were the Aggie Cadets. As the opening card, the promoters invited Sidney Lanier and Fox Tech to play. The fact that these two schools were chosen and that many of the attractions to the Municipal Auditorium were fight cards, it is likely that many of those who came to the city's premier auditorium were Mexican Americans, along with some soldiers and working-class whites.[46]

By this time, Fox Tech had started to become *the* rival for Lanier, if not in the athletic arena at least for the fact that it was beginning to attract a sizeable Mexican American student population. There is no available breakdown of Tech's student population, but the school's locality and its focus on vocational courses indicates that it served a chunk of the city's Mexican population. The school's boundaries encompassed much of the city center's West Side as well as most of the downtown area. While the numbers may have still been small compared to Lanier's, enough Mexican Americans attended Fox Tech to have five and possibly six Mexican American boys on the basketball team. Interestingly, one of them, Cesar Bernal, was related to Ramiro Bernal at Lanier.[47] This would not be the only case of family members divided among the schools. By the time I arrived at Lanier, Fox Tech was well established as the school we were all supposed to hate, mostly because they hated us. Our annual Chili Bowl—sportswriters' name for the Tech-Lanier football game—would in my high school years attract as many as twenty thousand fans to Alamo Stadium. Besides trying to tear each other apart on the football field, there were also fights among the Tech and Lanier students in the stands, parking lot, and even in downtown streets.

The rivalry would be part of the barrio tribalism that arose by the late 1940s with *pachucos* and gangs that roamed the west and central parts of the city. Eventually, beating each other became more important than beating the predominantly white schools on the North Side and South Side. "Beat Lanier" and "Beat Tech" became the battle cry for each school's fans when their team's fortunes in football declined dramatically. To measure ourselves against each other only underscored that by the 1960s neither Lanier nor Tech nor the other West Side high schools like Edgewood, Kennedy, and Memorial could compete in sports or much of anything else against their white counterparts. This caused the school fans to turn their focus and rivalry toward teams they felt they could beat, and so a circular firing squad commenced that sometimes got violent. I remember vividly once on the bus returning home to the West Side after the game and witnessing groups of Fox Tech supporters chasing someone with sticks, probably some unlucky Lanier fan who got off the bus to go downtown to celebrate or drown his sorrows.

The tenacity with which the teams went after each other helped put twelve hundred fans in the seats in the Municipal Auditorium to witness some fine individual basketball playing, though neither game proved to be close. The Camp Normoyle team improved its record to eight wins against one loss as they beat the hapless Aggies, 57–43, behind local favorite "Bo" Johnson's fourteen points. The Aggies showed heavy legs from the night before, when they had been drubbed 72–30 by the San Antonio Aviation Cadet Center. The Voks did not score as much as the Normoyle soldiers, but Kino matched Bo Johnson's night total with fourteen points to lead Lanier to a 46–34 win over the Buffaloes, who had been selected as possibly the top Class AA team in the city.[48] Joe Contreras added twelve, while Raul Gonzalez chipped in seven.[49] It was a balanced attack made necessary by Buddy Garza's "tight guarding" of David, whom he held to nine points.[50]

If district opponents had gotten any ideas from David's middling performance against Fox Tech, they quickly got a rude awakening when the tall center dominated the Hot Wells Blue Devils with numerous follow-up goals and short jump shots to lead Lanier to a 49–12 victory on their home court. Hot Wells simply had no answer for David, and when they double-teamed him, he simply flipped the ball to Frank, who added eleven points. While these two were scoring two-thirds of their team's points, their fellow Voks were shutting down the Blue Devils, holding them to five points in the first half and seven in the second.[51] The Voks followed their victory with another home win, this time by a slim margin against the South San Bobcats. The

Voks had to hold on to a two-point lead in the last forty seconds to record their second district win. In an uncharacteristic fashion, David lost the battle of the backboards. Ed Mattson, South San's center, was a "roaring demon" who limited the Lanier players to one shot at a time. David scored nine points, but all of those came in the first half. Lanier's narrow victory gave hope to all the district teams that the Voks were beatable.[52]

Again district and city opponents' hopes were raised only to be deflated when the Jefferson Mustangs stepped into the Lanier gym with a tall if greener team. The Mustangs were also the defending City Series champions, as Lanier had not played in the series the previous year. The game turned out to be much more exciting than any the Voks had played so far. The lead changed seven times and was tied three times as both teams sought to take the top spot of the City Series race. Throughout the game, neither team could open up more than a four-point lead. The Voks held a one-point lead after the first half, and by the start of the fourth quarter had been unable to increase it. But in the last three-and-a-half minutes of the fourth quarter, they made a furious final push and outscored the Mustangs 11–6 to win going away, 33–27.[53] Neither team shot well, but the Voks were able to make one goal and four more free throws than the Mustangs. David scored twelve points, six of them in the fourth quarter, to lead all scorers. More important, he kept the Jefferson big men from dominating the boards and scoring at will from under the basket. In support, Raul Gonzalez scored six points, and Kino and Frank and Joe Contreras each scored five for a balanced attack.

Although the Voks were riding high as leaders of both the district and city races and had some very impressive victories, they showed a bit of offensive inconsistency, leading one observer to remark, "The Vok attack is of the explosive variety with a flood of points swishing the hoop for a short period, followed by a letup."[54] This "explosive" play was complemented by their "6-feet, 3-inch tip-in artist" to make up the deficits they usually incurred due to their height disadvantage against most opponents, including their old nemesis Brackenridge, their next opponent. While the Eagles were green and had lost to Fox Tech, they were seen as a "fairly good team" with "good potentialities."[55] More crucial to their hopes of pinning Lanier with their first defeat was the ever-constant tenacity and downright hostility they brought to every clash with the Voks.

That intensity helped Brackenridge hold Lanier to one point in the second quarter, and the Eagles led 14–11 at halftime in front of their own screaming fans, who saw a chance to hand the Voks their first defeat by a city opponent in two years. But the Voks fought back with buckets by Kino, David, and Raul and went into the final quarter leading 21–16. The Eagles, however, reasserted themselves and scored ten points in the final quarter, limiting the

Voks to seven, the last a free throw by Raul Gonzalez. But those were enough to give Lanier a 28–26 victory. The top scorers for each team, David Rodríguez and Elmer Szafranski, guarded each other with such resolve and aggression that they mostly canceled each other out, though David did win the scoring battle 5–0. It took Raul and Kino, scoring nine points apiece, to help the Voks squeeze out a win in the very hostile Eagle gym.[56]

The close game seemed to awaken the Voks, and they went on a tear to win their fourteenth, fifteenth, and sixteenth games in a row, beating Burbank 49–19, Jefferson 34–22, and Fox Tech 33–27. Kino led the team with seventeen points in the first game, David scored eleven points in the Jefferson game, and point guard David Flores took scoring honors with thirteen against the Buffaloes.[57] The victories proved the Voks could find various high scorers when needed. With Flores's emergence, that made it four players—David Rodríguez, Raul Gonzalez, Kino Rodríguez, and now David Flores—who had taken turns as leading scorers in the sixteen games so far. More important, it meant that the Voks now had two guards who could score. There was no doubt about Kino's abilities, but Herrera had been waiting for the Class B star, David Flores, to show that he was not only able to distribute the ball but could score when needed. Complementing these four was Joe Contreras, David's old barrio friend who had the ability to score timely baskets, play solid defense, and reflect some of Escobedo's toughness. He would also be the star the following year.[58]

The three wins over City Series teams placed the Voks in position to win the title outright with a victory over Brackenridge. The Eagles were the only team still in the running to catch them for the title, but they trailed by two games and needed a victory over the Voks and then help from someone else. A Vok victory would put the title out of reach even though the Eagles would still have two more City Series games. According to one newspaper account, the "classy Mexican youngsters" had at least a fifty-fifty chance of winning the title on January 31. "A fortunate handful will see Wednesday night's classic, slated to be the most exciting game of what has been a closely fought season . . . fans are expected to be turned away with the small Lanier gym crammed to the rafters," said the local paper. But the game would be without two key individuals. The Eagles had lost starting forward George Collie to a sprained ankle, while Lanier's Raul Gonzalez also had an "ankle casualty."[59]

The game turned out to be another no-holds-barred contest, but this time it was the Eagles who were the more swift and aggressive team, "outshooting and outmaneuvering" the Voks. A shifting zone and a ball-hawking tenacity limited the Lanier quintet to one point in the first quarter and a scoreless eleven minutes during the first half when the Eagles took a 14–9 lead. Big Elmer Szafranski got his revenge on David by teaming up with forwards Ed

Kneupper and Herman Humble to completely dominate the boards and shut off the driving lanes. The tenacious zone did not allow the Voks to set up for their shots, and by the end "the Mexicans, totally disgruntled . . . ended the game tossing long, desperate shots at the basket." While the Voks were missing their shots, the Eagles were not, and they walked away with a convincing 31–23 win.[60] It was the worst defeat for the Voks in more than three years. To make matters worse for the fans who filled the gym, one-and-a-half hours before the game had started, their league-leading Class B team also lost to the third-place Eagles, 28–24.

David Rodríguez and David Flores tied for Lanier scoring honors with eight points apiece, but the other two Rodríguez boys could only tally seven points between them. It was a bitter defeat that the tall center would remember for years and one that he believed simply got away.[61] Though they were the City Series leaders and completely dominating their rivals, the Voks were not firing on all cylinders, and the players must have questioned whether they were better than the previous year's quintet. After a few days off, they came back to defeat South San Antonio 37–12 and followed that win with a 38–29 victory over the Edison Bears to clinch at least a tie for the district title.[62] An important game with the second-place Harlandale Indians remained, but before they played them, the Voks defeated Fox Tech 38–31 to tie for the City Series title.[63]

In that game, David Flores again led the scoring with 9, and Raul Gonzalez added 8. Again, the Voks showed a balanced attack that made it difficult for any team to concentrate on one or two players. And even if the Indians had been able to key on all four of the Voks' leading scorers, Kino was waiting in the wings, though in this game, his fellow Voks simply left no slack to pick up.[64] Things got even more complicated for opponents when the Voks found another gem in their lineup when they met the Harlandale Indians for the second time. An earlier meeting had been closer than expected, with the Indians falling 22–14 in a defensive struggle. This time, however, the Voks took an early lead and never looked back. Said a local paper, "The Mexican lads were hitting their shots . . . grabbing the rebounds of both baskets, alternating between a shifting zone and their usual man-to-man defense to give the Indians few cracks at the basket."[65] The easy 51–16 drubbing of Harlandale gave Herrera a chance to empty his bench, and to his surprise—or maybe not—"Tiny" Teddy Castellano, a star of the Class B team, came in and hit three buckets from long range and played tenacious defense, prompting one sportswriter to say, "The Voks can make good use of him in their drive toward a possible state crown."[66] Herrera must have smiled as he saw the tiny fellow play and realized that he now had two very good guards for the next season in Teddy Castellano and Joe Contreras.

The scoring in the second game against the Indians was again balanced, and Raul Gonzalez let it be known that he was as ready to make a splash in the playoffs as he had the year before. He led the team scoring with ten points, followed closely by Kino with nine, Frank with eight, and David, who celebrated his birthday that day, with seven. The District 28-A crown was the fourth in a row for the Voks and the third for David. In three years, he had not tasted defeat against district play opponents.[67] The Voks' dominance became official when they routed the Burbank Bulldogs 57–16 at their home gym to win both the district and City Series titles. The blowout was an outcome so expected that one reporter predicted that "an upset by the Burbankers . . . would cause the walls of Lanier gym to collapse."[68] The walls may well have seemed like they were collapsing under the approving roar of the Vok faithful, who were anxious to see their team go back to state and claim what should have been theirs the year before.

Seeking to put a cap on a brilliant career in district play, David used all his height, moves, and ambidextrous shooting ability to scorch the nets with thirteen goals and five free throws for a total of thirty-one points. This was the highest total for any Lanier Vok ever, surpassing Rivera's twenty-eight points in the state playoffs in 1943. More important, it gave David two scoring titles. His 153 points in the ten-game district schedule set a season scoring record, while his 94 points in City Series play made him the top scorer among the city schools.[69] It was a fitting end for David, who had already proved that he was the best big man in the city for two years in a row, and it left no doubt that he was as good a player as any that had donned a Vok uniform. More than any player in the past, David proved that he could place the team on his shoulders and will them to a win. Given his ability to rebound, block shots, and clog up the middle, he did not always have to carry the scoring burden, but when he needed to, he could score in high numbers.

The clinching of both the district and city titles gave Sidney Lanier one of the most impressive seasons of any school across all basketball classifications. Aside from the varsity team's two titles, the Class B team won the Alamo League title, the Class A junior high won its title, and the Class B junior high team just missed winning it all, losing to Mark Twain Junior High in the finals. No comprehensive record exists of junior high teams' titles, but a perusal of the years between 1939 and 1945 shows no other school getting even close to Lanier's achievement. It is possible Lanier itself had swept junior and varsity titles in previous years, as we know they won district titles four years in a row, at least three Alamo League titles, and one other City Series title. Either way, the 1945 season validated Herrera's basketball system and his legacy. There is no doubt that his coaching philosophy permeated all aspects of Lanier sports. In the last three years, he had also coached the football team and might have even helped out with the track team. In every sport, no matter the team, and with every boy, he had he stressed hard work, dedication, a will to succeed, and composure in the face of adversity.

With titles in hand, Herrera prepared his boys for the regional tournament and the state playoffs. In a warm-up game for the regional tournament to be held at Lockhart, the Voks traveled to the Central Catholic High School gym. The game proved an opportunity for Herrera to play the eight players most likely to go to regionals, and his Voks easily defeated the Buttons, 45–28. "Towering David Rodriguez . . . was the hottest man on the floor with 18 points and played an excellent defensive game," said one newspaper. Raul Gonzalez proved that he was ready to step up as he had done the previous year and help the Voks make a run for the title. He scored twelve points and helped in manning the boards. Frank Rodríguez added six points, but strangely, Kino does not appear in the box scores, which include even those players who did not score. Joe Contreras added five points to the total. The victory was the twenty-third in twenty-four games.[70]

After Central, the Voks had to wait a week for the start of the regional tournament, but rather than focusing on their tournament opponents—Brenham, Belton, and Lockhart—they directed their attention to their next warm-up opponent. Coming to town for the "best match of the year" were the Prairie Lea Indians, defending Class B champions, undefeated in twenty-two games and averaging fifty-six points per contest. Vilbry White, all-state point guard, led a team with all its starters back from the 1944 championship team, and it was the prohibitive favorite to repeat. White, said one writer, had "an uncanny eye for the basket on long shots," while the rest of the squad had "experience, polish and goaling ability."[71] The Indians were no strangers to San Antonio as they had earlier come to town and beaten the Jefferson Mustangs by a score of 42–31, a bit more convincing than Lanier's first defeat of the Mustangs, 33–27, but not as brutal as the second Lanier victory, 34–22.[72]

In the end, the game turned out as predicted, but not so in the first quarter, when the Voks raced to a 13–3 advantage. Led by Raul Gonzalez's four baskets, the Voks seemed on their way to a rout and may have "relaxed a bit," or so one sportswriter thought. Whether they did or the Indians simply got into form, the game changed by the second quarter as the Prairie Lea team matched the Voks' nine points in the second period but still trailed 23–11 at halftime (another newspaper reported it as 22–12). The third quarter saw lower scores, and the Voks went into the final quarter with a thirteen-point lead that they extended to sixteen (it may have even been seventeen, as the two newspaper accounts differ in their point totals and scores) within the first three minutes. And then the "Tribe" came alive as Vilbry White, who had been held scoreless in the first three quarters, exploded for fourteen points in the fourth quarter. The furious comeback saw the Indians score eighteen, while their impenetrable defense held the Voks to one free throw the whole quarter. Wrote one reporter, "In the last five minutes the Laniermen, who are hotshots . . . learned something about close-checking from the visitors, whose hustling tactics seldom allowed the Voks' possession of the ball for more than a few seconds, much less a clean shot at the basket."[73]

The Indians ended the game on an 11–1 run to end regulation time with a 37–37 tie. In overtime they limited Lanier to a free throw by Joe Contreras, while White and teammate James Gillis scored a bucket each to lead Prairie Lea to a 41–38 victory. In the last eleven minutes of play, the Indians had gone on a 22–2 run to "snatch victory from the jaws of defeat" and top a Herrera team that no one believed could squander such a lead and self-destruct in a crucial game. The Indian's George Carlisle, who became Prairie Lea's second all-state player, tied Vilbry White as top scorer with fourteen points. Depending on which newspaper account one reads, the Voks' leading scorer was either Raul Gonzalez with ten points or David Rodríguez with eleven.[74] David, however, "turned in one of the finest defensive tilts yet," especially in the earlier moments when the Voks kept the Indian scorers in check.[75]

The defeat stung for the Voks, who knew they had played one of the best teams—if not the best—in the state and had been on the verge of scoring a signature win. One more point in regulation or one more defensive stop, and the Voks would have clearly established themselves as one of the top teams in the state regardless of classification. "We should have beaten them," lamented David Rodríguez in 2011. But the team had simply gone cold, and David admits that the Indians had shown a quicker step than the Voks. "Vilbry White was a tremendous player," he recalled. The future University of Texas star was too fast, and his one-hand jump shot, a rarity in Texas high school basketball at the time, proved hard to stop.[76]

"There is no reason to be ashamed of that loss," asserted one sportswriter. "It came from one of the best high school teams to ever show the waves in San Antonio and from the greatest 'finishers' seen here in years."[77] Kino and Frank had tried to stop White, but neither could stay up with him. And while David played great defense, he could not stop George Carlisle, another future Longhorn player, from getting his fourteen points. Carlisle was a tall, hulky center with a soft touch. The close score and the excitement the game generated were, however, no consolation for the West Side players. They knew they were the better team for at least three quarters and that defensively they could play as good as anyone. They had been unable to find an answer for the Indian surge. For David, at least, it would remain a what-if game that would have eased the pain of the Brackenridge defeat.

After the game, Herrera kept the players for about hour to point out what they could learn from this defeat. He also chewed them out for the multiple errors and for wasting opportunities to score. It was a ritual for Herrera to sit his boys down and "teach" them—because if there was something that Nemo did well, it was to teach his boys to learn from life and experience. Yet these talks were also a way for the coach to unwind and vent his own frustrations with how he might have prepared them better. Coaches back then could not call time-out and gather their players to instruct them or set up a play. The players were taught their assignments in practice and further instructed during the halftime break, but once the game started, coaches were relegated to observers and substituters. David remembers that Herrera had also chewed them out after the Mount Vernon game, believing that they were a much better team than the Tigers. It was then that he told his team that they were going to work even harder and come back the following year and win it all.[78]

The disappointment must have lingered, as two days later the Voks struggled to get going against the Brenham Cubs, who led the Voks at halftime, 17–12, in the first game of the regional tournament. But that deficit would not last. Led by fourteen points from Ramiro Gonzalez—whom Herrera put in for Flores—the Voks went on a 23–11 run to storm back in the second half to beat the "big" Brenham Cubs 35–28. David added ten and Kino eight to advance the Voks to the championship game, where they had a much easier time winning, 53–31, over the Belton Tigers. After halftime, when the Voks led 29–16, Herrera let the subs play. Even so, the top scorers were the usual group, except this time Frank Rodríguez led the scoring with sixteen, followed by David with eleven, and Kino and Raul with seven each. Ramiro, soon to be seen by some as the hero of the tournament, also added six and Contreras four.[79] The victory made it four straight regional tournament titles for the Voks and five in seven years.

With the regional title theirs, the Voks prepared for the state tournament by taking on an independent team from St. Mary's University in the larger gym. The St. Mary's quintet was coming off a decisive 60–38 victory over the Central Catholic Buttons, who had lost twice to the Voks, but not by such a wide margin. Herrera decided to change the lineup by inserting Ramiro Gonzalez, who according to one newspaper, had "pull[ed] Lanier out of the doldrums" in the first regional tournament game. Gonzalez replaced David Flores. This meant, according to the newspaper, that he would be playing alongside his brother Raul and the three Rodríguezes. If that were the case, then Joe Contreras, the point guard, would be coming off the bench.[80] It is likely, however, that he would be coming on and off the bench and playing as many minutes as any other guard. According to David, Joe Contreras was the most important player on the team because without his passing and his floor management, the team would not have functioned the way it did.[81]

Ramiro played a game "good enough to earn a starting a berth in the state tourney," and his brother Raul led the team in scoring with fourteen points as the Voks ran away from the St. Mary's team in a 66–46 rout. David and Frank both scored twelve points, and Ramiro scored eleven while directing the team. Kino scored eight points, but Joe Contreras went scoreless. "Offensively, the Mexican lads never looked better, hitting the goal consistently, with all hands contributing to the score," said one reporter.[82] It was the highest score of the season for the Voks and possibly the highest score ever put up by a Lanier team. It was the game Herrera wanted to see from his team. They were playing together, scoring at will, and the lineup was interchangeable.

While Herrera now had five solid starters, he also had two others—Flores and Contreras—who could start and make a difference. Whether the rest of the state realized it or not, the San Antonio sportswriter did. In a headline that declared, "'Stop Rodriguez' Cry Lanier Foes," writer Johnny Janes said, tongue-in-cheek, "Stop Rodriguez and the Voks are licked. The only problem facing Lanier's opponents is that there are three Rodriguez boys on the starting quintet and if the defense gangs [up] on one of the trio the other two may go on a goaling spree that will run up the Voks score in a hurry." The three, he pointed out, had scored 717 of the team's 1,168 points. He warned that opposing teams had to learn the scoring style of the three "R's" if they wanted any chance to "turn back the San Antonio team's bid for another state championship."[83]

The three Rs, the Gonzalez brothers, their teammates, and their coach soon realized that the one team that could turn them back was their first-round opponent in the state tourney. David Rodríguez years later would call that game the "real state championship." In Texas City, Lanier faced a team with characteristics similar to their own—"not so large but ever so fast and with a tricky passing game that works the ball in for numerous lay-in shots." Texas City also came in with an impressive victory over El Campo, whom some sportswriters considered as having the best team in years, including the highly touted team that had played Lanier the previous year.[84] Leading the Texas City quintet was Derrest Williams, another future Texas college star who was capable of putting up big numbers. Herrera responded with the same team that had exploded for sixty-six points only two days earlier, and for once his team had the tallest guy on the court. The writers had to learn only two Spanish surnames—Rodríguez and Gonzales—as Ramiro, the "new find," was given the starting nod over David Flores. It would be a two-name team until the bench players entered the game.[85]

As the final minutes slipped away, the Voks must have felt history repeating itself. They started off quickly and led 12–7 at the end of the first quarter. They extended that to 23–16 by halftime and had a comfortable eleven-point lead going into the final quarter. But Texas City's Williams and teammate Eddie O'Donnell, who combined for thirty-four points, soon got going and brought their team to 36–31 with five minutes left. But Flores and Contreras, who were now coming off the bench after starting for most of the season, each hit a field goal in the space of five seconds, and with two minutes to go the Voks seemed ready to claim the victory. But in those two minutes, the Texas City five staged a ferocious comeback, scoring nine points while allowing Lanier only one free throw by Flores. While Williams and O'Donnell were scoring, their teammates "stole the ball time after time from the jittery Voks." This time, however, the Voks found composure. When Texas City made it 41–40, the Lanier Voks took a hold of the ball and held on to it for the game's last thirty seconds to win and advance to the semifinals.[86]

Unlike most of their previous games where they had faced much taller teams, the Voks dominated the inside "with nifty work" and scored at will. David's rebounding and defensive work had limited the Texas City teams to few follow-up shots, and no doubt his shot blocking had changed more than one shot. David put in eighteen, and serious-faced Frank added twelve more. The two Lanier inside men stayed up with the Texas City duo of Williams and O'Donnell. With Kino's six, Flores's three, and Contreras's two points from the outside, that proved enough for the Voks.[87] Raul Gonzalez was shut out, and so was Ramiro, who ended up not even taking a shot and not being on the floor in the last minutes of the game. At crunch time, Herrera went back to the guard tandem that had brought him to the playoffs and were his most capable dribblers. With them, he felt confident going into the semifinal game against a talented East Mountain squad.

CHAPTER TEN

An Era Comes to an End, but a School Remains

NEMO HERRERA STEPPED INTO THE LANIER GYMNASIUM, the "chicken coop," one last time in 1945. It was old, the floor worn, some of the bleachers overused, and if he listened carefully he could almost hear the cheers, boos, and quiet whispers that had echoed for the last seventeen years. He couldn't help the smile that came to his face when he thought of little Tony Cardona racing down court for a layup, of Joe Treviño pushing players out of the way with his broad shoulders, or of Tony Rivera smiling as he hooked the ball from an impossible angle that made everyone on the bench cringe. Then there was flashy Billy Saldaña, who may have been better than most remembered him if not for the weak team in his senior year that made him forgettable. There was Santos Belton, who worked hard but still found ways to bring out Herrera's white hairs. And, of course, there was Henry Escobedo, team leader and all-around tough guy who loved to sing while he practiced. Then there were Indio; Mosco; the Gonzalez brothers—Raul and Ramiro—heroes of the regional tournaments; the Camacho siblings, who would be friends forever; Gilbert Carrasco, not much for the books but an excellent team captain; "Rough House" Kelley; and many others. They were his Lanier boys, and he loved all of them.

He loved the school. It was a place with many friends and wonderful students. It was a home away from home. The activities, the patriotism, the humor, and the loyalty all came to mind as he walked across campus. He knew he'd miss his football players, too. They hadn't won state but had given him some district titles, and they worked just as hard. Hard work—maybe that is what stood out the most from these young men and women he had learned to love at *la garra*. They came from homes where the next meal was not a given but where expectations of a hard life after graduation were. But these students still managed to smile and find joy in being with their friends and learning from their teachers. Herrera knew that this quality of dedication in the face of adversity was what made some of his teams so good. These boys knew how to follow orders, show respect for authority, and work hard when asked to do so—or when told, as was the case in practice. Being the smallest team in most contests never gave them fear. No doubt part of their success was the strenuous practice he put them through—they were well prepared for battle—but another part was the quiet confidence they learned from surviving the harsh realities of poverty in the barrio. Others outside the school and the West Side of San Antonio may have found the students at Lanier wanting, but he found nothing in them that a good education and some tough training couldn't fix.

They were young men who went through a lot to accomplish what they did. Most fans, sportswriters, and opposing players did not know half of the challenges his Voks confronted daily, and through it all they remained composed. Some things were best left unsaid, but they were hard to forget. Herrera and his team had faced many a hostile place, but San Marcos would be etched in his mind as the worst place in which to play. In 1942, the team had won its second regional title, and they were hungry and anxious to celebrate with a nice dinner before heading home. But when they approached a diner on the road out of town, a crowd, or something more akin to a mob, soon formed around the bus. It had taken several area policemen to escort them safely out, frightened and hungry. This diner wasn't the first place to refuse them service, but it sure was the first where they got a police escort out of the joint.[1]

That incident paled compared to another that happened in that same town. He drove there with a policeman friend, Bob Cruz, and team helpers Joe Bernal and Bruno Herrera for opening day of the regional tournament. Upon arriving at the gym, a man in an adjacent car opened the door and pointed a shotgun at them. "Don't you move, you goddam Mexicans," he said. When the Lanierites explained that they were there to play a basketball game, he repeated something to the effect that "Mexicans don't play basketball." "Don't say anything, don't move," Bob had whispered. Then another man had come out of the car and told the fellow to put the gun down and, turning to them, said, "He won't shoot." In a few minutes, the men were gone. Herrera remembers Bernal having written something about this in the school newspaper, but he had done what he always did in those types of situations: he said nothing to the team.[2] It wasn't necessary, and he didn't want his team wondering what might await them. He wanted them to roll with the punches, to work their way through every problem. He drilled into them that it is not who you were born, it's what you become. They were there to play, and that's what they did, sweeping all their opponents to be crowned champs.

To be fair to memory, Herrera knew there were also unpleasant but funny things to remember about his Lanier Voks. One was the time he took the football team to play in Laredo, Texas. His boys had never been in a nice hotel, and their faces showed it, causing the Anglo manager at the Hamilton Hotel to tell him to "keep a sharp eye" on his boys so that they wouldn't steal anything. Herrera remembered being outraged and challenging the manager to inspect any of his boys at any time, which the manager proceeded to do after breakfast as they were checking out. Herrera remembered how confidently he ordered the reluctant boys to empty their duffle bags right there in the hotel lobby. To his surprise or, better said, shock, the boys dropped silverware, soap, towels, sheets, and even two pillows on the floor. Herrera chuckled as he revisited the story in his mind, but back then it had not been funny. He knew everybody expected the worst of these boys, but he knew them better. They were poor and at times unrefined, but they were good boys. Still, they were begging for mercy during the next week of practice.[3]

But there were other things that came to mind at this moment that were pleasant and not embarrassing. First and foremost was the recently concluded championship run. Here in this gym, the Rodríguez threesome—Kino, Frank, and, of course, David—had methodically dismantled many a visiting team, but it was in the state playoffs where they had truly shown their stuff. Prairie Lea had been a tough loss, but it gave the Voks what they needed to withstand the valiant run by the boys from Texas City. True champs knew how to play their best when it counted and win the close ones. The Rodríguezes had shone during that game as they led in scoring, rebounding, and playmaking. Against East Mountain, David simply took over the inside, scoring nineteen points, dominating the boards, and clogging up the middle. Whatever rebound he didn't get, Raul Gonzalez tucked away or put back into the basket to the tune of eight points. While the two big men were dominating inside, Kino, Frank, Joe, Ramiro, David Flores, Ted Castellano, and a couple of newcomers from the Class B team were suffocating the East Mountain squad, limiting them to eleven points in the first half, none in the third quarter, and only six in the final period to win 42–17.[4]

"The Voks' passing was as pretty as anything seen in the tournament's two days and they worked in for numerous close shots with a speed that baffled East Mountain," wrote Johnny Janes of the *San Antonio Light* after the game.[5] Nothing made Herrera happier than to hear things like that. Oh, he knew he had great players, but when they worked as a team it was then that he knew he had done his job. The fact that the team was setting records along the way was just as satisfying. In their first two games, they had scored eighty-three, a tournament record, while David's nineteen points against East Mountain ended up being the high for the Class A tournament and third best in all the contests that weekend.[6] He would have been named the best player in Austin had Paschal High School's Jack Robinson not wooed the fans, sportswriters, and coaches with his stellar play, causing "veteran observers" to declare him the best to have ever played in the tournament. Even then, Robinson scored only one more point than David in the three competitions.[7]

In the championship game against the Quitman Tigers, the Rodríguez threesome again led the scoring and the defensive play. David had "hung around the . . . basket and . . . punched in crisp shot after crisp shot" to put the Voks ahead in the early minutes of the game. He then took "control of the boards" to stave off a Tigers rally and seal Lanier's 30–24 victory. What made David's job particularly impressive was how he handled Quitman's Travis Gilbreath, a giant of a man at six-foot-four who was "deadly" under the basket.[8] David never allowed the big man to stake his position, forcing him instead to shoot from the outside, where he made only nine points, with eight of them coming in the first half.[9] The rest of Gilbreath's teammates failed to pick up the slack as Kino led a tenacious defense that limited the Tigers' passing and got some timely steals. Kino scored five points, Frank six, and David sixteen, as the Rodríguez boys scored all but three of the Lanier points. Raul scored one point and David Flores the other two.[10]

The play of David, Kino, and Frank brought the Voks a recognition that no other team could claim in the history of the tournament. The threesome that helped the Voks set a tournament record with 113 total points was placed on the all-state team, prompting one reporter to write, "The placing of three boys on the all-tournament team has never been exceeded." Neither had there ever been three boys with the same surname.[11] In 1945, for the first time ever, and possibly since, the all-state Class A team had more Mexican Americans than whites. It was an accomplishment that David Rodríguez, and surely Kino and Frank, would remember with pride. So would Herrera. He knew, and had probably reminded himself often during the early years, that few people believed he could take a team of Mexican boys to the tournament and win state. Of course, Herrera never talked about them as Mexican boys, just as young men who wanted to play and were willing to do everything they were told to get to the summit of Texas high school basketball.

There would not, however, be any trophies for the tournament champions or for the three all-state players. They received only scrip, to be redeemed at a future time when no war raged and tournament officials could buy a trophy and send it to the Voks. But while there were no trophies, the Voks received accolades and congratulations from members of the community. Shortly after their return, they were the honored guests of the local Lions Club at the prestigious Gunther Hotel. There, Principal Brewer introduced Herrera, who in turn recognized each one of the boys, including the four Rodríguezes on the team. This created a bit of a humorous situation, for the club's tail twister (a sort of jester), who was named Louis Rodríguez. That Lions Club feast was followed by another from the League of United Latin American Citizens (LULAC) Council no. 1. Among the invited guests were the district's athletic director, *Light* sports editor Harold Scherwitz, superintendent of vocational education L. W. Fox, Andres Rivera of the Good Neighbor Commission, as well as numerous dignitaries in the Mexican American community. There the team members were lauded as players, students, and sportsmen by numerous speakers. It was a celebration by a community that saw in his boys the characteristics necessary for Mexican Americans to move up in society.[12]

Herrera surely chuckled when he remembered asking the home economics teacher to spend some time teaching the boys how to eat properly in a fancy restaurant and how to behave in company of distinguished individuals. Most of the boys had never been to a restaurant or even a formal meal.[13] It took them a while to get it right, but as usual the boys did well. They were, after all, Lanier boys, and they knew how to act in public. Now, most of them were either in the armed forces or getting ready to join. Raul Gonzalez had passed his army physical and was inducted. So was Kino, who joined the Navy, both of them leaving even before graduation. David had gotten a deferment to finish schooling and was also now in the service. David Flores and Frank Rodríguez also went into the army, making the Voks' starting lineup five for five in serving their country.[14] In the armed forces, they joined Henry Escobedo, Tony Rivera, Refugio Olivares, and Walter Kelley of the 1943 and 1944 teams.

By then, one player—Richard Reyes—had already paid the ultimate price while participating in the liberation of France. He had survived fierce fighting in Africa and Italy before succumbing to German fire in the final push. Rivera and Olivares had also been wounded in action.[15] Herrera knew that there were others, like Tony Cardona, Joe Treviño, Jesse and Billy Saldaña, and Jesse and Carlos Camacho, who had served or were serving in the armed forces. None of them had shirked their responsibility to their country. Frank Rodríguez had worked extra hard after failing his initial army examination, and now he was proudly serving with the occupation forces in Germany.[16] There were others from earlier teams, many of whom he had driven himself to the depot station to be taken away to training and eventual combat.

The other thing that came to mind was the tough decisions he had made that spring. He was offered the job to coach the Texas A&M University Aggies but had turned it down. The contract offer had come during the run for state and was only for the duration of the season, possibly to be extended if things went well, but he could not take the risk, nor was he willing to sacrifice the team for a job he was "definitely interested [in] as anyone would be."[17] Herrera knew he was a good coach and that manning a college team would be another step in the progression of his career. The job also meant the possibility of finally making enough money in coaching to have something to show for all his efforts. Every summer, he'd head down to Mexico because his teacher's pay and his wife's job—when she was working—simply did not provide enough beyond the most basic necessities. But he could not afford to take a job that had no guaranteed future beyond the present season. As a high school coach, he made little, but it was steady employment.

Economics, however, was not the only challenge Herrera faced. His son William, a fragile child, needed to be in a drier climate because of respiratory problems. And according to some former players, Herrera's relationship with Principal Brewer had been tense during the last few years. No one knew why, though some, like Joe Bernal, speculated that Herrera did not like Brewer's efforts to extend administrative oversight to the locker room. Bernal would say years later, and Lanier alumni Raul Zuniga would confirm, that Brewer often sought to offer game advice to the players, only to have Herrera say, after the principal left, "Don't listen to him, I'm the coach."[18] He made a similar comment once when his wife, Mary Leona, volunteered some suggestions. Herrera never said anything publicly about why he left Lanier, and no one really had the inside scoop on his reasons, but by the end of the summer, he had accepted the coaching job at Class AA Bowie High School in El Paso, another predominantly Mexican American school.[19]

Shortly after Herrera walked out of Lanier in the summer of 1945, the school's storied runs at basketball supremacy would end. Only one starter, Joe Contreras, returned, along with several bench players who had seen some action during the championship run. When he still thought he would be back, Herrera had told one reporter that his team would "put up a great battle for . . . state honors in 1946. . . . We lose good players every year," he said, "but somehow more 'hot' ones always seem to show up the next season. We'll always have a lot of good material here at Lanier."[20] The 1946 team won the regional tournament for the sixth straight year and placed two players in the All District 28-A squad: Joe Contreras on the first team and Ramiro Gonzalez on the second. At center, they had another Rodríguez—Vidal—who, like his older brothers, knew how to play tough inside. David would later say that if Nemo had been there, either the 1946 or 1947 team might have won state. But it was not to be. The Vok run in 1946 ended in the first round of the state tournament when they met the Pasadena Eagles, who crushed them

59–25. It was the worst defeat in the school's basketball history. It would take the combined point total of all the losses that Lanier had suffered over the past four years to equal the thirty-four-point deficit that the team suffered that night.[21] A Herrera-coached team might have also lost to the very talented and tall Pasadena team, but it is unlikely that they would have been humiliated.

Lanier continued to be competitive under new coach Frank Rummels for another few years, but it never again reached the heights it did under Herrera. After their last regional title in 1951 they would not win another regional title until the 2000s. The steep decline led some Lanier parents to demand that Herrera be brought back in 1947, but that effort proved unsuccessful, even though Herrera had written some friends telling them he wanted to return. Brewer simply replied that he had tried to keep Herrera from leaving and now had no slot for him. The district responded that they had only an opening for a coach who would teach part-time, a situation Herrera found totally unacceptable.[22]

For Coach Nemo Herrera, there were still twenty-five more years of triumphs in the high school sports world, like winning a state baseball championship in 1949, placing fourth in the state basketball tournament (which he might have won had not his best player become ineligible), producing one of the all-time great coaches of college basketball in Nolan Richardson, and coaching numerous athletes with fruitful college careers. He would be inducted to the Texas Sports Hall of Fame and eventually return to San Antonio to work as a recreational director for Kelly Air Force Base.[23]

For Lanier, however, its days of sports glory were gone. Not until 2001 and 2002 did Lanier make it back to the finals of the state basketball championships, though it was unable to win the title. When I came to Lanier in the 1960s, we fielded mediocre sports teams and did not win, with an exception of one or two, championships of any kind. Not until years after I graduated would I learn that Lanier had once been a sports giant. But the players that Herrera coached never forgot, and they kept remembering and honoring the man. In 1967, while on a trip to San Antonio for a coaching clinic, Herrera expressed to some of his ex-players a desire to see "all of the old Lanier gang," their families, and grandkids. He probably believed it wishful thinking, but his former players made it a reality in just two days, setting up a testimonial dinner at the city's famed La Villita Assembly Hall that attracted 1,200 people who came to honor the man and reminisce about the glory years of Lanier sports.

Shortly before the testimonial dinner, one of his former football players, Mike Machado, then a municipal court judge, expressed the feelings of all his players when he said:

> I love that man. He gave me things money will never buy. Inspiration, understanding, self-respect and perhaps most important of all, happiness. In later years I was fortunate enough to go on to Yale, Southern Cal and Denver University. But so help me, the happiest days of my life were spent at Lanier with Coach Herrera. We were bound together in a bond of poverty but his friendship and guidance made us rich kids.[24]

In honoring Herrera, the players were recognizing their own achievements and affirming their own struggles. The coach would have been the first to admit that he didn't invent a new breed of men in the barrios. He only took what parental instruction and a hard life of poverty gave him and helped mold it into winning teams. He showed his players the way, but they had been the ones to expose their bodies to the intense practices and hostile crowds and to make the plays to win games, claim championships, and build character. He saw something in them that only a few caring and perceptive teachers had. These were young men who caught the vision of what could be done despite the limitations they faced and the low expectations that people had of them. And with them, he accomplished his own dreams.

There would be other success stories that came out of Herrera's teams. There was Frank Sepulveda, head of the major produce-distributing company in the region; Joe Bernal, one of Texas's great civil libertarians; and high school coaches like Santos Belton, Henry Escobedo, and David Rodríguez, who was also a principal. His alumni also included a number of civil service employees, such as Tony Rivera and Carlos Camacho, and businessmen like Jesse Camacho and Tony Cardona. Countless others in various walks of life were better men because of Nemo and their experience at Lanier.

Machado's sentiments expressed the feeling of many other Lanierites that came after the Herrera years. Sidney Lanier High School was a special place for those who lived in the West Side of San Antonio. It was their home, a place where they made friends, found spouses, developed their politics, and found their identity as Mexican Americans. The school had its limitations, and few would attend without having some gripe: too strict, few counselors, old facilities, hand-me-down teachers, few college preparatory courses, and a host of other problems that made this the "Mexican" school. Yet Lanier was always theirs—and ours—and it provided a space that they navigated and that allowed many of them to find their way. My own generation would produce its teachers, college professors, writers, a university president, and businesspersons, as well as many a fine printer, body and fender expert, commercial artist, and other skilled citizens of the community. Subsequent generations have done as well even as they, too, have faced many limitations.

Lanier provided Mexican American youth a space that was unavailable anywhere else in segregated San Antonio before World War II and for years after. There, West Side residents navigated the complicated road of assimilation and cultural maintenance. Students experienced what it was to be American within a protected educational bubble; they also decided how much of their Mexicanness they should keep. This was particularly so for the basketball players, who played the American game of basketball while representing the hopes of the Mexican and Mexican American residents of the Latin Quarter. Herrera taught them the American sports creed of hard work, discipline, and exemplary behavior on and off the court, with a promise that it would bring them benefits after they left the courts behind. But the Mexican ball players soon found that those characteristics were not so different from those that their parents had taught them about surviving in the harsh American reality of poverty and discrimination. Hard work and discipline in the workplace were what allowed their parents to bring home meager but much-needed funds. And what parent had not instructed their child to respect their teachers and to behave in school? Even in the 1960s when gangs were plentiful in the West Side of San Antonio, Lanier students were known as the best-behaved students in the city, or at least we gave ourselves that title because we could see how our parents' instruction to behave played out on campus.

In many ways, the basketball players and their classmates were not learning anything new at Lanier in terms of character, but they were discovering that these ideals worked in a larger arena. What they gained was a space in which to see the application of those ideals. While their school facilities were not always up-to-date, they were better than anything they knew on the outside. The shop equipment was as good as that of any other school simply because of Lanier's vocational focus. And in Brewer and Tafolla, they had administrators who, while often limited in their views of what Lanierites could do, believed in their charge and sought to protect their students from the hostilities of the outside world.

On the basketball court, the Voks were provided spatial parameters, rules that were basically fair for all, and opponents with no more advantage than what personal talent and possibly greater height might provide them. The crowds might be hostile on the road, but the Voks also at times had home-court advantage. In that "chicken coop" of an arena, they were usually unbeatable, the crowd was on their side, and the visiting white players often got a taste of their own medicine. Herrera taught his team to play hard, play by the rules, play quicker than their opponents, and play smarter—and thus avoid having the referees decide the game. Outhustling their opponents, pivoting around them to score, stealing their balls, suffocating them on defense, and, most important, beating them provided them a slightly skewed but important sense that they could similarly find success in the outside world. Becoming winners in a society that valued winners was something they could fully appreciate. It was as close to equality as the Lanier players were going to get in an unequal America, and it taught them much about how the world should be.

The value of Lanier was not that it was a perfect world but, rather, that it provided experiences its students could use to navigate the larger world. Because it did not serve as a stepchild to a larger school—like most rural "Mexican schools"—Lanier stood on its own and thus had to be included, if not as an equal school, at least as one with the full rights of participation in the University Interscholastic League activities. This allowed Lanier students to be a part of a larger educational and sports world in San Antonio—something rare for most Mexican American students in Texas before the 1948 ruling that desegregated schooling for "Spanish-speaking" students.

Lanier was a second home to the children of the West Side because there they learned a view of American society that did not always conform to the asymmetry of the outside world. At Lanier, surrounded by fellow brown bodies, with Mexican neighborhoods as far as the eye could see, they felt secure and capable of being what their talents and efforts could make them. The atmosphere of inclusion, optimism, and potential inside Lanier rarely carried to the world outside Lanier, but by bringing success and dedication from the barrio to the outside world, the players Herrera coached as well as other bright students began to change the view that West Side residents had of themselves and the world. Today, Lanier remains a place dedicated to educating the youth of the West Side and helping them come to grips with who they are in American society. It remains far from perfect, but many years ago, it was place that taught many others not of Lanier and those far away from the Latin Quarter that Mexicans could play ball. And win!

Notes

INTRODUCTION

1. "Voks Go into Tie for Top in City Series; Brackenridge Meets Burbank Today," *San Antonio Express*, January 13, 1939; emphasis in original.

2. For an in-depth discussion of Fiesta Week, see Hernández-Ehrisman, *Inventing the Fiesta City*.

3. Monograph-length works are particularly rare, the available literature being limited mostly to articles, a couple of anthologies, and some general works on Latino sports. The top scholars in this field are Jorge Iber, Samuel O. Regalado, José M. Alamillo, and, more recently, Richard Santillan. These scholars have begun to unravel an activity within the barrio that most people knew existed but that few scholars had acknowledged in their work. Earlier historians such as Juan García, Thomas E. Sheridan, and Douglas Monroy had mentioned Mexican American participation in sports in their community histories. These authors saw this participation as an important aspect of the Mexican American community's efforts to build internal communal activities and structures to maintain the vibrancy of the segregated barrios. Sheridan's *Los Tucsonenses* mentioned bullfighting, cockfighting, and horse racing; Juan García's *Mexicans in the Midwest, 1900–1932* talked about baseball leagues in the Midwest; while Monroy's *Rebirth* spoke to the role of sport as recreation among Mexican Americans in Los Angeles. None of the authors, however, delved deep into the activities of sports or even the role sports played in their studied communities, other than to mention sports as recreational and leisure-time activities that helped maintain a sense of community within the Mexican barrios. Balderrama and Santillan, in *Mexican American Baseball in Los Angeles*, and Santillan, Ocegueda, and Cannon, in *Mexican American Baseball in the Inland Empire*, have looked at Mexican American baseball leagues in Southern California and the Midwest, as well as other teams and leagues across the country. These works, however, are more pictorial histories than in-depth studies of particular teams or communities. Two other works that mention sport as a leisure activity among Mexican Americans are Alamillo's *Making Lemonade*

Out of Lemons and Jimenez-Innis's "Beyond the Baseball Diamond and Basketball Court." For a discussion of the political implication of sport in the Mexican American community—a still undeveloped topic—see Piece's "More than a Game." The first discussion of where sport fit within the evolution of the Mexican American community was presented in the anthology by Iber and Regalado, *Mexican Americans and Sports*. In the introduction, titled "Athletics and Chicano/a Life, 1930–2005," Iber argues that sports have often been an afterthought in Chicano history, particularly when discussing historiography, and he notes that most of the treatment is superficial and uncritical.

4. Iber and Regalado, *Mexican Americans and Sports*, 133–139. See also Marin's "Courting Success and Realizing the American Dream," which tells the story of a predominantly Mexican American basketball team that captured the state title and established a national scoring record on the road to an undefeated season.

5. Iber et al., *Latinos in U.S. Sport*, 278.

6. My approach also differs in that it provides the first book-length treatment of one team and one school in one sport and focuses on the subject across a period of nearly seventeen years. The previously mentioned works provide a framework by which we can understand larger aspects of the role that sport played among Mexican Americans, but they do not provide specifics for an in-depth narrative because they lack the kinds of details over time necessary to understand the story of sports in a community.

7. Three books that influenced my approach, though I ended up not patterning my work on any of them, are Gorn, *The Manly Art*; Levine, *Ellis Island to Ebbets Field*; and Grundy, *Learning to Win*. The first was appealing because it dealt specifically with the sport and the people participating. Gorn's description of the men involved in pugilism and his analysis of how their struggles reflected much about American working-class life are superb. One can almost smell the sweat on the fighters' bodies and hear the pounding of fist against flesh. All the characters that come in and out of each chapter add to our understanding of how sport reflected the changes occurring among working-class white men and their families throughout most of the nineteenth century.

8. Richard A. García, *Rise of the Mexican American Middle Class, San Antonio, 1929–1941*, 16.

9. Ibid., 39.

10. Murray, *A Socio-cultural Study of 118 Mexican Families*, 9–15. For an in-depth study of the Alazan–Apache federal housing projects, see Zelman, "Alazan-Apache Courts."

11. Murray, *A Socio-cultural Study of 118 Mexican Families*, 14–21.

12. Tony Rivera, interview [Spring 2009], 6; Rudy Bernal, interview, April 9, 2009, 1–3.

13. Murray, *A Socio-cultural Study of 118 Mexican Families*, 83–85.

14. Ibid., 86, 100–101.

15. Ibid., 89–92.

16. Stella Molina, interview, August 2009, 5.

17. Rudy Bernal, interview, 7–8.

18. We can understand this better if we place those Lanier players within the generational mode that Chicano historian Mario T. García developed in his work on the "Mexican American generation," *Mexican Americans*. In this work, García argues that middle-class Mexicans born on this side of the border were beginning to shift emotionally and intellectually toward an Americanism that they were themselves constructing. It was an Americanism that took into consideration their life experiences but contextualized those experiences within their own desires to fit and succeed in an American society that "offered" them a lot even while creating obstacles for them.

19. See Kelly, "Physical Anthropology of a Mexican Population in Texas."

20. Ibid.

21. Murray, *A Socio-cultural Study of 118 Mexican Families*, 106–107.

22. Kibbe, *Latin Americans in Texas*, 8.

23. Ibid., 26.

24. Richard A. García, *Rise of the Mexican American Middle Class*, 72–73.

25. Ibid., 54–56.

26. David Mercado Gonzalez, interview, June 10, 2010, 18–19.

27. Ibid.

28. Grundy, *Learning to Win*, 7.

29. Like Grundy, I sought to "build chapters from collections of . . . overlapping stories, seeking less to construct explicit arguments than to throw athletic narratives and events into relief . . . to convey . . . the creativity and passion with which [Lanierites] approached their sporting endeavors." *Learning to Win*, 9.

30. This negotiation often took the form of labor organizing, cultural promotion through celebrations and fiestas, civil rights activism, educational reform, and a refusal to accept discrimination without pushback.

31. In my research, I have "discovered" numerous other teams of Mexican Americans that achieved the ultimate goal in their sports but that still remain unknown to the general public. Jorge Iber, Samuel O. Regalado, Richard Santillan, and other historians have brought some of these to light, but much more is "known" through the oral recollection of old-timers.

CHAPTER 1

1. See "1992 Annual Nemo Herrera Memorial San Antonio High School Boys-Girls All-Star Games," brochure/program. Also see "Grand Opening Ceremony for the Alumni Center and Gymnasium Dedication," program.

2. For an extensive explanation of this generation of Mexican Americans, see Mario T. García, *Mexican Americans*, esp. chap. 1. Also see Griffith, *American Me*, for a discussion of a generation coming of age during the Depression and after massive deportations slowed immigration from Mexico and made American-born Mexicans the majority of "Spanish-speaking" people.

3. See Balderrama and Rodríguez, *Decade of Betrayal*.

4. See Victor Rodríguez's *Bell Ringer*, a memoir in the third person.

5. For more on this generation, see Mario T. García, *Mexican Americans*; and Ignacio M. García, *Hector P. García.*

6. Frank Hinojosa, e-mail to Charles Herrera, July 9, 2011. Hinojosa gathered this information from his mother, who was a member of the Herrera family, possibly from the father's side.

7. William Carson Herrera, scrapbook. This old scrapbook is literally falling apart and was passed on to Herrera's youngest son, Charles, and is in his possession.

8. See Mario T. García's *Mexican Americans* for a more substantive discussion of the contradictions Mexican Americans often battled within themselves and among each other.

9. Herrera scrapbook.

10. See "A Scrappy, Gutsy and Winning Coach."

11. "Brackenridge High Takes Another Step toward Championship," *San Antonio Light*, March 21, 1918.

12. "Sidney Lanier Coaches Produce Winning Clubs," *San Antonio Express*, June 4, 1939, 4B.

13. For the story of Mario "Mike" de la Fuente, see his *I Like You Gringo—But!*

14. For more on E. C. Lerma, see Iber, "Mexican Americans of South Texas Football." Also see E. C. Lerma, interview, 1980.

15. In the scrapbook is a picture of Herrera with his certificate of initiation into the Phi Delta Theta Fraternity below it.

16. "Basketball Season Successfully Closed," undated clipping, Herrera scrapbook.

17. Herrera scrapbook.

18. For a discussion of these teams and the life of a minor leaguer, see *Professional Baseball Teams in Texas*; also see Johnson and Wolff, *The Encyclopedia of Minor League Baseball.*

19. "A Scrappy, Gutsy and Winning Coach."

20. Most of this information comes from his scrapbook, where he has pictures of himself in the baseball leagues as well as pictures of the aforementioned stars with whom he played. The scrapbook also has a short blurb on his "semi-pro career."

21. "Nemo Herrera Joins Texas Hall of Fame," *San Antonio Light*, March 14, 1967, 14.

22. For one of the few in-depth discussions of violence toward Mexicans, see Carrigan and Webb, "The Lynching of Persons of Mexican Origin or Descent."

23. See "Tales from the Morgue," *El Paso Times*, March 27, 1969.

24. "Beaumont's New Cage Coach Here; Believes He Has Best Material," Herrera scrapbook.

25. "A Trophy for Change," *Port Arthur Daily News*, January 30, 1923.

26. Grundy, *Learning to Win*, 4–9, 70–71.

27. Ibid.

28. For more on the Gulf Oil Company, see Thompson, *Since Spindletop*; and Yergin, *The Prize.*

29. For more on Herrera's time with the Basketeers, see "Second Aggie-Good

Gulf Tilt Promises to be Sensational Clash," *Port Arthur News*, January 23, 1923; "On the Firing Line," "Challenge of Texaco Basketeers Accepted," and "Houston Team Meets Gulfers," all from the *Port Arthur Daily News*, January 30, 1923. Also see "Good Gulf Teams Looms Up as Possible Champ at S.A.A.U. Tournament," *Port Arthur News*, March 10, 1923, and "Pirates Foe of Local Cage Team Tonight," *Port Arthur News*, December 27, 1923.

30. There are numerous clippings in Herrera's scrapbook about the Gulf Coast Basketeers, and they all show him as one of their best players.

31. See "Nemo Herrera Joins Texas Hall of Fame."

32. See "Sidney Lanier Coaches Produce Winning Clubs."

33. Jesse Sánchez, "History of Baseball in Mexico."

34. Ibid.

35. Charles Herrera, personal conversation with the author.

36. Herrera scrapbook, which has several pictures of him dressed as an umpire and attending the hall of fame opening, as well as a picture of his umpiring credentials for the Mexican baseball league.

37. Charles Herrera, phone interview with the author, July 1, 2011.

38. For a succinct discussion of oil companies in Mexico during the 1920s, see Coerver, Pasztor, and Buffington, *Mexico*, 353–354, 487–489.

39. Ibid.

40. Tony Rivera, interview with Benjamin Dominguez, August 1, 2009, 8.

41. Ibid.

42. Rudy Bernal, interview with the author, November 12, 2009.

43. Jesse Camacho and Carlos Camacho, joint interview, November 13, 2009, 2–4.

44. For a scholarly explanation, see Waterhouse, "Mexican Spanish Nicknames." For a more humorous discussion, see Arellano's "How Do Mexicans Get Such Ridiculous Nicknames?" See also "Mexican Nicknames" for a list of the many hilarious descriptive nicknames among Mexicans and Mexican Americans. This list tends to be about names used to describe someone's looks rather than the nicknames that come from shortening or changing a word or two from a regular name.

45. Rudy Bernal, interview with the author, November 12, 2009, 10.

46. Jesse Camacho and Carlos Camacho, joint interview, November 13, 2009, 4.

47. Domingo Vasquez, e-mail to the author, January 17, 2010.

48. Rosie Peña, e-mail to the author, January 21, 2011.

49. "Chino" is the nickname of the young man who kills Tony, one of the protagonists of the film (1961) and play *West Side Story*.

50. On the Mexican cinema, see Paranagua, *Mexican Cinema*; and Mora, *Mexican Cinema*.

51. See Alvarez, *The Power of the Zoot*; Pagan, *Murder at the Sleepy Lagoon*; and Mazon, *The Zoot-Suit Riots*.

52. Dan Cook, "West Side's Little Giant," *San Antonio Express/News*, August 6, 1967.

53. "Nemo Herrera Joins Texas Hall of Fame."

54. Heer, "Little Nemo in Comicsland."

55. Ibid.
56. Ibid.
57. Charles Herrera, phone interview with the author, July 1, 2011.
58. "Life Begins at 70 For Texas Coach," Herrera scrapbook.
59. Cook, "West Side's Little Giant."
60. "A Scrappy, Gutsy and Winning Coach."
61. Ibid.
62. Ibid.
63. Ibid.
64. Ibid.
65. Jesse Camacho and Carlos Camacho, joint interview, November 13, 2009, 20–21.
66. Ibid., 20.
67. See Victor Rodríguez, *The Bell Ringer*, 175–178, for the story of Victor Rodríguez, a track star in high school and college, a successful coach, and the first Mexican American superintendent of a major Texas school district.
68. Nicolas Rodríguez and Benjamin Dominguez, e-mails to the author, January 22, 2011. Benjamin was on the junior high basketball team.
69. Domingo Vasquez, Patricia Jacobs, and Rosie Peña, e-mails to the author, January 21, 2011.
70. David Rodríguez, interview with author in El Paso, Texas, June 15, 2011.
71. Rudy Bernal, interview with the author, November 12, 2009, 5.
72. "A Scrappy, Gutsy and Winning Coach."
73. Ibid.
74. Rudy Bernal, interview with the author, November 12, 2009, 3.
75. Tony Rivera, interview with Benjamin Dominguez, August 1, 2009, 4.

CHAPTER 2

1. "Riley to Be Assigned to Lanier Hi," *San Antonio Light*, September 16, 1929.
2. Untitled article, *San Antonio Express*, August 26, 1929.
3. "Senior Schools Have Extra Coach," *San Antonio Express*, August 29, 1929.
4. There are no real significant articles on Wright "Toady" Riley, but there are bits and pieces in numerous articles that mention him. See "Kellum to Coach Brackenridge High," *San Antonio Light*, August 23, 1929; "What Ho? Wright Riley Spouts Some Grid Dope," *San Antonio Light*, March 20, 1927; "Championship Hangs on Lanier-Main Game," *San Antonio Light*, February 14, 1930; "Main-Eagles Feud Renewal First on Bill," *San Antonio Express*, January 20, 1930; and "Riot Imperils City Basketball League," *San Antonio Light*, February 4, 1932.
5. "Riley to Be Assigned to Lanier Hi."
6. See "Guarantee Sportstraits," *San Antonio Light*, November 20, 1931; "Championship Hangs on Lanier-Main Game"; and "Frio County Champs Meet Lanier Here," *San Antonio Light*, February 10, 1932, as examples.

7. "Guarantee Sportstraits."

8. For information on Lanier junior high sports, see "Lanier 'A' Class Junior High Team Division Champs," *San Antonio Light*, March 8, 1925; "Lanier Lads Give St. Mary's a Run for School Game," *San Antonio Light*, January 15, 1925; "Lanier Eleven Junior High Champions," *San Antonio Light*, n.d. (in author's possession). There are other scattered articles on Lanier athletics in the years from 1924 to 1929, before Riley took over as head coach.

9. "Lanier 'A' Class Junior High Team Division Champs."

10. See Putney's *Muscular Christianity*.

11. "Golf Champs to Battle Saturday," *San Antonio Light*, May 25, 1928; and "Lanier Hi Boy Wins Light Golf Title," *San Antonio Light*, May 27, 1928.

12. "Lanier High Will Get Football Tags Friday," *San Antonio Express*, September 25, 1924.

13. For a good discussion of educational reform activities by Mexican Americans, see San Miguel's *"Let All of Them Take Heed."*

14. "13 Star Teams Off for State High Meet," *San Antonio Light*, March 5, 1931.

15. See Ratlief, *Texas Boys' Basketball, A History*.

16. "Voks Place Four Men on All-City Selection," *San Antonio Express*, February 7, 1931. Also see "Voks Win Way in to District Title Scramble," *San Antonio Express*, February 7, 1931. Other information on Farias comes from his son George Farias, who compiled a list of newspaper comments on his father from the *San Antonio Express* dated January 27, 1931, January 30, 1931, February 4, 1931, and February 16, 1931. Unfortunately, no article titles are available. Also George Farias, "Anastacio 'Stacy' Farias," biographical sketch, in the author's possession.

17. See George Farias, "Anastacio 'Stacey' Farias."

18. George Farias, phone conversation with the author, February 2012.

19. See the sports front page, *San Antonio Light*, March 17, 1931.

20. George Farias, "Anastacio 'Stacy' Farias."

21. See "Times Selects Its All-City Cage Team. Stacey Farias, Forward, Central," *Laredo Times*, March 4, 1935.

22. "Edison 'Iron Man' Meet Lanier for Title," *San Antonio Light*, October 26, 1932.

23. Ibid.

24. "Win Virtually Assures Jefferson Title," *San Antonio Light*, February 9, 1933.

25. Ibid.

26. See "Central Buttons Loom as City Basketball Threat" and "Voks Play Randolph," *San Antonio Express*, January 6, 1933.

27. "Mustangs Ride High after 39–31 Win," *San Antonio Light*, February 1, 1933.

28. See San Miguel's *"Let All of Them Take Heed"* for a discussion of how Mexican children were perceived to be good with their hands but not their brains.

29. See Putney, *Muscular Christianity*, for a fuller discussion of these notions of sports and physical fitness and how those were an integral part of being a Christian.

30. Interestingly, Jewish basketball players who dominated in the early years of the sport in the northeast were also accused of "tricks" as they were not seen as

"physical or athletic enough" to compete with white players. See Levine, *Ellis Island to Ebbets Field*, for the stereotypes Jewish players confronted.

31. "Lanier Seeking Title Cinch in District," *San Antonio Light*, November 20, 1935.

32. Ibid.

33. Ibid.

34. "Lanier Seeking Title Cinch in District."

35. "Mustangs, Voks in Large Game," *San Antonio Express*, January 17, 1936.

36. Ibid.

37. "Latin American," *San Antonio Express*, November 30, 1936, 9.

38. "Lanier 58, Heights 17," *San Antonio Express*, January 20, 1938.

39. "Brackenridge Wins Overtime Verdict to Gain 2nd Place," *San Antonio Express*, February 16, 1938, 11.

40. "John Saldaña," Obituary, *San Antonio Express*, June 11, 2010. Also see "Sidney Lanier Voks Nose Out Central," *San Antonio Express*, December 16, 1938.

41. "Voks Need Win or Tie to Own Crown," *San Antonio Light*, November 17, 1938.

42. "Win for Lanier Would Mean Championship While Loss Probably Would Throw Voks into Tie with Edison," *San Antonio Light*, November 13, 1938.

43. "Edison Files Protest against Lanier Voks," *San Antonio Light*, November 13, 1938.

44. Ibid.

45. See "Brewer, 97, Led Blue Jackets at Lanier in the '30s," obituary on Marian Brewer, *San Antonio Express-News*, November 5, 2009.

46. "Edison Protest Is Disallowed," *San Antonio Light*, November 16, 1938.

47. "Voks Capture District Flag Twice in Row," *San Antonio Light*, November 18, 1938.

48. "Sidney Lanier Coaches Produce Winning Clubs," *San Antonio Express*, June 4, 1939, 4B.

49. "Lanier Voks Honored," *San Antonio Light*, December 22, 1938.

50. "Trades School Ready for Opening," *San Antonio Light*, August 28, 1924.

51. Ibid.

52. See San Miguel's *"Let All of Them Take Heed,"* 39–47, for a discussion of how Texas educators saw Mexican American students as mostly capable of vocational education.

53. See "Trades School Ready for Opening."

54. "School Overcrowded as Enrollment Takes Leap," *San Antonio Light*, January 27, 1939.

55. Ibid.

56. "Wrestle with Lanier Hi Jam," *San Antonio Light*, January 28, 1939.

57. Ibid.

58. "Tax Rate for Schools to Be Aired," *San Antonio Light*, February 1, 1939.

59. "$1 Tax Rate Is Retained by Board of Education," *San Antonio Light*, February 2, 1939.

60. Ibid.

61. "Public Schools Hear Credit Loss Warning Lifted," *San Antonio Light*, December 2, 1938.

62. Ibid.

63. "Boon to Youth," *San Antonio Light*, February 14, 1939.

CHAPTER 3

1. "International Clubmen Beat Lanier 39–26," unattributed newspaper clipping, December 21, 1938, in author's possession.

2. Ibid.

3. Tony Rivera, interview with the author, June 9, 2011. This is the second interview with Rivera.

4. "Watching the Hi Cage Teams," *San Antonio Light*, January 6, 1939.

5. Ibid.

6. Ibid.

7. Ibid.

8. Ibid.

9. Ibid.

10. "Interest Keen as High Cagers Square Off," *San Antonio Light*, January 6, 1939. Also see McLemore, *Texas High School Basketball Scrapbook*, 19, for Reagan's run at the state title.

11. "Champions Fall by Wayside in Cage Tourney," *San Antonio Light*, January 7, 1939.

12. Ibid.

13. "Jeff Davis Hi Cage Winner," *San Antonio Light*, January 8, 1939, 1, 4.

14. "City High Cage Series Opens with Pair," *San Antonio Light*, January 11, 1939.

15. Photos in *San Antonio Light*, January 11, 1939, 6A.

16. "Jefferson Off to Battle in Houston Cage Tourney," *San Antonio Light*, January 13, 1939.

17. "Voks Go into Tie for Top in City Series; Brackenridge Meets Burbank Today," *San Antonio Express*, January 13, 1939.

18. "Jefferson Off to Battle in Houston Cage Tourney."

19. Ibid.

20. Ibid.

21. Ibid.

22. "Lanier Meets Brackenridge," *San Antonio Light*, January 17, 1939.

23. "Brewer Blasts Hays in Edison-Lanier Row," *San Antonio Light*, January 18, 1939.

24. Ibid.

25. "Hays Says Edison Firm in Its Stand on Lanier," *San Antonio Light*, January 20, 1939.

26. Joe Bernal, interview with Stephen Casanova, January 6, 1987.

27. Lackey's Stars in Close Win," *San Antonio Express*, January 19, 1959.

28. At this time, students often became ineligible during the season either through age or through mid-term graduations, and sometimes teams would lose a good size of their roster before the season ended. See "Graduation Set at S.A. Schools," *San Antonio Light*, January 19, 1939, for an example of a mid-term graduation.

29. Bill Michaelis, "Lackey Stars in Close Win," *San Antonio Express*, January 19, 1939.

30. Ibid.

31. See Acuñas, *Occupied America.*

32. "Lanier Moves Up to Undisputed Possession of Second Place by Beating Tech 35–21; Indians Beat Burbank," *San Antonio Light*, January 21, 1939. For the Tivy victory, see "Lanier Beats Tivy," *San Antonio Light*, January 24, 1939.

33. "Jefferson Plays Lanier Tonight," *San Antonio Light*, January 25, 1939.

34. "Voks Shade Jeff, Stay Right on Eagles' Heels," *San Antonio Light*, January 26, 1939.

35. "Mustangs Fight Uphill Battle, Nearly Make It," *San Antonio Express*, January 26, 1939.

36. "Voks Set New Scoring Mark for Year, Beating Bulldogs 53–21; Mustangs Beat Buffs 31–20," *San Antonio Light*, January 28, 1939.

37. "Now It'll Be Eagles and Voks Neck and Neck," *San Antonio Light*, January 28, 1939.

38. "Joe Treviño Tallies 16 points to Lead Voks into Tie for First Place with Brackenridge," *San Antonio Light*, February 9, 1939.

39. "Burbank and Tech Play This Afternoon for Cellar Title; Four 'B' Teams in Action," *San Antonio Light*, February 10, 1939.

40. "Lanier High Favored to Win City Cage Championship," *San Antonio Light*, February 10, 1939.

41. Ibid.

42. "Come through in Overtime to Win, 26–24," *Express and News*, February 11, 1939.

43. Jesse Camacho and Carlos Camacho, interview with the author, March 20, 2011.

44. "Stab Boy in School Riot," *San Antonio Light*, February 11, 1939.

45. Ibid.

46. "Come through in Overtime to Win, 26–24."

47. "Stab Boy in School Riot."

48. See Mazon, *The Zoot-Suit Riots.*

49. "Stab Boy in School Riot."

50. Tony Cardona, interview with the author, spring 2011.

51. This information is from the Tony Cardona interview with the author. During this interview, Rebecca Jimenez (Cardona) answered several questions about her Lanier experience. Initially she agreed with Cardona, but on further discussion she admitted that "you heard a lot and saw a lot" that dealt with discrimination.

52. Cardona interview.

53. Jesse and Carlos Camacho interview.

54. Rivera interview.

55. The details of the taunting were not covered in the newspapers but were discussed on the Internet and the KENS5 television station on their sports blog. That blog does not exist anymore, but the incident is referred to in another KENS5 blog covering a similar incident the following year with another predominantly Mexican American school. Ironically, the school was the old Lanier nemesis, Edison High School. See Flores, "SAISD Files Complaint over Taunting."

56. "Voks Breeze to Easy Win over Tech Five," *San Antonio Light*, February 14, 1939.

57. Ibid.

58. "Lanier Needs Two Wins to Cop Title," *San Antonio Light*, February 18, 1939. Also see "Lanier Romps to Easy Win over LaVernia," *San Antonio Express*, February 18, 1939.

59. "Bobcats Make Battle of It, Bowing 34–28," *San Antonio Express*, February 19, 1939.

60. "South San Antonio Gives Lanier Hi Fight in District," *San Antonio Light*, February 19, 1939.

61. "Fanning Trims Lanier High Champions," *San Antonio Express*, February 24, 1939.

62. "Lanier Cagers Favored in Regional," *San Antonio Light*, February 25, 1939.

63. "Lanier Voks Go after Place in State Playoffs Today in San Marcos," *San Antonio Express*, February 25, 1939.

64. "S.A. Boys Cop 25–20 Decision in Title Game," *San Antonio Light*, February 26, 1939.

65. "State Basketball," [*San Antonio Light* or *Express*], February 27, 1939.

66. "Lanier Drawn to Oppose Gilmer," *San Antonio Light*, February 28, 1939.

67. Ibid.

68. "Rodriguez Out Voks Wind up Cage Work," *San Antonio Light*, March 2, 1939.

69. "Sidney Lanier Scraps Seven Other Quints," *San Antonio Light*, March 3, 1939.

70. "Lanier Off to Cage Meet," *San Antonio Light*, March 3, 1939. Also see "Sidney Lanier Scraps Seven Other Quints."

71. See "Lanier Battles Abilene in State Tourney," *San Antonio Light*, March 4, 1939; and "Voks Turn Back Gilmer Quintet in First Game," *San Antonio Express and News*, March 4, 1939.

72. "Voks Go Down in Title Game by 37–35 Count," *San Antonio Express*, March 5, 1939.

73. For a composite of the game, see ibid.; and "Lanier Nosed Out in Finals," *San Antonio Light*, March 5, 1939.

74. See "Voks Go Down in Title Game."

75. "Herrera, Proud of Lanier Boys, Says: 'No Alibis,'" *San Antonio Light*, March 6, 1939.

76. Ibid.

77. Cardona interview.

CHAPTER 4

1. Jessie Vargas Camacho, interview by the author, March 22, 2011.
2. See *Los Recuerdos*, 1940.
3. See *Los Recuerdos*, 1942.
4. Ibid.
5. *Los Recuerdos*, 1940.
6. "Dedication," *Los Recuerdos*, 1941, 7.
7. Rosie Peña and Irene Ramirez, interview by the author, March 22, 2011.
8. Jessie Vargas Camacho interview.
9. For the best work to date on this educational battle, see San Miguel's *"Let All of Them Take Heed."*
10. See "Clubs," *Los Recuerdos*, 1940.
11. Ibid.
12. See "The Stamp Club," *Los Recuerdos*, 1941, 45.
13. Sidney Lanier, "The Symphony," in *Poems of Sidney Lanier* (C. Scribner's Sons, 1891).
14. See "Clubs," *Los Recuerdos*, 1940.
15. *Los Recuerdos*, 1941, 47.
16. Ibid., 45.
17. "School Life," *Los Recuerdos*, 1942, which has a longer biography of each club and organization at Lanier.
18. See *Los Recuerdos*, 1941, 45.
19. Ibid.
20. Ibid. Also see "School Life," *Los Recuerdos*, 1942.
21. *Los Recuerdos*, 1941, 45.
22. Ibid.
23. See ibid., 47.
24. Jessie Vargas Camacho interview.
25. See Richard A. García, *Rise of the Mexican American Middle Class*, 73–83.
26. "Latin American Pupils Learn Americanism via Mexico Route," *San Antonio Light*, December 4, 1938.
27. Ibid.
28. See "School Life," *Los Recuerdos*, 1940.
29. Ibid.
30. See "Clubs," *Los Recuerdos*, 1940.
31. Ibid.
32. See "Latin American Pupils Learn Americanism via Mexico Route."
33. See "Clubs," *Los Recuerdos*, 1940.
34. Ibid.
35. Jesse Camacho mentioned this while I interviewed his wife Jessie about her experience at Lanier. While she thought that she was learning much at the school, he differed by saying that the teaching of English was particularly poor, even though admittedly his English was perfect.

36. For a discussion of this adoption of "Spanish culture" by whites, see McWilliams, *North from Mexico*; and Padilla, *My History, Not Yours.*

37. For a good discussion on how immigrants become "white," see Roediger's *Working toward Whiteness.* For a much more in-depth and academic study of "whiteness," see Delgado and Stefancic, *Critical White Studies.*

38. See "Brewer, 97, led Blue Jackets at Lanier in the '30s," *San Antonio Express and News*, November 5, 2009, for son's discussion of his mother's love for the school and the dinner discussions about Lanier.

39. Richard A. García, *Rise of the Mexican American Middle Class*, 182. For a view of what Mexican American reformers were saying about segregation see Manuel, "Education of Mexican and Spanish-Speaking Children in Texas." Also see George I. Sánchez, *Concerning Segregation of Spanish-Speaking Children in the Public Schools.*

40. See Richard Rodriguez's *Hunger of Memory.*

41. See Ignacio M. Garcia, *White but Not Equal.* Also see Chafe, *Civilities and Civil Rights*, for a discussion of what desegregation did to black teachers and black elite students and others who were likely to participate in an all-black school but rarely had the same opportunities in desegregated schools.

42. All of this information—interpreted with creative license—is found in "Seniors," *Los Recuerdos*, 1940.

43. See *Los Recuerdos*, 1941, 21–26, for the senior pictures and comments. The names and pictures are not in alphabetical order.

44. Jesse Camacho remembers the team players calling Riojas "Alitas," which also means "little wings," though he doesn't remember for sure why they called him that, though he does remember him as a good leaper.

45. *Los Recuerdos*, 1941, 23.

46. Ibid., 24.

47. Ibid., 26.

48. Ibid., 27.

49. Richard A. García, *Rise of the Mexican American Middle Class*, 181.

50. "P.T.A. Council to Meet Friday," unattributed newspaper clipping, January 22, 1939.

51. See "Uniforms Issued to School Cadets," unattributed newspaper clipping, January 11, 1939.

52. See *Los Recuerdos*, 1941, 42.

53. See "The Girl Reserve Club," *Los Recuerdos*, 1942.

54. See "As a Girl Reserve," ca. 1920s, Portland YWCA Archives, Portland, Oreg. Most of the information is found in the archives of local YWCAs that sponsored a Girl Reserves.

55. Ibid.

56. Ibid.

CHAPTER 5

1. Jesse Camacho and Carlos Camacho, interview by the author, November 13, 2009.

2. "Jefferson Meets Lanier in Feature City Series Game Tonight," *San Antonio Express*, January 15, 1940, 2A.

3. "Lanier Nips San Marcos," *San Antonio Express*, January 9, 1940.

4. Ibid.

5. "Lanier and Brackenridge Maintain Positions in City Series Race," *San Antonio Express*, January 23, 1940.

6. "City High School Basketball Race Gets Going Tonight," *San Antonio Express*, January 10, 1940, 1A. See also "Brackenridge and Lanier in Important Game Tonight," *San Antonio Express*, January 19, 1940.

7. Carlos Camacho and Jesse Camacho interview, March 20, 2011.

8. See "Lanier and Brackenridge Maintain Positions in City Series Race."

9. "City Series Race Winds Up with Twin Bill at Jefferson," *San Antonio Express*, February 17, 1940.

10. Ibid.

11. Jesse Camacho and Carlos Camacho, interview by the author, November 13, 2009.

12. See Menchaca, *Guardian Angel*. This is a side I never saw of Coach Belton. Not all of his former athletes, however, remembered him as fondly. Raul Zuniga, who played for Belton and later became his friend, remembers him as moody, at times difficult, and not a very good basketball coach. In almost twenty years of coaching basketball, he rarely had a winning season. Zuniga also remembers him as coaching a "slow game," compared to Herrera's fast-tempo approach.

13. "Brackenridge and Lanier in Important Game Tonight."

14. See "City High School Basketball Race Gets Going Tonight," for a mention of these two players' new role.

15. Tony Rivera, interview by the author, June 9, 2011.

16. Tony Rivera, interview by Benjamin Dominguez, August 1, 2009, 2.

17. Ibid.

18. Ibid., 3.

19. Ibid., 4.

20. Ibid., 7.

21. "Sidney Lanier Will Afford Antlers Ample Competition in Basketball Game at Tivy Gymnasium Monday Eve," *Kerrville Mountain Sun*, January 2, 1941.

22. "Tivy Basketeers Fall before Lanier Voks Monday Night 45–30," *Kerrville Mountain Sun*, January 9, 1941.

23. "Jefferson Beats Brackenridge to Maintain City Series Lead," *San Antonio Express*, January 18, 1941.

24. "Lanier Voks Meet Tivy in Vok Gym Practice Game," *San Antonio Express*, January 27, 1941.

25. "Tivy Antlers Scare Lanier Voks before Losing Close Game," *Kerrville Mountain Sun*, January 30, 1941.

26. "Tivy Antlers Grab Kerr County Basketball Championship; Whip Center Point Thursday Eve, 40–7," *Kerrville Mountain Sun*, February 20, 1941.

27. "City Series Basketball Chase Heading for Title Game," *San Antonio Express*, February 9, 1941, 5A.

28. See "Basketball," *Los Recuerdos*, 1941 and 1942, for names of returning players.

29. Jessie Vargas Camacho, interview by the author, March 22, 2011; also Jesse Camacho and Carlos Camacho interview, March 20, 2011.

30. José Angel Gutiérrez, unpublished manuscript. I reviewed this manuscript for a university press, but it hasn't been published to date; it is in the possession of José Angel Gutiérrez, who was a close acquaintance of Peña.

31. See Ignacio M. García, *Hector P. García*. Also see Carroll, *Felix Longoria's Wake*.

32. See Ignacio M. García, *Hector P. García*.

33. Jessie Vargas Camacho interview.

34. On playing basketball in Mexican tournaments and leagues, see Jesse and Carlos Camacho interviews, November 13, 2009, and May 20, 2011, as well as Margaret Treviño (Joe's wife) and David Rodríguez, phone conversations with the author, both in April 2011.

35. See Perdew, "The Secondary School Program in World War II." See also "The Nation's Schools after a Year of War."

36. See "The Nation's Schools after a Year of War."

37. Perdew, "The Secondary School Program in World War II," 47.

38. Ibid.

39. Ibid., 47–48.

40. Ibid., 45.

41. Ibid.

42. See Cohen, "Schooling Uncle Sam's Children." I found a mention of this document in Noboa, "On the West Side."

43. For a discussion of the Good Neighbor Policy, first see Roosevelt, "First Inaugural Address." See also Nixon, *Franklin D. Roosevelt and Foreign Affairs*, 1:559–560. For a history of the Texas Good Neighbor Commission, see Kinrea, *History of the First Ten Years of the Texas Good Neighbor Commission*. Also see Green, "Good Neighbor Commission."

44. For Castañeda's political and intellectual views, see Mario T. García, "Carlos E. Castañeda and the Search for History." For a longer biography on the man and his work, see Almaráz, *Knight without Armor*. For a closer look at his time as director of the Fair Employment Practices Committee, see Zamora's *Claiming Rights and Righting Wrongs in Texas*, 125–157.

45. Noboa, "On the West Side," 69.

46. *Los Recuerdos*, 1942.

47. Noboa, "On the West Side," 85.

48. Rafael Castillo, personal communication with the author, no date.
49. For a discussion of the Mexican muralists, see Rochfort, *Mexican Murals.*
50. "Vocational Arts and Crafts Shop," *Los Recuerdos*, 1942.
51. "Auto Mechanics After Noon Class," *Los Recuerdos*, 1942.
52. "Vocational Dressmaking," *Los Recuerdos*, 1942.
53. Ibid.
54. See Noboa's "On the West Side." Jesse Camacho made that comment during my interview with Jessie Vargas Camacho. Jessie also agreed that no college education was ever promoted, though she argued that over time Brewer and the rest of the faculty would begin selectively promoting that as an option to the brighter students.
55. See Richard A. García's *Rise of the Mexican Middle Class.*
56. "Clubs—Activities," *Los Recuerdos*, 1942.
57. "The R.O.T.C. Band," *Los Recuerdos*, 1942.

CHAPTER 6

1. See "Activities of the Senior Class," *Los Recuerdos*, 1942.
2. Ibid.
3. See Ignacio M. García's *Hector P. García* for a discussion of the concern that Mexican American reformers had about their own people's rejection for military service.
4. See "The American of Mexican Descent, a Statement of Principle," 2. For a discussion of this document, see Ignacio M. García's *Viva Kennedy*. Also see Bray and Ginsberg, *The Uneducated.*
5. See Manuel, *The Education of Mexican and Spanish-Speaking Children in Texas*, 92; also see Sánchez, "Concerning Segregation of Spanish-Speaking Children in the Public Schools."
6. See "The American of Mexican Descent," 6.
7. George Wright, "Basket Ball Year 'Round, Lanier Sport," *San Antonio Light*, April 4, 1943, 2.
8. Ibid.
9. Ibid.
10. Tony Cardona, interview by the author, June 9, 2011.
11. Tony Rivera, interview by the author, June 9, 2011.
12. Walter Kelley, interview by the author, June 9, 2011.
13. "Basket Ball Year 'Round, Lanier Sport."
14. Three books of value in understanding this phenomena are Grundy, *Learning to Win*; Levine, *Ellis Island to Ebbets Field*; and Gorn, *The Manly Art*. The last is a study of boxing in American society, but it provides some view of the rise of ethnic American participation in the sport.
15. For a discussion of one less traditional immigrant group's involvement in sports, see Yep, *Outside the Paint*. For a story of a nonimmigrant group but one still considered outside the mainstream in sports, see Peavy and Smith, *Full-Court Quest.*

16. The information on the former Lanier players playing in Mexico comes from conversations held over several years with the Camacho brothers, David Rodríguez, and Margaret Treviño and from some of the players' press clippings from Mexican newspapers. Carlos Camacho joked that, in one of the Mexican tournaments, his brother Jesse was named the "dirtiest" player of the event. For one of the few academic works done on American-born Mexicans playing south of the border, see Alamilla, "Playing across Borders."

17. Raul Zuniga, e-mail to Felix Urrieta, January 17, 2009. This e-mail was pointed out to the author by Charles Herrera, who sent the e-mail to me.

18. Raul Zuniga, interview with author, June 7, 2011.

19. Joe Bernal, e-mail to Felix [no last name given], May 30, 2011, in the author's possession.

20. Joe Bernal, interview by the author, June 10, 2011.

21. David Rodríguez, interview by the author in El Paso, Texas, June 15, 2011.

22. Kelley interview.

23. Rodríguez interview.

24. Tony Rivera interview, June 9, 2011. At the time of the interview, Rivera had lost custody of himself, and his affairs were being executed by a family member.

25. Ibid.

26. Both Rivera and Kelley spoke glowingly about Escobedo in their respective interviews.

27. The pictures in the 1942, 1943, and 1944 yearbooks all show a very serious young man. Most players remembered him as quite serious.

28. Rivera interview, June 9, 2011.

29. *Los Recuerdos*, 1943.

30. See Rudy Bernal, interview by the author, November 12, 2009.

31. Kelley interview.

32. Rivera interview, June 9, 2011.

33. Kelley interview.

34. Rivera interview, June 9, 2011.

35. Ibid.

36. Ibid.

37. "Invitation Basketball Tourney Starts Today at Brackenridge," *San Antonio Express*, January 2, 1942, 4A.

38. "Jefferson Cagers Win High Tourney," *San Antonio Light*, January 4, 1942, pt. 6.

39. Ibid.

40. "Favored Vok Cagers Idle as District 26-A Starts," *San Antonio Light*, January 6, 1942.

41. Ibid.

42. "Lanier Rated Third Best in Houston Meet," *San Antonio Light*, January 9, 1942.

43. "Lanier Tackles Mules Tonight," *San Antonio Express*, January 8, 1942, 8.

44. "Jeff, Voks Tied Up in City Hi Race," *San Antonio Light*, January 7, 1942.

45. Ibid.

46. Harold Scherwitz, "Sportlights," *San Antonio Light*, January 6, 1942, 11A.

47. Ibid.

48. Phone conversation with David Rodríguez on September 13, 2012.

49. Scherwitz, "Sportlights."

50. "Lanier Loses in First Round of Cage Meet," *San Antonio Express*, January 10, 1942.

51. "Lanier Still in Houston Consolation," *San Antonio Light*, January 10, 1942.

52. Ibid.

53. Rivera interview, June 9, 2011.

54. Charles Herrera, phone conversation with the author, June 1, 2011. Charles remembers the meeting with his cousin as being quite emotional. He expressed regret over not having known his grandmother—in fact, he could not remember her maiden name—but felt comfortable with his ethnic heritage and proud of his father's work with the Mexican youth of both San Antonio and El Paso.

55. Rodríguez interview.

56. All the players I spoke to remember her as an avid fan. Some remember meeting her and her children, and Charles Herrera remembers the Lanier players rubbing his hair every time they saw him. A couple of them—Jesse Camacho and Walter Kelley—even remember driving her home a couple of times.

57. Herrera phone conversation.

58. "Lanier Beats Edison 34–15," *San Antonio Express*, January 17, 1942. Also see "Edison Bears Meet Lanier in Golden Jubilee Game Tonight," *San Antonio Express*, January 16, 1942.

59. "Voks Win Fourth Straight Game by Defeating Hot Wells 67–13; Burbank and Heights Also Win," *San Antonio Express*, January 20, 1942.

60. "Lanier Takes on Burbank in District 28-A," *San Antonio Light*, January 21, 1942.

61. "Buttons Lick Lanier 25–24," *San Antonio Express*, January 27, 1942.

62. "Lanier Voks Face Bobcat Challenge," *San Antonio Light*, January 30, 1942.

63. See "Voks Wallop Edison 34–11 in 28-A District," *San Antonio Express*, February 5, 1942; and "Lanier Beats Burbank 35–20," *San Antonio Express*, February 10, 1942.

64. "Lanier Tackles Lampasas in Jeff Gym," *San Antonio Express*, February 25, 1942.

65. "Lampasas Badgers Upset Lanier Voks by 35–33 Score," *San Antonio Express*, February 26, 1942.

66. Ibid.

67. See "Basket Ball," *Los Recuerdos*, 1942.

68. "Lanier Takes Region Crown by 31–25," *San Antonio Express*, March 1, 1942.

69. "Voks Capture Title, Beating Badgers, 31–25," *San Antonio Light*, March 1, 1942.

70. "Lanier Passes Up Chance to Practice," *San Antonio Light*, March 4, 1942.

71. Ibid.

72. "State Schoolboy Basketball Play Opens Today at Austin," *Corpus Christi Caller*, March 5, 1942.

73. Ibid.

74. "Houston, Dallas, Lufkin in Cage Semi-finals," *Galveston Daily News*, March 6, 1942.

75. Ibid.

76. Ibid.

77. "Lanier Wins First Game in State Tournament," *San Antonio Express*, March 6, 1942.

78. "Lanier Loses to Nederland in Semi-final 31–28," *San Antonio Express*, March 7, 1942.

79. "AA Cage Title to Jeff Davis of Houston," *San Antonio Express*, March 8, 1942.

CHAPTER 7

1. See "Basketball," *Los Recuerdos*, 1942.
2. Ibid.
3. Ibid.
4. David Rodríguez, interview with author, June 15, 2011, El Paso, Texas.
5. Ibid.
6. Both Walter Kelley and David Rodríguez, as well as Tony Rivera, in their respective interviews remembered fondly those tournaments. Kelley, in particular, believed that those allowed him to get an invitation to the varsity team, though he was already on Herrera's radar with his play in the junior varsity.
7. Rodríguez interview, June 15, 2011.
8. Charlie Herrera, phone interview by the author, July 1, 2011.
9. Rodríguez interview, June 15, 2011.
10. Ibid.
11. Tony Rivera, interview by the author, June 9, 2011.
12. Rodríguez interview, June 15, 2011.
13. Ibid.
14. Ibid.
15. David Rodríguez, phone interview with the author, August 3, 2011.
16. Ibid.
17. Ibid.
18. Ibid.
19. *El Nopal*, untitled and undated clipping, David Rodríguez scrapbook.
20. Rodríguez interview, August 3, 2011.
21. *El Nopal*, untitled and undated clipping.
22. Rodríguez interview, August 3, 2011.
23. "South San Antonio Tourney Slated for Friday and Saturday," *San Antonio Express*, December 13, 1942.
24. "Voks Beat Buttons with Score of 27–21 to Win S.S. Tourney," unattributed clipping, [likely *San Antonio Light*], December 20, 1942.
25. "Lanier Cops South San Tourney by Defeating Central 27–21," *San Antonio*

Express, December 20, 1942. This article has Rodríguez scoring eight points and Rivera nine, but "Voks Beat Buttons" has Rodríguez with eleven.

26. "Voks Beat Buttons."

27. "Burbank Duels South San; Tech Battles Lanier," unattributed clipping, [likely *San Antonio Express*], January 4, 1943, David Rodríguez scrapbook.

28. "Tech Tackles Lanier in Feature," *San Antonio Light*," January 4, 1943.

29. "City School Leaguers Play Double Bill," unattributed clipping, January 6, 1943, in the author's possession.

30. Joe Bernal, "Sports Spotlights," *El Nopal*, no date, located in the Sidney Lanier High School library. Also see "Hot Wells and Edison Meet in 28-A Contest," *San Antonio Express*, January 5, 1943; and "Four Hi Teams Stand Out at Week's End," *San Antonio Light*, January 9, 1943.

31. "Schoolboys in Twin Bill Tonight," unattributed clipping, January 6, 1943, David Rodríguez scrapbook.

32. For a compilation of tidbits on the Brackenridge game, see "Jeffs, Voks Tied Up in City Hi Race," *San Antonio Light*, January 7, 1943; Joe Bernal, "Sports Spotlights"; and "Four Hi Teams Stand Out at Week's End."

33. "3 Tussles Booked in Lanier Gym," unattributed clipping, Rodríguez scrapbook. For more on Martinez, see "Four Hi Teams Stand Out at Week's End."

34. "Basketball," unattributed sports news wrap-up column from Rodríguez scrapbook.

35. Ibid.

36. "28-A Basketeers Battle," *San Antonio Light*, January 15, 1943.

37. David Rodríguez, phone conversation with the author, November 1, 2011.

38. "28-A Basketeers Battle."

39. "Lanier Leads 28-A; Plays Jeff Monday," unattributed clipping, Rodríguez scrapbook.

40. Ibid.

41. "Voks to Cage Bears," unattributed clipping, Rodríguez scrapbook.

42. Ibid.

43. For pregame coverage of the match between the teams, see "Jeff Ponies Tackle Voks for Top Spot"; "Jeff to Play Brackenridge Friday Night"; and "Jeffs Battle Voks," January 18, 1943; unattributed clippings, Rodríguez scrapbook. The Winkle quotes are from "Jeff Ponies Tackle Voks for Top Spot."

44. "Winning Voks Ready for Brackenridge," *San Antonio Light*, January 26, 1943.

45. Ibid.

46. For those two games, see "Voks Smother Tech 46–5," unattributed clipping, Rodríguez scrapbook; also "Sport Spotlights."

47. "Voks Smother Tech 46–5."

48. "Sports Spotlights."

49. Tony Rivera, interview with the author, June 9, 2011.

50. Much of this assessment comes from talking to his son Rudy Bernal (interview on November, 12, 2009), who at the writing of this book had been coaching the Lanier Voks for over twenty-five years, and from new articles and conversations with

some of the other players. Without doubt Bernal was a more likeable guy and one very much in the easygoing mode of most of the Lanier players.

51. "Winner to Be Front Runner in Flag Chase," unattributed clipping, Rodríguez scrapbook.

52. Ibid.

53. "Voks Win District Championship," Rodríguez scrapbook.

54. "Lanier Short of Talent for Tough Tourney," *San Antonio Light*, March 2, 1943.

55. "Lanier Plays Lakeview in First Tussle," *San Antonio Light*, March 4, 1943.

56. "Lanier Short of Talent for Tough Tourney."

57. Ibid.

58. "State Tourney for Highs Holds Cage Spotlight," *San Antonio Light*, March 1, 1943. See also, "Lanier Top Class A Team in State Meet," *San Antonio Express*, March 1, 1943.

59. "Lanier Short of Talent for Tough Tourney."

60. "Lanier Plays Lakeview in First Tussle."

61. Unattributed clipping, March 5, 1943 [probably *San Antonio Light* or *San Antonio Express*], in Rodríguez scrapbook.

62. "Rivera's Right," unattributed clipping [probably March 5, 1943], Rodríguez scrapbook.

63. "Jeff Davis, Lanier Look Good at Austin," unattributed clipping, Rodríguez scrapbook.

64. "Austin and Lanier Win to Move into State AA and A Cage Finals," unattributed clipping [possibly March 6, 1943], Rodríguez scrapbook.

65. "Lanier, Austin Survive to State Finals," *San Antonio Light*, March 6, 1943.

66. Walter Kelley, interview by the author, June 9, 2011.

67. "Lanier Wins Class B State Title; Jeff Davis Beats Austin in Class AA," *San Antonio Light*, March 7, 1943. This article erroneously says that Lanier won the Class B title when it was the Class A title that the Voks won.

68. "Lanier Wins State Class A Title by Defeating French, 30–18," *San Antonio Express*, March 7, 1943.

69. Ibid.

70. "Lanier Places Two on All-State," *San Antonio Light*, March 7, 1943. Also see "Lanier Wins State Class A Title." For Rivera's point total, see "Lanier Wins Class B State Title."

CHAPTER 8

1. Quotations from Margaret E. Sangster, poem; and Thomas Bailey Aldrich, "Unguarded Gates," poem, in *Los Recuerdos*, 1943, on the first page following the hard front cover.

2. "Wide Walls" (author unknown); see "Our Guides and Friends," *Los Recuerdos*, 1943, 4.

3. These words are spoken in the movie *Casablanca* (1942) when Rick, after trick-

ing Ilsa into going with her husband to America, says, "I'm no good at being noble, but it doesn't take much to see that the problems of three little people don't amount to a hill of beans in this crazy world."

4. See Mario T. García, *Mexican Americans*, 166, for a discussion of the National Spanish-Speaking Congress and other Mexican American organizations that became part of a left-of-center Popular Front.

5. Ibid., 29.

6. See Rivas-Rodriguez, *Mexican Americans and World War II*, for a discussion of Mexican American pride in their service to the nation during the war.

7. "ROTC Enrollment at All-Time High," *San Antonio Light*, October 3, 1943.

8. Ibid.

9. "Lanier Students Push Jeep Purchase Plan," unattributed clipping, April 14, 1943 [likely from one of the San Antonio newspapers], in the author's possession.

10. "Bond Drive Nets 170 Jeeps Here," unattributed clipping, March 18, 1943, in the author's possession.

11. See "All Paths Lead to the Stamp Windows," *Los Recuerdos*, 1943.

12. Following "Our Classmates" and the section on vocational shops, "A Song of Victory" was the first section to introduce student activities and clubs; *Los Recuerdos*, 1943.

13. See "Scrap! Tons of It! Lanier Brought It In!" *Los Recuerdos*, 1943.

14. See "The Student Council's Newest Committee," *Los Recuerdos*, 1943.

15. "The Student Council's Newest Committee," *Los Recuerdos*, 1943.

16. "Zoom, Rat, Tat, Tat, Boom! That Is What You Get," *Los Recuerdos*, 1943.

17. "The Paint and Trim Shop," in the larger section "On the Vocational Side," *Los Recuerdos*, 1943.

18. See "Body and Fender Work Morning Class" and "The Body and Fender Shop—Afternoon Class" in "On the Vocational Side," *Los Recuerdos*, 1943.

19. See "Auto Mechanic Shop Morning Class" and "Auto Mechanics Afternoon Class," *Los Recuerdos*, 1943.

20. Ibid.

21. See "Print Shop" and "Art Shop" sections in "On the Vocational Side," *Los Recuerdos*, 1943.

22. See "Vocational Dressmaking," *Los Recuerdos*, 1943, which has a large picture of some young women using sewing machines, others sewing by hand, and still others standing and watching.

23. Ibid.

24. This is a two-page section with three rows of names in each page.

25. See Rivas-Rodriguez, *Mexican Americans and World War II.*

26. Walter Kelley, interview by the author, June 9, 2011.

27. See sport section, *Los Recuerdos*, 1943, for information on the Class B team; also see "Basketball Champions," *Los Recuerdos*, 1944.

28. David Rodríguez used the term "big dog" in a phone conversation with the author, September 15, 2011.

29. Ibid. Rodríguez played with Escobedo for two years and became one of the main recipients of his passes when Rivera left.

30. Ibid.

31. See "Last Will and Testament," *Los Recuerdos*, 1944.

32. "Vocational Basketball Team to Get First Try-out in South San Tourney," unattributed clipping, David Rodríguez scrapbook.

33. Ibid.

34. For coverage on the tournament, see "Charlotte Joins 3 City Clubs in Semifinals" and "Lanier Wins South San Cage Tourney," both unattributed clippings, [likely December 16–18, 1943], Rodríguez scrapbook. The scrapbook has the box scores for the semifinal game.

35. "Lanier Defeats Burbank, 50–2," *San Antonio Light*, January 5, 1944. See also, "Lanier Stops 'Em Cold," *San Antonio Express*, January 5, 1944.

36. "Lanier Breezes in for Win over Hot Wells," *San Antonio Express*, January 7, 1944.

37. See "Lanier Downs South San, 35–15," *San Antonio Express*, January 12, 1944; and "Lanier Defeats Edison Bears in 28-A Tilt," *San Antonio Express*, January 15, 1944.

38. See "Jeffs, Lanier in Battle of Unbeaten Fives," unattributed clipping, Rodríguez scrapbook.

39. Ibid.

40. "Second Round Starts in City Hi Series," unattributed clipping, Rodríguez scrapbook. Also see "Lanier Hands Jefferson Crushing 30–18 Defeat," *San Antonio Express*, January 19, 1944.

41. "Second Round Starts in City Hi Series."

42. "Lanier Stomps Harlandale Five," *San Antonio Light*, January 22, 1944.

43. See "Lanier Easily Beats Burbank," *San Antonio Express*, January 26, 1944; and "Jefferson AA Basketball Champ Again," unattributed clipping, Rodríguez scrapbook.

44. "Lanier Defeats Blue Devils in 28-A Go, 40–5," *San Antonio Express*, January 29, 1944.

45. "Austin Visits Eagles; Title for Lanier," unattributed clipping, Rodríguez scrapbook.

46. Ibid.

47. "Lanier Whips Edison Quint," *San Antonio Express*, February 5, 1944.

48. "Lanier Hikes Win Streak to 31 in Row," unattributed clipping, Rodríguez scrapbook.

49. "Basketball Team Seeks to Match Last Year's State Champ Record," unattributed clipping [probably from *El Nopal*].

50. Rodríguez phone conversation.

51. Ibid.

52. "Lanier and Brackenridge in Hi Feature," unattributed clipping, Rodríguez scrapbook. Also see "Eagles, Jeffs Meet in City Series Windup," unattributed clipping, Rodríguez scrapbook.

53. "Lanier Defeats Eagles in Close One, 19–17," *San Antonio Express*, February 8, 1944. Also see "Eagles, Jeffs Meet in City Series Windup."

54. "Lanier Edges Harlandale," *San Antonio Express*, February 11, 1944.

55. See "Lanier Defeats Central, 32–16," *San Antonio Express*, February 16, 1944; and "Lanier Whips Central, 37–14," *San Antonio Express*, February 24, 1944.

56. See "Class A Cage Teams Begin Region Play," "Lanier Seeks Region Title at Lockhart," "Lanier Shoots for Region Cage Laurels," and "Lanier Plays LaGrange in Friday Opener," unattributed clippings, Rodríguez scrapbook.

57. Their names are included in a program published for the regional tournament. In that program, Ramiro Gonzalez is incorrectly referred to as Romero; Rodríguez scrapbook.

58. "Lanier Takes Fine Record to State Tourney," unattributed clipping, Rodríguez scrapbook.

59. Rodríguez phone conversation.

60. Ibid.

61. "Voks Gallop through Meet at Lockhart," unattributed clipping, Rodríguez scrapbook.

62. Ibid.

63. Tony Rivera, interview with the author, June 9, 2011.

64. Kelley interview.

65. Rodríguez phone conversation.

66. Ibid. David recounted that Nemo Herrera kidded Ramiro and told him that if he did not change his ways he was "going to get killed."

67. "Lanier Takes Fine Record to State Tourney," unattributed clipping, Rodríguez scrapbook.

68. Ibid.

69. "Lanier Opens Defense of State Title," unattributed clipping, Rodríguez scrapbook. Also see "Voks, El Campo Risk Unbeaten Cage Records," *San Antonio Light*, March 2, 1944.

70. "Lanier Plays Mt. Vernon in Second Round," unattributed clipping, Rodríguez scrapbook. Also see "Escobedo Paces Voks to 38–21 Cage Victory," *San Antonio Express*, March 3, 1944.

71. For a mention of Smith's state championship team before World War II, see McLemore, *The Texas High School Basketball Scrapbook*, 19. For the team record of the championship team, see Onley, *Coach "Catfish" Smith and His Boys*, inside cover flap.

72. "Lanier Plays Mt. Vernon in Second Round."

73. Onley, *Coach "Catfish" Smith and His Boys*, 118–119.

74. For constructions of the game, see "Lanier Loses to Mt. Vernon in State Meet" and "Voks End Basketball Season with Third Place in State Tourney," both unattributed clippings, Rodríguez scrapbook. Also see "Austin Beaten by Childress in State Meet," *San Antonio Express*, March 4, 1944.

75. See "Lanier Loses to Mt. Vernon in State Meet."

76. Joe Bernal, interview by the author, June 10, 2011.

77. Raul Zuniga, interview by the author, June 8, 2011.

78. Joe Bernal, interview by the author, June 10, 2011.
79. "Voks End Basketball Season with Third Place in State Tourney."
80. "All State Cagers," *San Antonio Express*, March 5, 1944.
81. Escobedo declined to be interviewed for this book, even when I expressed his critical role in the team's story.

CHAPTER 9

1. This comment was one repeated several times during my conversations with David Rodríguez, including my interview with him on June 15, 2011.
2. "Sports Eye: Adventures of Three Lanier Students on Trip to Austin as Told by Herbert Kelley," undated clipping [probably from *El Nopal*], David Rodríguez scrapbook. There is no collection of *El Nopal* left in any known depository, so it is difficult to confirm though it is in the style of the *El Nopal* newspaper.
3. Ibid.
4. Ibid.
5. Ibid.
6. Ibid.
7. Onley, *Coach "Catfish" Smith and His Boys*, 117.
8. This is part of larger introduction to the yearbook, *Los Recuerdos*, 1945, 2.
9. Ibid., 3, in the section on the administration.
10. See "Seniors," *Los Recuerdos*, 1945, where beside each name is listed not only the student's club affiliations and offices but also their "life ambition."
11. See Campbell, *Women at War with America*, chap. 2.
12. *Los Recuerdos*, 1944. The information comes from the captions that accompanied the senior pictures.
13. Joe Bernal, interview by the author, June 10, 2011.
14. The black-and-white yearbook pictures are not always clear-cut in terms of skin lightness, but some show students with markedly lighter or darker complexions. The comments in the "Last Will and Testament" section as well as other pictures in the yearbook make it possible to make assumptions about students' racial and ethnic orientation. The difficultly comes in deciphering which were part-white students and which were white students with no Mexican lineage.
15. *Los Recuerdos*, 1943.
16. "Seniors," *Los Recuerdos*, 1945.
17. See "Last Will and Testament," *Los Recuerdos*, 1944.
18. Junior and sophomore picture section, *Los Recuerdos*, 1945.
19. *Los Recuerdos*, 1943.
20. David Rodríguez, phone interview with author, October 19, 2011.
21. This was told to me by Carlos Camacho during one of the breaks in my interview with Jesse Camacho and Carlos Camacho on March 20, 2011. The "word" was that Tony was accused of "something" and was either expelled or pressured to leave.
22. Bernal interview.

23. "South San Cage Tourney Opens Local Basketball," unattributed clipping, Rodríguez scrapbook.

24. "Athletes in Service," unattributed clipping, Rodríguez scrapbook.

25. Rodríguez, phone interview, October 19, 2011.

26. This perception comes from a picture in David Rodríguez's scrapbook that features the three Rodríguez boys kneeling down. The picture is above an article by Johnny Janes titled, "'Stop Rodriguez' Cry Lanier's Foes," *San Antonio Light*, no date, clipping in David Rodríguez scrapbook.

27. Ibid.

28. One reason for his lower profile may be that he did not get all-state honors or come to many of the award or recognition ceremonies that the players of the '43, '44 and '45 teams received.

29. "South San Cage Tourney Opens Local Basketball."

30. "Lanier Gets Off to Fast Start," December 14, 1944, unattributed clipping, Rodríguez scrapbook.

31. David Rodríguez, phone conversation with the author, November 1, 2011.

32. Ibid.

33. Ibid.

34. "South San's Cage Meet Set to Go," unattributed clipping, Rodríguez scrapbook.

35. "Annual South San Cage Tourney Opens Today," *San Antonio Express*, December 15, 1944.

36. "Lanier and South San Win First Round Tourney Tilts," *San Antonio Light*, December 16, 1944.

37. "Lanier Voks Capture Cage Tournament at South San," *San Antonio Light*, December 17, 1944.

38. Ibid.

39. Ibid., see box scores.

40. David Rodríguez, phone conversation with the author, November 1, 2011.

41. Ibid.

42. A good number of his players took physical education classes with him, and it was there that he identified them as talented enough for the team. While there is nothing in the yearbook or any other publication on his abilities as a teacher, it would have been out of character for Herrera to be anything different in the gym or classroom than he was at basketball practice.

43. David Rodríguez, phone conversation with the author, November 1, 2011.

44. Margaret Treviño, phone conversation with the author, April 2011.

45. Raul Zuniga, interview by the author, March 2011.

46. "Tech and Lanier Meet in Opener of Twin Card," *San Antonio Light*, December 28, 1944.

47. For the names of at least four of them and possibly five, see "Tech Buffs Preseason Cage Choices," unattributed clipping, Rodríguez scrapbook. Another player, named Joe Barron, might have also been Mexican American. The sixth name is that

of Buddy Garza, who is mentioned in "Lanier Continues Unbeaten by Edging Tech Buffs, 46–34" *San Antonio Light*, December 29, 1944.

48. "Lanier Continues Unbeaten by Edging Tech Buffs, 46–34." For the story on the pre-season selection of Fox Tech as one of the top teams in the city, see "Tech Buffs Pre-season Cage Choices."

49. "Normoyle Beats Aggies, 57–43, at Auditorium," unattributed clipping, Rodríguez scrapbook.

50. "Auditorium Basket Ball Big Success," unattributed clipping, Rodríguez scrapbook.

51. "Lanier Wallops Devils, 49–12" and "Lanier, Edison Open with Cage Victories," unattributed clippings, Rodríguez scrapbook.

52. "Lanier Barely Wins; Hopes of Others Rise," unattributed clipping, Rodríguez scrapbook.

53. For game coverage, see "High Goalers in Another Big Program" and "Lanier Voks Edge Jefferson, 33–27," unattributed clippings, Rodríguez scrapbook. The game was played around January 10, 1945.

54. "Voks Eagles Clash," unattributed clipping, Rodríguez scrapbook.

55. Ibid.

56. See "Eagles Scare Lanier but Voks Win, 28–26" and "Close Games in City High Basket Ball," unattributed clippings, Rodríguez scrapbook.

57. For the wrap-up of the three games, see "Lanier Stretches Leads with Win over Burbank," "Lanier Voks Rack Up 15th Straight Victory," and "Lanier Topples Tech, 33–27 for 16th Win," all unattributed clippings, Rodríguez scrapbook.

58. Joe Contreras would be selected as a District 28-A first team selection at guard on February 24, 1946. See "Coaches Pick All-District Class A Basketball Squad," *San Antonio Light*, February 24, 1946.

59. "Lanier Seeks Title Cinch in Eagle Contest," *San Antonio Light*, January 31, 1945.

60. "Kenridge Upsets Lanier," unattributed clipping, Rodríguez scrapbook.

61. David Rodríguez, phone conversation with the author, November 1, 2011.

62. See "Lanier Nears Flag Cinch in District 28-A," *San Antonio Light*, February 7, 1945; and "Lanier Puts Clamp on Tie in 28-A," *San Antonio Light*, February 10, 1945.

63. "Lanier Quint 'I' as City High Champs," *San Antonio Light*, February 13, 1945.

64. Ibid.

65. For information on the earlier matchup, see "Harlandale Hi Blocks Vok Title Path," *San Antonio Light*, February 14, 1945; and for coverage of the second game, see "Lanier Packs Away 28-A Cage Crown," unattributed clipping, Rodríguez scrapbook.

66. "Lanier Packs Away 28-A Cage Crown."

67. "Voks 28-A Champs," unattributed clipping, from Rodríguez scrapbook.

68. "Lanier, Edison Games Close Local Leagues," *San Antonio Light*, February 20, 1945. For a roundup of the game, see unattributed clipping, Rodríguez scrapbook.

69. "Lanier Champs Play Central," *San Antonio Light*, February 22, 1945; see photo caption.

70. "Lanier Defeats Central, 45–28," unattributed clipping, Rodríguez scrapbook.

71. For all the game hype, see "Prairie Lea to Play Lanier," "Prairie Lea's Unbeaten Five Faces Lanier," and "Prairie Lea Plays Voks Wednesday," all unattributed clippings, Rodríguez scrapbook.

72. See ibid.

73. "Prairie Lea Cops Thriller from Lanier," unattributed clipping, Rodríguez scrapbook.

74. The discrepancy seems to have occurred when the scorekeeper gave an extra four points to either Frank Rodríguez or David Rodríguez.

75. "Prairie Lea Nips Lanier," unattributed clipping, Rodríguez scrapbook.

76. David Rodríguez, phone conversation with the author, November 23, 2011.

77. "Prairie Lea Cops Thriller from Lanier."

78. David Rodríguez, phone conversation with the author, November 23, 2011.

79. "Lanier Takes Region 7-A Laurels Again," unattributed clipping, Rodríguez scrapbook.

80. "Lanier Plays St. Mary's in Warm-Up," *San Antonio Light*, March 4, 1945.

81. David Rodríguez, phone conversation with the author, November 23, 2011.

82. "24 Games on High School Cage Schedule," *San Antonio Light*, March 6, 1945.

83. Janes, "Stop Rodriguez' Cry Lanier's Foes."

84. "Lanier Faces Texas City in 8:30 Game," unattributed clipping, Rodríguez scrapbook.

85. Ibid.

86. "Lanier Wins; Next Faces East Mountain," *San Antonio Light*, March 9, 1945.

87. Ibid.

CHAPTER 10

1. This story comes from David Rodríguez, who told it to the author in a phone conversation in the spring of 2012. David heard it from his brother Johnny ("Indio"), who was quite shaken up by the incident.

2. This story came from Joe Bernal, interview by the author, June 10, 2011. Asked about Herrera's reaction, Bernal simply said, "Some people don't react to this [kind of thing]."

3. See Dan Cook, "West Side's Little Giant," *San Antonio Express/News*, August 6, 1967, for the incident in the Laredo hotel.

4. Johnny Janes, "Lanier Favored to Capture State Title," *San Antonio Light*, undated clipping, David Rodríguez scrapbook.

5. Ibid.

6. Ibid.

7. "Paschal's Star Acclaimed by Cage Experts," unattributed clipping, Rodríguez scrapbook.

8. "Lanier Favored to Capture State Title."

9. Johnny Janes, "Lanier Brings Class A State Basket Ball Title to S.A.," *San Antonio Light*, undated.

10. Ibid.

11. "Lanier Home with 'Scrip' for Trophy," unattributed clipping, Rodríguez scrapbook.

12. For information on the dinners honoring the coach and players, see "Lanier Boys Lions' Guests," "Lions Honor Lanier Voks," "Lanier Champions Feted by LULAC," and "Lulac Honors Lanier Champs," all unattributed clippings, Rodríguez scrapbook.

13. David Rodríguez phone conversation, Spring 2012.

14. For information on Kino, Frank, Raul, and David, see "Lanier Looks Forward to 1946 Cage Season," unattributed clipping, Rodríguez scrapbook.

15. For information on Reyes's death and the wounding of Rivera and Olivares, see "Reyes, Lanier State Champ, Dies in Action," *San Antonio Light*, January 16, 1945.

16. "Vok Cage Champs Still in Service," *San Antonio Light*, December 26, 1945.

17. "Frankie Gets Ag Job Passed Up by Herrera," unattributed clipping, Rodríguez scrapbook.

18. Charles Herrera, phone conversation with the author, June 1, 2011.

19. "Vok Cage Champs Still in Service."

20. "Lanier Looks Forward to 1946 Cage Season."

21. "Lanier Crushed by Pasadena 59–25," *San Antonio Express*, March 8, 1946.

22. "Movement Afoot to Oust Lanier Principal, Coach," *San Antonio Express*, March 2, 1947.

23. For this information, see the William Carson "Nemo" Herrera scrapbook, which provides many details on his post-Lanier career.

24. See Cook, "West Side's Little Giant."

Bibliography

INTERVIEWS AND CORRESPONDENCE

Joe Bernal, interview with Stephen Casanova, January 6, 1987, San Antonio, Tex.

Joe Bernal, e-mail to Felix Yruega, May 30, 2011, in author's possession.

Joe Bernal, interview by the author, June 10, 2011, San Antonio, Tex.

Rudy Bernal, interview with the author, April 9, 2009, San Antonio, Tex.

Rudy Bernal, interview with the author, November 12, 2009, San Antonio, Tex.

Jesse Camacho and Carlos Camacho, interview with the author, November 13, 2009, San Antonio, Tex.

Jesse Camacho and Carlos Camacho, interview with the author, March 20, 2011, San Antonio, Tex.

Jessie Vargas Camacho, interview with the author, March 22, 2011, San Antonio, Tex.

Tony Cardona, interview with the author, June 9, 2011, San Antonio, Tex.

Benjamin Dominguez, e-mail to the author, January 22, 2011.

George Farias, phone conversation with the author, February 2012.

David Mercado Gonzalez, interview with the author, June 10, 2010.

Charles Herrera, personal conversation with the author, no date.

Charles Herrera, phone conversation with the author, June 1, 2011.

Charles Herrera, phone interview with the author, July 1, 2011.

Frank Hinojosa, e-mail to Charles Herrera, July 9, 2011; in the author's possession.

Patricia Jacobs, e-mail to the author, January 21, 2011.

Walter Kelley, interview with the author, June 9, 2011.

E. C. Lerma, interview with the author, 1980.

Stella Molina, interview by Benjamin Dominguez, August 2009; in the author's possession.

Rosie Peña, e-mail to the author, January 21, 2011.

Rosie Peña and Irene Ramirez, interview with the author, March 22, 2011, San Antonio, Tex.

Tony Rivera, interview with Benjamin Dominguez, August 1, 2009, San Antonio, Tex.; in the author's possession.
Tony Rivera, interview with the author, June 9, 2011, San Antonio, Tex.
David Rodríguez, phone conversation with the author, April 2011.
David Rodríguez, phone interview with the author, August 3, 2011.
David Rodríguez, interview with author, June 15, 2011, El Paso, Tex.
David Rodríguez, phone conversation with the author, September 13, 2011.
David Rodríguez, phone conversation with the author, September 15, 2011.
David Rodríguez, phone conversation with the author, October 19, 2011.
David Rodríguez, phone conversation with the author, November 1, 2011.
David Rodríguez, phone conversation with the author, November 23, 2011.
David Rodríguez, phone conversation with the author, Spring 2012.
Nicolas Rodríguez, e-mail to the author, January 22, 2011.
Margaret Treviño, phone conversations with the author, April 2011.
Domingo Vasquez, e-mail to the author, January 17, 2010.
Domingo Vasquez, e-mail to the author, January 21, 2011.
Raul Zuniga, e-mail to Felix Urrieta, January 17, 2009; in the author's possession.
Raul Zuniga, interview with the author, March 2011.
Raul Zuniga, interview with the author, June 7, 2011, San Antonio, Tex.
Raul Zuniga, interview with the author, June 8, 2011, San Antonio, Tex.

ARCHIVAL MATERIALS CONSULTED

"1992 Annual Nemo Herrera Memorial San Antonio High School Boys-Girls All-Star Games," a brochure/program used to promote a June 1992 fundraiser for the Nemo Herrera Scholarship Fund, in author's possession.
"The American of Mexican Descent, a Statement of Principle," Texas chapter of the Viva Kennedy Clubs organization, Special Collections, Texas A&M University, Corpus Christi.
"As a Girl Reserve," ca. 1920s, Document 2, Portland YWCA Archives, Portland, Oreg.
William Carson "Nemo" Herrera, scrapbook, in the possession of Charles Herrera.
George Farias, "Anastacio 'Stacy' Farias," biographical sketch, in the author's possession.
"Grand Opening Ceremony for the Alumni Center and Gymnasium Dedication," program, October 12, 2009, in which the gym was named after Herrera; in the author's possession.
José Angel Gutiérrez, unpublished manuscript; in the author's possession.
El Nopal, newspaper. There is no collection of *El Nopal* left in any known depository. Citations in text are from clippings in the personal scrapbook collections of William Carson "Nemo" Herrera and David Rodríguez.
Ratlief, Harold V. *Texas Boys' Basketball, A History*. Pamphlet, University Interscholastic League of Texas, 1976; in the author's possession.

Los Recuerdos, the yearbook of Sidney Lanier High School, San Antonio. Years consulted: 1940–1945, Provided by the San Antonio Independent School District.

David Rodríguez, scrapbook; in his possession; copy in the author's possession.

NEWSPAPERS

Corpus Christi Caller
El Nopal
El Paso Times
Express and News
Galveston Daily News
Kerrville Mountain Sun
Laredo Times
Port Arthur Daily News
Port Arthur News
San Antonio Express
San Antonio Express/News
San Antonio Light
Southwest Airlines Magazine

BOOKS, BOOK CHAPTERS, ARTICLES, AND WEBSITES

Acuñas, Rudolfo. *Occupied America: A History of Chicanos*. New York: Pearson Education, 1972.

Alamilla, José M. "Playing across Borders: Transnational Sports and Identities in Southern California and Mexico, 1930–1945." *Pacific Historical Review* 79, no. 3 (August 2010): 360–392.

Alamillo, José A. *Making Lemonade Out of Lemons: Mexican American Labor and Leisure in a California Town, 1880–1960*. Urbana: University of Illinois Press, 2006.

Almaráz, Felix D. *Knight without Armor: Carlos Eduardo Castañeda, 1896–1958*. College Station: Texas A&M University Press, 1999.

Alvarez, Luis. *The Power of the Zoot: Youth Culture and Resistance during World War II*. Berkeley: University of California Press, 2009.

Arellano, Gustavo. "How Do Mexicans Get Such Ridiculous Nicknames from Seemingly Normal Names?" Pitch.com, January 1, 2009. http://www.pitch.com/kansascity/how-do-mexicans-get-such-ridiculous-nicknames-from-seemingly-normal-names/Content?oid=2192857.

Balderrama, Francisco E., and Raymond Rodríguez. *Decade of Betrayal: Mexican Repatriation in the 1930s*, rev. ed. Albuquerque: University of New Mexico Press, 2006.

Balderrama, Francisco, and Richard A. Santillan, *Mexican American Baseball in Los Angeles*. Charleston, S.C.: Arcadia Publishing, 2011.

Bray, Douglas W., and Eli Ginsberg. *The Uneducated.* New York: Columbia University Press, 1953.

Campbell, D'Ann. *Women at War with America: Private Lives in a Patriotic Era.* Cambridge, Mass.: Harvard University Press, 1984.

Carrigan, William D., and Clive Webb. "The Lynching of Persons of Mexican Origin or Descent in the United States, 1848 to 1928." *Journal of Social History* 37, no. 2 (Winter 2003): 411–438.

Carroll, Patrick J. *Felix Longoria's Wake: Bereavement, Racism, and the Rise of Mexican American Activism.* Austin: University of Texas Press, 2003.

Chafe, William H. *Civilities and Civil Rights: Greensboro, North Carolina, and the Black Struggle for Freedom.* Oxford: Oxford University Press, 1981.

Coerver, Don, Suzanne B. Pasztor, and Robert M. Buffington. *Mexico: An Encyclopedia of Contemporary Culture and History.* Santa Barbara, Calif.: ABC-CLIO, 2004.

Cohen, Richard D. "Schooling Uncle Sam's Children: Education in the USA, 1941–1945." In *Education and the Second World War: Studies in Schooling and Social Change*, edited by Roy Lowe, 46–47. London: Falmer Press, 1992.

de la Fuente, Mario. *I Like You Gringo—But!* Phoenix: Phoenix Books, 1972.

Delgado, Richard, and Jean Stefancic. *Critical White Studies.* Philadelphia: Temple University Press, 1997.

Johnson, Lloyd, and Miles Wolff, eds. *The Encyclopedia of Minor League Baseball: The Official Record of Minor League Baseball.* Durham, N.C: Baseball America: 1997.

Flores, David. "SAISD Files Complaint over Taunting at Edison-Alamo Heights Playoff Game." KENS5.com San Antonio, March 6, 2012. http://www.kens5.com/on-tv/kens-reporters/david-flores/Ethnic-taunting-mars-Alamo-Heights-postgame-celebration-141646503.html.

García, Ignacio M. *Hector P. García: In the Relentless Pursuit of Justice.* Houston: Arte Público Press, 2002.

García, Ignacio M. *Viva Kennedy: Mexican Americans in Search of Camelot.* College Station: Texas A&M University Press, 1969.

García, Ignacio M. *White but Not Equal: Mexican Americans, Jury Discrimination, and the Supreme Court.* Tucson: University of Arizona Press, 2009.

García, Juan. *Mexicans in the Midwest, 1900–1932.* Tucson: University of Arizona Press, 2004.

García, Mario T. "Carlos E. Castañeda and the Search for History." Chapter 9 of *Mexican Americans: Leadership, Ideology, Identity, 1930–1960*, 231–251. New Haven, Conn.: Yale University Press, 1989.

García, Mario T. *Mexican Americans: Leadership, Ideology, Identity, 1930–1960.* New Haven, Conn.: Yale University Press, 1989.

García, Richard A. *Rise of the Mexican American Middle Class, San Antonio, 1929–1941.* College Station: Texas A&M University Press, 2000.

Gorn, Elliott J. *The Manly Art: Bare-Knuckle Prize Fighting in America.* Ithaca, N.Y.: Cornell University Press, 1986.

Green, George N. "Good Neighbor Commission." *Handbook of Texas Online.* Austin:

Texas State Historical Association. www.tshaonline.org/handbook/online/articles/mdg02.

Griffith, Beatrice. *American Me*. New York: Pennant Books, 1954.

Grundy, Pamela. *Learning to Win: Sports, Education, and Social Change in Twentieth-Century North Carolina*. Chapel Hill: University of North Carolina Press, 2000.

Heer, Jeet. "Little Nemo in Comicsland." *Virginia Quarterly Review* 82, no. 2 (Spring 2006): 104–121.

Hernández-Ehrisman, Laura. *Inventing the Fiesta City*. Albuquerque: University of New Mexico Press, 2008.

Iber, Jorge. "Mexican Americans of South Texas Football: The Athletic and Coaching Careers of E. C. Lerma and Bobby Cavazos, 1932–1965." *Southwestern Historical Quarterly* 55 (April 2002): 616–633.

Iber, Jorge. "Athletics and Chicano/a Life, 1930–2005." In *Mexican Americans and Sports: A Reader on Athletics and Barrio Life*, edited by Jorge Iber and Samuel O. Regalado. College Station: Texas A&M University Press, 2006.

Iber, Jorge, and Samuel O. Regalado, eds. *Mexican Americans and Sports: A Reader on Athletics and Barrio Life*. College Station: Texas A&M University Press, 2006.

Iber, Jorge, Samuel O. Regalado, José M. Alamillo, and Arnoldo De León. *Latinos in U.S. Sport: A History of Isolation, Cultural Identity, and Acceptance*. Champaign, Ill.: Human Kinetics, 2011.

Jimenez-Innis, Michael. "Beyond the Baseball Diamond and Basketball Court: Organized Leisure in Inter-war Mexican South Chicago." *International Journal of the History of Sport* 26, no. 7 (2009): 906–923.

Kelly, Arthur R. "Physical Anthropology of a Mexican Population in Texas." Ph.D. diss., Tulane University, New Orleans, 1947.

Kibbe, Pauline R. *Latin Americans in Texas*. Stratford, NH: Ayer Company Publishers, 1974.

Kingrea, Nellie Ward. *History of the First Ten Years of the Texas Good Neighbor Commission: Discussion of Its Major Problems*. Fort Worth: Texas Christian University Press, 1954.

Lanier, Sidney. "The Symphony." In *Poems of Sidney Lanier*, New York: Charles Scribner's Sons, 1891.

Levine, Peter. *Ellis Island to Ebbets Field: Sport and the American Jewish Experience*. Oxford: Oxford University Press, 1992.

Manuel, H. T. "Education of Mexican and Spanish-Speaking Children in Texas." In *Education and the Mexican American*, edited by Carlos Cortes. New York: Arno Press, 1974.

Manuel, Herschel T. *The Education of Mexican and Spanish-Speaking Children in Texas*. Austin: University of Texas, 1930.

Marin, Christine. "Courting Success and Realizing the American Dream: Arizona's Mighty Miami High School Championship Basketball Team, 1951." *International Journal of the History of Sport* 26, no. 7 (June 2009): 924–946.

Mazon, Mauricio. *The Zoot-Suit Riots: The Psychology of Symbolic Annihilation*. Austin: University of Texas, 1988.

McLemore, Ivy. *Texas High School Basketball Scrapbook.* Austin, Tex.: Eakin Press, 1989.

McWilliams, Carey. *North from Mexico.* New York: Greenwood Press, 1968.

Menchaca, Richard. *Guardian Angel.* Dubuque, Iowa: Kendall Hunt Publishing, 2012.

"Mexican Nicknames." blogadilla.com, July 25, 2009. http://www.blogadilla.com/2009/07/25/mexican-nicknames/, site discontinued.

Monroy, Douglas. *Rebirth: Mexican Los Angeles from the Great Migration to the Great Depression.* Berkeley: University of California Press, 1999.

Mora, Carl J. *Mexican Cinema: Reflections of a Society, 1896–2004.* Berkeley: University of California Press, 1990.

Murray, Sr. Mary John. *A Socio-cultural Study of 118 Mexican Families Living in a Low-Rent Public Housing Project in San Antonio, Texas.* Washington, D.C.: Catholic University of America Press, 1954.

"The Nation's Schools after a Year of War." *National Education Association Research Bulletin*, vol. 21, no. 2 (April 1942).

Nixon, Edgar B., ed. *Franklin D. Roosevelt and Foreign Affairs.* Cambridge, Mass.: Belknap Press of Harvard University Press, 1979.

Noboa, Julio. "On the West Side: A Portrait of Lanier High School during World War II." In *Mexican Americans and World War II*, ed. Maggie Rivas-Rodriguez, 67–92. Austin: University of Texas Press, 2005.

Onley, Glen. *Coach "Catfish" Smith and His Boys: A Novel Based on the Life of Coach Milburn "Catfish" Smith.* Santa Fe, N.M.: Sunstone Press, 2004.

Padilla, Genaro M. *My History, Not Yours: The Formation of Mexican American Biography.* Madison: University of Wisconsin Press, 1994.

Pagan, Eduardo Obregon. *Murder at the Sleepy Lagoon: Zoot-Suits, Race and Riot in Wartime Los Angeles.* Buchanan, N.Y.: ReadHowYouWant, 2009.

Peavy, Linda, and Ursula Smith. *Full-Court Quest: The Girls from Fort Shaw Indian School, Basketball Champions of the World.* Norman: University of Oklahoma Press, 2008.

Perdew, Phillip W. "The Secondary School Program in World War II." *History of Education Journal* 3, no. 2 (Winter 1952): 43–48.

Piece, Richard. "More than a Game: The Political Meaning of High School Basketball in Indianapolis." *Journal of Urban History* 27 (November 2000): 3–23.

Paranagua, Paulo Antonio. *Mexican Cinema.* London: British Film Institute, 1996.

Professional Baseball Teams in Texas: Texas Rangers, Houston Astros, Amarillo Dillas, San Angelo Colts, El Paso Diablos, San Antonio Missions. Memphis, Tenn.: General Books LLC, [2010].

Putney, Clifford. *Muscular Christianity: Manhood and Sports in Protestant America, 1880–1920.* Cambridge, Mass.: Harvard University Press, 2001.

Rivas-Rodríguez, Maggie. *Mexican Americans and World War II.* Austin: University of Texas Press, 2005.

Rochfort, Desmond. *Mexican Murals: Orozco, Rivera, Siqueiros.* San Francisco: Chronicle Books, 1994.

Rodriguez, Richard. *Hunger of Memory: The Education of Richard Rodriguez.* New York: Bantam, 1982.

Rodríguez, Victor. *The Bell Ringer.* San Antonio: Watercress Press, 2005.

Roediger, David R. *Working toward Whiteness: How America's Immigrants Become White: The Strange Journey from Ellis Island to the Suburbs.* New York: Basic Books, 2006.

Roosevelt, Franklin Delano. "First Inaugural Address of Franklin D. Roosevelt." Washington, D.C., March, 4, 1933. Transcript at *The Avalon Project: Documents in Law, History, and Diplomacy.* New Haven, Conn.: Lillian Goldman Law Library, Yale Law School. http://avalon.law.yale.edu/20th_century/froos1.asp.

Sánchez, George I. *Concerning Segregation of Spanish-Speaking Children in the Public Schools.* Inter-American Educational Occasional Papers, no. 9. Austin: University of Texas Press, 1951.

Sánchez, Jesse. "History of Baseball in Mexico." MLB.com. January 7, 2004. http://mlb.mlb.com/news/article.jsp?ymd=20040107&content_id=626058&vkey=news_mlb&fext=.jsp&c_id=null.

San Miguel, Guadalupe. *"Let All of Them Take Heed": Mexican Americans and the Campaign for Educational Equality in Texas, 1910–1981.* College Station: Texas A&M University Press, 1987.

Santillan, Richard A., Mark A. Ocegueda, and Terry A. Cannon. *Mexican American Baseball in the Inland Empire.* Charleston, S.C.: Arcadia Publishing, 2012.

"A Scrappy, Gutsy and Winning Coach, San Antonio's 'Nemo' Herrera Is Still a Fighter at Age 80," *Southwest Airlines Magazine*, February 1980, 103–108.

Sheridan, Thomas E. *Los Tucsonenses: The Mexican Community in Tucson, 1854–1941.* Tucson: University of Arizona Press, 1992.

Thompson, Craig. *Since Spindletop: A Human Story of Gulf's First Half-Century.* Pittsburgh: Gulf Oil, 1951.

Waterhouse, Viola. "Mexican Spanish Nicknames." In *Linguistics across Continents: Studies in Honor of Richard S. Pittman*, edited by Andrew B. Gonzalez and David D. Thomas. Manila: Summer Institute of Linguistics and Linguistic Society of the Philippines, 1981.

Yep, Kathleen S. *Outside the Paint: When Basketball Ruled at the Chinese Playground.* Philadelphia: Temple University Press, 2009.

Yergin, Daniel. *The Prize: The Epic Quest for Oil, Money and Power.* New York: Simon & Schuster, 1991.

Zamora, Emilio. *Claiming Rights and Righting Wrongs in Texas: Mexican Workers and Job Politics during World War II.* College Station: Texas A&M University Press, 2009.

Zelman, Donald L. "Alazan-Apache Courts: A New Deal Response to Mexican American Housing Conditions in San Antonio." *Southwestern Historical Quarterly* 87, no. 2 (October 1983): 123–150.

Index

Page numbers shown in italics indicate figures or illustrations.

acculturation
Herrera and, 20–21
Lanier and, 4–5, 10–11, 91–92, 176–177, 197–198, 226–227
student clubs and, 93–97
vocational education and, 127–129
war as impetus for, 16, 109, 120, 122–124, 131–133, 177–178
administration (of Lanier High School), 89–92, 103–104
Alazan/Apache Courts, 8–9
Americanization
Herrera and, 20–21
Lanier and, 4–5, 10–11, 91–92, 176–177, 197–198, 226–227
student clubs and, 93–97
vocational education and, 127–129
war as impetus for, 16, 109, 120, 122–124, 131–133, 177–178
assimilation. *See* Americanization

basketball
commercial leagues and, 62–63
community and, in San Antonio, 29–31, 44, 63, 115, 156–160, 205–206
discrimination and, 22
eligibility to play and, 69–72
evolution in style of play and, 28–29
oil company teams and, 25–28
racial identity and, 3–5, 15–16, 71–72, 75–76, 226
racial stereotypes and, 48–50
See also Voks basketball
Bears. *See* Thomas A. Edison High School
Belton, Santos, 113–114, 145–146
Bernal, Joe, x–xi, 137, 193
Bernal, Ramiro, 139–140, 168
biculturalism, 20, 97–101, 198–200
bilingualism, 90–91, 119–120
Boys Club, 29–30, 115, 159–160
Brewer, Principal R. H. "Dick"
background of, 89–90
bicultural education and, 72–73, 98–103, 122
and defense of Lanier, 50–54, 59, 69–70
Buffaloes. *See* Fox Tech High School

Camacho, Carlos, 30–31, 81, 107
Camacho, Jesse, 30–31, 81, 107
Camacho, Jessie Vargas, 118–119
Cardona, Tony, x, 1, 52, 79–81, 201
Carrasco, Gilbert, 140, 145, 150, 152
Civil Rights Movement, 16, 19, 118

clubs, student, 93–97, 99, 109–110
commercial leagues, 62–63
Contreras, Joe, 203, 210, 215, 223

Del Toro, Joe, 140
discrimination
against players, 22
at sports events, 82–83, 136–137, 140–141, 149–150, 153, 219–220
See also eligibility disputes; racial hostility

Eagles (G. W. Brackenridge High School), 1–2, 68–81, 163–164, 208–210. *See also* Voks basketball
education
influenced by war, 120–121
race issues and, 9–11, 176–177
vocational, 57–58, 125–129, 179–181
See also Sidney Lanier High School
eligibility disputes, 50–54, 69–72
Escobedo, Henry, 139, 182–184, 194, 202

Farias, Anastacio "Stacey," 45–46
Flores, David, 210, 217
football
eligibility issues and, 50–55
Herrera's coaching of, 25, 28, 46, 55, 220
at Lanier, 43–44, 48, 52, 57, 75
Fox Tech High School, rivalry with Lanier, 113, 117, 161, 207–208

Gonzalez, Manuel, 140
Gonzalez, Raul, 186, 189–190, 202
G. W. Brackenridge High School, 1–2, 68–81, 163–164, 208–210

Hays, D. G., 69–72
Hernández, Raul, 64, 67, 77, 84, 112
Herrera, William Carson "Nemo"
career after Lanier of, 222–224
coaching strategies of, 29, 39–40, 63–65, 114–115, 169–170
coaching to overcome disadvantages by, 29, 143–144, 172
disappointment after losses of, 114, 193–194, 214–215
early years of, 18, 20–22, 23–28
football coaching by, 25, 28, 46–47, 55
Mexican American society and, 146–147
origin of nickname of, 33–35
players' reminiscences of, 37, 134–135, 161–162, 224–225
promoting college education by, 200–201
scouting new players by, 156–157
on sportsmanship, 81–82
teaching character by, 35–37, 200–203
See also Voks basketball

integration
Herrera and, 20–21
Lanier and, 4–5, 10–11, 91–92, 176–177, 197–198, 226–227
student clubs and, 93–97
vocational education and, 127–129
war as impetus for, 16, 109, 120, 122–124, 131–133, 177–178

Kelley, Herbert, 195–200
Kelley, Walter, x, 134, 156, 164
Kellum, Claude, 41–42, 51, 70

Lanier High School. *See* Sidney Lanier High School
Latin Quarter. *See* San Antonio
Lerma, E. C., 19, 22–23

Martínez, Albert, 164, 166
masculinity
sports and, 20–21, 43–44, 49
war effort and, 182
Mexican Americans
Anglo views of, 11–12, 15
educational issues and, 9–11

identity of, 1–4, 6, 20–21, 97–100, 108–109, 119
sports and, 3–5, 15–16, 22–23, 71–72, 75–76, 226
stereotypes of, 48–50
war and, 16, 109–110, 120, 122–124, 131–133, 177–178
See also Americanization; discrimination; racial hostility
military
Mexican Americans in, 133, 177–178
service of players, 181–182, 222
student organizations, 109–110, 177–182
Muscular Christianity, 43–44, 49

nicknames, 31–35

oil companies, 25–28

paddling, 37–39
patriotism, during wartime, 137–138, 177
pecan-shelling factories, 13–14, 181

race. *See* Americanization; Civil Rights Movement; discrimination; Mexican Americans; racial hostility
racial hostility
during World War II, 137
riot at championship game, 1, 79–81
in San Antonio, 14–15
See also discrimination
Reyna, George, 150, 170
Riley, Wright "Toady," 28, 41–43, 45–47
rivalries
with Fox Tech High School, 113, 117, 161, 207–208
with Thomas A. Edison High School, 46, 137, 148
Rivera, Tony
early career of, 115–116, 117
play of, 147–152, 154, 164, 166–169, 171, 173–174
reminiscences of, 9, 30, 81, 134, 140
shooting style of, 138–139
team leadership of, 183
vocational education of, 127
Rodríguez, Alfonso, 79, 85
Rodríguez, David
childhood of, 157–159
college plans of, 201
early play of, 157–158, 160
play of, 161–162, 185, 203–204, 205–206, 212
reminiscences of, x, 10, 38–39, 137, 188–189
Rodríguez, Frank, 170, 202
Rodríguez, Kino, 186, 202
ROTC, 60, 109, 130–131, 178

Saldaña, Billy, 80, 218
San Antonio
community sports in, 29–31, 44, 63, 115, 156–160, 205–206
economic divides in, 9, 12–13
living conditions in, 8–9
Mexican culture in, 1–2, 33, 98
1960s, 7–9
pecan-shelling factories, 13–14, 181
racial issues in, 14–15, 72
sports and community identity in, 4–5
See also Sidney Lanier High School
segregation. *See* Americanization
Sidney Lanier High School
administration of, 89–92, 103–104
assimilation efforts of, 4–5, 10–11, 91–92, 176–177, 197–198, 226–227
basketball after Herrera, 223–224
bilingualism at, 90–91, 119–120
clubs, 93–97, 99, 109–110
doors and gates in, 175–176
homeroom tournaments, 154–156
1960s, 75–76, 97–98, 108, 113, 176–177
origin of Voks, 18
overcrowding at, 58–60, 73

patriotic activities at, 109–110, 118–119, 123–124, 130–132, 177–182, 222
race and, 4–5, 56–57
ROTC, 60, 109, 130–131, 178
students' views of, 9–10, 89–90, 225
teachers of, 11, 92
vocational education in, 57–58, 125–129, 179–181
See also education; San Antonio
Smith, Milburn "Catfish," 192, 197
sports
race and, 1–4, 6, 43–44
racial discrimination in, 22, 136–137
racial hostility and, 79–83, 140–141, 149–150, 153, 219–220
See also basketball; football; Voks basketball
state championship, 1943, 154, 161–174. *See also* Voks basketball
student clubs. *See* clubs, student

Tafolla, Fidel, 90–91, 197
teachers, at Lanier, 11, 92
Texas A&M University, 22–23
Thomas A. Edison High School
eligibility disputes and, 50, 53–54, 69–71
rivalry against Voks, 46, 137, 148
Treviño, Joe,
adult league, 205–206
play of, 68, 77–78, 83–84, 87, 112

Vandervort, Charles, 198–199
Vargas, Jessie. *See* Camacho, Jessie Vargas
vocational education, 57–58, 125–129, 179–181. *See also* Sidney Lanier High School
Voks basketball
1933 season, 47–48
1936 season, 51–52
1937 season, 52
1938 season, 62–69
1939 season, 1, 69–81, 83–88
1940 season, 111–113
1941 season, 115–118
1942 season, 138–145, 147–153
1943 season, 154, 161–174
1944 season, 182–194
1945 season, 201–217, 220–221
discrimination against, 36–37, 82–83, 140–141, 149–150, 153, 219–220
after Herrera, 223–224
influence of, on community identity, 3–5, 15–16, 22–23, 71–72, 75–76, 226
origin of name, 18
scuffle at championship game, 1, 79–81
state champions, 172–174
style of play, 29, 39–40, 63–65
See also basketball; Herrera, William Carson "Nemo"; Sidney Lanier High School

Woodall, Belle, 91
World War II:
effect of, on educational standards, 120–121
Lanier students and, 109–110, 118–119, 123–124, 130–132, 177–182, 222
Mexican Americans and, 16, 109, 120, 122–124, 131–133, 177–178
patriotism during, 137–138, 177

YMCA basketball, 205–206